In Counterpoint

In Counterpoint

Diaspora, Postcoloniality, and Sacramental Theology

KRISTINE SUNA-KORO

PICKWICK *Publications* · Eugene, Oregon

IN COUNTERPOINT
Diaspora, Postcoloniality, and Sacramental Theology

Copyright © 2017 Kristine Suna-Koro. All rights reserved. Except for brief quotations in critical publications or reviews, no part of this book may be reproduced in any manner without prior written permission from the publisher. Write: Permissions, Wipf and Stock Publishers, 199 W. 8th Ave., Suite 3, Eugene, OR 97401.

Pickwick Publications
An Imprint of Wipf and Stock Publishers
199 W. 8th Ave., Suite 3
Eugene, OR 97401

www.wipfandstock.com

PAPERBACK ISBN: 978-1-62564-710-8
HARDCOVER ISBN: 978-1-4982-8831-6
EBOOK ISBN: 978-1-5326-1990-8

Cataloguing-in-Publication data:

Names: Suna-Koro, Kristine.

Title: In counterpoint : diaspora, postcoloniality, and sacramental theology / Kristine Suna-Koro.

Description: Eugene, OR : Pickwick Publications, 2017 Includes bibliographical references.

Identifiers: ISBN 978-1-62564-710-8 (paperback) | ISBN 978-1-4982-8831-6 (hardcover) | ISBN 978-1-5326-1990-8 (ebook)

Subjects: LCSH: Postcolonial theology. | Liturgics.

Classification: BV176.3 .S86 2017 (paperback) | BV176.3 .S86 (ebook)

Manufactured in the U.S.A. 04/11/17

For here we have no lasting city,
but we are looking for the city that is to come.

HEB 13:14

Contents

Acknowledgments

THIS MONOGRAPH WOULD NOT have been possible without the support of family, friends, colleagues, and institutions. I am grateful for the faculty research time that Xavier University, Cincinnati, OH, and the Beckman Fund have granted me to complete this project. It grew out of and far beyond my initial explorations of postcolonialism in conversation with liturgical studies in my doctoral dissertation at Emory University (with particular gratitude to my *Doktorvater* Don E. Saliers among other outstanding mentors and colleagues).

I would like, in particular, to thank the Critical Theories and Liturgical Studies seminar members at the North American Academy of Liturgy (NAAL) for fruitful conversations and lots of inspiration as I presented some initial fragments of this project in progress (particularly Drs. Claudio Carvalhaes and Bruce Morrill, SJ).

I am grateful to my Pickwick Publications editor Dr. Charlie Collier for guiding me through the publication process and Dr. Andy Buechel for editorial support with the manuscript.

With lots of joy I thank a circle of precious colleagues at Xavier University from across the disciplines for their friendship and collegiality—Drs. Sarah Melcher, Anna Miller, Karen Enriquez, Minerva Catral, Carol Winkelmann, Martin Madar, and James Helmer. To Sr. Rosie Miller, OSF, goes my deepest gratitude for her unwavering encouragement throughout the whole process of writing. I thank my husband Philip "Arkiv" Koro whose enduring support accompanied me through the ups and downs of the project. Last but not least, most of what appears in this book has been written with at least one of our parrots—Pippy and Papageno—perching on my shoulder and cheering me on with squawks and beak prompts; for that companionship I also joyfully give thanks.

Palm Sunday, 2017
Cincinnati, OH

Introduction

It is permissible not to say all that can be said on a topic, but to deal with it from one particular standpoint.[1]

Yves Congar

We are all strands of energy connected to each other in the web of existence. Our thoughts, feelings, experiences affect others via this energy web. Our pervasive, excessive sense of woundedness compels us to erect barriers that create knots on the web and block communications. When conflict . . . disrupts a sense of connectedness, las nepantleras call on the 'connectionist' or web-making faculty, one of less structured thoughts, less rigid categorizations, and thinner boundaries that allows us to picture . . . similarities instead of divisions. Las nepantleras develop esta facultad, a realm of consciousness reached only from an 'attached' mode (rather than from a distant, separate, unattached mode), enabling us to weave a kinship entre todas las gentes y cosas.[2]

Gloria E. Anzaldúa

What does postcoloniality have to do with sacramentality? It may seem odd to talk about these allegedly disparate fields of human experience and knowledge in one breath within the present postcolonial and theological milieu. Sacramental theologians, especially in the West, have so far

1. Congar, *The Mystery of the Temple*, xi.

2. Anzaldúa, *Light in the Dark*, 83. Anzaldúa writes without using italics for Spanish words in the original text.

showed remarkably little interest in postcolonial modes of critical analysis and theological imagination. Postcolonial studies have returned the compliment with an equivalent vacuum of interest. The reasons for such "little traction" and even deliberate mutual distancing are rather complex.[3] But by no means should they thwart more vigorous conversations in the future.

The aspiration of this study is to offer a hybrid peregrination through the borderlands of both postcolonialism and sacramental theology through the prism of a diasporic imaginary. The underlying question here is: how does one, then, do sacramental theology precisely as a diasporic theology and as a postcolonial theology? As things currently stand, postcolonial sacramental theology as a sustained critical and constructive exploration of historical and contemporary sacramental imaginaries, discourses, and liturgical expressions is not just in its infancy—it is probably only in a gestational stage. Meanwhile sacramental theology, particularly in its Occidental expressions, is, as it were in a state of profound emergency. My study does not and cannot aim to tackle all the multidimensional challenges that sacramental imagination and reasoning face today. Rather, I proceed here with Yves Congar's counsel: "It is permissible not to say all that can be said on a topic, but to deal with it from one particular standpoint."[4] In this book, that "particular standpoint" is postcolonialism with a diasporic twist.

Postcolonial sacramental theology is still an uncharted terrain. I hope to at least scratch the proverbial surface of this embryonic field of theological inquiry to invite deeper and broader explorations and transdisciplinary conversations. Above all, my study is an invitation for both Christian theologians and postcolonial theorists to move beyond sporadic and mostly ethnographic engagements to initiate mutually enriching conversations at the level of the inner sanctum of both disciplines—postcolonial theory and Christian doctrine.

ON THE (OCCIDENTAL) POSTMODERN SACRAMENTAL EMERGENCY

Outside of specialized theological guilds of sacramental and liturgical studies, sacramental theology is often (mis)perceived and (mis)represented as a mighty fortress of an entrenched Christendom-type of churchiness where the church's most conservative and reactionary elements find their defensive and rarefied refuge. As David Brown observes, "it is still true that for the

3. Bill Ashcroft provides a brief and helpful overview of the paradigmatic tensions between Christian theology and postcolonialism; see his "Threshold Theology," 1–6.

4. Congar, *The Mystery of the Temple*, xi.

most part the sacraments are treated as the most 'churchy' or ecclesiastical part of a theology course. Left to the end, the sacramental is thus treated as an issue for the inner circle, as it were, those most committed to the specifics of Christian belief."[5] Hence, arguably, the postcolonial hesitation to engage this segment of Christian theology more vigorously.

Additionally, a regrettable modern inertia still packs a punch in the dominant Occidental division of theological labor: sacramental theology is still often dismissed, together with its allegedly more dynamic twin, liturgical theology, as "a swamp" for theological lightweights. Aidan Kavanagh's picturesque description captures the dominant modern mood with sarcastic accuracy:

> Sacramental discourse in fact is often thought of as theological adiaphora best practiced by those with a taste for banners, ceremonial, and arts and crafts. It is regarded as an academically less than disciplined swamp in which Anglican high churchmen, Orthodox bishops, and many if not all Roman Catholics and others are hopelessly mired.[6]

Most significantly, contemporary (Late postmodern? Post-postmodern?) Western sacramental theology is a theology in the state of emergency. Despite the unflinching formal affirmations of the "sacramental principle" in Roman Catholicism, there is an unavoidable recognition that it is not just Protestants and Evangelicals but also large numbers of Western Catholic and Eastern Orthodox faithful who feel profoundly alienated from sacramental worldviews. Or, at least, they feel alienated from the historically developed and ecclesiastically authorized conventions of sacramental imagination and practice.

The theme of sacramental crisis, particularly in its Western ecclesiocentric shape, only keeps getting louder with persistent regularity and increasing urgency.[7] Most ironic, perhaps, is the realization that experientially meaningful encounters with the Divine in these postmodern times—together with angels and other inhabitants of the (re)enchanted participatory universe of earthy and sensual mysticism—"have migrated from their home

5. Brown, *God and Enchantment of Place*, 6.

6. Kavanagh, *On Liturgical Theology*, 46.

7. Danneels, "Liturgy 40 Years After the Council," 11–14 and "Liturgy Forty Years After the Second Vatican Council," 7–26; and Martin, "Post-Christendom Sacramental Crisis," 57–75. See also Martos, *Doors to the Sacred* (updated and revised edition) and his *The Sacraments* among other Roman Catholic voices. However, A. Orobator, S.J. clearly outlines the geo-cultural specificity of the sacramental crisis as something peculiar to Western cultures, see for example, Orobator, "A Global Sign of Outward Grace," 14–22.

in the Church to populate the postmodern marketplace, recognizing perhaps that they are more welcome in that world of fantasy, creativity and imagination than in the constipated rituals of the Christian Church."[8]

And it is also true, as David Toolan noted, that today most of us—and not only in the supposedly secularized West—enjoy nature and see God's grandeur in it while perhaps on vacation, but then go back to work where rigid utilitarianism quickly takes the driver's seat. This results in a schizophrenic sacramental consciousness which continues to underwrite the planetary environmental crisis: "A sacramental consciousness of earth survives—just barely and in a somewhat schizophrenic fashion."[9]

The lamentations about a crisis in sacramental worldview, particularly in its ecclesiocentric shape, usually blame the overall secularization of Western/Occidenal cultures. I do not, however, see the modern secularization as the sole cause (scapegoat?) of the current sacramental predicament. Such a claim would be an easy escape route. Especially, because it tempts the so-called "liturgical" church traditions to prematurely abdicate a much needed and profound soul-searching and courageous examination of their own dualistic entrapments both on the level of theological imagination and doctrinal orthodoxies as well as authoritarian ecclesiastical power and gender dynamics.

Indeed, it is Occidental sacramentality that is struggling to come to terms with the crescendoing crisis of sacramental consciousness and imagination—at least in its conventional and institutionally authorized versions. Is, then, sacramental imagination and theological inquiry into it a fading territory on the map of Christian theology? Indeed, some traditional forms of sacramental theology and practice today live in an anxious land of trepidation concerning what may be lost or at least suffer substantial change. The present ecclesiastical predicament of sacramentality is a felt and lived reality in many Christian contexts. Yet, historically speaking, today's contested sacramental waters do not constitute an unprecedented experience of volatility. This is true even if the focus is no longer so much on the precise nature of, say, the controversial mechanics of eucharistic change during the consecration that creates the biggest theopolitical waves today.

The unique razor's edge of current sacramental predicaments cuts deep into the scar tissues of hierarchical authoritarianism, cultural imperialism, social injustice, and ecological degradation interfacing with a whole cluster of varying contextual challenges surrounding race, gender, sexuality, cultural diversity, and multiple religious belonging. And these are far from

8. Beattie, *New Catholic Feminism*, 295.

9. Toolan, "The Voice of the Hurricane,"96.

being parochially Western or specifically whitefeminist or ecofeminist concerns in the current spiritual climate of World Christianity![10]

On the other hand, is sacramentality not anxious to be rejuvenated, reclaimed, enacted, embodied, and proclaimed in new ways as a genuine "promised land"[11] of post-West-centric World Christianity? This is the reason why, perhaps ironically, the sacramental crisis is lamented by such diverse and even contradictory perspectives as institutional ecclesiocentrism (mourning the past and fearing what else it is going to lose in terms of authority, membership, and organizational solidity) as well as by emancipatory Christian movements such as church-oriented feminism (mourning what many faithful women have already lost by being marginalized and even demonized in a sacramental context).

And yet, sacramental theology—especially if willing to enter into creative and interdisciplinary conversations with other wisdom traditions and various critical discourses such as postcolonialism—may well be a theology in the process of emergence. As the Greek origins of the notion of crisis suggest, it is an emergency that forces one to face limitations, assumptions, and deep angst while also potentially harboring promises of breakthrough and evolution. Hence the two-pronged predicament of contemporary (Occidental) sacramental theology: 1) it is confronted by the emergency of sedimented sacramental conventions slipping into unintelligibility and irrelevance and, 2) at the same time, it is facing a crisis from which a cathartic renewal might emerge to benefit the whole planetary community.

Not that such a cathartic renewal is an easy matter. As Tina Beattie notes, for disenchanted "postmodern Christians the recovery of sacramentality requires a conscious linguistic act, for only through the medium of language might we liberate creation from its (post)modern captivity to language, and speak an opening into the silence of rupture between faith and reason."[12] I remain unconvinced that the recovery of sacramentality has much—let alone primarily—to do with linguistic acts but rather with what Beattie elsewhere describes as a "rediscovery of a lost enchantment, a new mysticism of the earthy, sexual being before God" through "the bodily music of the liturgy."[13] But the lesson to be remembered by all who engage in sacramental inquiry today, postmodernly, postcolonially, or otherwise, is

10. For example, see African and Asian sacramental reflections on these contentious issues by Jesuit theologians such as Orobator in "A Global Sign of Outward Grace" and Francis X. D'Sa, "The World as Sacrament," 24–39.

11. I am referring to Teresa Berger's rich Trinitarian metaphor in "Spying in the Promised Land," 41.

12. Beattie, *New Catholic Feminism*, 294–95.

13. Ibid., 294, 299.

that it is an effortful and countercultural endeavor—at least in the West and wherever the modern Occidental epistemological fingerprints are present.

Where the crisis talk really becomes contentious is where the colonial and imperial structures within Christianity—the "Christendom" style of belief, worship, salvation, communion, and authority—are being questioned or outright jilted. The modern, let alone postmodern, changes in cultural imagination, scientific worldview, and social economy alone cannot explain the growing disenchantment with—yes, indeed, with what exactly?—institutionalized sacramental practices. For many contemporary Christians the primary difficulty is not with sacramentality or worship *per se*. Rather, the question is about what kind of sacramentality and whose worship? In other words, what some versions of sacramental nostalgia do not want to recognize is that "problems with the sacraments are often problems with the Church."[14]

What seems to be on the way out to meet gnawing atrophy are the dualistic, disembodied, and imperialistic aspects of Occidental sacramentality that have operated in the West and wherever else those aspects have been imported, imposed, or downloaded—and wherever they remain sequestered behind the protective walls of intractable institutional traditionalism.[15] But is this sort of voyage out something to be mourned univocally and inconsolably?

ON THE EMERGENCE OF A NEW CONVERSATION: POSTCOLONIALISM AND SACRAMENTALITY

Sacramentality, as I will constructively explore it in the present study, is a matter of relational ontology. Indeed, to appropriate a term from the Russian postmodernist philosopher Mikhail Epstein, it could be called a relational "chamber metaphysics."[16] Epstein rightly argues that in the late

14. Padinjarekuttu, "Sacrament in Catholic History," 32.

15. For example, Emmanuel Y. Lartey summarizes such a dynamic of theological colonization and globalization in the African context as follows: "Christians have been made to see God exclusively in European terms. This has meant that we have been restricted to only one aspect of the divine mystery. Postcolonial analysis of particularly western Christian formulations that were transmitted and imposed on African peoples suggests that we have been made to worship a European crafted 'idol'—a creation made in the image of the philosophies, anthropologies, intellectual and emotional preferences of Europeans to fit their felt needs and provide remedies for their foibles," *Postcolonizing God*, 124–25. The colonizing dynamic Lartey describes here applies with equal accuracy to the Occidental sacramental theologies and practices in all their "inculturated" ambivalence.

16. I refer here to Mikhail Epstein's work on the philosophy of the possible, see Эпштейн, Философия возможного, 219–29.

postmodern era, metaphysics cannot and should not be resuscitated in its earlier dogmatic, deterministic, totalizing, or even totalitarian expressions. Instead, we can speak of a multiplicity of, as it were, small scale, compact, or chamber metaphysics which are constantly at play among themselves. These chamber metaphysics are well aware of their limits as (almost apophatic) gestures of the possible that do not preclude multiple other alternatives to play out and rub off one another.[17]

Postcolonial imagination and critical endeavors are also matters of relationality. In both its critical and constructive modes, postcolonialism gravitates toward and around relations. It is about scrutinizing the ontological, epistemological, cultural, spiritual, economic, political, social and imaginative webs of often grossly asymmetrical relationality that engender our world as we know and experience it. As Robert Young recapitulates, the objectives of postcolonialism are

> to reconstruct Western knowledge formations, reorient ethical norms, turn the power structures of the world upside down, refashion the world from below. The postcolonial has always been concerned with interrogating the interrelated histories of violence, domination, inequality, and injustice . . . Postcolonial theory . . . has never involved a singular theoretical formation, but rather an interrelated set of critical and counterintuitive perspectives, a complex network of paronymous concepts and heterogeneous practices that have been developed out of traditions of resistance to a global historical trajectory of imperialism and colonialism.[18]

Postcolonialism is a critical path of discerning life-giving and life-denying patterns of relationality in the world that is being chronically structured in domination and hegemony. Never mind how dense its theoretical and conceptual jungle may appear, postcolonial discernment is a worldly and practical enterprise. Its gaze is trained onto the incessant collusions of imperial imaginaries and colonial power dialectics as they mutate through endlessly self-justifying games of indifference toward human and planetary suffering.

The overall critical thrust of postcolonial endeavors is historical and axiological at once. As Achille Mbembe has argued,

> we must therefore reread the history of the West against the grain of Western accounts of its own genesis, reading against its fictions, its obvious and sometimes empty truths, its disguises,

17. Ibid., 220.

18. Young, "Postcolonial Remains," 20.

> its ploys, and—it bears repeating—*its will for power*. For, beyond the compilation of empirical detail, the critique of colonialism or imperialism still has nothing to say about colonialism and imperialism until it confronts this will for power and the constant obfuscation of its ontological, metaphysical, theological, and mythological dimensions. As will for power, colonial reason is simultaneously religious, mystical, messianic, and utopian. Colonization is inseparable from the powerful imaginary constructions and the symbolic and religious representations that are integral to the depiction of a terrestrial horizon in Western thought.[19]

Even though postcolonialism critically probes the roots of asymmetrical power and the routes of disempowerment, the constructive aspirations labor toward relations, imaginaries, and practices of life-affirming empowerment. While it interrogates the copious fruits of hegemonic power as it is felt primarily "from below" and among the "wretched of the earth" (Frantz Fanon), it simultaneously seeks fruitful and workable ways to unscramble imperial imaginaries and colonial incarnations as they endure throughout the whole global postcolony.

Postcolonial theology emerges out of historical imagination and this historical imagination, as Kwok Pui-lan puts it, "aims not only to reconstitute the past, but also to release it so that the present is livable."[20] Ultimately, the strategic aspiration of postcolonial theology is to continue unmasking, resisting, and, above all, transforming the patterns of colonial dominance and its warring will to unilateral and hegemonic power.

Broadly speaking, the work of postcolonial imagination is to develop the habits of mind which Gayatri Spivak refers to as "teleiopoiesis"—the conscious structures "that interrupt the past in the name of the future"[21] beyond the ingrained dualistic master-slave dialectic of colonial imaginary. As Mayra Rivera elaborates, in theological context teleiopoiesis engenders "a relation to past witnesses that bears a messianic structure, 'affecting the distant other,' 'future companions,' 'unknowingly, without guarantees.'"[22] Consequently, in resonance with Johann Baptist Metz's insistence, a theology that is conceived and performed in teleiopoetic mode "entails 'creative remembering' grounded in a re-understanding of history in which 'vanquished and forgotten *possibilities* of human existence—to which we give

19. Mbembe, "Provincializing France," 116. Italics in original.
20. Kwok, *Postcolonial Imagination*, 37.
21. Spivak, *An Aesthetic Education*, 302.
22. Rivera, "Ghostly Encounters," 131.

the name 'death'—will neither be revoked nor sublated by the course of future history."[23]

The goal of teleiopoetic imagination and its emancipatory modulations is to birth a "dialogic of accountability."[24] The dialogic of accountability is precisely a dia-logic: a "freedom of contradiction without synthesis—critical of the comforts of both dialectics and pluralism"—that foregrounds the new planetary ethical imperatives "that structure all of us, as giver and taker, female and male, planetary human beings."[25]

An indispensable, although not exclusive, part of such postcolonial modulations is the *hermeneutic of resourceful vigilance*. Such a hermeneutic is necessary considering the historical abuses and misuses of Christian sacraments during the era of the "high" colonialism as well as their resiliently malformative metastases during the present neocolonial milieu. But here an important caveat must be underscored at once to avoid further misunderstandings: the hermeneutic of resourceful postcolonial vigilance does not automatically equal a metaphysical, ideological, or religious anti-Westernism or some sort of crude reverse Eurocentrism. Such a simplistic reversal would be much too reductionistic an escape route for conscientious postcolonial sensibilities that, after all, have worked so hard to move beyond the temptations to homogenize and essentialize identities, histories, relationships, and cultures.

The hermeneutic of resourceful postcolonial vigilance should be applied toward the liturgical and sacramental dimensions of Christianity to distinguish between the mystical and symbolic forms of spirituality, and the predatory mystifications of both human and divine reality in the service of cultural, patriarchal, and economic imperialism in the past as well as in the present. The point is not to judge the past anachronistically from some presumed moral, intellectual, or cultural high ground of the present. Rather, it is to ensure that the Occidental sacramental and liturgical traditions finally grow into a fuller planetary awareness of their own deeply ambivalent colonial and imperial histories under whose shadows they (and all those touched by their impact) still live and move today—and still often in ignorance or denial. In the end, the point is to work toward making sure that these traditions truly own—and own up to—the full gamut of their own histories precisely in order to learn, discern, and not to carelessly repeat their past foibles. The goal is not to simply expose and oppose but even more so to kindle the creative and transformative contribution of Western

23. Ibid. Italics in original.

24. Spivak, *An Aesthetic Education*, 350.

25. Ibid., 335–36.

Christian sacramental imagination toward the survival and well-being of the planetary community of creation through its overarching evolutionary relation with God—with the Holy Mystery underlying all that exists.

The transformative path of postcolonial imagination leads through modulations of coercive, competitive, unilateral and hegemonic dialectics of power toward progressively reciprocal—even though not always symmetrical—power relations. This is not a path that glorifies weakness and romanticizes vulnerability and marginality as if in a simplistic dialectical reversal. The postcolonial modulations are to engender equitable, accountable, non-coercive, inter-logical, life-giving and whole-making interfaces of empowerment for all, especially those already—and not by their own choice or deliberate fault—indwelling the many disinherited undersides of the present global postcolony.

That being said, I proceed with the presupposition that a postcolonial retrieval and reenvisagement, indeed a constructive *ressourcement*, of sacramentality offers a fecund and perhaps even a uniquely therapeutic space in which the twenty-first century Christian theology can constructively heal the metastases of its historical enmeshments with the imperial and colonial structures of dominance. Sacramentality can be a genuinely decolonial crucible within which theological imagination can be profoundly challenged and empowered to facilitate a liberating and whole-making transformation.

This project rests on the conviction that a sacramental imaginary is also a methodological comportment that can enable the emergence of a radically relational, pluriversal, and decolonial cosmovision. A sacramental imaginary is particularly suited, especially if working synergistically with other emancipatory discourses, to engender a meaningful and genuinely planetary "chamber metaphysics" of creation and salvation. Even though sacramentality is a marginal discourse in modern and even postmodern theology, such a vision nevertheless glimmers throughout the crevices of Christian theological traditions. It resiliently glimmers around, above, and under the occlusions, distortions, and all the violent zigzags that cross the social, cultural, and political terrains of Christian history, and that sacramental imaginary must necessarily traverse this side of the beatific vision. Challenges notwithstanding, postcolonial theological *ressourcement* can—and should—judiciously reclaim and reaffirm the revelatory and transformative promise of non-coercive and synergistic relational interface between God and the world that sacramental imaginary is uniquely positioned to advance.

My constructive goal is to rekindle the idea of the sacramental *as* the ethical. In light of postcolonial historical *anamnesis*, the only fair conclusion is that the vital and primordial entanglement of the sacramental with the ethical has been molested with a lamentable regularity in the history of Christianity. Past and present molestations notwithstanding, my motivation for this postcolonial retrieval of sacramentality is the conviction that this providential entanglement is not extinct despite its lack of celebrity. Therefore postcolonial *ressourcement* can and should try to prudently recuperate and wisely repurpose all and any ethically fecund fragments and impulses of both magisterial *and* marginal sacramental imaginaries to find out, as Gayatri Spivak iconoclastically suggested, if "the magisterial texts can now be our servants, as the new magisterium constructs itself in the name of the Other."[26]

The constructive itinerary of this study proceeds by connecting the robust incarnational commitment in Christian theology with the notion of contrapuntal hybridity in postcolonialism through a diasporic imaginary to seek for new paths of transformative crosspollinations. Granted, some of these paths will most likely appear "exotic" to a good deal of Occidental theological conventions and narrowly cultivated denominational identities. Sacramentality and postcolonialism seem to be strange bedfellows for the conventional procedures in theology as well as in postcolonial theory. This state of affairs, however, is neither the only possible nor the most desirable one. In fact, such an impasse deserves a shakeup. My study is a step toward such a constructive trajectory.

IN COUNTERPOINT: THE WAY OF PROCEEDING

Catherine Keller has aptly remarked that "theology is never anything but an open-ended activity between many voices, living and dead."[27] The methodological itinerary of this study is intentionally polyphonic and contrapuntal: it relentlessly weaves together both theological and postcolonial voices, themes, perspectives, resonances, and dissonances.

As in diasporic life, for every "on the one hand" there is a corresponding "on the other hand" that inescapably—and for some, of course, annoyingly—marks every interdisciplinary discourse. The reflections I present in this monograph always carry the branding of my "dual citizenship" in theology and postcolonial theory, and all of that with a diasporic twist. Hence my hope is that this study may prove useful for both of my two intellectual and spiritual homelands as I constantly migrate from diasporic spirituality to postcolonialism, onto theology, and back again in the polyvocal language of a *nepantlera*, a cultural and confessional border crosser and linguistic

26. Spivak, *A Critique of Postcolonial Reason*, 7.

27. Keller, *On the Mystery*, 177.

code-switcher. And it is also to invite a conversation on sacramentality, diaspora, and postcolonialism not only in the North American context but also in Europe, South America, and wherever else diasporic theologians ponder over the Divine and its many sacramental mysteries unfolding in their migratory lifeworlds.

Multiple languages have played out, at least in my mind, as poignantly as in Gloria Anzaldúa's magnificent epigraph, even as I have attempted to render the actual written text reasonably manageable. All of these languages—ancient and modern, dominant and marginal, native and adopted, forced or willingly acquired—have left their footprints in my sentence structure and the jumbled poetics of vocabulary.

The three opening *Preludes* contextualize my study from incarnational, ethnographic/ historical, and sacramental perspectives. No theological reflection happens in a cultural vacuum. The *Preludes*, to use the Ignatian framework, "compose a place" for analysis, reflection, critique, and constructive imagination by situating my critical and constructive explorations in the diasporic lifeworld of Baltic and North American postcoloniality.

Part I sketches the theoretical and interdisciplinary framework of diasporic and postcolonial analysis that underwrites my theological reflections on sacramentality. It performs a theoretical *compositio loci* for the constructive segments of this study. It explores the contours of diasporic subjectivity and imagination through Latvian diasporic spirituality and sacred art, and surveys the methodological expressions which characterize such a fabric of imagination. In Part I, the emphasis falls on conversations with postcolonial theory and diasporic discourses. The concluding chapter of Part I advances the notion of diasporic imaginary as a "braided" and "kluge"-like theoretical comportment which embodies the hybrid ontology of connections rooted in the diasporic homing desire which contests the imperialistic ideologies of authenticity. This diasporic imaginary will be applied in Part III as the methodological framework for my constructive explorations in postcolonial sacramental theology.

Part II explores a range of resonances between theological inquiry and postcolonialism. Above all, it foregrounds the distinctive significance of ethics for postcolonial theology. It focuses on the multifaceted notions of postcolonial hybridity, contrapuntality, and Third Space as gateways for postcolonial re-envisioning of ethical relationality with otherness and transcendence, particularly through the (theologically hitherto underappreciated) work of Edward W. Said.

Part III offers several constructive trajectories for emerging postcolonial sacramental theology from a diasporic perspective. My constructive thrust is grounded in the historical excursus of colonial sacramental practices in the context of the Latvian history of Christianization and its complex postcolonial aftershocks. In that context, I proceed to discuss the ethics of theology as an irrevocable theopolitical prolegomenon for postcolonial imaginaries of sacramentality, relationality, and divine transcendence. These are followed by my constructive reflections. They take shape as a polyphonic interdisciplinary conversation between Chalcedonian Christology and the ideas about the world as *Ursakrament* as well as the notions of postcolonial planetarity, contrapuntality, hybridity, and Third Space. Out of this conversation emerge my constructive proposals of sacramental pluriverse and the understanding of Christ as its sacramental crescendo. My reflections conclude with a constructive retrieval of the notion of eucharistic transubstantiation as a postcolonial avenue for reimaging a non-hegemonic and non-coercive transformation.

A brief *Coda* wraps up this study with concluding reflections on diasporic method and an appeal for renewed attention to the notion of sacramentality as a methodological "chamber metaphysic" for an ethically and ecologically committed sacramental theology.

Finally, a couple of terminological clarifications are also in order. The term "imaginary" figures prominently throughout the whole text. I use the term "imaginary" in the way Édouard Glissant did: namely, as a shorthand for "all the ways a culture has of perceiving and conceiving of the world"[28] and God, and everything that transpires across that transontological and epistemological interval.

I also use a terminological distinction, admittedly blurry more often than not, between the adjectives "Western" and "Occidental." The adjective "Western" typically denotes those ideas, actions, and events which have originated and exert influence in the geopolitical "West"—itself a very slippery category, of course. The adjective "Occidental" denotes the ideas, attitudes, and practices that have originated in the "West" yet have been colonially imposed on or imported to cultures and societies elsewhere through neocolonial globalization, and which these cultures have now assimilated and made their own to a significant degree.

All references to the Scriptures are from the New Revised Standard Version unless explicitly indicated otherwise. All translations from Latvian, Russian, German, and French are my own unless the translator of an English edition of any foreign language text is indicated in the bibliography.

The lived complexity of diasporic life in conjunction with multiple sacramental and liturgical lifeworlds has led me to question the reign of visual and textual metaphors in Western critical discourses, including

28. Wing, "Translator's Introduction," xxii.

postcolonialism and theology. Hence, in this study, I have often deliberately turned to music for a more aurally evocative language and authors like Edward W. Said who extensively use musically inspired semiotic practices. It is part of my larger quest for signifying practices that are not hegemonically ruled by competitive visualism and the logocentric fixation on the written word in linguistically infatuated Western modernity. As Vladimir Jankélévitch observes,

> the experienced simultaneity of opposites is the daily regime, incomprehensible as it might be, of a life full of music. Music, like movement or duration, is a continuous miracle that with every step accomplishes the impossible. The superimposed voices of polyphony realize a *concordia discors*, of which music alone is capable. . .[29]

In the following pages, saluting Paul Gilroy's analysis, I have sought to draw on music precisely to question the "privileged conceptions of both language and writing as preeminent expressions of human consciousness" thereby challenging the "ideology of the text and of textuality as a mode of communicative practice which provides a model for all other forms of cognitive exchange and social interaction."[30]

In the end, it is indeed right and salutary, as Jean-Luc Marion insists, to remember that "one must obtain forgiveness for every essay in theology."[31] Indeed, even with the best intentions of apophatic awareness, there is so much that can always be missaid, misperceived, misrepresented, and misjudged in the audacious and ever so inescapably historical and human enterprise of trying to imagine and speak of the Ultimate, the Holy Mystery that undergirds, permeates, and transcends all that is. Hence my reflections do not presume to be anything more final than peregrinations-in-progress toward a sacramental imaginary that can aid our shared human ability to desire and lean into the fullness of life for all planetary creatures, now and forevermore.

29. Jankélévitch, *Music and the Ineffable*, 18–19. There is also an ethical connection with music that philosopher Kathleen Marie Higgins suggests in her book on philosophical ethics and music. She argues that music provides models of "flowering and resolution of tension" through "the possibility of graceful navigation within a texture of external and internal tensions"—thus music suggests desirable modes of ethical social interaction. Most importantly, "reflection on music suggests that satisfaction need not be construed as a drastic reduction or elimination of tension. Instead, satisfaction can be found in controlled and coordinated manipulation of tension itself. Musical experience also suggests the fallacy involved in making satisfaction our overriding ethical concern. Risk itself has a positive value in both musical and ethical experience," *The Music of Our Lives*, 194.

30. Gilroy, *The Black Atlantic*, 74, 77.

31. Marion, *God Without Being*, 2.

Prelude I

I firmly believe that theology does not float above culture and context. Doing theology is not an exercise in conceptual weightlessness.[1]

Agbonkhianmeghe E. Orobator, S.J.

Our bodies are geographies of selves made up of diverse, bordering, and overlapping 'countries.'[2]

Gloria E. Anzaldúa

The calling of any theology worth its salt is to stir up a cognitive, imaginative, affective, and sensory foretaste of that wholeness that can only be fathomed in relation to that glory divine which alone uniquely renders all sentient beings truly, fully, and abundantly alive. Theology is, if rarely truly wholistic in its actual historical manifestations, then at least a thoroughly synthetic undertaking. It plumbs the most intimate crevices of mind and soul to search for the meaning and destiny of human life. And it surely struggles with buried and unhealed fears and anxieties—sometimes precisely through ignoring them or zealously fighting people and ideas that seem to trigger their unwelcome arrival. Theological imagination does all this and much more, albeit sometimes under the institutional and doctrinal radar screen, as it reflects on all things in relation to God.

At the same time—and this gets perilously forgotten far too often—theology is an intrinsically embodied endeavor. Even as the imagination

1. Orobator, *Theology Brewed in an African Pot*, 153.

2. Anzaldúa, *Light in the Dark*, 69.

soars with desire to discern the mysteries of life, and even as the intellect very audaciously seeks to taste the richness of the Divine through the most exigent apophatic leaps and bounds of the human mind, all the soaring and seeking inevitably happens in and through the body. But all bodies have histories! No matter how detached and speculative such a soaring and seeking may appear, for each one of us it happens through our own inimitable pattern of "the fundamental consanguinity of the intelligible and sensible."[3] In other words, theological reflection is incarnate in and through a historically and culturally embedded body: in, through, with, and around a gendered body, a body of a certain race, class, ethnicity, ability, linguistic legacy, sexual orientation, affectivity, temperament and many other relational and historical vignettes of one's existential tapestry of personhood. As the South African theologian Denise Ackerman succinctly puts it, "everything starts with our bodies" since they are "the intricate tracery of all that is ourselves, the good and the bad."[4]

Who we are as enmattered spirits (or ensouled bodies) in the jumbled gamut of cultural and political histories is not merely a matter of detached and inconsequential interiority that sometimes even gets paraded as spirituality in theological discourse. Rather, we are an amalgam of visibility and invisibility, of materiality and spirituality, and of identity and difference—and all of it matters profoundly. Our theological reasoning and imagination "are personal and private, political and public, bone, flesh, blood, and spirit"[5] throughout all our conscious and unconscious terrains of experience, memory, and desire. When all is said and done, "all theological reflection starts with the body. To think that theology is an activity separate from the concreteness of the human body and concerned solely with some abstract realm of the spirit is nonsensical."[6]

And so I imagine, act, perceive, think, discern, reflect, hope, fear, pray, eat, love, and write this book fully aware of my diasporic female enfleshment that is colored by the postcolonial transitions in the Eastern Europe of the 1990s after the dissolution of the Soviet Union as well as my subsequent habitations within the orbit of the Western metropolises of knowledge and power. Wherever my theological imagination might want to soar historically or proleptically, I must start with my diasporic, hyphenated

3. Miles, "Foreword: The Eye of the Beholder," xx.

4. Ackerman, *After the Locusts*, 65, 67.

5. Ibid., 67.

6. Ibid., 78. Ackerman adds: "Sadly, traditional Christian theology has either ignored, denied, or denigrated the human body. . . Sadly, shame in regard to the 'lowly nature of the body' has permeated Christian thought," ibid.

Latvian-American, female, (and "off-white"[7]) clerically ordained Lutheran body and mind in the second decade of the twenty-first century.

When it comes to postcolonial theology, embodiment is not a mere spill-over of Occidental postmodernism with its penchant for the (previously repressed) carnivalesque, the somatic, and the erotic. Nor is it a ludic fancy of high postcolonial theory clinging to its (allegedly Francophile) roots in deconstruction. Regardless how hard Christian theology has struggled with its own incarnational origins, it remains true that the lifeworld of Christian revelation gravitates around the Word becoming materiality, indeed becoming flesh, *sarks* (John 1:14). No matter how ambivalent our bodies may feel to ourselves and others on this side of the beatific vision, embodiment in all its complex historical materiality remains the pivotal and the irreducible site of nothing less than incarnation, salvation, and revelation.

Within the incarnational economy of creation and salvation, revelation is precisely "the revelation-in-embodiment."[8] Embodied reality, as Tertullian noted long ago, is nothing less than the hinge of salvation. Through the incarnation of the Word/Wisdom,

> humanity, precisely in its embodied subjectivity (and by extension all creation in its materiality), is deemed a fitting locus for God's revelation. Revelation thereby influences the parameters of all thought and action. The event of God's unique self-revelation, occurring as it does within a particular human life at a particular place and time, also indicates God's positive judgment on the suitability of humanity, human embodiment, and the particularity of its historical situatedness for the mediation of divine love and salvation.[9]

In the postcolonial milieu, however, one must immediately ask which bodies, which minds, and whose historical particularity is judged to be suitable to express divine revelation? Obviously, the very reason why postcolonial sensibilities have come to exist at all is due to Western colonial assumptions about the (fabricated) "natural" hierarchies of embodied human life, intelligence, ability, and value. The totalizing constructs of colonialist

7. A postcolonial identity like mine is further complicated by what Mita Banerjee describes as "off-white" in the European context where I, for instance, clearly do not belong to the "old" Europe and cannot pass for a "real" American either. Banerjee observes that "Eastern Europeanness verges on the racial difference of an off-whiteness" and this "different whiteness" is ethnically inscribed. Particularly in the British context, "the postcommunist takes the place of ethnicity; the postcommunist is the new ethnic" as it also suggests "the new erotic of the postcolonial," see Banerjee's "Postethnicity and Postcommunism," 314–17.

8. Godzieba et al, "Resurrection-Interruption-Transformation," 778.

9. Ibid., 779.

imagination about human value and ability have been buttressing racial, religious, cultural, sexual, economic, and political subjugation and abuse of those peoples and individuals who have been deemed "primitive," "deficient," "derivative," "different," "weaker," or "underdeveloped" all the way into the present neocolonial formations of power and knowledge.

Despite its incarnational imperatives, Christianity has a very "ambiguous history" with anything enfleshed due to its presumed connotations with sin, death, sexuality, and desire.[10] The imperialistic missionary ideology of Western Christendom has often participated in the very production, proliferation, and imposition of oppressive colonial hierarchies of being, knowing, and loving. Against this historical background and its colonial cosmologies of divine power, any discourse invoking flesh—or carnality—is indeed "risky" as Mayra Rivera suggests.[11]

It is risky indeed, yet it is also necessary: a meaningful and ethically answerable theology in the postcolonial era can fulfill its transformative vocation only if it originates through existential engagements with the material and relational specificity of human lifeworlds. Of particular importance today are the voices and material networks of meaning-making that the Occidental theological mainstream has so far left by the wayside or delegated to its (still exotic) footnotes. The constructive vector of this project proceeds from the tricky, messy, and risky particularity of diasporic and postcolonial lifeworld, as it is nudged on by the still unrealized incarnational imperatives of the Christian vision of reality and theological inquiry.

Following the incarnational matrix of contextual "suitability," I start with *compositio loci* from the Ignatian spiritual tradition. *Compositio loci* is an imaginative and meditative "composition of place" to create a space for a potentially life-changing encounter with otherness, divine and otherwise. In the beginning of his *Spiritual Exercises*, Ignatius of Loyola outlines two practices for an imaginative composition of place. These are the so-called preparatory "preludes." The first practice entails surveying the "history" of the matter at hand that a person is about to contemplate. Secondly, the goal is to envision a physical/material place where the visible or embodied objects (such as Christ or Mary or other Gospel figures) of one's attentive contemplation are located and where the encounter might take place.[12] The third practice aspires to call into awareness and to inhabit an imaginative space wherein one can stay present to realities such as one's desires, intentions, thoughts in the mind and its dispositions, affects, and truths of the moment—yet with an eye to the eternal divine "now."

10. Rivera, "Flesh of the World," 52–53.

11. Ibid.

12. Ignatius of Loyola, *Spiritual Exercises*, [47], 136.

The Ignatian practice of the composition of place is an intensely imaginative journey above and beyond disembodied speculation about God. It deliberately flows into the realms of sensuous and affective knowledge. The practice enables precisely that often elusive awareness of the fundamental consanguinity of the intelligible and sensible. Ignatius' specific focus for the First Week of Spiritual Exercises falls on the realities of sin accompanied by a traditional yet rather vexing dualistic juxtaposition of body and soul in the opening lines of the First Week exercises.[13] Such an approach can, if used without proper discernment and mature spiritual and psychological contextualization, quickly thin out or even antagonize the holistic thrust of this spiritual practice.

What matters most, however, is the importance of a deliberate and sustained embeddeddness of imagination in both historico-material as well as the emotional, intellectual, and ethical space to intentionally facilitate a meaningful encounter with otherness, across time and space. In other words, before any sort of fruitful encounter with realities other than one's own, various personal fixations can materialize if not brought into awareness, probed and acknowledged for what they truly are. It is worth recognizing that one's location matters here. Location is the specific socio-historical and cultural landscape that has been personally appropriated through the intricately relational terrains of body and soul over the years of one's life. Spiritual life and theological imagination is not chained to these multifaceted and relational terrains. Yet both remain anchored *within* specific materialities of embodied experience through all its complex exigencies of suffering, (dis)empowerment, and hope. Indeed, doing theology is not an exercise in conceptual weightlessness—nor is it an exercise in affective, political, or socio-economic weightlessness.

The composition of place is, then, a practice of intentionally foregrounding the pivotal connection between God-talk, contextual imagination, and historical materiality. Consequently, theological reflection weaves itself through the "place" so composed by participating in meaningful conversations across the widest spectrum of human knowledge, experience, and creativity. Within a "place" so composed, the Divine can be found, to use another Ignatian motto, in all things, even in those that do not seem to offer immediate spiritual, intellectual, emotional, doctrinal, or political gratification.

13. It must be noted, especially in light of Ackerman's argument, that the second kind of "composition" with its preparatory emphasis on sin carries a dualistic perception of "soul as imprisoned in this corruptible body, and my whole compound self as an exile in this valley [of tears] among brute animals," ibid. But Ignatius also indicates the flexibility of the object of "composition" depending on the focus of meditation so that sin is not the only subject matter of the second practice, *Spiritual Exercises*, [49], 137.

Prelude II

But it's history that matters, what keeps you together in the tight ball of nerves and flesh that you are and what makes you you and not someone else.[1]

Bret Lott

How many people live today in a language that is not their own?[2]

Gilles Deleuze and Felix Guattari

The history that makes me me or "composes" my place in the world started in Latvia—on the southern Baltic rim, in the North-Eastern corner of Europe. What matters most in the context of this study is that Latvia is a multiply conquered and colonized interstice of Europe, currently enjoying only its fifth decade of sovereignty in one thousand years. The colonial enmeshment for Latvia started with the crusade inspired *Drang nach Osten* in the twelfth century. It brought medieval Europe and its Latin Christianity to the southern Baltic lands and peoples—the last "pagan" frontier of Europe. The most recent colonial afflictions were doled out by the Nazis and, above all, the Russo-Soviet empire up until just a few decades ago. Bearing the memories and legacies of various imperial subjugations, Latvia remains as one of the routinely unrecognized dark undersides of colonial modernity.

The history of Latvian Christianity is inseparable from the impact of numerous colonial conquests from both West and East (more about the theological implications of that in Part III Ch. 1). The medieval crusades

1. Lott, *Jewel*, 5.

2. Deleuze and Guattari, "What is a Minor Literature?" 19.

trampled over and tried to extirpate the "idolatries" of the indigenous spiritual traditions alongside bringing political and economic subjugation. Ever suspended in the crossroads of modern Euro-Asian empires, the peoples of the Baltic did what others in similar situations have done: in order to survive they simultaneously appropriated and resisted the Western Christian trajectories of Roman Catholicism and Lutheranism while both of these religious cultures clashed and mingled with the Russo-Byzantine trajectory politically, spiritually, and economically.

Unsurprisingly, Latvian Christianity was and is syncretistic: it is a hybrid, if one just bothers to scratch the conventional West-centric surface. It was syncretistic long before the early waves of Latvian dispersal into diasporas eastward and westward commenced in the late nineteenth century under the Russian imperial squeeze. It is growing increasingly and innovatively syncretistic amid the current historically unprecedented and economically motivated upsurge of Latvian emigration to the "Old Europe" and elsewhere. These waves of political and economic migrations compose my present habitat—the worldwide Latvian diaspora and its Lutheran communities of faith.

Contemporary Latvia and its global diasporas—like the whole Baltic region—carries the ingrained memories and legacies of a contested, pragmatically desired, and multi-conquered (play)ground of clashing imperial ambitions throughout the centuries of colonial modernity.[3] All that was to be trumped only by the Nazi and Soviet genocidal apogee of totalitarianism in the twentieth century. In the words of Timothy Snyder, the Baltic postcolonies are indeed the "bloodlands" of Europe:

> In the middle of Europe in the middle of the twentieth century, the Nazi and Soviet regimes murdered some fourteen million people. The place where all of the victims died, the bloodlands, extends from central Poland to western Russia, through Ukraine, Belarus, and the Baltic States. During the consolidation of National Socialism and Stalinism . . . mass violence of a sort never before seen in history was visited upon this region. The victims were chiefly Jews, Belorussians, Ukrainians, Poles, Russians, and Balts, the peoples native to these lands. The fourteen million were murdered over the course of only twelve years, between 1933 and 1945, while both Hitler and Stalin were

3. To underscore and fine-tune the (arguably) dramatic hierarchical differences in power configurations among various modern Eurasian empires, the term "subaltern empires" is occasionally applied to empires such as, for example, the Russian Czarist and Austro-Hungarian empires. See Tlostanova, "The Imperial-Colonial Chronotope," 406–27.

> in power. The Second World War was the most lethal conflict in history, and about half of the soldiers who perished on all of its battlefields all the world over died here, in this same region, in the bloodlands. Yet not a single one of the fourteen million murdered was a soldier on active duty. Most were women, children, and the aged. . .[4]

The memories and legacies of "bloodlands" constellate Latvia's peculiar postcolonial predicaments. In light of the dominating experiences of back-to-back totalitarian conquests during and after World War II, a terminological shift must be flagged to better understand the unique mutations of Eastern European, particularly Baltic, postcoloniality. Here I must comment on the pivotal theoretical and ideological conundrums regarding the murky variety of Eastern European postcoloniality that continue to baffle the more canonized expressions of Asian, African, or South American postcolonialisms. Nancy Condee provides a useful summary of what it at stake: in the postsoviet era across the ethnoscapes of Eastern and Central Europe, "a descriptor more familiar than *Soviet colonialism*—given the geographic, historical, and conceptual proximity to Nazism—has been *Soviet occupation*."[5] Thus in many Eastern and Central European milieus, the "postsoviet" often virtually equals the "postcolonial"—at least in practical implications.

For the most part, Latvia today is seen as a member of the so-called "New Europe" which has risen as an unlikely Phoenix out of the Soviet occupation or the former "Eastern Bloc." But Europe as a geopolitical entity has always been a complicated concoction. As a geographical entity, Europe has never completely coincided with the "West"—except in some imperialistic self-aggrandizement or reductive conflations.[6] With Russian neo-imperialism marching across Eurasia again, the imaginary of the "New East" is starting to compete with the turn of the millennia imaginary of the "New Europe" as the Western metropolises struggle to make sense of the perplexities of the postsoviet/postcolonial world.[7] The postcolonial fault lines between European "East" and "West," however, are rather demoralizingly playing out in the disastrous divisions over what to do with the current refugees fleeing the contemporary "bloodlands" in the Middle East and Africa. The present toxic mix of fear and the un-remedied sense of historical

4. Snyder, *Bloodlands*, vii–viii.

5. Condee, "The Anti-imperialist Empire and After," 830.

6. I have elaborated on the historical and ethical necessity for making that distinction, particularly in the postcolonial context, in "Once More on (the Lightness of) Postcolonial Naming," 1–58.

7. For example, the newly formed online "New East Network" by *The Guardian* is an apt illustration here.

injustice, colonialism, and totalitarianism, as well as the pragmatic amnesia in the "West" about the relatively recent frightening traumas of the Eastern European "bloodlands" once again testifies to the stubbornly undigested—and often neurotically repressed and underinterrogted—postcolonial complexity of Europe.

But what about the spiritual landscape of the postcolonial crevices in the European "Orient" such as Latvia? At this point in history it is rather impossible to locate any "original" or "pure" Latvian Christianity even if one attempts to painstakingly dig through multiple strata of colonization-*cum*-Christianization.[8] The distinctive marker of Latvian Christianity is precisely its (often unconscious) postcolonial hybridity. Centuries after the Christianization/Europeanization of Latvia was technically completed, indigenous pre-Christian religious practices continue to endure alongside and throughout various versions of "inculturated" German and Swedish Lutheranisms, Polish Catholicism, and Russian Orthodoxy. After all, these traditions rubbed against one another within the same tight geopolitical and religious space as wave after wave of colonial incursions rolled over the Baltic peoples and lands.

It is a common observation among Latvian historians and theologians that only with the arrival of the Pietist (The Brethren) movement in Latvia in the eighteenth century is it possible to discern the first "inculturated" type of indigenous Latvian Christian spirituality and even some popular theology. In light of its history of colonization, the Latvian theological vision is more implicit than explicit; more whispered than trumpeted. It remains predominantly homiletic, local, and expressed in poetic and pastoral vernacular that weaves itself around the textures of dominant colonial languages and their cultural and theological imaginaries. From a standard Occidental perspective, the academic archive of Latvian religious scholarship, that is, the texts that have been originally produced in the Latvian language or even those produced by ethnic Latvian theologians writing in the dominant languages remains comparatively embryonic. Today it is aimed at the milieu of approximately two million speakers of the Latvian language worldwide.

Latvian postcolonial Christianity continues to harbor the ambivalence of centuries of economic, political, and spiritual apartheid. Only during the early decades of the twentieth century, as Solveiga Krūmiņa-Koņkova observes, "we can speak of professional [Latvian] scholars in the field of theology and philosophy."[9] It is telling that, to summarize the greatest challenges

8. For a more detailed account of the internal tensions of this creolized spirituality, see my "Not With One Voice."

9. Krūmiņa-Koņkova, "Ievads/Foreword," *Reliģiski filozofiskas idejas Latvijā 20.gs.*, 11. Even though Krūmiņa-Koņkova has detected a reciprocal participation of Latvian

and accomplishments of early twentieth-century "professional" Latvian Lutheran theologians, Māra Grīnfelde has this to say:

> During the first half of the twentieth century, the question of religion was particularly relevant for Lutheran pastors. The new Latvian state inherited the Lutheran Church as an institute of German nobility and now it had to accommodate itself to the new situation—to "reorient itself from the unattractive German 'masters' church' into a nationally oriented 'folk church.'" While doing that it was necessary to answer the question as to how to make religion closer to the Latvians.[10]

The hybridity and ongoing challenges of "Latvianizing"[11] Christianity are powerfully played out on the cover of the *Hymnal of the Evangelical Lutheran Church of Latvia and in Exile* (1992). There a golden cross overlays the Latvian symbol of *Auseklis* (Morningstar) to create a powerful symbolic palimpsest of two rather different religious and cultural systems—Christianity and the polytheistic, indigenous cosmological traditions of wisdom. According to these spiritual traditions, *Auseklis*, among other things, was an ancient deity.

Similar symbolic creolizations can be observed on diasporic Latvian gravestones particularly in North America where indigenous symbolism intertwines with more mainstream Christian semiotics. The former President of Latvia, Vaira Vīķe-Freiberga, has aptly described such symbolic

twentieth century philosophers and theologians in "the development of the Western European theologically philosophical ideas" (11), the assessment of that participation, especially its reciprocal nature, does not appear persuasive. Rather, it seems that what is really present is an unacknowledged and under-interrogated dynamic of the dreaded postcolonial derivativeness (which I will address later in more detail). A summary by Māra Grīnfelde certainly hints at such a situation by arguing that "the Latvian religious-philosophical thinkers were well aware of the discussions obtaining in Western European theological thought and religious studies of their time. However, there are no indications of attempts to further develop and problematize these ideas. With the exception of G. Mensching, no one [. . .] attempted to join the on-going discussion in Europe on the theme of religious studies," "Definitions of Religion," 185–86. It has to be mentioned that Gustav Mensching was actually a German theologian working in Latvia in the 1920s-1930s. He wrote and lectured in German.

10. Grīnfelde, "Introduction,"18.

11. See, for example, the reflection originally published in 1937 by Alberts Vītols, "Latviešu reliģiskā īpatnība un kristiānisma latviskošanas iespējas," ("Latvian Religious Particularity and the Feasibility of the Latvianization of Christianity") and the essay by the then leading Latvian Lutheran systematic theologian Voldemars Maldonis, "Nacionālie un internacionālie elementi reliģijā" ("National and International Elements in Religion"), both available in the recent anthology *Reliģiski filozofiskās idejas Latvijā*. Grīnfelde, "Introduction," 18.

creolizations in Latvian culture and spirituality as a "layer cake" (with a heavy dose of implicit postcolonial overtones) in which "all the various cultural eras have left a significant substratum."[12] As a result, contemporary postcolonial Latvian cultural and religious DNA is hybrid or, in Vīķe-Freiberga's words, "successfully syncretistic"[13] despite ongoing cultural and theological scuffles to distill the "ethnographically correct" style of folk costumes, cuisine, aesthetic taste, musical preferences, orthography, or religion.

When the notorious "Iron Curtain" separating the Eastern European "bloodlands" finally came down in the late 1980s, what emerged from the widely open post-totalitarian religious wilderness was what the Russian postmodernist Mikhail Epstein insightfully called the "minimal" or "poor" religion of post-atheist religiosity.[14] In Latvia it emerged alongside two other less popular, while more zealous and vocal, alternatives: a confessional Christian "traditionalism" and a much vaguer New Age "neopaganism."[15] Meanwhile minimal religion manifested itself as a seeker-type, eclectic habit of theological inquisitiveness—often without the rock-solid precincts or irresistible desire for a single church, single tradition, and single orthodoxy. The wilderness experience, according to Epstein's apt analysis, manifests as "a striving for a fullness of spirit, transcending the boundaries of historical denominations. Those people who have found God in the wilderness feel that the walls of the existing temples are too narrow for them and should be expanded."[16]

Theological inquiry in early postsoviet Latvia was a curious hybrid, too. On the one hand, it was modeled after the speedily defrosted pre-World War II (mostly German) traditions of theological scholarship. On the other, it was shaped by the freshly repatriated expertise of the modern Anglo-American theological edifice through retired diaspora theologians. But

12. Vīķe-Freiberga, *Kultūra un latvietība*, 159.

13. Ibid., 172.

14. Mikhail Epstein, "Minimal Religion." The essay was originally written in 1982 and the term for "minimal religion" is actually "bednaya religiya," or "poor religion." Its poverty is a metaphor for a radical inclination toward apophaticism and a "new life of God beyond the confines of the Church" and "has no worldly possessions: neither temples, nor rituals, nor doctrines. All it has is a relationship with God. . .," in Epstein, et al., *Russian Postmodernism*, 165.

15. Ibid., 386.

16. Ibid. In his later reflections on minimal religion Epstein adds that "spirituality, as it emerges from the ruins of totalitarianism, recognizes the dignity of diverse ethnic and religious traditions but is not satisfied by any single one. Rather it seeks to establish a sacred space across the boundaries of culture," 388. Although Epstein's analysis concerns the Russian postmodern religious landscape in the aftermath of totalitarian atheism, it applies rather well to the similar political specifications of Latvia.

there was also a third force: the Russian Orthodox theological and liturgical tradition was alive and around to be explored by those who knew Russian. I savored Russian theological treasures amidst the piles of slightly outdated English and German theological texts weeded out from various Western libraries and airmailed to the fledgling Eastern European theological libraries by generous expats and various charitable organizations. The stylistic, temperamental, and thematic difference alone provided an exciting and unforgettable contrast that continues to shape my theological mindscape and liturgical sensitivities.

But even this three-pronged hybridity is a rather unruly one. In a twist of true postcolonial irony, Russian Orthodoxy, despite its "exotic" (at least from Western perspectives!) spiritual, contemplative, and liturgical vision, is indelibly imbricated in the centuries of Russian imperial conquest and colonial subjugation of the Latvian people, language, culture, and religion. Again, Latvia's geopolitical location—and its spiritscape—expresses rather hauntingly its location as the borderzone or bufferzone between the "West" (i.e., the Euro-Atlantic orbit of power) and the "East" (i.e., the resurgent Russian neo-imperialist orbit of power). It is here that I owe my readers a further clarification: my study is deeply influenced by the Eastern Orthodox theological vision, its soteriology, and its (pan)sacramentality of creation. But remember the "bloodlands!" The history of calamitous twentieth-century clashes of imperialism and totalitarianism during both World Wars on Latvian soil cannot but complicate any serious theological rendezvous with Eastern Orthodoxy.

As I write, the Russian Orthodox Church once again stands in unholy "symphonic" unity with the Russian neo-imperialist regime. The widely shared and politically cultivated Russian nostalgia for the restoration (creation?) of a hybrid Czarist-*cum*-Orthodox empire is mutating into a new neocolonial imaginary—and into new "hybrid" wars of imperialistic conquest in Georgia, the Crimea, and now also Ukraine. No one knows where else this resurgent "second class" or "subaltern"[17] empire might strike next in Europe or in Asia as some Cold War frontiers are being resuscitated to prevent further Russian incursions into its former colonies. As a whole, Russian Orthodoxy has endorsed and legitimated these neocolonial movements. Eastern Orthodoxy in general has yet to come to terms with its own multiple imperial(istic), colonial, and postcolonial entanglements across a

17. Madina V. Tlostanova and Walter D. Mignolo have explored the interimperial and intercolonial dynamic of modern empires by theorizing Russia and Austro-Hungary as second class/subaltern empires—yet empires nevertheless whose cultural and political posteriority is far from extinct. See Tlostanova and Mignolo, *Learning to Unlearn*, Ch. 2.

wide span of imperial formations that the Orthodox traditions have inhabited, both "from above" and "from below."[18]

The heavily creolized Latvian spiritscape[19] is marked by a weighty postcolonial religious ambiguity toward Russian Orthodoxy. Albeit diasporically, I still inhabit that creolized spiritscape and its inescapable postcolonial ambivalence. If postcolonial history is messy then a self-aware and embodied postcolonial theology cannot possibly expect to be ahistorically idyllic and methodologically pristine. Rather, such theology sooner or later effectively becomes a kind of border thinking once it realizes its hybrid intellectual and cultural pedigrees as well as its often disavowed workings of mimicry. Walter Mignolo helpfully observes that, for those dwelling in the cracks of imperial power constellations,

> theories are where you can find them; and now you can find them all over the world, not just in Europe or the United States. The difference is that theories all over the world, or emerging from "minorities" in Western Europe and the United States, imply border thinking, and for border thinkers the reference point is no longer Greece or Rome; or if it is. . . it is only half of the story.[20]

Well, yes: there are no singular, monotopic, monologic, monochromatic, monolinguistic, or monodoctrinal reference points for a self-aware diasporic and postcolonial imagination, including theological imagination. And thus to be absolutely clear: even as I draw from the treasures of Orthodoxy, often perhaps more implicitly than explicitly, I univocally decry the past and present imperial ecclesiologies and theopolitical entanglements of Russian Orthodoxy with Russian imperial ambitions wherever and however they metastasize today.

At the end of the day, no unambiguous loyalty to any Christian tradition, "Eastern" or "Western," is possible in the environment of a reflective and self-aware Latvian or, for that matter, Eastern European postcoloniality. As Ivana Noble has eloquently explained:

> Now more than during preceding centuries we can see that who we are as Central or East Europeans are is a texture woven from the threads of many cultures, but also many religious expressions. In this sense, it would be foolish to search for one

18. On this topic, see Papanikolaou, *The Mystical as Political*.

19. Recent research shows that Latvia is the most religiously diverse among the postsoviet countries in Europe, see the report by LETA, "Latvijā reliģiskā dažādība visaugstākā starp postpadomju valstīm," April 18, 2016.

20. Mignolo, *The Darker Side of Western Modernity*, 251.

> symbolic tradition that could interpret the whole plurality. We could not all participate in such a tradition. Yet we share one world in which we live and move.[21]

By the same token, no unambiguous *ressourcement* from either the "East" or the "West" will ultimately be credible in Eastern European post-coloniality. And so there is little surprise that like the diasporic biblical scholar, Osvaldo Vena, I too, "have this feeling of not being able to pin down my theology. To many I am a sort of theological chameleon. . ."[22] The history that makes me me comes to fruition in a hybrid theological temperament that virtually instinctively crosses borders—to survive, to seek fulfillment and liberation, to reflect on its own psychospiritual enigmas, and to let life and revelation unfold and flourish.

The darker undersides of such hybridity deserve a mention. My constellation of hybridity—like many other postcolonial lifeworlds from the Caribbean to the Sulu Sea—entails a good dose of what the late Martiniquan poet and theorist Édouard Glissant called "forced poetics," *poétique forcée.*[23] Glissant described "forced poetics" as any "collective desire for expression that, when it manifests itself, is negated at the same time because of the deficiency that stifles it, not at the level of desire, which never ceases, but at the level of expression, which is never realized."[24] What can be done in such circumstances is to:

> cut across one language in order to attain a form of expression that is perhaps not part of the internal logic of this language. A forced poetics is created from the awareness of the opposition between a language that one uses and a form of expression that one needs.[25]

Crucially, "forced poetics exist where a need for expression confronts an inability to achieve expression. It can happen that this confrontation is fixed in an opposition between the content to be expressed and the language suggested or imposed."[26] Mine is a diasporic hybridity of *forced* poetics—and hence it does not feel and may not come across as particularly *poetic* at all.

21. Noble, *Theological Interpretation of Culture*, 199.
22. Vena, "My Hermeneutical Journey," 99.
23. Glissant, *Caribbean Discourse*, 120–21.
24. Ibid.
25. Ibid.
26. Ibid.

For a diasporic sensibility, history is not a past that can be recalled and strategically deployed when the need or desire arises. Rather, for good and for ill, it unintentionally and spontaneously comes alive, on its own, sometimes utterly uninvited and frustratingly burdensome, as a "cultural memory *in* the present."[27] Hence, many a diasporic person usually ends up as if perpetually fidgeting at a crossroads: they are always already in the process of trying to make sense of the relational traffic of languages, (dis/re) locations, theologies, traditions, politics, and moralities as they constantly coalesce in migrant lives and migrant soulscapes. And they must continue to keep making sense and ever tuning into their own homing desire, however unfulfilled or simply fleeting and improvisational it may ever remain. This study charts one possible course of what happens when these diasporic perplexities of belonging voyage into theological reflection. The upcoming parts of this study aim to flesh out the itinerary of a diasporic crossroads-mindscape as it winds through the landscapes and soulscapes of sacramental imagination.

27. Here I refer to Mieke Bal's notion of history in *The Practice of Cultural Analysis*. Italics added.

Prelude III

God's creative energies are echoed and reflected in all that he has made.

Elizabeth Theokritoff[1]

What does it mean to engage in sacramental discourse in the present day of global postcolony—so asymmetrical, so convoluted, and yet so interconnected and interdependent? How does it feel to do theology sacramentally through a diasporic imaginary which is intentionally rooted in postcolonial experience and its ethical exigencies? What can it offer to postcolonial and diasporic Christianity? Most importantly, what can it do, to borrow Alexander Schmemann's famous intention, "for the life of the world"[2] and not just for the liturgical and sacramental orthodoxies presently in (academic and ecclesiastical) vogue?

The three parts of this study comprise a meandering peregrination, indeed a quest, for at least some modest answers to these questions. But where does one start? The first two preludes have foreshadowed two grounding *Leitmotifs* of my study: the incarnational charge of embodied history and the hybrid mindscape of a postcolonial diaspora. In the third prelude the third *Leitmotif* must be briefly introduced: sacramental imaginary. More will be said about sacramental imaginary in Part III.

The most life-giving theological "pearls of greatest value" (Matt 13:46) for constructive postcolonial sacramental reflection do not reside on the level of rituals and devotional observances alone. Why? Because "unfortunately, the sacraments are often reduced to ritual observances"[3] in both modern and postmodern liturgical milieu, and no, the West is not the

1. Theokritoff, *Living in God's Creation*, 169.

2. Schmemann, *For the Life of the World.*

3. Cryssavgis, "A New Heaven and a New Earth," 160.

only place where it happens! But I don't want to overstate the case either. Undoubtedly, these "pearls" do encounter us within and through religious rites. But the point is that what really matters in sacramental theology today dwells still deeper and broader—ontologically, epistemologically, and eschatologically—than the rubrics of hitherto institutionalized rituals, be they "Western" or "Eastern." In other words, the "pearls" I am diving for exceed their performative actualizations and enactments in historically codified and authorized ecclesial rites.

The "pearls" I am after throughout my peregrinations in this study are not confined to rituality or language as privileged as these liturgical modalities are for the dominant Western postmodern spiritual senses and intellectual proclivities. Rather, they pertain more to something I call sacramental imaginary: a sensibility, a rationality, a fabric of imagination, a structure of feeling, a "habitus"—"the constellation of instincts, both individual and collective, which shape the ways of feeling, thinking, observing, understanding, approaching, acting and relating."[4] As such, sacramental imaginary is neither exhausted by its historically known enactments nor incarcerated in the current forms of institutionalized rites. In fact, a fuller fleshing out of postcolonial sacramental imaginary will challenge the self-sufficiency of specific rites, numbers, and habitual definitions of sacraments in the concluding chapters. In that sense, postcolonial sacramental imaginary can be described as sharing in the post-ecclesial condition. Post-ecclesiality, according to Brannon Hancock, is a contemporary socio-cultural context for theological imagination in which, he argues, "sacramentality cannot and will not be circumscribed by the Church. And for this reason we might call sacramentality 'post-ecclesial,' not because it has left the *ecclesia* behind, but because it is constantly moving beyond the ecclesia, superseding and transcending its (seemingly necessary) limits."[5]

Sacramental imaginary is a term for what happens if and when human beings reflect on the nature of reality out of a sacramental lifeworld, a sacramental pluriverse/multiverse. And the sacramental pluriverse is many things at the same time: a planetscape, an ideascape, a sensescape, a soundscape, a touchscape, and a lifepath. It emerges out of life's radical and original openness toward the holy mystery of the triune God. Sacramental imaginary is a way of making sense of the world in which God reveals godself as a creative and salvific mystery within, without, and throughout all that we humanly know and intuit to have been sourced from and sustained by it.

4. Yap Fu Lan, "Living the Eucharist in Asia: A New Habitus."

5. Hancock, *The Scandal of Sacramentality*, 182.

Sacramental imaginary as a worldview and a style of inquiry errs on the side of connections: it holds creation and salvation, Christology and sacraments, history and eschatology together. It is positively predisposed toward the whole creation and not just humanity being made whole and longing for a conviviality with God to become partakers of divine life, no matter how crooked the path toward eternity may be. It is constructively predisposed toward a panentheistic rationality that perceives all of that unfolding and evolving, as it were, within the One in whom the whole creation "lives, moves, and has our being" (Acts 17:28). Sacramental imaginary opens up and down, across and ahead toward the ongoing, coalescing, and synergistic Mystery of creation and salvation ever on the way to when the Holy Mystery will be "all in all" (1 Cor 15:28). It doggedly seeks to find the Divine in all things and all things in the Divine.

But what, then, are the sacraments? At this point, suffice it to say, by "sacraments" I do not exclusively—or even primarily—mean the officially approved and ecclesiastically demarcated ritual observances of various Christian denominations, be they seven or two, or whatever other number. In cases where I specifically refer to these institutionalized rituals/observances, I will use adjectives "ecclesiastical" and "ritual" to explicitly name them as such. Rather, the broader notion of sacrament is a shorthand for the relational and interactive mysteries of divine self-disclosure, human receptivity, and creaturely response that are rooted in and derived from that sacramental interface of creation, revelation, and transformation which grounds, contextualizes, and interconnects the Uncreated and the created. In the biblical imaginary this foundational interface of relationality is usually described as the all-encompassing cosmic *mysterion* of creation and salvation (Col 1:26; Rom 16:25; 1 Cor 2:7, 4:1, 13:2; Eph 1:9, 3:3–4).

But the crux of the matter is this: a sacrament, whatever else it may be, is, as Jean-Jacques von Allmen puts it, never a "thing" (*une chose*) but a "'situation' (*une situation*): it is where our world is visited, or better: it is inhabited and transformed by the presence of the future eon."[6]

Sacramental imaginary hatches when the Holy Mystery and human beings touch, embrace, and intermingle in a myriad of historically specific and culturally individuated ways. Sacramental imaginary breaks open when the Holy One is discerned in the depths of lived encounter and tasted in sensed knowledge. It unfolds at the crossroads of culturally embodied,

6. Von Allmen, *Prophétisme sacramentel*, 13. Von Allmen links this understanding of the sacraments with the re-presencing of Christ as the *Ursakrament*: "*il y a sacrament là où le sacrament par excellence, le Christ incarné, se re-présente*," 13. Even though I do not follow this linkage without reservations, I appreciate the interactive and processual character of von Allmen's contrast.

historically embedded, and psychospiritually textured human lives on their unique evolutionary paths. Every moment of time and every millimeter of space can harbor sacramental revelations and sacramental interactions. As Walter Benjamin has so poignantly remarked, every moment of history might be a narrow gate through which the Messiah could enter![7]

The hermeneutical gateway or harmonic key for a specifically Christian sacramental imaginary gravitates around nothing other than the divine Word/Wisdom becoming incarnate, becoming Emmanuel—God with us, God becoming flesh, Christ Jesus. Christian sacramental imaginary is rooted in a history that is "deeply" indwelled by the Holy Mystery made flesh, energy, matter, stuff. . .[8] Of course, history does not equal the past: the sacramental triple helix of creation, revelation, and salvation is not a nostalgic memoir of spiritual antiquity. Sacramentality and its incarnational crescendo in Christ are about past, present, and the future, all of them together and even more so about the whole of history as an evolutionary, and therefore, as yet a decidedly unfinished, symphony.

And so, proceeding from the sacramental triple helix, what happens after Christ's Ascension is nothing less than the Incarnation continuing its intimate, interpersonal, and salvific unfolding through the "derivative" mysteries, or the spin-off mysteries, or the offshoot mysteries in time and space—the relational events that we traditionally call "sacraments."[9] What we have historically been naming "sacraments" in Western Christianity or "mysteries" in Eastern Christianity are but rhythmic resonances or melodic variations on the paradigmatic sacramental cadence already present in creation and crescendoing in the hypostatic mystery of Christ. Christian sacramental discourse is, as Louis-Marie Chauvet has put, "necessarily rooted in Christology, which no less necessarily opens onto a Trinitarian discourse."[10]

7. Benjamin, "Theses on the Philosophy of History," 264.

8. Niels Henrik Gregersen summarizes the "deep incarnation" approach as the incarnation of Logos into the depths of materiality since the "New Testament nowhere says that God became human. Rather, it says that "the Word (Logos) became flesh (sarx) and lived among us," see "The Extended Body of Christ," 228.

9. The crucial connection between Ascension and interpersonal *incarnatio continua* was concisely pointed out by Leo the Great in his Sermon 74:2 "On the Lord's Ascension, II." Leo did not, however, highlight other *continuous* variables and innovative dimensions of the interconnected and ongoing fugue of creation, incarnation, and salvation. Yet Leo emphasized the visible presence of Christ having transitioned into sacraments after Ascension very clearly: "*Quod redemptoris nostri conscpicuum fuit, in sacramenta transivit*"—what in our savior had become visible, has transitioned into sacraments. The Christian Classics Ethereal Library translation offers a rather flippant interpolation of later terminology in the English translation; see online footnote #1131 giving the original Latin to clarify the meaning.

10. Chauvet, *Symbol and Sacrament*, 155–56.

It is the same cadence that continues to unfold in ever more complex, profound, and intimate ways through Christ and in the Spirit while we journey into what the Eastern Christians so aptly call *theosis*—being saved, being made whole and healed, being transformed and becoming fulsome partakers of the divine life and thus also growing into our true human potential of being fully alive.

Amid all these resonances and variations, the Eucharist of the incarnate Word/ Wisdom through the life-giving vitality of the Spirit is the fulcrum of the whole sacramental galaxy. We humans indwell this open-ended galaxy, this pluriverse of sacramentality, to a more self-aware and reflective degree—at least sometimes—but always not merely on our own and for our own sake. We are indwelling it amid and alongside the rest of creation. Hence the Eucharist is not a sacramental sign and instrument for us alone, by us alone, and among us alone. Above all, the Eucharist communicates and transposes[11] the triune Holy Mystery, our cosmic source and the intimate summit of the whole planetary life and hope, into a uniquely, though not exclusively intense, salvific, and convergent interface for intersubjective and planetary transformations—for the whole creation and for the life of the world to come.

All things sacramental begin and end not in theological manuals or even pristine and shielded ritual spaces but rather in the middle of the serpentine paths of life—in experiences, sensibilities, interactions, frustrations, and imaginaries. For some of us life happens in postcolonial diaspora. And that is where a postcolonial, down-to-earth (back-to-earth?) and earnestly and judiciously "worldly"[12] sacramental theology must begin its long and winding peregrination to seek the Holy Mystery of creation and salvation in the global postcolony.

What might a "worldly" sacramental reflection sound like? If nothing else, it deliberately flares forth from the messy lifeworlds of history. And that history is not to be whitewashed into defensive, disembodied and ultimately unaccountable symbolism. Nor is it to be spirited away into some decadent fiefdom of otherworldly ritualism. These two insular temptations tend to

11. Analogically, to be sure, and always already through the irreducible counterpoint of kataphatic and apophatic rhythms of revelation.

12. "Worldliness" is one of the signature critical metaphors in Edward W. Said's postcolonial humanism and literary theory. Said explains that "worldliness originally meant to me. . . some location of oneself or one's work, or the work itself . . . in the world, as opposed to some extra-worldly, private, ethereal context. Worldliness was meant to be a rather crude and bludgeon-like term to enforce the location of cultural practices back in the mundane, the quotidian, and secular," in Said, *Power, Politics, and Culture*, 335–36.

accompany sacramental-liturgical theology as doggedly as linguistic idealism plagues the poststructuralist imagination of Occidental postmodernity.

First of all, any sacramental imaginary worth its salt cannot be otherwise than profoundly worldly, earthly, and fleshy. Sacramental ontologies and epistemologies are relational and incarnational if they are at all sacramental; they function as an antidote to the binary logic of dualism. Kevin W. Irwin has helpfully underscored the distinctiveness of sacramental outlook as follows:

> Sacramentality is a worldview, a way of looking at life, a way of thinking and acting in the world that values and reveres the world. Sacramentality acts as a prism, a theological lens through which we view creation and all that is on this good earth as revelations of God's presence and action among us here and now. The premise of sacramentality means that in fact we do not live in "two different worlds," the sacred and the secular, but that we live in one graced world named "good" by God in Genesis 1:3 . . . Sacramentality is a worldview that invites us to be immersed fully in the here and now, on this good earth, and not to shun matter or avoid the challenges that such earthiness will require of us, even as we pray through liturgy and sacraments (and other means) to enter into heaven when this earthly pilgrimage has ended.[13]

This understanding of sacramentality, Irwin rightly argues, "presumes engagement in the world and the use of the things on this earth; and this engagement in and through the sacred liturgy leads us to experience that which transcends this world, the transcendent yet immanent triune God."[14]

But we must go even further in postcolonial sacramental reflection. To appreciate the ethical claim of Said's "worldliness" is, then, nothing other than to take seriously "the world as real, empirical messy, contradictory, contingent, crisscrossed and crosshatched by uneven flows of power."[15] As R. Radhakrishnan summarizes, without necessarily amplifying Said's nonchalance toward all things religious, a Saidian take on "worldliness" suggests that it is "a way of submitting" even "other-worldly privileged moments to a genealogical analysis that demonstrates . . . that even the epiphany was a result of worldly circumstances" since, like great works of art, the greatest artifacts of theological inquiry and spiritual insight also are "not marooned in some never-never land of idealism."[16]

13. Irwin, *The Sacraments*, 210.

14. Ibid., 213.

15. Radhakrishnan, *A Said Dictionary*, 148.

16. Ibid., 151.

A Saidian "worldliness" in theological context puts a premium on what David Ngong has recently called the "ethics of theology." Namely, in distinction from theological ethics, the ethics of theology "examines the ethics of theological discourses, focusing on how salutary a particular theological discourse might be to communities and individuals"[17] since "depending on how we do it, our theology may kill us or give us life"[18]—sometimes literally. This sort of "worldliness" in theology always calls for scrutiny—in this context, through a postcolonial lens of discernment—"by asking what could be the possible outcomes of particular theological constructions" with a full recognition that "the actual outcome may be different from the imagined one."[19]

Last, but not least: to do a "worldly" postcolonial sacramental and liturgical theology is to recognize, as intimidating and embarrassing as it may be for us theologians, that any and all theological reflection takes place precisely in this "worldly" world of tumultuous and ambiguous history. In fact, theological imagination is manipulated, often far more deeply and far more strongly than many dare to admit, by the functional dark sides and even neurotic blindspots within our sociocultural, political, and religious imaginaries.

Our shared global history was and still remains, on this side of the beatific vision, mired in the wounding structures of dominance and competitive dualism: racism, sexism, classism, and a legion of cultural imperialisms and religious fundamentalisms to mention just the most obvious ills. Even under the summons of grace, a messy history can only engender messy theology and messy worship that are, at best, profoundly aware of their own limits and inadequacies throughout their poignant *epektasis* toward wisdom. And this history, including the pages written by Christianity, as Walter Benjamin ever reminds us with such daring lucidity, is very far from being uncritically "citable in each of its moments"—moments past, present, and alas many still to come—especially if Christian theologians take the eschatological perspective of resurrection as seriously as Benjamin did.[20]

17. Ngong, *Theology as Construction of Piety*, xxi.

18. Ibid., xvii.

19. Ibid., 2.

20. Benjamin, "Theses on the Philosophy of History," 254.

PART I

Compositio Loci

Exploring Diasporic and Postcolonial Lifeworlds of Theological Imagination

1.1.

Diasporic Sights and Sounds

A Fugue of Christ, Blue Cornflowers, and Wild Carrots

How does a theologian live with a haunted history—disjointed, constantly shifting, and refusing to be fitted into one piece?[1]

Kwok Pui-lan

Whatever else it might mean, being "haunted" does not stand for being settled comfortably in any geographical, linguistic, cultural, or confessional location. "Haunted," that is, by the perplexities of belonging among divergent cultural memories, political allegiances, and theological traditions that co-inhere rather spontaneously in an intellectual sensibility marked indelibly by the experience of migrancy and diasporic life.

In this study, my critical peregrinations through the terrain of theological method and its Occidental colonial attraction to dualistic imaginaries of divine transcendence, sacramentality, and agency are "haunted" by the polyphony (cacophony?) of diasporic life. The polyphonous (and sometimes cacophonous!) diasporic life is almost instinctively drawn to interrogate the modes of relationality between the multiple, coexisting and conflicting, dimensions of experience and knowledge that so often seem altogether disagreeable at first glance. In this regard, being "haunted" stands for being

1. Kwok, Pui-lan, "A Theology of Border Passage," 110.

always already embedded in a specific diasporic hybridity of cultural, linguistic and theological code-switching.[2]

But being "haunted" by cultural and theological hybridity is not necessarily a liability within a religious worldview that strives to affirm the Incarnation as its quintessential revelatory paradigm. If the culturally embodied human person as a historically enmattered soul or ensouled body indeed is the archetypical locus of encounter between divinity and humanity, then the "materiality of the particular"[3] can and should be vigorously affirmed as a foremost interface of revelation and grace. The incarnate, crucified, and resurrected body of Christ intensifies the innate "sacramental potential of the particular" throughout the whole economy of creation and thus also the "perduring presence of God's salvific power as mediated by particularity."[4] In other words, the sacramental potential of the particular is present in creation through primordial divine generosity. Its inclusive scope of diversity is nothing short of planetary. It permeates, liturgically speaking, "all times and all places"[5] without any ideologically, politically, or historically imposed omission and segregation.

Furthermore, the sacramental potential of the particular is actually indispensable for a meaningful revelation within the incarnational hermeneutic: precisely through their sacramental potential particular forms of human embodiment engender nothing less than "true *loci theologici*."[6] Even though the Roman Catholic theological trio of Anthony Godzieba, Lieven Boeve, and Michele Saracino do not specifically delve into the geopolitical intricacies of embodiment that are inescapably configured through glaringly inequitable power dynamics that postcolonial critiques would highlight, their hermeneutical thrust begs material elongation beyond unspecific "embodiment" into the realm of precisely those intricacies that shape particular human lives and agencies so uniquely and consequentially. Hence the incarnationally intensified sacramental capacity of material realities to mediate divine revelation indeed embraces a whole palooza of particular configurations of postcolonial hybridity and diasporic experience.

2. Code-switching is a linguistic and socio-cultural term that describes affiliated use of words from more than one language by a multilingual person in the same sentence or throughout a whole conversation.

3. Godzieba et al., "Resurrection-Interruption-Transformation," 780.

4. Ibid.

5. The phrase is part of a traditional formula in eucharistic prefaces in a number of Christian liturgical traditions, including the Lutheran *ordo*, that often runs similar to this: "It is truly good, right, and salutary that we should at all times and in all places give thanks to you, holy Lord, almighty Father. . ."

6. Godzieba et al, "Resurrection-Interruption-Transformation," 782.

Both constitute a *locus theologicus* in their own right, not just a fashionable vignette of "context" according to the presently solidifying scholarly etiquette in the Occidental academy. Without doubt, the sacramental potential within the particular facilitates an "always-vulnerable mediation."[7] But what avenue of revelation can ever achieve more, even if it manages to steer clear of idolatrous self-indulgence and hegemonic presumptuousness?

POSTCOLONIALITY BEYOND MONOCHROMATIC ESSENTIALISMS

And yet there is another dimension to the predicament of being "haunted." The postcolonial connotations and connections which are so pivotal for hybrid theological sensibilities such as mine—namely, being a white person of Eastern European origin—might appear rather puzzling outside of Europe. Of course, even Eastern European postcoloniality—one type of postcoloniality "from below" among others—can never be unambiguous.

In the context of my study, postcoloniality "from below" refers to the peoples, territories, cultures, and groups that have been on the receiving end of colonial subjugation and conquest not only politically and economically but also spiritually, culturally, intellectually, and affectively. Today, in the aftermath of the classic colonial era, both the formerly colonized and the former colonizers share the deeply ambivalent realities of postcoloniality. This sort of reciprocal entanglement in the colonial regimes of power is precisely what the postcolonial condition expresses and what postcolonial analyses interrogate. Yet both parties share the present global postcolonial condition differently; their reciprocity remains asymmetrical and their interconnection is often lopsided and always very complex.

Obviously, one must tread very carefully here. Taking the history of Western European colonialism into account, it comes as little surprise that today virtually all white people of European ancestry are often seen as inhabiting global postcoloniality "from above" almost by default. But if one asks, say, the Irish, or the Estonians, or the Roma—to choose the most geographically distant and culturally diverse examples of intra-European colonial histories—then their (usually unheard) stories may add some important nuances to postcolonial analysis. If attention is paid to the geocultural "small voice[s] of history,"[8] even in Europe and Eurasia, then the racial anatomy of global colonial escapades must be further problematized

7. Godzieba, "'Stay with us. . .' (Luke 24:29)," 793.

8. I am referring to the groundbreaking articulation of postcolonial subaltern historiography by Ranajit Guha, "The Small Voice of History," 1–12.

to avoid precisely what postcolonial critiques have always deplored so incessantly—a reductive essentialization of identities and histories.

To remain vigilant about some quite entrenched postcolonial clichés, it is helpful to recognize that the globalized world of the early twenty-first century is a postcolonial world *in toto* by virtue of so many societies and countries having been involved—triumphantly or sorrowfully—in the global colonial system over many centuries of Western conquests. As I have argued elsewhere, several formerly colonized cultures in Europe, for reasons too complex to elucidate here, are typically ignored by postcolonial scholarship. On top of that, quite a few are not at all eager to join the postcolonial club "from below." In Eastern and Central Europe this attitude is due to the simmering conundrum of racism (just think about the current refugee crisis in Europe and the racial and ethnic strife exemplified by Brexit!) that intermingles with a sense of cultural violation, memories of spiritual and political victimhood, and resurgent ideologies of nationalism. These lived paradoxes shape the postcolonial/postcommunist space in Eastern, Southern, and Central Europe since the collapse of the Soviet Union—a colonial empire that was "internally imperialist but (in its declared animosity to First World predation) externally anti-imperialist. . ."[9]

Perhaps nothing could serve this postcolonial/postsoviet milieu of Europe—at least from the diasporic North-American perspective—more fruitfully than entering into a dialogue with other postcolonial treasuries of critique and wisdom to help at least name the deeply unsettling colonial traumas as well as ambivalent imbrication in Western ideologies of imperialism. Such a dialogue draws from the widest range of postcolonial resources of imagination and wisdom with a sense of subaltern (horizontal) solidarity and with the sense of kinship in "minor transnationality."[10] The outcome is, not surprisingly, a certain kind of border thinking.

9. Condee, "The Anti-imperialist Empire and After," 830.

10. I refer here to Françoise Lionnet and Shu-Mei Shih's notion of minor transnationality that "points toward and makes visible the multiple relations between the national and transnational" that creates "a space of exchange and participation wherever processes of hybridization occur and where it is still possible for cultures to be produced and performed without necessary mediation by the center," *Minor Transnationalism*, 8, 5. Minor transnationality emphasizes the need for postcolonial communities to understand the lost potential of mutual empowerment if "our battles are always framed vertically, and we forget to look sideways to lateral networks that are not readily apparent" (1) but through which minoritarian subjects can fruitfully interact in lateral ways. Transnationality is enacted through cultural, political, and epistemological border-crossing.

WHICH BORDERS AND WHOSE BORDER THINKING?

It is precisely through the "border thinking" which unfolds across the planetary curvatures of subaltern solidarity and empathy, that postsoviet-*cum*-postcolonial lifeworlds can come to terms with their own deeply ambiguous and multilayered colonial past and move toward an earnest and meaningful decolonial renewal. According to Walter Mignolo,

> Border thinking is grounded not in Greek thinkers but in the colonial wounds and imperial subordination and, as such, it should become the connector between the diversity of subaltern histories (colonial and imperial—like Russia and the Ottoman empires) and corresponding subjectivities . . . we want to include the perspective and . . . the foundation of knowledge subjectivities that have been subjected in and by the colonial matrix of power.[11]

Strange as it may sound, the ancient Greek tradition—as well as the ancient Hebrew tradition, for that matter—is not native to all Europeans, especially those of us who find ourselves in the postcoloniality "from below" end of the spectrum. Both are part of the colonial matrix of power despite their prophetic theological potential, revelatory wisdom, and philosophical acumen. Thus, considering postsoviet versions of postcoloniality, only a multi-pronged border thinking will be intricate enough to "enact the de-colonial shift" as it connects precisely the "different experiences of exploitation" within "different colonial histories entangled with imperial modernity."[12] And here dwells the crux of the matter, in Mignolo's précis of postcolonial difference:

> Decolonizing knowledge and being from the perspective of Japan's or Russia's colonies will be quite different from the perspective of England's colonies. In the first two cases, decolonization from the epistemic and existential conditions imposed by Japanese and Russian languages leaves still another layer to deal with, which is the epistemic and epistemic conditions growingly imposed world wide by Greco-Latin and the six vernacular imperial languages of Western empires. . . Any project of decolonization must operate in full awareness of its location within the complex relations structured by imperial and colonial differences.[13]

11. Mignolo, "Delinking," 493.
12. Ibid., 498.
13. Ibid.

In other words, quite a few postsoviet-*cum*-postcolonial imaginaries face the sensitive task of making a critical inventory of multiple and oftentimes culturally and ideologically opposed layers of coloniality and imperiality that have been inscribed in their histories to discern sustainable and genuinely restorative models of decolonial integrity. To return to Glissant's poignant trope of *poétique forcée*, such discernment is ridden with complex hierarchies of oppression, hegemony, victimhood, and mimicry.

Mita Banerjee highlights the fact that there is often "no sense of a shared history or kinship between the ex-postcolonial and the postcommunist."[14] Reflecting on the swelling racial tensions within the "old" or Western Europe, Fatima El-Tayeb observes: "White Christian migrants to the European Union from eastern Europe are also frequently racialized as not properly European" even though they can "visually pass" while being "forced to remain silent in order not to betray their otherness."[15] The recent British propaganda campaigns on television and in the cyberworld to discourage the influx of impoverished Romanian and Bulgarian migrants, especially the Roma, from the "new" Europe by threatening them with awful weather conditions among other alleged ills of the British lifestyle, illustrate these attitudes rather bluntly. As I write, ethnoracial resentment against postcommunist Eastern European migrant workers is percolating throughout the brave new world of Brexit. It is not only Muslims or Caribbean immigrants but also Eastern European immigrants who are increasingly targeted by hate speech and hate crimes. Despite differences in racial dynamic between Europe and the United States, similar developments are not inconceivable in the US considering the ideology which propelled Donald Trump to the office of the President.

In light of Banerjee's observations, there is a need to acknowledge the emergence of metastasizing forms of postcolonial subalternity. Among those forms "the Eastern European appears as the "un"-or-"precivilized" while the whole of "Eastern Europe has become the other of a now civilized postcolonial world"[16] as it continues to provide relatively cheap labor in the strawberry fields, mushroom farms, and healthcare services of the United Kingdom and elsewhere in "old" Europe.

The present study is diasporically emplaced within the materiality and imaginary of the often unnoticed yet "tantalizing off-whiteness of Eastern

14. Banerjee, "Postethnicity and Postcommunism," 315. The same issue is also relentlessly problematized in *Baltic Postcolonialism*. See also my analysis of the postcolonial ethics of naming and politics of recognition in "Once More on (the Lightness of) Postcolonial Naming."

15. El-Tayeb, "The Forces of Creolization," 235–36.

16. Banerjee, "Postethnicity and Postcommunism," 316–17.

Europeanness" which routinely continues to fall "outside the 'ethno-racial pentagon' of both US racial discourse and postcolonial studies."[17] Constantly slipping off the charts of both colonial and postcolonial routines and orthodoxies leaves a thinker like me suspended somewhere alongside the routes of the North-Atlantic and Euro-Asian metropolitan vortexes of power; suspended somewhere in the stubbornly disagreeable interstices of cultural and historical memory. Nevertheless, as Nancy Condee argues, "the Soviet case (Eurasia, after all) is an important crossroads for postcolonialist debates, a site where familiar terms encounter each other anew."[18]

To make it absolutely clear: I tout neither diasporic identity nor my particular configuration of postcolonial "forced poetics" as a badge of cultural honor, inverse privilege, or esoteric insight. The recent decades of postcolonial studies alongside other minoritarian discourses have shown that sometimes it is academically titillating to explore and theorize margins and migrancy—but usually from an economically and politically safe distance. However, to live within these interstitial and fuzzy outskirts is not nearly as much fun as to theorize them. The only reason why I highlight these historical and contextual prolegomena for theological inquiry is this: they cannot but permeate theological reflection in a decisive way as I voyage into the realm of Christian sacramentality. They play an existentially grounding role in the *compositio loci* for theological praxis. To conclude the *compositio loci*, two brief interludes to further illustrate the gravitational vortices of this particular historic and diasporic mindscape may be helpful here.

EXILES AND THEIR TRANS-ATLANTIC CHRIST

First, I turn to the altarpiece at the Latvian *Trimdas* (Exile) Evangelical Lutheran Church of Boston, Massachusetts. I invoke it not because I consider it to be particularly beautiful or to comment on my taste in visual arts. The author of the monumental altarpiece[19] is the prolific Latvian-American painter Augusts Annus (1893—1984) who came to the United States, as the majority of Latvians in the Americas once did, as a World War II refugee. In the center of the altarpiece is a stern, blond, and rather Nordic-looking Jesus Christ who is depicted as walking on water right in the middle of the Atlantic Ocean. The ocean's stormy waters have parted and Christ walks

17. Ibid., 316.

18. Condee, "The Anti-Imperialist Empire and After," 830.

19. The altar painting can be seen on the website of the Latvian Center of Boston: http://bostonlatviancenter.org/facilities_rental_3.html?frm_data1=8&frm_data1_type=large.

victoriously, as if in a tunnel of light, toward the viewer under a colorful rainbow that connects a contour of Latvia in the right upper corner with the shape of North America in the left upper corner. Of course, these images are instantly recognizable to those who know where and how to look—to a casual observer who cannot recognize geographical shapes of various countries and continents these signs will most likely remain obscure without an explanation.

Christ's outstretched hands gesture toward both locations—Latvia and North America—to acknowledge, connect, and gather both sides of the ocean in him as the incarnate covenant of divine love. This is not just an awe-inspiring yet generic depiction of Christ conveying calm, composed, and majestic—if somewhat detached and static—divine power to anchor the scattered and downtrodden exiles who pray around the altar below. This Christ is always betwixt and between continents, histories and temporalities, under the covenantal rainbow that weaves together loss and hope, memory and promise, survival and faith. This Christ is neither in the Old World nor in the New. Christ's outstretched hands do not have a firm grip on either side of the ocean even as they appear to hold and balance both. Christ is in the very connection of both sides of the partition, walking confidently on the fluid and treacherous waters of the Atlantic that connect as much as they separate.

Christ is in the middle of the "passage" as he voyages toward the souls of those who view the altarpiece. This Christ walks on the waters of uncertainty, partitions, displacements and emplacements. Precisely from there, from the sinuous chasm of the Atlantic, Christ meets the eye and soul of those who find themselves on a voyage into a new place, language, culture, and history and also those who see in this Christ a spiritual affirmation of the voyages of their migrant forebears. Among other things that could be said about the Boston altarpiece, this is a Christ of those and for those who, as Edward Said put it, are not "purely *one* thing"[20]—as heartbreaking as it often has been, especially for the post-World War II political refugees, to reconcile with this outcome of their displaced lives. Nevertheless, this is a paradigmatic Christ of migrants and refugees and for migrants and refugees.

CREATION AND ITS DIASPORIC CORNFLOWERS

Secondly, I turn to the magnificent stained glass windows in the sanctuary of the Latvian Evangelical Lutheran Church of St. John in the Western suburbs of Philadelphia, Pennsylvania. The windows reflect salvation history

20. Said, *Culture and Imperialism*, 336.

from Creation to Pentecost, a seemingly universal pattern of pivotal Christian themes and narratives from the Hebrew Bible and the New Testament and designed by the contemporary Latvian artist Sandra Utāne from Rīga, Latvia, in 2001.[21]

The artistic rendition here, as contrasted to Annus' neo-classical and monumental strokes, is tantalizingly contemporary. The theme of the first window is the Creation: luscious green colors saturate the highly stylized artistic rendition of cosmological plenitude and goodness, as well as earth and water, flora and fauna. A rainbow as the sign of the covenant graces the light-permeated upper part of the window, but this time the most intriguing element of this diasporic sacred art is located in the dark green fecundity of the corners and chromatic interstices. There a casual gaze might miss two flowers that are very near and dear to Latvian hearts: a small blue cornflower (*centaurea cyanus*) and a stylized and very unpretentious Queen Anne's lace or wild carrot (*daucus carota*). These two flowers certainly do not dominate the bountiful Creation scene with its intense colors and plethora of life forms. Rather, they claim the deepest crevices of creation with the subtle elegance of a fragment, yet with a profoundly meaningful presence of nuance that once noticed will not be forgotten or ignored.

It is important to note that the unexpected fragment does not force itself on a distracted eye. These gossamer nuances that one has to look for very attentively signify most immediately the particular, indeed sacramental, inscription of Latvian cultural memory and history in the providential economy of divine creation and salvation. The whole array of universal Judeo-Christian sacred symbols is succulently present in the stained glass window. And yet, in the semiotic space of diaspora and exile it is the small blue cornflower and the ethereal wild carrot that incarnate (bear the burden of!) existential profundity and the simultaneous fragility of God's redemptive relation to Latvian cultural roots and routes of life and faith through the twists and turns of a rather unforgiving history.

A FUGAL ENCOUNTER

Why do these two images of Latvian sacred art matter? First of all, encountering the Divine through the incarnate Christ and in the movement of the

21. Sandra Utāne is a stained glass artist at the Academy of Arts in Rīga, Latvia. Some of her work at the Latvian Lutheran Church of St. John can be seen online: http://www.latvianluthchurchphila.org. I was delighted to collaborate with Sandra and the architect of St. John's sanctuary, the late Janis Freijs, in the creation of the interior design while serving as the pastor at St. John's.

Spirit—imaginatively, aesthetically, theologically, discursively, affectively, and historically—is something that for a diasporically embodied soul happens particularly meaningfully within their own hybrid borderland between cultures, languages, histories, and traditions.[22] The traditional and the innovative, the unitary and the fragmentary, the shared and the particular, and both global and local elements and techniques weave themselves together not just in discursive theological imagination and liturgical practice but equally so in art. In fact, in the Latvian diasporic milieu, art expresses the theological and spiritual mindscape in a most concise and accessible way.

These two instances of Latvian diasporic visual theology show that the provisional home of hybrid diasporic spirituality and imagination is most akin to the visual fugues that "play" out in sacred communal and individual spaces alongside equally hybrid (culturally fugal) musical expressions. In music, a fugue is a figure of polyphonic complexity, intertwinement, and interaction of voices and melodic lines that can accommodate dissonant tensions as well as harmonic resolutions. In a fugal composition of music—and by metaphoric stretch, also in visual images, spaces, tastes, smells, affects, and intellects—the moments of resolution and harmony can be generated without obliterating the inherent polyphonic and even dissonant texture. All these multivalent, eclectic, and ultimately hybrid artscapes convey the sacramental potential of the particular.

The diasporic and postcolonial particularity is what it is together with—and despite of—all the colonial burdens, legacies, and ambiguities. Precisely as such, in all its genealogical impurity and "inauthenticity," this sort of particularity nevertheless fully participates in the sacramental economy of revelation. Without doubt, there are myriads of ways how such a sacramental *commercium admirabile* can happen. Diaspora is one historico-cultural itinerary among many other experiences and expressions. Within this diasporic itinerary, however, the migrant Christ who walks under the rainbow in the middle of the parting Atlantic is an imaginative, affective, artistic and discursive sacrament of diasporic lifeworld of in-betweenness, interconnectedness, and (often undesired and uncelebrated yet inescapable) hybridity.

Secondly, small blue cornflowers and gossamer wild carrots can unlock the uniquely creative potential of diminutive analytic metaphors to explore postcolonial and diasporic modes of theologizing and the nature of their critical and constructive contributions. I will return to these images

22. Here Godzieba's insight is pastorally crucial: "The presence of God's love and grace can be salvific for human persons only when that divine presence in some way appears within the field of their embodied lived experiences and particular categories of understanding, even while it exceeds these categories," Godzieba, "'Stay with us. . .,'" 792.

as analytical and constructive metaphors at the conclusion of Part I. At this juncture, suffice it to say that in certain diasporic and postcolonial contexts, the very integrity of theological inquiry is all about nuances, diminutive and minuscule as they may be. Nuances are deployed as critical, subversive, constructive, and sometimes even redemptive pivots around which postcolonial migratory lives and imaginations can thrive outside of and otherwise than hegemonic spiritualities and imaginaries. But what exactly is meant by postcoloniality and postcolonialism here?

1.2

Postcoloniality, Postcolonialism, and Decoloniality

Beyond Revolutions and Reversals

Postcolonialism is at once a response to the Western colonial spirit and a symptom of its own decadence.[1]

Vítor Westhelle

Unsurprisingly, postcolonialism means different things to different people depending on their cultural background, historical memory and academic allegiance. What are "postcolony," "postcoloniality," and "postcolonialism"—words that I have allowed to leak into these reflections without rushing to define them? The precise beginnings, meanings, and transgressions of the "post" in post(-)colonial/ity/ism have remained under unrelenting interrogation and critique since the earlier in-depth analyses in the 1990s. The "post" in "postcolonial" is most definitely not a simple matter of chronological time.[2] The "post" does not celebrate the end of "classic" fixed territorial colonialism as a complete victory of genuine decolonization. Rather, with Françoise Lionnet, it continues to be useful to think of postcoloniality "in terms of 'postcontact': that is, as a condition that exists

1. Westhelle, *After Heresy*, 65.

2. Chow, *Ethics After Idealism*, 150–51.

within, and thus contests and resists, the colonial moment itself with its ideology of domination."[3]

COLONIALITY AND POSTCOLONIAL REASONING

To understand the nature of postcolonial reasoning it is important to remember that colonialism is much more than mere bureaucratic exercise of direct colonial rule of one political entity over another. In the words of Stuart Hall, it signifies "the whole process of expansion, exploration, conquest, colonization and imperial hegemonisation which constituted the 'outer face,' the constitutive outside, of European and then Western capitalist modernity."[4] In light of the colonial penchant for omnipresent binary juxtapositions, it is particularly ironic to remember that under the aegis of colonialism "differential temporalities and histories have been irrevocably and violently yoked together."[5] Hence at the present historical moment, Hall reminds us, "no site, either 'there' or 'here,' in its fantasied autonomy and in-difference, could develop without taking into account its significant and/or abjected others."[6]

Historical manifestations of modern colonialism as ideology and as intertwined political, economic, military, epistemic, and religious practices are rooted in the imaginary of coloniality. Coloniality is a relationality imagined, legitimated, and executed in the mode of violence, hegemony, inequality, and coercion. It obtains as the colonial matrix of power, knowledge, and being. Coloniality, according to Walter Mignolo's summary, is:

> the logic of oppression and exploitation hidden under the rhetoric of modernity, the rhetoric of salvation, progress, civilization, development. . . [it] is precisely the triumphal and persuasive rhetoric of *being*: being as success, being someone, being on top of another (e.g., Benjamin Franklin's celebration of competition as an improvement for all).[7]

Coloniality is enacted upon social bodies and individual bodies not just politically, militarily, and economically but also spiritually, intellectually, and affectively. In other words, colonialism grounded in the coloniality of power, knowledge, and being is a mode of relating to other(ness), usually

3. Lionnet, *Postcolonial Representations*, 4.
4. Hall, "When Was 'The Post-Colonial'?" 249.
5. Ibid., 252.
6. Ibid.
7. Mignolo, "Introduction: Immigrant Consciousness," xix. Italics in the original.

constructed and perceived as deficient yet instrumentally profitable, without a life-affirming recognition of respectful reciprocity. Coloniality obtains as the enshrinement of presumptuous and allegedly "natural" asymmetry of agency, dignity, identity, values, knowledge, beauty, and ability based on the racial, ethnic, cultural, geo-political, and sexual origins and markers of human lives. This asymmetry of power (authority and economy!) is "grounded and supported by patriarchal racialization."[8] Under the auspices of coloniality, as Nelson Maldonado-Torres observes, life becomes "an imperial project of existence"—"a modality of being" forced into the aggressive power grid of social and geopolitical divides, all bound together in the competitive dualism of war.[9]

POSTCOLONIALITY AND POSTCOLONIALISM

Postcoloniality, then, is what has been unfolding across all of the above mentioned terrains of life throughout very diverse locations around the globe in the deeply ambiguous wake of the "high" or "classic" colonialism of modernity. Postcoloniality or postcolony, as Achille Mbembe fittingly emphasizes, "encloses multiple *durées* made up of discontinuities, reversals, inertias, and swings that overlay one another, interpenetrate one another, and envelope one another: an *entanglement*."[10] As an analytical term, postcolony is a concept-metaphor that conveys the "figure of a fact—the fact of brutality, its forms, its shapes, its markings, its composite faces, its fundamental rhythms and its ornamentation."[11]

Postcoloniality refers to the geo-political, socio-cultural, and religious lifeworlds on our planet during the ongoing aftermath of the formal decline of mostly, but not exclusively, Western territorial empires. Postcoloniality is a historical, economic, and psychic condition that has been substantively carved into the lifestyles and value systems for both the colonized and the colonizers, albeit asymmetrically, by the heterogeneous ideologies and practices of colonial power. While the formal structures of political and spiritual hegemony are technically gone, the "concealed persistence of unfreedom" on the political and economic level endures in tandem with the "perverse longevity of the colonised [that] is nourished, in part, by persisting colonial hierarchies of knowledge and value which reinforce what Edward Said calls

8. Ibid., xiv.

9. Maldonado-Torres, *Against War*, 245, 239.

10. Mbmebe, *On the Postcolony*, 14.

11. Mbembe, "On the Postcolony: a brief response," 151.

the 'dreadful secondariness.'"[12] The postcolonial nature of the present era, in Deepika Bahri's nimble summary, is like "a watermark left on the text of cultures after the experience of colonialism. It is the way in which the governance, political systems, and cultural expression bear the impact of the historical period of colonial rule."[13]

How does postcolonialism relate to postcoloniality? In the context of this book, postcolonialism is the body of transdisciplinary critical dispositions and strategies of inquiry that study the manifestations of the coloniality of power, being, and knowledge in the era of colonial modernity and the present condition of postcoloniality. Postcolonialism interrogates the constellations of asymmetrical relations—economic, political, and cultural as well as religious and theological—and the ethical qualities of empowerment and agency involved in the performance and legitimization of these relations.

Postcolonial critiques describe, according to Robert Young, "a theoretical and political position which embodies an active concept of intervention within . . . oppressive circumstances. It combines the epistemological cultural innovations of the postcolonial moment with a political critique of the conditions of postcoloniality."[14] The postcolonial critical trajectory is an intellectually and politically "unashamedly committed stance."[15] As R.S. Sugirtharajah aptly characterizes it, postcolonialism, to name just the most obvious interlocutors and inspirations,

> unlike other theoretical categories . . . is not too preoccupied with detachment and neutrality. It emerged from both indigenous and diasporic contexts. Its critical stance is a creative adoption of the practical insights gleaned from those involved in anti-colonial and neo-colonial struggles and the theoretical tools and perspectives gained from a wide variety of disciplines. This includes a combination of clashing and contradictory voices from literary theory, philology, psychology, anthropology, political science, and feminist studies, with a view of exposing the collusive nature of Western historiography and its hidden support for imperialism. It is an attempt to explore the often one-sided, exploitative, and collusive nature of academic scholarship.[16]

12. Gandhi, *Postcolonial Theory*, 7.
13. Bahri, "Raising the Profile of Southeastern Studies," 22, 24.
14. Young, *Postcolonialism*, 57.
15. Sugirtharajah, *Exploring Postcolonial Biblical Criticism*, 13.
16. Ibid.

Postcolonial critiques do not operate as metaphoric blanket terms for any diffuse contemporary cultural differences and marginalities with the goal to simply spice up the weary categories of multiculturalism. Postcolonialism describes a "specific set of practices that are grounded in 'the discursive and material effects of the historical 'fact' of colonialism' "[17] in its various manifestations. In other words, to be historically vigilant and ethically accountable, postcolonial imagination must remain attuned to the "from below" aspect of lived postcoloniality. Postcolonialism, if it desires to engender an ethically accountable intellectual and political comportment, has to exercise vigilance lest it degenerate into just another trendy theoretical game in the academic global village—a prodigiously frequent temptation in the corporatized academic world.

Some critical voices, mostly outside the British-Indian postcolonial orbit, have warned about precisely that: Lionnet and Shih point out that "postcolonial cultural studies have been overly concerned with a vertical analysis confined to one nation-state, such as the effect of British colonialism in India" while sidelining those cultures that remain effectively colonized and thus reinforcing "the hegemony of English as the language of discourse and communication."[18] Walter Mignolo echoes these sentiments by questioning the postcolonial enamouration with Euro-centered poststructuralist theories and cautions that the discourse of postcoloniality remains limited as a "project of scholarly transformation within the academy."[19] What is needed beyond the Western ivory tower theories, according to Mignolo, is rather a shift toward decoloniality.

FROM POSTCOLONIALITY TO DECOLONIALITY

Decoloniality, as Maldonado-Torres summarizes, entails a "confrontation with the racial, gender and sexual hierarchies that were put in place or strengthened by European modernity as it colonized and enslaved populations through the planet."[20] The ethos of decoloniality embodies an epistemic

17. Thieme, *Post-Colonial* Studies, 123.

18. Lionnet and Shih, "Introduction," *Minor Transnationalism*, 11.

19. Mignolo, "Delinking," 452. Mignolo and Madina Tlostanova do not oppose postcoloniality but aspire to "move postcolonial critique out of the celebratory in which it has been cajoled by the book market in the English language and for an Engish-speaking market audience," see their "The Logic of Coloniality and the Limits of Postcoloniality," *The Postcolonial and the Global*, 109.

20. Maldonado-Torres, "On the Coloniality of Being," 261. The notion of coloniality/decoloniality is addressed by a number of influential postcolonial thinkers, mostly from South American countries and their diasporas in the Western hemisphere such

shift that "denounces the pretended universality of a particular ethnicity (body politics), located in a specific part of the planet (geo-politics), that is, Europe where capitalism accumulated as a consequence of colonialism."[21] According to Mignolo, decoloniality is enacted through "ethically oriented, epistemologically geared, politically motivated and economically necessary processes" that have "the damnés as its central philosophical and political figure."[22] The ethos of decoloniality advocates both the resistance to and the transformation of coloniality—the enduring imaginary of dominance, hegemony, coercion, and competitive dualism—of power, knowledge, and being.

These critiques of postcoloniality have merit. Yet, what some thinkers call "decoloniality" resonates very strongly with what I have presented here as postcolonialism. In fact, I will argue in the opening chapter of Part II that the so-called ethical pre-text in postcolonialism overlaps with the critical and transformative thrust of the decolonial trajectory. This is why prudent postcolonial thinkers have not ceased to call attention to the recurrent problematic connotations of the "post." It is clear that sometimes the "post" has been deployed prematurely and overly celebratory. This is what happens if and when the academic postcolonial critique slips into textual or aesthetic suspension of history and politics that continues to plague real life postcolonial individuals and communities today. Nevertheless the constructive thrust of postcoloniality-as-postcolonialism is envisioned to be nurture something quite different. Homi Bhabha's vision still rings true because a perceptive postcoloniality

> is a salutary reminder of the persistent 'neo-colonial" relations with the 'new' world order and multinational division of labour. Such a perspective enables the authentication of histories of exploitation and the evolution of strategies of resistance. Beyond this, postcolonial critique bears witness to those countries and communities—in the North and the South, urban and rural—constituted, if I may coin a phrase, "otherwise than modernity."[23]

as Anibal Quijano, Walter Mignolo, Arturo Escobar, Ramon Grosfoguel, Chela Sandoval, Maria Lugones, and the trans-diasporic Madina Tlostanova from Russia. The influence of Enrique Dussel is prominent in the movement. For a good summary see the essay collection *Globalization and the Decolonial Option* edited by Mignolo and Arturo Escobar. For a perspective beyond South American locales, see Tlostanova's Деколониальные гендерные эпистемологии.

21. Mignolo, "Delinking," 453.

22. Ibid., 458.

23. Bhabha, *The Location of Culture*, 9.

The persistent scuffling around the meaning of "post" in postcolonial circles attends to the unfinished and messy dialectics between the past and the present. Despite recent academic quarrels, alas, as Robert J. C. Young pointed out, "the real problem lies in the fact that the postcolonial remains." He argues:

> The desired dissolution of postcolonial theory does not mean that poverty, inequality, exploitation, and oppression in the world have come to an end, only that some people in the U.S. and French academies have decided they do not want to have to think about such things any longer and do not want to be reminded of those distant invisible contexts which continue to prompt the transformative energies of the postcolonial.[24]

Amidst the efforts to resist selling out to the corporatized academic industry and the false consciousness of neo-colonial globalization, the tedious and nitpicking buzz around the "post" serves the purpose of keeping it on the razor's edge of due ethical diligence. The "post" has a difficult task: it performs a simultaneous "epistemological break with and an ironic continuity of"[25] the coloniality of power, knowledge, being and relating. In a historical perspective, "postcolonialism has always been about the ongoing life of residues, livings remains, lingering legacies."[26] Its ambivalence and ongoing incompleteness is simultaneously its strength and Achilles' heel.

Postcolonialism is not invested in fabricating a historical or discursive space of cleanly and self-righteously executed reversals of unjustifiable hierarchies of subjugation with some utopian final victory already in sight. Far from it. Rather, it is a quest for a lifeworld of repositioned relationality in which the relations among unevenly spread empowerment, agency, and resources can be renegotiated and wrenched out of the colonial gridlocks of unproductive and oppressive binarisms.

Pushing beyond the typical academic aspirations, postcolonialism is also "an ameliorative and therapeutic theory" as Leela Gandhi has suggested.[27] To that end, postcolonial theory, at least in some manifestations, has appropriated certain psychoanalytically geared procedures of "anamnesis" to commit itself to "a complex project of historical and psychological 'recovery.'"[28] Concomitantly, postcolonial analyses have also attested to "an equally compelling political obligation to assist the subjects of postcolonial-

24. Young, "Postcolonial Remains," 19–20.

25. Yang, "Theorizing Asian America," 146.

26. Young, "Postcolonial Remains," 21.

27. Gandhi, *Postcolonial Theory*, 8.

28. Ibid.

ity to live with the gaps and fissures of their condition, and thereby learn to proceed with self-understanding."[29]

The therapeutic aspirations of postcolonialism and decoloniality underscore the commitment and desire to transcend self-centered and insular academic agendas. Instead, there is a deep awareness of an ethical or visionary pre-text in postcolonial critiques. The transformative dimension of postcolonialism must not be overshadowed by its deconstructive clichés as it calls attention to the unfinished business of both enduring colonial inertias and genuine decolonization. As Young argues, "the postcolonial is in many ways about such unfinished business, the continuing projection of past conflicts into the experience of the present, the insistent persistence of the afterimages of historical memory that drive the desire to transform the present."[30]

It is this facet of postcolonialism, I submit, that engenders the crucible of the distinctively postcolonial fabric of imagination and its transformative energy longing to envision and enable a life-affirming and equitable planetary conviviality. But such a postcolonial conviviality will not be possible without an ethically reinvigorated spiritual, religious, and theological praxis.

Speaking theologically, it is here that a particularly meaningful connection has a potential to emerge: as I will argue in Part III, the deep undertow of ethics in postcolonialism can resonate most fruitfully with sacramental imagination in the Christian theological vision. Before getting there, however, some preliminary theoretical questions beckon. Where exactly is the connection between postcolonialism and diaspora? How does diaspora enter postcolonial reflection? What might be the critical, ethical, and spiritual purchase of diasporic subjectivities and their theoretical sensuality for theological inquiry?

29. Ibid.

30. Young, "Postcolonial Remains," 21.

1.3.

Diasporic Lives and Hybrid Homing Desires

Migration is a one-way ticket. There is no home to go back to.[1]

STUART HALL

. . . if you have to think about belonging, perhaps you are already outside.[2]

ELSPETH PROBYN

AS WITH ALL THINGS postcolonial, wildly diverse definitions of diaspora abound. Among varied descriptions of diaspora, Lingyan Yang's approach stands out as a judicious attempt to portray the intricacies of negotiation between losses and gains that permeate diasporic subjectivity and socio-cultural position. Yang suggests that diaspora is:

> the material conditions and dialectical process of negotiating with the historical conditions, geographical relocations, cultural displacements, emotional alienation, trauma or relief, symbolic representations, artistic imaginations, philosophical conceptions, or political dispossessions of leaving homes, homelands,

1. Hall, "Minimal Selves," 44.
2. Probyn, *Outside Belongings*, 8.

> home cultures and mother tongues, by necessity or by choice, due to a variety of reasons in different historical epochs. Simultaneously diaspora is also the forced or chosen making, creating, and articulating of their new cultural existential selves in the NEW adopted homes (such as America), new cultures, new nations, and new m(O)ther tongues.[3]

Some recent psychoanalytically and textually bent theories of diaspora come grievously close to distancing diaspora from the actual historical experiences of the "dispossessions of leaving" that Yang highlights so acutely. Yang's definition does not underestimate the scope of change and transformation that takes place amidst the struggle of creating and articulating nothing less than "new cultural existential selves." The struggle is both forced and chosen; it can be exciting and genuinely liberating, yet often comes at the high cost of estrangement and sometimes ends in unrelieved heartbreak.

Viewed from the experiential angle, but certainly *not at the expense* of the material, historical and socio-political ingredients of displacement, diaspora can also be understood in humanistic terms as a condition of subjectivity. In the words of Lily Cho, diaspora is "a subjective condition marked by the contingencies of long histories of displacements and genealogies of dispossession."[4] Precisely from within these personal histories and genealogies, "diasporic subjects emerge in turning, turning back upon these markers of the self, homeland, memory, loss—even as they turn on or away from them."[5]

DIASPORA AS A LOCATION OF IDENTITY

Diaspora is as auspicious a location of postcolonial identity and agency as it is contentious. A few standard challenges to the postcolonial diaspora need to be addressed right away to minimize confusion. It is clear that postcoloniality and its predicaments are as immediate and pressing for diasporics, exiles, and migrants as they are for those who stay put and remain stable, willingly or unwillingly, in their homelands. Granted, some hyper-metaphoricized

3. Yang, "Theorizing Asian America," 153.

4. Cho, "The Turn to Diaspora," 11.

5. Ibid. The context of Cho's argument is literary and cultural studies. While I appreciate Cho's meticulous analysis and endorsement of diaspora as a "tremendously enabling" (13) resource in postcolonial studies, among other fields, I do hesitate to agree that diaspora is "first and foremost a subjective condition" (14). Without doubt, it is a condition of subjectivity. But such a privileging of interiority makes the valuable insight disproportionately vulnerable to disembodied and ludic metaphorizations that have already cast a cloud of suspicion about the usefulness and adequacy of the term.

and weirdly romantic fascinations with postcolonial displacements and abstract homelessness have seeped into rather self-absorbed versions of "high" postcolonial theory.[6] Such theoretical flights of fancy understandably score very low on the scale of compassionate critical integrity. It should be clear that postcoloniality cannot be adequately identified with diasporic life. To claim or imply such an identity would be nothing short of presumptuous. It is exactly these hyper-metaphorizing tendencies that have prompted some postcolonial critics to dismiss diaspora as useless for social transformation and for "bringing history back" into overexcited theoretical and textual idealism.

While it is indeed the case that some hyper-metaphoric constructions of diasporas do look quite thrilling in the writings of self-absorbed elite postcolonial theorists, the problem is that these hyper-metaphorizing approaches fail to discern and honor the material and psychic constraints of physical displacement and uprooting that more often than not come with a share of deep wounding in the lives of actual diasporic subjects. As a result, the genuinely creative and transformative potential of lived diasporic experience and knowledge to progressively modulate the ways we live, think, and interact with different others is in danger of being (mis)perceived not only as elitist and manipulative but also, as some fear, tacitly neocolonial.

Diasporic existence is not an exclusive attribute of travelling diplomats, celebrities, globe-trotting corporate executives, or affluent cosmopolitan tourists. These groups undoubtedly possess certain transnational fluency. Yet having mastered and feeling at ease in the elite circuits of voluntary transnational movements for profit or fame is significantly different from having lost a home or from searching for a new one out of necessity. To push the point further, and against the tenor of some prominent theoretical claims in postcolonial circles, it is really hard to see the present world of postcoloniality as "postnational"—except for (neocolonial) corporate, political, and intellectual elites. But then again, the world has always been "postnational" for those groups anyway . . . Meanwhile, in the present world of very real and sometimes closely guarded borders and citizenship systems of nation states (some even with border fences!), diaspora does engender a rather distinct lifeworld within the broader postcolonial reality.

Before looking into what intimations of wisdom diasporic imaginary can deliver, it is necessary to reiterate that privileging interiority or mobility

6. Quite a few postcolonial thinkers have observed that the "obsession with diaspora" is one of the analytical metaphors that betray the metropolitan biases of postcolonial theory that focus excessively on identity issues rather than on the arguably more pressing economic and political exigencies. For a condensed version of these critiques, see Sugirtharajah, *Exploring Postcolonial Biblical Criticism*, 24–27.

(often directly or indirectly forced mobility) over history or stability (often directly or indirectly forced stability) should be immediately recognized as a false dichotomy in postcolonial diaspora studies. It is a straw juxtaposition and has little analytical or practical valence. Diasporas do not exhaust the whole of postcolonial reality; diasporic reality is not identical with postcoloniality. Postcoloniality is a much more pervasive condition of life than diaspora. Within postcoloniality there are both stable and moving communities which coexist and interact without one type of community or individual being somehow more "authentically" postcolonial than others. Hence the diasporic imaginary that I will spell out at the conclusion of Part I is just *one* historically habituated version of postcolonial experience and imagination—no more and no less.

Meanwhile, it *is* very tricky to articulate a good enough and fair enough description of diaspora as a uniquely idiosyncratic form of postcolonial migrancy and agency. The seminal postcolonial critic Edward W. Said, a Palestianian Arab-American scholar and a postcolonial migrant and diasporic, wrestled with this challenge with theoretical acumen and autoethnographic insight. In Said's work, the experience and the imaginary of exile plays a powerful critical and imaginative role. His musings on exile are prolific but frequently they are heavily metaphorical, virtually metaphysical. On the one hand, Said took care to underscore the perils of runaway metaphorizations of realities like exile, migrancy, and diaspora. On the other hand, Said's own proclivity to metaphorically valorize "exile" as the alleged authentic condition of dedicated intellectuals[7] also displays the difficulty of trying to keep theory and histories of disempowerment and vulnerability together in an ethically accountable way.

In Said's work, the image of "exile" denotes various types of contemporary migrancies marked by forced choice. Precisely in this context it is important to notice that Said's renowned essay "Reflections on Exile" begins with a somber observation that exile is "strangely compelling to think about but terrible to experience."[8] Elsewhere he argues most sagaciously that,

7. See, for example, Said's 1993 essay "Intellectual Exile: Expatriates and Marginals." It is beyond the scope of this project to expose the transitions and extensions between various interpretations of exile in Said's work. In this essay Said's sense of exile shows an obvious postmodern privileging of mobility and restlessness projected onto "exile" as the most desirable state of intellectual life in a thinly disguised elitist manner. But it does not erase other dimensions of migrancy that Said addresses elsewhere with a much tighter grip on historical experiences of migrancy and their anguished vulnerabilities.

8. Said, *Reflections on Exile,* 173. I must note that I do not refer to Said's more "metaphorical" or "metaphysical" conceptualization of exile in which Said equates, for all practical purposes, exile with the vocation and predicament of transnational intellectuals.

even metaphorically and theoretically speaking, "marginality and homelessness are not, in my opinion, to be gloried in; they are to be brought to an end, so that more, and not fewer, people can enjoy the benefits of what has for centuries been denied the victims of race, class, or gender."[9] I could not agree more.

DIASPORA AND HYBRIDITY: A POSTCOLONIALLY SATURATED PHENOMENON

In postcolonial theory, diaspora is often perceived as denoting locations of in-betweenness which are the spontaneous abode of hybridity. Those who indwell the diasporic in-between locations hover, as it were, in between the demands of assimilation in the society of arrival but, are also set, as Arif Dirlik argues,

> against the society of origin, which likewise denies political and cultural citizenship to the migrant on the grounds that emigration is inevitably accompanied by distancing and degenerations from the culture of origin. Thus placed at the margins of two societies, the migrant is denied cultural identity and autonomy [. . .] Hybridity . . . releases the imagination to conceive the world in new ways.[10]

Two elements of Dirlik's observations merit a brief elaboration. First, the hybrid newness which characterizes the diasporic universes of personhood and relationships is akin to what Salman Rushdie has whimsically called mongrelization, *mélange*, hotchpotch—"a bit of this, a bit of that is how newness enters the world" producing "change-by-fusion, change-by-conjoining."[11] It can be good news for some (those hoping for healing transformation through relatively more open cultural interaction) and bad news for others (those aspiring to restore the nativistic purity of lost "golden ages" among both the victims and victimizers of colonialism). This sort of hybridity broadly denotes cultural and racial syncretism, creolization, or *métissage* that indeed increasingly characterize intensifying transnational migration.

Of course, especially in the present moment of high-speed globalization, the reach of cultural *métissage* or hybridity is virtually universal. Yet there are notable differences when it comes to specific diasporic hybridities.

9. Said, *Reflections on Exile*, 385.
10. Dirlik, "Bringing History Back In," 103–4.
11. Rushdie, *Imaginary Homelands*, 394.

Cultural *métissage* does not yield commensurable and equally intense results in all instances of encountering difference and being affected, empowered, or limited by it. Indeed, diasporic hybridity is, at it were, a forced state of being.

In postcolonial diasporas hybridity is a mode of resilience, endurance, and continued existence amidst differences that are "in one's face"—they are not optional. On the contrary, they are palpable and much deeper than short and often superficial exposures to otherness that a traveler encounters but can always choose to ignore or forget. Hence a kind of hybridity obtains by its own inexorable logic. It is primarily a logic propelled by the need to survive and the desire to humanly thrive. It obtains through the pressures and sometimes also pleasures of unavoidable intertwinement of diverse identities, knowledges, languages, races, ethnicities, and many other factors that shape our irrevocably relational lives. This unavoidable intertwinement is not necessarily celebratory or constructive. Sometimes it happens rather conflictually or traumatically as I have observed. To mention just one example: for numerous World War II political refugees living in the Latvian diaspora in North America the trauma of displacement and alienation remains more unhealed than healed despite their more or less successful physical and economic survival.

The second element Dirlik pointed out was the double cultural dispossession or double marginality affecting those who are no longer organically moored in one culture and society by birth, language, citizenship, spirituality, or allegiance. This is the case particularly in those diasporic contexts where the experience of migrancy is still recent and undomesticated. Indeed, migration is a one-way ticket: a certain estrangement from where one comes from and where one has arrived never quite dissipates. This is why diasporic hybridity is a life form that bears a certain resemblance to homelessness: no place, no culture, no language, and no religious tradition feel entirely "native" anymore—or yet.

The existential actualities of diasporic life and all its hybridities have occasionally been appropriated as theoretically titillating metaphors of endless deferral and infinite negative dialectics in postmodernism. However, for those who actually live and move, and have their whole psycho-spiritual being in the diasporic existence, the ratio of pleasures and pains of postcolonial diaspora and its complex displacements is not at all so clearly squared away. As Wonhee Anne Joh poignantly observes, a thoroughly postcolonial version of hybridity often entails "foremost an extreme sense of pain, of loss, of agonizing dislocations and fragmentations."[12] Cho underscores it with a laudable amount of prudence:

12. Joh, *Heart of the* Cross, 70.

> To turn to diaspora is to turn to the power of relation and the enabling possibilities of difference. To turn to diaspora is to turn away from the seemingly inexorable march of history and towards the secret of memories embedded within the intimacies of the everyday. To turn to diaspora is to turn to restless specters of sorrow bound by that which is lost and to obscure miracles of connection marked by that which is found.[13]

In some cases, migrancy and diasporic existence carries a certain sense of mourning until one's last breath. Exiles and refugees are the most agonizing case in point as I have seen time and again in the context of my ministry among refugees, exiles, asylum seekers, and migrants. From the depths of such diasporic experience, spirituality and theology emerges, to borrow Wendy Farley's expressive words, as "pain seeking understanding"[14] but also as pain ultimately seeking recognition, restoration, and transformation.

A DIASPORIC ONTOLOGY OF CONNECTIONS?

Diasporic ontology is an ontology of interconnectedness and hybridity. In a universe such as ours, relations have the power to create life, sustain it, and transform it for human and planetary flourishing—or to destroy it. Our reality is a reality of interrelatedness, for good and for ill. Relations are constitutive for our planetary life.

Diasporic hybridity does not shy away from the jagged incongruities that permeate the "intimacies of the everyday" with an immediacy and an intensity that knows virtually no equal. Diasporic life gravitates toward discovering connections among peoples (while differences are already obvious). Discovering relational links and making connections requires effort in diasporic contexts and yet, paradoxically, it is an instinctual effort. The goal of the effort is to survive and eventually to flourish on both individual and communal levels. Amidst these instinctual and yet deliberate efforts diasporic hybridity subsists like a distinct identity—but an identity that is like "a noun of process."[15]

Diasporic hybridity bodies forth as new—but not necessarily better—configurations of wisdom, attitudes, imagination, authority, and agency. These configurations keep emerging from personally embodied or relationally remembered experience of migration and difference. But all these elements subsist within a yet deeper underlying matrix of relationality in

13. Cho, "The Turn to Diaspora," 28.

14. Farley, *Gathering Those Driven Away*, 8.

15. Gilroy, *Against Race*, 252.

which countless deeply personal and contextual elements of displacement and emplacement, the old and the new, the familiar and the different, constantly generate new webs of connections. In many contexts, to connect and to network is simply an imperative for survival. Relational networks frequently assume the stabilizing role of places. It is not to say that physical and geographical proximity as the most embodied forms of relationality cease to be desired. Rather, finding "home," solace, and solidarity in diasporic networks is, above all other gains (and losses), a creative survival technique. As all survival techniques, this one too, may come at a cost: separation and even further estrangement from physical neighbors, ghettoization, and ethnic or religious absolutism.

Amidst all this, there also resides a grand—and sad—irony in many diasporic lives. What stands out among the vices of diaspora is an inflated and compensatory rhetoric of superiority vis-à-vis other, often equally diasporic, communities. Often it comes in tandem with a jealous—indeed, a self-ghettoizing—policing of one's own community's cultural, religious, and social boundaries.[16] Alongside the promises and small relational miracles that diasporic lifeworlds engender, diasporic life can also accommodate the shrillest rhetoric of nativism. It labors extremely hard to suppress and, as it were, extirpate, the real and organic flesh-and-blood hybridity that it fears and yet cannot stop anyway. In these situations, diaspora can function as a terrain in which the most parochial ideologies of nostalgic purity clash with the actual hybridizing practices of everyday life. It is truly odd how such ethnocentric navel-gazing can willfully overlook the facts of life since the actual diasporic communities are far more enmeshed in the transcultural cross-fertilization of the "diaspora space"[17] than some diasporic acolytes of nativist authenticity dare to admit even to themselves.

THE DIASPORIC HOMING DESIRE

In diasporic lifeworlds, the focus on relationality is not limited to a theoretical critique of essentialized understanding of being, feeling, knowing,

16. In the context of Latvian diaspora, the astute essay by the former President of Latvia (1999–2003), Vaira Vīķe-Freiberga "Trimdas psicholoģija/The Psychology of Exile," continues to be relevant as it unmasks the conflictual conundrums of diasporic life. See Vīķe-Freiberga, *Pret Straumi*, 21–47.

17. Brah, *Cartographies of Diaspora*, 181. Even though I find Brah's concept very pertinent and helpful, I nevertheless question the "equality" of inhabitation of diaspora space as too casually utopian at the expense of the lived realities of immense inequality between diasporas themselves, as well as among the "indigenous" and the "diasporic" segments of Western societies.

and acting. There are good historical and cultural reasons for that critique, of course. But such foregrounding of relationality materializes out of the school of lived diasporic experience in which a complex and sometimes heartrending dance of hybridity always already colors our acts and affects.

It is very tricky to generalize diasporic experiences due to the immense diversity of diasporic positionalities. These are variously situated across the interfaces of race, gender, class, ethnicity, religion, sexuality, education, language, ability, education, and age. Millions of refugees who do not have an opportunity to be resettled are trapped in camps or half-way countries for years and even decades, living, as it were, in a permanent transit without even a provisional zip code. Many more, primarily economic refugees, float or are trafficked from region to region with or without travel and employment documents. They, too, do not often have a zip code with at least some provisional durability and safety.[18] Obviously, these are just some of the most destitute subaltern faces of diasporic life-forms.

Considering these caveats, one summary observation of diasporic subjectivity appears to be warranted. Diasporic subjectivity routinely lives what one cannot automatically and effortlessly reconcile in purely discursive or analytical ways. Diasporic subjectivity and imagination is akin to what Kwok Pui-lan calls the "border subject," who is not a "hero or villain, but . . . a much more complex, three-dimensional subject situated in the enthralling plots or irony, between satire and despair, between rage and empathy, between absurdity and hopefulness."[19]

Additionally, these border-passage efforts at living together what one cannot neatly coordinate by purely intellectual means usually are not glamorous—even when lauded and marketed as such by some intellectual elites. More often than not,

> diasporic consciousness "makes best of a bad situation." Experiences of loss, marginality, and exile (differently cushioned by class) are often reinforced by systematic exploitation and blocked advancement. Thus constitutive suffering coexists with the skills of survival. . . Diaspora consciousness lives loss and hope as a defining tension.[20]

18. The recent essay collection *Home and Away*, edited by Burns and Pearson, attends to the variations of migrant experience from a theological perspective.

19. Kwok, "A Theology of Border Passage," 113.

20. James Clifford, "Diasporas," quoted from *The Postcolonial Studies Reader*, 454. I must add the categories of race, ethnicity, and generation to Clifford's ladder of "cushioning."

Perhaps a notion from the field of engineering might be helpful here to grasp the jerry-rigged, improvising nature of diasporic consciousness: "kluge." Kluge is a makeshift, quick-and-dirty solution in circumstances where a permanent solution to a problem at hand has not yet been devised. As a rule, kluges are often inelegant and clumsy—but they work when nothing better is available. It may well be that with kluges, "adequacy, not beauty, is the name of the game."[21] On the other hand, doesn't this kind of makeshift, hands-on, creativity radiate its own kind of quirky magnificence?

Diasporic consciousness is often marked by the tension of loss and hope. Hence diasporic imaginary is an imaginary of "both" and, perhaps to a degree, of "neither/nor"—"neither home nor not-home."[22] Is it then a life of permanent negation? Not at all. What holds diasporic life and its multiple belongings together is a "homing desire."[23] Here it is worth remembering Avtar Brah's distinction between the "homing desire" from the desire for a homeland which is accompanied by an ideology of return that some diasporas and some diasporic subjects sustain, but others do not. There are situations when the geo-political or cultural "home" is more a place of terror than nostalgic longing.[24] Diaspora is more often than not a space of both trauma and relief, a space of tension. At the same time, diaspora is also a space where ingenious and resilient life energies cluster into "kluges" of identity and consciousness expressing their own unfinished and imperfect fortitude.

And yet: precisely from a diasporic perspective, the value of tension and contradictions should be viewed with caution. It seems disconsolate to choose contradiction as the definitive element of the Janus-faced migratory lives. Surely, contradictions abound in diasporic lifeworlds! Indeed, the tension between loss and hope is woven through diasporic habitats. And without doubt, contradictions are very fascinating to theorize and poeticize. But at the same time, diasporic people arguably know better than others that contradictions are difficult to live with. Do scholarly theories account for these complexities of displacement in an adequate way?

To imply that contradiction and tension capture the heart of diasporic existence parallels the presumptuous argument that the central emancipatory function of diasporas is to disrupt the dominant cultural and geopolitical regimes. Both approaches place a *theoretical* premium on Western postmodern negative dialectics of tension. Can it be simply assumed that

21. Marcus, *Kluge*, 6.

22. Radhakrishnan, "Postcoloniality and the Boundaries of Identity," 765.

23. Brah, *Cartographies of Diaspora*, 16.

24. Ibid., 192–93

migrants and diasporic subjects indeed revel in the difficult tensions as enthusiastically as the scholars extolling the critical sublimity of these same tensions? Does not such valorization of tension devalue the very difficult experiences of those who live these tensions as forced upon them or as a result of forced choices? To privilege contradictions, negations, and fragmentations is to overlook the redemptive longing for reconciliation, wholeness, and peace that is also abundantly present in diasporic lifeworlds despite the agonizing contradictions and estrangements. The trouble with diaspora, after all, is that it is neither home nor not-home!

The diasporic homing desire is not necessarily an ideology of return or a nativistic melancholy. Rather, is it the ever sticky glue that holds together the diasporic ontology of relational hybridity, all the jagged incongruities included. Diasporic selfhood is akin to what the pastoral psychotherapist Pamela Cooper-White has described as "braided self."[25] According to Cooper-White, the "braided self" is a subjectivity of healthy and non-hegemonic multiplicity in human personhood. The "braided self" acknowledges and honors the increasingly widespread postmodern, postcolonial, diasporic, exilic, and queer experiences of hybridity. Precisely as "braided" out of experiential multiplicity, this kind of diasporic subjectivity has a certain composite fluidity about it. It facilitates and holds contradictions and disruptions together while not being exhausted or solely defined by them.

25. Cooper-White, *Braided Selves*, 195–221.

1.4.

Braiding a Diasporic Imaginary

Sola experientia facit theologum.[1]

Martin Luther

Survival in fact is about the connections between things.[2]

Edward W. Said

Diasporic imaginary—of which I offer here only one particular stanza out of a host of existential experiences and imaginative possibilities—is a whirlpool of legacies, rationalities, sensibilities, allegiances, affections, and ethical exigencies. As a mindscape—and therefore as a methodological sensibility—it bears the historical and existential watermarks of migrancy and hybridity. Diasporic imaginary emerges through the transposition of lived experience into a matrix of theoretical sensuality and a pattern of perception and reflection. Embedded and embodied in cultural, racial, linguistic, and religious hybridity of the global postcolony, diasporic imaginary is, as it were, "polygamist" in its resourcefulness. Postcolonial diasporic imaginary is perhaps the most concerted manifestation of multiply organized postco-

1. Luther, "Table Talks, Nr. 46," *Luther's Works*, 54:8. English translation: Experience alone makes the theologian.

2. Said, *Culture and Imperialism*, 336

lonial subjectivity as outlined by Françoise Lionnet: it simultaneously feeds and poaches from many pastures as it lives and moves by "braiding all the traditions at its disposal, using the fragments that constitute it in order to participate fully in a dynamic process of transformation."[3]

HOMING DESIRE AND INTERSTITIAL INTEGRITY

The *telos* of the diasporic braiding is to find a home-away-from-home. It is an experiential and reflective space wherein the homing desire gravitates toward integration and integrity. As the embodied and interpersonal terrain where the diasporic homing desire materializes, this kind of imaginary is a delicate equilibrium: here the integrity of body, mind, imagination, behavior, values, affects, traditions, allegiances, and beliefs is interstitial. In fact, diasporic imaginaries are sustained by, in Rita Nakashima Brock's eloquent phrase, "interstitial integrity."[4] For diasporic individuals, the most realistic, honest, and self-aware version of integrity available out there is interstitial. Now this kind of integrity indeed "has to do with moments of entireness;" but for real life diasporic people it comprises "the monumental task of making meaning out of multiple worlds by refusing to disconnect any of them, while not pledging allegiance to a singular one."[5]

The crux of the theoretical sensuality that is grounded in this kind of lived interstitial integrity abides in the recognition that "interstitiality is not an integrity of yes or no despite the context;" moreover, it is "not a sense of honor that guards the self from relational influence that might corrupt its purity."[6] The refusal, or perhaps simply an incapacity, to disconnect those multiple worlds that congregate in diasporic subjectivities instinctually permeates the whole imaginary including theological imagination and spiritual practices. Speaking from a lived diasporic experience, Brock thoughtfully concludes that interstitial integrity is

> this spirit in us, our struggle to hold the many in the one. We endeavor to make sense and meaning out of the multiple social

3. Lionnet, *Postcolonial Representations*, 5. Lionnet uses the image of braiding to specifically describe the creativity of postcolonial women writers who are compelled to speak "several different languages (male and female, colonial and indigenous, global and local, among others)." There is a good reason to expand her keen metaphor of braiding, without diluting its specific pertinence and acuity for postcolonial women's creative agency, to better understand various gendered locations in postcolonial and diasporic contexts beyond women.

4. Brock, "Interstitial Integrity,"190.

5. Ibid., 190–91.

6. Ibid.

> locations, the hybrid cultures, and many powers of death and life that are placed before us. Interstitial integrity is our ability to lie down, spread-eagled, reaching to all the many worlds we have known, all the memories we have been given, tempered in the cauldrons of history and geography in our one body.[7]

Diasporic imaginary performs its fugal, indeed its contrapuntal, *compositio loci* as an ongoing bodying forth of an insatiable homing desire. It emerges from an embodied interstitial integrity that is composed of trans-incarnations of bodies and minds in migration amidst dominant and subjugated knowledges and spiritualities, amidst various registers of sound, vision, fashion, and etiquette, amidst sensory memories of movement, speech, smell, and taste. Diasporic imaginary is a space wherein, to borrow Edward Said's pertinent phrase in relation to exile, one is "neither completely at one with the new setting nor fully disencumbered of the old, beset with half-involvements and half-detachments, nostalgic and sentimental on one level, and adept mimic or a secret outcast on another."[8]

DIASPORA AND THE FORCED POETICS OF POSTCOLONIALITY

But where exactly does the Latvian and Baltic postcolonial nuance of this diasporic imaginary come into play? As sketched in Chapter 1.1, postcolonial hybridity describes its location well as a *forced* habitat of life and mind. This kind of imaginary never loses its internalized and reflectively "processed" *poétique forcée*. It is part and parcel of the historical Baltic postcoloniality "from below." It has not exactly been "picked out" from among other equally thrilling and available options. Moreover, it often feels quite arduous since hybridity is again one of those things that are fascinating to theorize but rather more demanding to live in everyday life.

Without doubt, contrapuntal postcolonial hybridity marks diasporic spirituality to the same degree as if affects all other arenas of life and thought. Primarily, it means ecclesial and liturgical fluidity as well as confessional code-switching. It is impossible to discard, except by disavowal or hypocrisy, this hybrid attunement in favor of a singularly ensconced allegiance—culturally, politically, or theologically. Again, the contrapuntal hybridity here is not a studied posture: it consciously, but perhaps mostly unconsciously, creolizes identity regimes and perceptions of reality,

7. Brock, "Cooking Without Recipes," 140.

8. Said, *Representations of the Intellectual*, 49.

including ecclesiastical identity, without *a priori* discarding them or declaring them entirely obsolete. The outcome is indeed, as Wilson Harris puts it, a "complex counterpoint between partial origins, between partial imprints of unfinished genesis, partial absolutes."[9]

The diasporic imaginary in question here is heterolocal or translocal[10] not only as a way of life but also as a way of creativity—including theological creativity. It lets all of its historical, cultural, religious, and experiential "footprints" play off one another in theological method, rhetoric, and in the substance of its arguments and analyses. As I emphasized before, diasporic imaginary is rooted in the desire for survival and for recognition without reduction as well as deep-seated hope for wholesome flourishing.

Naturally, these hopes and desires migrate into theological mindscapes and bodyscapes. When it comes to theological or liturgical allegiances, a seemingly simple question for example—in which liturgical and which doctrinal tradition are you exactly at home?—can prompt a hesitant pause before venturing an answer. Living and thinking diasporically issues into theologizing or participating in any particular liturgical, contemplative, or charitable act with all of the various legacies, knowledges, and experiences simultaneously permeating and braiding together every sensation, insight, emotion, thought, action, reaction, word, sound, movement, and gesture. To expect or even demand that a postcolonial diasporic subject should be fully at home in only one doctrinal tradition, or swear allegiance to only one theological and liturgical language, or only one ecclesial culture is, ironically, yet another manifestation of imperialistic "forced poetics." It proliferates the *faits accomplis* of colonial violence with more, if subtler, violence and alienation.

To throw the nuances of diasporic ambiance and its theological methodology into a sharper relief within the broader postcolonial orbit, two analytical metaphors are particularly resonant in the Baltic context of "small numbers": Gyan Pandey's notion of "fragment" and Wilson Harris' notion of "diminutive poles." The two analytical metaphors by Indian and Caribbean postcolonial thinkers serve as hermeneutical hinges for the Latvian postcolonial whirlpool of diasporically "composed place" that is populated

9. Harris, "The Fabric of the Imagination," 177.

10. Ato Quayson helpfully indicates that "the implications of translocality cannot be limited to the two locations that have most framed migrants' identities. The translocality of migrants means that their senses of themselves draw on inflections and emphases of different ethnic communities in other parts of the world. As [Khachig] Tölölyan points out in his definition of diasporas, "diasporas are resolutely multilocal and polycentric, in that what happens to kin communities in other areas of dispersion as well as in the homeland insistently matters to them," in "Introduction: Area Studies, Diaspora Studies, and Critical Pedagogies," 588.

by both Occidental cultural and theological conventions as well as obscure and marginal cornflowers and wild carrots that carry a virtually equal existential weight to Moses and John the Baptist.

CARDINAL FRAGMENTS AND DIMINUTIVE POLES

The notions of fragment and fragmentation are unsurprisingly among the hallmarks of both the postmodern and postcolonial lexicons. Proceeding from the minuscule Latvian crevice of postcoloniality, I specifically invoke Gyan Pandey's multivalent notion of fragment. Pandey's notion of fragment exudes a striking subaltern tang. The fragment,

> resists the whole . . . it cannot be assimilated into the narrative and its claims to wholeness. It speaks to us of what *cannot* be written of the whole (and indeed of the fragment), and in that sense becomes symptomatic of a particular claim to wholeness or completeness.[11]

The thorny, undisciplined fragment can materialize in such simple things as blue cornflowers or wild carrots in the Latvian stained glass Creation scene or the barely traceable contours of pivotal geo-cultural locations in otherwise conventional altar paintings of Christ. In this sense, the fragment indeed disturbs and ruptures, as Pandey suggests, the smoothly polished totalities of progress and authenticity. A paradoxical disparity ought to be obvious here: something small and seemingly negligible functions as a catalyst of integrity, interstitial as it may be, in resistance to the premature claims to wholeness. It is through the cracks in dominant metanarratives that the small voices of history can whisper or shout their truth, their anguish, their beauty, and their hopes to God and to all who have ears to hear. Seeing a fragment as the catalyst of integrity affirms the sacramental, i.e., revelatory and transformational, potential of particularity even when that particularity is barely visible and audible. Postcolonial integrity does not depend on the shock and awe of numbers or decibels; its vocabulary of genuine authenticity contains not only *forte fortissimo* but also *pianissimo*, to use a musical analogy.

Wilson Harris' "diminutive poles"—or even more aptly, "fields of uncanny diminutives"—push even deeper.[12] The diminutive poles bring out the re-visionary potential in the imaginaries of reality in a way that recognizes the intuitive elements of reality and imagination. The diminutives, be

11. Pandey, *Routine Violence*, 66–67.

12. Harris, "The Fabric of the Imagination," 180.

they a blade of grass or a grain of light appearing in the living "imageries and texts of reality," (re)shape the imaginary in a profound, if not always rationalizable and quantifiable, way.[13] They attend to the "hidden numinous proportions within the mechanisms of colonialism and post-colonialism;" it is from these uncanny depths that the diminutive poles surface, "numinous and intact in the midst of aridity" so that "the unconscious may gestate and bring fertile motifs and clues" out in the reflective and narrative daylight of art, literature, rationality, and (also theological) imagination.[14]

The differences that the uncanny diminutive poles can germinate are genuinely cardinal and life-giving differences. But they don't have to always be grand, loud, obvious, and imposing. This difference is substantial but subtle. In spaces of encountering otherness within and without, it is precisely the diminutives—like those blue cornflowers and wild carrots—that bear the brunt of re-visionary potential. Here it is worth quoting Harris at length to show how the diminutive yet cardinal fragments of, in this case, diasporic hybridity bring out new apprehensions, new rhythms of possibility, and new rhythmic edges to the ways of reading reality:

> It is the life of "diminutives" that may offer a peculiar key to the cross-cultural imagination. Each "diminutive" exists as it were in a certain field, or upon a certain frontier or margin of being, to apprise us of the polar life of other fields, to warn us of the necessity to *read* the mutual attraction of apparently remote poles of existence, to warn us to create a new space or interrelationship in which to transform a threat that may overwhelm us if we adhere to block, institutional habit. . .[15]

The diminutives or fragments may be small and may speak *sotto voce*. Yet they are nothing less than cardinal fragments or cardinal diminutives—the hinge elements that carry the capacity to create new images and enactments of relationality that honor the depths and appreciate the intuitive dimensions of life and imagination. For Harris, this constitutes an explicit antidote to Western postmodernist nihilism. But one does not need to look far to see how it also challenges the camouflaged postcolonial nihilism that sometimes manifests in hyper-metaphorization of such palpably embodied (and often suffered) spaces of global postcolony as diaspora, hybridity, and exile.

Furthermore, cardinal fragments are not only dynamic and uncanny carriers of re-visioning of reality, relationality, and imagination. Their

13. Ibid., 177, 179.

14. Ibid., 179.

15. Ibid. Italics in original.

function and impact is therapeutic. The uncanny diminutives unshackle "the logic of perpetual nightmare, perpetual ordeal" of relating to otherness within and without.[16] The diminutives signify and enable a therapeutic relief, however frail or threadbare it may be: what is unbearable can be rendered bearable. Honoring and fostering the presence and action of uncanny diminutives can nudge the ordeal of living with otherness without and within, in Harris' passionate estimation, toward a "genuine diversity-in-universality" as it struggles to unfold "within a theatre of unfathomable wholeness."[17]

The theater of unfathomable (in more than one sense) wholeness is not possible without imagination. The diminutive poles perform a twofold mission when it comes to the intuitive canvas of imagination: they bear the seeds of both change and healing. Reaching beyond the transformative power of literature or art, Harris' diminutives bring out the capacity to re-orchestrate the rhythms of reality and possibility far deeper than just textually. Hence, it is worth paying attention to the diminutives in order to

> unravel a thread in the dense loom or economy of being (density means economy), to unravel a thread that may sustain us to cope with an abysmal otherness whom and which we dread but which may also bring resources to alter or change the fabric of imagination in the direction of a therapeutic, ceaselessly unfinished genesis.[18]

In Harris' postcolonial canvas of intuitive imagination, transformation happens in a diminutive—and hence, cardinal—mode. It may be as gossamer as a thread, and yet it is these frail and thread-like apertures of vision and the obscure connections of healing that hold the space of that never finished interstitial integrity which so aptly marks the exigencies and hopes of diasporic life-forms.

16. Ibid.

17. Ibid., 180. Reflecting on the poignancy of postcolonial suffering in his novel *Carnival,* Harris underscores that the field of uncanny diminutives can facilitate a process of attraction among differences and that, in our world, amounts to facilitating "a therapeutic community, therapeutic genius of love within one and other, within parallel existences and non-existences." Harris does not shy away from calling such interaction "progress" (ibid.).

18. Ibid., 182.

ON THE DIMINUTIVE SIGNS OF SALVIFIC RELATIONALITY

How can the postcolonial diasporic sensibility of diminutive poles be transposed into a theological key? Emerging here are the first contours of the analogical resonance between a postcolonial diasporic lifeworld and sacramental modes of perception, imagination, and rationality. Before addressing the analogical resonance in a sustained way in Part III, suffice it to say at this juncture that cardinal fragments and diminutive poles function as sacramental signs, indeed mysteries, of salvific relationality. They signify and effect meaning, vitality, affirmation, and genuineness. Of course, they challenge and disrupt but they also, even more evocatively, connect and heal. They may appear as mere footnotes or accidental oddities and irregularities to other imaginaries and knowledges that are built on dominance, transparency, and aggression.

To the dominant regimes of knowledge and power these cardinal fragments can sound like mere whispers. But the casualness, the opacity, and the "small numbers" quality here can be deceptive: diminutives' stealthily creative agency is more akin to what theologians call a cardinal virtue in the spiritual geography of diasporic imaginary. Namely, here they are and act as an existential hinge (*cardo*) of recognition, empowerment, and sustenance for the diasporic homing desire. They enable the interstitial integrity of diasporic mindscapes and landscapes, and therefore shape and nurture that particular diasporic claim to spiritual, cultural, and theoretical wholeness in which even subaltern whispers count and small numbers, small languages, and small differences matter and even ingeniously disturb superficial and reductive hegemonies of culture and spirit in order to vigilantly body forth life.

The vocation of the "undisciplined fragments of subaltern history"[19] in the composition of diasporic mindscapes and landscapes across the global postcolony is both prophetic and restorative. It is prophetic because a fragment as inconspicuous as a blue cornflower in a stained glass pane can destabilize the common Judeo-Christian narrative of Creation *ex nihilo et ex amore* in a way that acknowledges and values both the universal kerygma of that narrative as well as the dark ambivalence surrounding its colonial arrival into the histories of postcolonial diasporas. Simultaneously, these cardinal fragments and diminutives pivot the shared narrative subtly yet effectively to interrogate and provoke resistance to the still largely unrepentant triumphalism of Western Christianity through a contestation, stealthy

19. Pandey, *Routine Violence*, 67.

as a whisper as it may be, of its violent history of crusades, conquests, and subjugation by "fire and sword." This is why postcolonial diasporic integrity is impossible without the hermeneutic of vigilant, though non-violent and perhaps even beautiful, resistance when it comes to the most redemption-laden images and narratives of Christianity such as creation, God, salvation, Christ, love, and heaven, to name just a few.

The restorative or therapeutic vocation of the cardinal fragments encompasses honoring and acknowledging those many truncated histories and deeply ambivalent memories and hopes that today swirl within the postcolonial spaces amidst the current interregnum[20] of waning and rising imperial formations. The diminutive poles are restorative when they affirm and enliven the incarnational and sacramental potential of subjugated and marginalized historical and cultural experiences and lifeworlds as unapologetically full participants in the economy of divine love, revelation, and redemption. They weave in an irreducibly specific layer of providential intimacy and possibility for renewal into postcolonial diasporic lives and fabrics of imagination. Soteriologically speaking, through the unruly diminutive poles, the undisciplined postcolonial and diasporic memories and hopes, in their fully dangerous historical concreteness of suffering and resilience, "voyage in" into the redemptively "composed place" where the triune God welcomes all landscapes, bodyscapes, and mindscapes to live, move, and have their being in the crosshairs of the sacramental mystery of salvation.

DIASPORIC "VOYAGING IN" INTO POLLUTION

But what about the epistemological implications of the diminutive poles beyond postcolonial diasporas and their imaginaries? Some cardinal fragments and diminutive poles can erupt like firecrackers when they "voyage in" to disrupt colonial and imperial imagination and behavior. Some even make it onto the academic shortlists of, as it were, "canonized" or "token" margins. But do all postcolonial and diasporic fragments have to be loud? Must they all fit one cliché of volume, timbre, and exoticized difference? In fact, in what sense *can* these fragments and diminutive poles be loud enough to be noticed at all when their small voices continue to struggle to speak and be heard? What happens when postcolonial knowledges and imaginaries previously classified as peripheral or marginal "voyage in"? What constitutes the postcolonial and diasporic twist of theological imagination and

20. I am referring here to the Gramscian notion of interregnum, recently appropriated by Zygmunt Bauman, *44 Letters*, 119–22.

its potentially creative reverberations—especially within the still dominant Euro-Atlantic theological orbit?

As postcolonial and diasporic themes and sensibilities slowly enter the mainstream of Western theological discourses, it is easy to overhear quite a bit of grumbling about the lack of "authenticity" and critical purchase of postcolonial trajectories. I have been asked numerous times about what, on earth, constitutes an "authentic" postcolonial identity. What is a "true" postcolonial difference? What is a diasporic "originality?"

Postcolonial and diasporic trajectories are questioned by indigenous Westerners on the grounds of being insufficiently un-Western. They are criticized for being insufficiently remote and insufficiently unaffected by postmodern Western critical theories and therefore, insufficiently "authentic" and insufficiently "original" in their desired or perceived difference. In other words, the diasporic mindscapes with all their postcolonial variations are still habitually measured against the hazardous notion of non-Western "sense of specialness."[21] When so measured, they often fail to satisfy the cravings for exoticized and reified difference. What is the spectrum of difference that postcolonially colored diasporic "voyages in" can offer?

Edward Said's notion of the postcolonial "voyage in"[22] can help to clarify some great and seemingly unfulfilled expectations of the Western theo-cultural edifice which continue to pontificate over the criteria of production, recognition, normativity, and the legitimacy of theological knowledge.

Said highlights the routes of hybridity in the world which, on the one hand, remain enmeshed in the historical legacies of imperialism and are, thus, still far away from a truly liberating polycentric reality. On the other hand, the world has become sufficiently porous to allow at least a certain reciprocity of wisdom and creativity through hybridizing cultural exchange. Hence:

> The voyage in, then, constitutes an especially interesting variety of hybrid cultural work. And that it exists at all is a sign of adversarial internationalization in an age of continued imperial structures. No longer does the logos dwell exclusively, as it were, in London and Paris. No longer does history run unilaterally, as Hegel believed, from east to west, or from south to north, becoming more sophisticated and developed, less primitive

21. Trinh, *Woman, Native, Other*, 87–90. This, now classic, dissection of an ongoing problem of exoticized difference and "specialness" is part of the chapter discussing the problematic issue of exoticized otherness and is tellingly titled "Difference: 'A Special Third World Women Issue.'"

22. Said, *Culture and Imperialism*, 239–61.

> and backward as it goes. Instead, the weapons of criticism have become part of the historical legacy of empire, in which the separations and exclusions of 'divide and rule' are erased and surprising new configurations spring up.[23]

The sanguinity of Said's evaluation of the imperial legacy of the Western cultural edifice may well be premature. Indeed, it does seem more and more obvious that "the logos" no longer dwells exclusively and triumphantly in the geo-political West. However, it remains subtly and pervasively yoked to the recognizable constellations of knowledge, civility, legality, wealth, wisdom, prestige, and beauty that continue to imprint the techno-globalized presence of the Occident throughout all continents. This process builds precisely on the already existing foundation of colonial globalization .

The historical legacy of modern colonial empires is a lifeworld of forced enmeshment that cannot be simply reversed except, theoretically at least, by equally violent efforts. In this lifeworld, Said's hoped for "surprising new configurations" can only spring up as always already polluted, impure, and intermingled as long as and insofar as any cultural imaginary has been touched by the cultural and spiritual Occident of colonial modernity. Consequently, the "new configurations" can be neither chemically purified "new" nor annoyingly "old." They are rather akin to Rushdie's mongrelization: "a bit of this, a bit of that is how newness enters the world" within the global postcolony producing "change-by-fusion, change-by-conjoining."[24]

DIASPORA AND EXOTICIZED "AUTHENTICITY"

Postcolonial and diasporic imaginary will utterly disappoint if what one desires is something akin to the planned authenticity and dialectic of absolute and automatically antagonistic differences. The postcoloniality that today surrounds many a diasporic location of enunciation, including my own, cannot be otherwise than "a form of double consciousness;" the double consciousness is "not an act of secession from the metropolitan regime"[25] since such a clean detachment is historically and psycho-spiritually impossible. Therefore the diasporic postcoloniality in question here is not a sphere of being simply "outside" or "over-against" the dominant culture in its present or past domicile. Rather, the diasporic fugue of postcolonial cultural experience, languages, politics, and racial and economic legacies translates

23. Ibid., 244–45.

24. Rushdie, *Imaginary Homelands*, 394.

25. Radhakrishnan, "Postmodernism and the Rest of the World," 37.

into "new"—in a Rushdian sense—configurations in intellectual, political, spiritual, and creative life.

These new configurations are poised among overlapping and sometimes contestatory cultural legacies, confessional alliances, socio-political imperatives, and moral visions. Ultimately, to speak meaningfully about authenticity in the context of diasporic postcoloniality is to speak with utter fidelity to one's experience of reality as lived and often suffered in the world that remains stubbornly structured by dominance. Authenticity here does not reside in any formal adherence to cultural, political, or religious codifications of normativity and normality but rather in the courage to name and honor one's lived experience in all its puzzling multiplicity and hybridity. It is a fidelity to lived reality that "forbids the bearing of false witness."[26]

When it comes to innovation, the diasporic fugues of imagination and reasoning are not quite the triumphantly elective polyphonies of the Occidental postmodernist *bricolage* although certain similarities are undeniable. The epistemological trajectory of diasporic avenues of newness and creativity resembles a certain "litany of pollution" in Paul Gilroy's words.[27] It poaches boldly and shrewdly from all available sources. But this sort of newness, to emphasize once more, is not a matter of calculated choice out of an abundance of equally attractive options. It could be more adequately called a "looser temporality"[28] of nifty survival—yet embellished with an always ambiguous spontaneity of drinking from diverse wells of inspiration, empowerment, and knowledge. The kind of "polluted" newness in postcolonial diasporic imaginaries manifests mostly through various forms of border epistemology. Rooted in political and ethical exigencies, border epistemology bears a constructive thrust. Thus, as aptly characterized by Tlostanova and Mignolo, it

> should be distinguished from anti-Western and anticapitalist doing and thinking. Anti-Western options are forms of

26. In my reflection on the murky theme of postcolonial authenticity I am indebted to Sandra Schneiders,' explorations of the Gospel of John where she poignantly links authenticity and the human capacity for salvation with a person's "openness and utter fidelity to reality and to his own experience of it, a fidelity that perhaps reflects a lifelong practice of Torah, which forbids the bearing of false witness." Authenticity as fidelity to the experience of reality "opens up one to God's action in one's life." See Schneiders, *Written that You May Believe*, 156, 168.

27. Gilroy, *The Black Atlantic*, 2.

28. David Parker suggests that the difference between merely cosmopolitan and diasporic subjectivities consists in their different experiences vis-à-vis loneliness arguing that "a cosmopolitan would never be lonely, or would see potentially anywhere, anyone, anything as capable of assuaging such sentiments. . . diasporic identities in contrast carry the weight of embodied, racialised histories and a more collective orientation," in "Diaspora, Dissidence and the Dangers of Cosmopolitanism," 166–67.

> resistance, while border epistemologies, in and from different local histories confronting imperial Western designs, not only oppose but mainly think forward, imagining and building a pluriversal and nonimperial world order(s).[29]

How do diasporic imaginaries tackle the ever edgy conundrum of difference? Difference is addressed in the borderzones of authenticity/originality and inauthenticity/mimicry. It is here that the axiologies of difference remain tricky. Trinth's classic observation about the colonial habits of postmodern difference still holds true today, especially for those of us who do not organically and univocally belong in the Occidental metropolitan cultures. Some decades ago she mused that:

> My audience expects and demands [difference]; otherwise people would feel as if they have been cheated: We did not come to hear a Third World member speak about the First (?) World, we came to listen to that voice of difference likely to bring us *what we can't have* and to divert us from the monotony of sameness. They, like their anthropologists whose specialty is to detect all the layers of my falseness and truthfulness, are in a position to decide what/who is "authentic" and what/who is not.[30]

Interestingly, the Occidental inertia of conceiving difference according to the image and likeness of competitive binarity perseveres in the ongoing treasure hunt for "authenticity"—be it the "Third World," the Native American, the postcolonial, or the diasporic authenticity. What is reflected in such a problematic demand for "authentic," immediately obvious, and blunt difference is the same dualistic rationale that postcolonial hybridity challenges since "differences made *between* entities comprehended as absolute presences—hence the notions of *pure origin* and *true* self—are an outgrowth of a dualistic system of thought peculiar to the Occident (the 'onto-theology' which characterizes Western metaphysics)."[31] In this context, diasporic imaginary cannot fail but to disappoint the desire for *pure* difference since the "spirit of diasporic thought" reflects resistance to "absolutist demarcation between authentic and inauthentic, pure and impure, real or fake."[32]

29. Tlostanova and Mignolo, *Learning to Unlearn*, 218.

30. Minh-ha, *Woman, Native, Other*, 88. Italics in the original. Vítor Westhelle attends to another famous theological squabble involving Jürgen Moltmann and South American Liberation theologians that illustrates the potent inertia that exoticized concepts of difference can exert even on the most daring Western theologians, Westhelle, *After Heresy*, 128.

31. Ibid, 90.

32. Ien Ang, "Can One Say No to Chineseness?" 225–27.

Regardless of its theological merits and pitfalls, is such a model anything "new," i.e., anything "original," anything postcolonially and diasporically "authentic" and unprecedented? In other words, is the voice of this itinerary "natively informative" enough, exotic enough, different enough? Here another possible disappointment may beckon for those steeped in what Catherine Keller calls "dominological" imagination within and without Christianity and its self-serving fabrication of *ex nihilo* as the "logos of lordship."[33] The "dominological" logos—unilateral, dualistic, arbitrarily omnipotent, overpowering, interventionist—underwrites not only patriarchal oppression, racial injustice, and theological legitimation of colonial conquest but also how difference, authenticity, and originality is envisioned. The theologically lording *ex nihilo* vision of creative agency, Keller argues, did not remain limited to matters of theological authority alone: rather, it "gradually . . . took modern and then secular form, generating every kind of western originality, every logos creating the new as if from nothing, cutting violently, ecstatically free of the abysms of the past."[34]

Historically speaking, no diasporic imaginary today can be either completely inside or completely outside the Occidental cultural and intellectual orbit and its *colonially* established global reach. Decolonial aspirations toward "unlearning" and "delinking" from the colonial matrix of power, knowledge, and being notwithstanding, there is no way around the fact that "Western modernity is inscribed in all of us (Westerners and non-Westerners)."[35] Diasporic imaginaries, insofar as they are vectored toward earnestly postcolonial/decolonial transformation, embody the potential of a contrapuntal border imagination to the fullest precisely as they straddle cultures and continents. The postcolonial diasporic both/and vector of imagination and creativity recognizes "that modernity is in all of us;" yet with a postcolonial twist, it also recognizes that while coloniality is constitutive of modernity, "Western contributions to world history must be celebrated, but the self-appointed role of modern actors and institutions to demand that the rest of the world follow their example has been and will always be totally illegitimate."[36]

Furthermore, to explicitly locate diasporic imaginaries within the postcolony is to reiterate that "the general mode of the postcolonial is citation, reinscription, rerouting the historical."[37] This inevitable general mode is due

33. Keller, *Face of the Deep*, xvii.

34. Ibid., xvi.

35. Tlostanova and Mignolo, *Learning to Unlearn*, 224.

36. Ibid.

37. Spivak, *Outside in the Teaching Machine*, 244.

first and foremost to the fact of Western modern *colonial* globalization and its postcolonial hybridity: the imaginary of Occident as the self-appointed center of power, knowledge, and being is not limited to the geo-political West as Édouard Glissant memorably retorted: The Occident is indeed not a just place but a project![38]

From the ivory tower of Western dominance the hybrid "newness" of a postcolonially colored diasporic imaginary may well appear to be *a priori* "fated to unoriginality"[39] in Derek Walcott's haunting observation. It is no accident that the presumed unoriginality has been acknowledged in postcolonial theory as stigmatizing and even as "dreadful secondariness" (Said) and the "curse of 'derivativeness'" (Radhakrishnan).[40] What is at stake here is the issue of legitimacy and recognition in relation to non-Occidental and marginally Occidental people to merit respect for their creative and scholarly endeavors if they dare to trespass beyond the confines of their supposedly "pure" and "authentic" cultures and knowledges. Thus, if one is, say, a Nigerian, then only Nigerian sources and references will do; similarly, to evaluate the originality of a Latvian, only Latvian sources and references will make the cut to satisfy Trinth's lamented Western demand for the diversion from its self-generated and self-proliferated monotony of sameness. This typical ivory-tower trap of Occidental reason is described with tormenting accuracy by Robert Bernasconi in his assessment of the African philosophical vision:

> Western philosophy traps African philosophy in a double bind: either African philosophy is so similar to Western philosophy that it makes no distinctive contribution and effectively disappears; or it is so different that its credentials to be genuine philosophy will always be in doubt.[41]

38. Glissant, *Le Discours antillais*, 14. In a brilliant footnote Glissant remarks that "the Occident is not in the West. It is not a place, it is a project," (*L'Occident n'est pas à l'ouest. Ce n'est pas un lieu, c'est un projet*). In the French language the crucial nuance is obvious.

39 Walcott, "The Caribbean: Culture or Mimicry?" 261.

40. Radhakrishnan, "Derivative Discourses," 790. Elsewhere Radhakrishnan has advanced Partha Chaterjee's notion of "derivative discourse" as resonating with Ranajit Guha's "small voice of history" both of which are caught in the profoundest ambiguity as "incapable of achieving systematicity on their own behalf. The best they can do to authorize their own sense of agency is to chip away, to 'signify' their intentions on a pre-existing and often alien text," see, "Globalization, Desire, and the Politics of Representation," 320.

41. Bernasconi, "African Philosophy's Challenge to Continental Philosophy," 188.

Africa is not alone in this ongoing entrapment of cultural imperialism; nor is philosophy as a discipline. A similar predicament overshadows theological inquiry with equal urgency. Theological assessments as to what counts as "real" and "true" theology and what pertains to the fuzzy sphere of inculturated spirituality, popular religion, or "local" religious practices are trapped in a similar colonial logic of binarity and narcissism. Furthermore, it only gets more complicated for the rest of us in diaspora who fall into the category of "not quite" only this or only that. Instead, I suggest, it might be more productive to direct the desire for diversion away from fantasies about ghettos of exoticized authenticity and focus on the critical analysis of what seems to be, for all practical purposes, a skillfully camouflaged "fulfillment of anthropological fantasy to condemn the native to some indigenous or autchtonous content and in the process den[y to] her the formal or fictive freedom to invent her own realities, affiliations and narrative trajectories."[42]

FROM THE CARIBBEAN TO THE BALTICS: SEARCHING FOR THE WOBBLE OF POSTCOLONIAL ORIGINALITY

To move beyond adversarial, indeed binaristic, constructs of authenticity and originality requires keeping in mind that the "great imperial experience. . . is global and universal; it has implicated every corner of the globe, the colonizer and the colonized together."[43] As knowledges, values, and sensibilities "travel" through diverse geo-historical arenas, and as variously colored diasporic experiences "voyage in" the Occidental cultural edifice, hybridity crescendos rather than diminishes. What emerges in the postcolony is "the wobble of assimilation or alterity"[44] on the part of those who "voyage in" as well as on the part of those Occidental theoretical and ethical axiologies that "travel" into landscapes and mindscapes previously seen as primitive, marginal, exotic, and, at best, derivative from the colonial point of view. However derivative and unoriginal such hybrid commerce of ideas, values, and sensibilities may be, in the postcolonial milieu it may well be the most organic way of how newness, meaning-making, and truth-telling are born. Two examples might be helpful here.

First, I turn to the Caribbean archipelago. In his study of the mid-twentieth century Afro-Caribbean poets and their engagement with Euromodernism, Jahan Ramazani suggests that postcolonial "authenticity" and "originality" have an idiosyncratic relation with repetition. Namely,

42. Radhakrishnan, "Derivative Discourses and the Problem of Signification," 792.

43. Said, *Culture and Imperialism*, 259.

44. Ramazani, "Modernist Bricolage, Postcolonial Hybridity," 459.

the Caribbean poets crafted their distinctive poetry through an uncanny process of appropriation and selective and critical reinvention through non-identical repetition. Such an approach "has helped the postcolonial poets encode aesthetically the intersections among multiple cultural vectors;" precisely by strategically and creatively redeploying Euromodernism, these poets also refashioned it in order to resist "local and imperial monisms."[45] Here is not a case of Euromodernist wannabes running short on so-called originality!

What happened in the poetic circles of the Caribbean archipelago is rather emblematic for many forced colonial contexts. This is a creative procedure that can be employed equally in literature and in theology—or other fields of inquiry. The fruit of such strategic redeployment is a vintage postcolonial newness in the key of postcolonial hybridity which,

> "confirms yet alters," reworks yet revalues . . . Only by breaking out of exclusionary models of tradition as either Eliot's "mind of Europe" or its postcolonial obverse ("an autonomous entity separate and apart from all other literatures") can we begin to grasp the continuous remaking of "traditions" by one another across the twentieth century and beyond, the mutually transformative relations between the poetries of metropole and margin.[46]

The other example of postcolonial remaking I would like to invoke is the Latvian musical tradition of the Song and Dance Festivals (*Dziesmu un deju svētki*). The Latvian Song Festival movement is considered today by many to be the most potent and sacred symbol of ethno-cultural identity. Approximately 40,000 singers from approximately one thousand choirs across the country, together with folk dancers and brass orchestra musicians—roughly 2% of the population, not counting the spectators—have participated in the summer Festival every five years since 1873. As the Latvian Lutheran theologian Guntis Kalme recently put it, the Song Festival is the "festive celebration of the Latvian nation" and "our identity" in which "our unique Latvian selfhood is being affirmed, voiced in song and expressed in the harmony of dance."[47] In 2008, the Latvian Song Festival together with similar traditions in Estonia and Lithuania was included by UNESCO in the Representative List of the Intangible Cultural Heritage of Humanity.

In the present context it is interesting to note that while the Song Festival is recognized as the foundation of Latvian ethno-cultural and national

45. Ibid., 448–49.

46. Ibid., 460.

47. Guntis Kalme, "Izdziedāt, svinēt un apliecināt."

identity, its origins signal yet another instance of the postcolonial "confirm yet alter" pattern of mimicry. In this case, the Latvian postcolonial mimicry has been subversive, invigorating, and astoundingly fruitful: the idea of the Song Festival is of a German origin. It was the German colonial diaspora who organized the first German song festival in Latvia in 1861[48] without, however, leaving a lasting impact on German singing culture.

The story could not be more different for Latvians. The first Latvian Song Festival took place in 1873, coinciding with the First National Awakening. It was one of the rare opportunities for Latvians to do something meaningful in their own language under the imperial Czarist regime. The Song Festival movement grew into a unique way of cultural and political empowerment that eventually led to national independence in 1918 and all the way to the Third Awakening and liberation from Soviet colonial occupation in 1991. It is telling that the events of the 1988–1991 struggle for Latvian independence during the collapse of the Soviet empire are known as the "Singing Revolution." Meanwhile, the Song Festival movement continues in the Latvian diasporas worldwide as it had done throughout the decades of Cold War exile with similar mythological/mystical prowess and emancipatory daring even as the symbolic heart of the tradition has now shifted back to the homeland.

What marks this trajectory of postcolonial creativity and empowerment in and through music is precisely the dynamic of confirming yet altering/ reworking yet revaluing the German colonial cultural impulses in an uncanny resonance with the indigenous creative genius in word and sound. The awe-inspiring cultural and spiritual life force of postsoviet Latvia, the symbolic celebration of Latvian identity in the homeland and in diaspora, is actually a fruit of an intricate postcolonial hybridity!

It is the subtle ambiguity of nuanced modulations (the *modus operandi* of diminutives!), as well as meticulously timed cultural quotations that "confirm yet alter" as they express the hybrid fabric of postcolonial imagination. Postcolonial diasporas amplify and intensify this dynamic. The hybrid imagination might not always be new enough for dominant regimes of knowledge, "authenticity," and beauty. But it is often good enough and genuine enough to be nothing less than life-giving for postcolonial peoples and individuals both in their homelands and diasporas. It is also good enough to carry the thrust of the diasporic homing desire further as it seeks to embody, among other things, the truth, the pain, and the beauty of its own longing for wholeness and interstitial integrity.

48. See the online resource "Dziesmusvētki."

DIASPORIC HYBRIDITY AND ASYMMETRICAL RECIPROCITY

Another crucial aspect deserves to be mentioned. Diasporic hybridity and reciprocity, as far as it is postcolonial, cannot be otherwise than asymmetrical. To claim equality for reciprocity in the present state of global postcolony, all its complex hybridities included, is idealistic naiveté or sheer hypocrisy. Asymmetrical reciprocity, not least in terms of the asymmetries of prosperity, agential power, self-determination, and wellbeing, is the hallmark of global postcolony. On top of that, the fiddly relations of diasporas with their valorized or abject homelands are always asymmetrical regardless of who ends up in the position of advantage in the complex dance of "here" and "there," "better" or "worse," and "authentic" or "polluted."

The relational complexity and disparity of diaspora spaces migrates into the mindscapes of diasporic imaginary. As pivotal as relationality and reciprocity are in postcolonial and diasporic lifeworlds, they are irrevocably colored by multi-layered asymmetry.

Postcolonial and diasporic relationality is not a paradisiacal state of affairs: some relations bless us and some torment. Nor does the notion of postcolonial relationality fit neatly into certain anti-essentialist postures that privilege relational ontologies and epistemologies—yet in a swooning manner without discerning the inherent power dynamics of any and all relational interfaces.

In the postcolonial milieu, no matter how unnerving and intimidating the relational asymmetry may be on socio-political and interpersonal levels, it can be recuperated for theological critiques as a blessing in disguise. As a midrash on the diasporic practice of "making the best" out of what cannot be undone by a simple act of will, it can serve postcolonial theology really well as a particularly hardnosed and judicious resource for theological reflection precisely regarding the haunting dilemmas of relational interfaces, divine and human. Suffice it say at this juncture that theology, too, deals with asymmetrical reciprocity—and the host of concerns about the use of power it raises—in every instance the notion of the monotheistic God is invoked. In Christian theological imagination, a profound asymmetrical reciprocity dwells at the very core of the economy of creation and salvation: it permeates the relations between the uncreated (transcendence) and the created (immanence), between nature and grace within the transontological God-world interface. The same dynamic can be found in sacramental discourse. Here, too, we find a similar asymmetrical reciprocity in action when the facets of material reality synergistically work together with the uncreated agency of grace that conjointly render a sacrament—and all that sacraments are called to signify and enable.

A BRAIDED IMAGINARY OF PLACES, SELVES, AND RELATIONS

Diaspora is not an intrinsically messianic location as opposed to other socio-cultural locations and subjectivities. Diasporic mindscapes are not so much colored by some kind of primordial innocence but rather by tenacious practices of survival rooted in the homing desire for wholeness. And diasporic imaginary is not an automatic panacea for rejuvenating imagination—theological or otherwise. While walking the razor's edge between glorification and demonization of diaspora, it does seem justified to conclude that diasporic lifeworlds and imaginaries do bear a particular sacramental potential as locations of divine revelation through their particularly intense entanglement with the ecology of relationality, as I have already argued above, for the sake of survival and the attempt to make the best out of whatever situation is at hand. When it comes to relating to difference, diasporic imaginaries live the paradox of "already, but not yet" in a uniquely strenuous way. A sustained and judicious discernment of that experiential and reflective paradox comprises the most constructive gift of diasporic imaginaries.

The critical and constructive contribution of postcolonial and diasporic imaginaries will never be uniform, equally loud, equally exotic, or equally "distracting" *vis-à-vis* the Occidental monotony of self-sufficiency. Some postcolonial diasporic voices find their natural habitat while speaking *sotto voce*—softly, through a whisper; through cardinal fragments that affirm both the roots and routes of their bodies and minds; through diminutive poles, overlooked as they routinely are by the Occidental mainstreams of imagination and authenticity, that disrupt yet do not destroy and connect yet do not absorb—just like sacraments do in order to bring about transformative change and redemptive restoration. The fabric of transformation that is braided together through cardinal fragments and diminutive poles is a real—yet stealthy—transformation.

To conclude, the *compositio loci* of the postcolonially colored diasporic imaginary of survival, displacement, relations, and new beginnings is an itinerary of braiding together dissonances and asymmetries while also nurturing the irrepressible homing desire for the contrapuntal harmony of a non-violent wholeness. It foregrounds the ethical pre-text of postcolonialism through meditation upon the genealogies of how "relationships and historical events intersected to inflict wounds"[49] even if an organized consensus as to how these wounds can be alleviated and prevented from being inflicted again and again is nowhere in sight. In the end, postcolonial diasporic imaginary is an ever maturing articulation of both estrangements and re(dis)coveries of selves, bodies, relations, histories, sins, desires, and hopes. As such, diasporic imaginary stands humbly under the proviso of its own unfinished genesis. As such, diasporic imaginary also stands under the apophatic proviso as rigorously as all and every theological mindscape must.

Postcolonially attuned diasporic imaginary offers a Christian theological method that is permeated by tenacious interstitial integrity. It is a space for a polyvocal, polycentric, pluriversal, and polymarginal—and in more explicitly theological terms also "polydox"[50]—homing desire This homing desire is vectored toward a salvific consummation of God being all in all through Christ in the Spirit without violence, without coercion, without conquest, and without abuse and humiliation. Diasporic imaginary recognizes dissonance and tension—yet without valorizing it as "a lasting city" (Heb 13:14). It acknowledges and embodies both the pain of disjointedness and the yearning for transfigurative *salus*—salvation, healing, wholeness, *theosis*. While yearning it walks through the hybrid postcolonial waters of experiences, theories, and theologies under the transcontinental rainbow and together with the diasporic Christ against the inconspicuous yet cardinal background of blue cornflowers and wild carrots in all their stealthy beauty.

49. Nesaule, *A Woman in Amber*, 279.

50. I refer to the emerging theological movement of "polydoxy" as a theological imaginary of multiplicity, relationality, and uncertainty in relation to divinity and its various revelatory modes. Polydoxy is considerably influenced by postcolonial discourses among other traditions of thought. The prefix "poly" underscores the emphasis on the logic of relational multiplicity and the necessity to "remain mindful of the toxic by-products of any doxic certainty," see Keller and Schneider, *Polydoxy*, 3.

PART II

Hybridity, Ethics, Theology

Some Postcolonial Resonances

2.1

Ethics, Theology, and the Postcolonial Fabric of Imagination

Feminism and postcolonial theory have a certain concern for social justice. I would like to think that this would be the case for all Humanities and Social Science work, perhaps for all work.[1]

GAYATRI CHAKRAVORTY SPIVAK

The relation with the Other is accounted for. . .in ethical and not epistemological terms.[2]

NELSON MALDONADO-TORRES

THE EPOCH OF so many "posts"—post-totalitarian, post-Holocaust, post-modern, post-secular, post-Christendom, post-liberal, post-institutional, post-ecclesial, and so forth—situates any critical and creative reasoning, including theology, within the limelight of irretrievably lost innocence regarding its true motivations, capabilities, limitations, and implications. Genealogically speaking, the Holocaust has been the decisive unsettling ethical challenge for late Western modernity and particularly for its theo-

1. Spivak, "In Memoriam: Edward W. Said," 7.

2. Maldonado-Torres, *Against War*, 239.

logical traditions. Christian theologies that are genuinely conscious of their age and their own deeply ambiguous legacies of violence continue to mature in their responses to the internal Western critiques of racism, totalitarianism, sexism, imperialism, and capitalism in a variety of motivating ways. The postcolonial approach, however, brings to the fore even more divergent and disagreeable histories, experiences, epistemologies, and anthropologies from other (dis)empowered locations outside of or—which is an even more complex and ambivalent story—from the fuzzy margins and interstices of the antithetical modern West versus non-West/the Rest gridlock.

TURNING AWAY FROM THE "VICIOUS" ASPECTS OF MODERNITY

The post-Holocaust era engendered a compelling "turn to the ethical" at least in some segments of Western philosophical and theological inquiry. During the past couple of decades postcolonialism has been confronting both philosophy and theology with a similarly nonnegotiable claim for the enlargement of ethics beyond the traditional intra-Western "others." Despite potential convergences, in the early twenty-first century it remains true that the gap between the studies of antisemitism, the Holocaust, racism, and postcolonialism is still not closed. As of yet, these histories of victimization and sources of critique still have not been rigorously and systematically interrelated in either field.[3] Against this background, the paramount postcolonial question for theology is really about the importance of being consistent in the ethically grounded theological lament about the horrors of Western modernity. These horrors are by no means limited to the Holocaust. The lament can no longer revolve only around emblematic Western preoccupations with itself (even including its predictable "others"!) and itself alone as the sole center of values or at least, the most sublime center of universal tragedy if more congratulatory self-centering gestures are no longer feasible.

The theological significance of recognizing the violence of colonialist imaginary and praxis lies, ethically speaking, in a penitential acknowledgment of colonialism as "the vicious aspect of modernity"[4] in the words of R. S. Sugirtharajah. Ashis Nandy was more specific: he pointedly described colonialism as "the armed version of modernity."[5] The armed viciousness of

3. The work of scholars like Bryan Cheyette and Ella Shohat is informative here. See their respective essays "White Skin, Black Masks" and "Columbus, Palestine and Arab Jews" in *Cultural Readings of Imperialism*.

4. Sugirtharajah, *Postcolonial Configurations*, 4.

5. Nandy, *The Intimate Enemy*, xiv.

modernity was historically embodied, more often than not, by the tandems of crown and cross, the Gospel and the sword, and of *ecclesia* and *mercatura* through the centuries of the globally proliferated unholy "synergy of conquest, commerce, and Christ."[6]

From a postcolonial perspective, Christian theology is intrinsically and undeniably part and parcel of the overall Occidental socio-cultural and political edifice. This edifice includes its overt and covert global colonial ambitions and their legitimizing (theo)ideological apparatus that was and, to a certain degree, remains camouflaged under the soteriological pretext of saving unbelieving souls through "mission." To briefly restate what has been elucidated by postcolonial critiques over the past three decades: "the culpability of the church is twofold: first, as an ally in the political dispensation of 'divine sanction' to Western imperialism; and second, as a tyrant in absolutizing the binarism of God/servant aligned with the civilized West/primitive East"[7] or whatever construct of the peripheral other was culturally profitable and theologically ingratiating in any particular situation.

Furthermore, in some Western theological contexts it still needs to be explicitly underscored that the colonial regimes of power do not subsist in economic policies, military strategies, or ideological postures alone. Colonial regimes of power, knowledge, and being do not neatly interlock with the modern Western mythology of an unambiguous church-state separation. The seemingly "secular" avenues of exercising and materializing the cultural imaginary of colonialism are uncannily enmeshed with violent and arrogant cosmologies of divine power and agency. In fact, the "secular" practices of colonialism find their inspiration, legitimation, and sublimation in violent and arrogant cosmologies of divine power and agency. As Namsoon Kang summarizes, too often in history Christian communities

> have perceived Christianity in an exclusive way as the only true religion in the world and portray God as the Emperor of the world. Theopolitically speaking, how one perceives God provides a ground for Christians' self-understanding in the world. In this sense, Christian theological construction of God as, for instance, Father, Lord, or King conveys the colonial image of an Emperor with an untouchable absolute authority. For those who perceive God in an exclusive, militant, hierarchical way, Christian mission always means dominating and colonizing the religious or cultural others and the heathen of foreign land [. . .] Although Christians have claimed that God is beyond human

6. Keller et al., *Postcolonial Theologies*, 14.

7. Bong, "Theologies of, for, and by Asians," 81–82.

> attributions such as gender, race, sexuality, or age and beyond human comprehension, it is hard to deny that people shape and mediate the symbol for God by the values inherent in a social matrix, in which the values of patriarchy, hierarchy, or colonial mentality prevail.[8]

Thus it is hard to imagine how contemporary Western Christian theologians, especially those inhabiting the global postcolony from "above," could escape living and working *coram Deo* otherwise than kenotically and penitentially (consider the deeply transformative rationale of *metanoia*!) if the "evangelical"[9] integrity of theological enterprise is a virtue to be truly affirmed.

Kenosis is not an innocuous notion in postcolonial imagination. As it already has been argued in feminist, womanist, *mujerista*, and various liberation critiques, it is also the case for postcolonial theologies that *kenosis* must be carefully and contextually calibrated. Against the historical backdrop of patriarchal and colonial abuses of *kenosis* imaginary, an extreme caution needs to be exercised when it is invoked in the postcolonial context.[10] *Kenosis* invokes the Trinitarian movement of generous, compassionate, and freely willed vulnerability out of the abundance of divine love, power, and redemptive agency. *Kenosis* starts in plenitude and empowerment—not scarcity, disenfranchisement, and imposed vulnerability. Hence, *kenosis* cannot be the universally recommended comportment or tool of choice for the already weak. When misused and enforced upon those already powerless and abused, it is one of the most blasphemous and perverse conceptual and imaginative weapons of psychospiritual victimization across the interconnected terrains of colonial oppression—be they racial, cultural, political, economic, or gendered. In the postcolonial context, *kenosis* as well as conversion, that is, *metanoia*—the movement beyond the corrupting power of self-absorbing attachments and compulsions, and the struggle of becoming open to changing one's culturally ingrained habits of perception and action—have little to do with stewing in (post)colonial guilt. Instead, it has

8. Namsoon Kang, *Diasporic Feminist Theology*, 115.

9. Here I use the arguably confusing term "evangelical," at least in the Anglo-Saxon cultural and linguistic context, to refer to the Gospel-based vision of the Reign of God as revealed by Jesus Christ. The German "*evangelisch*" and the Latvian "*evaņģēlisks*" express the "good news" aspect of Christianity's Christ-centered kerygmatic integrity less ambiguously.

10. Profoundly relevant critiques of the dangers of valorizing allegedly redemptive kenotic and imitative suffering that has been habitually imposed on the already disadvantaged and oppressed (women, racial minorities, the colonized) in Christian history are summarized in the essays by Marit Trelstad, Katryn Kleinhans, and Anna Mercedes in *Transformative Lutheran Theologies*.

much to do with cardinal virtues like justice and courage to look at oneself through the eyes of previously ignored and caricatured others.

At the same time, it is important to reiterate here that the value of postcolonial challenges does not consist in a simplistic dismissal or wholesale "defrocking" of Western theological traditions. As I have already noted before, they are not singularly invalid or automatically irrelevant *vis-à-vis* non-Western religious traditions and spiritual sensibilities. To claim so would lead to a mere proliferation of arbitrary hierarchical dualism (i.e., such as "Orientalism") albeit in the reverse gear. Tragic blind spots and blasphemous failures notwithstanding, the Western theological tradition is rich, beautiful, and intricate. It accommodates diverse genealogies of spiritual, intellectual and artistic influences, including powerful internal critiques and dissents. Even the specific theological and spiritual traditions of the Western colonial modernity are not one-dimensional villains of world history and world Christianity. Nor are all of its theological images, concepts, practices, and aspirations irremediably beyond repair and doomed forever.

Instead of one-dimensional vendettas, postcolonial explorations and spiritual quests into Christian and other religious terrains are currently cross-fertilizing into a deliberately unmonitored and unmanaged force-field of theological creativity. This force-field of spiritual longing, vigilant discernment, and creativity relentlessly contests the enduring colonial hierarchies of theological dominance, arrogance, non-accountability, and self-righteousness. Today it encompasses both theologies of postcolonial displacement (diasporic modes) and postcolonial stability (indigenous modes), to use a rough distinction, and much in between without privileging either pole of the spectrum.

Without denying the existing deep entanglements of Christianity in the ideologies of colonialism and imperialism, it is not simply an unmitigated march of imperial conquests and messianically tinted genocidal violence. Christianity's colonial histories and imperial genealogies have certainly distorted and obscured, yet not extinguished, the salvific sway of the coming Reign of God so uniquely embodied and so copiously shared through the life of Jesus Christ. It is here that the most profound and fruitful resonance between postcolonialism and the Gospel is to be found. The proverbial *Anknüpfungspunkt*, or the reverberating creative interface between these two, obtains through the dimension of postcolonialism that can be summarized as an "ethical pre-text" or "the appeal to an ethical universal."

THE HYPERSENSITIVE "ETHICAL PRE-TEXT" OF POSTCOLONIALISM

What, then, is the ethical pre-text in postcolonialism? Or, to use the language more prevalent in the context of the Americas, where does decolonial commitment dwell in postcolonial imagination and praxis? The ethical pre-text of postcolonialism—*vis-à-vis*, say, postmodernism—resides, to quote Kwame Anthony Appiah's classic formulation, "in the appeal to an ethical universal" which in turn is grounded "in an appeal to a certain simple respect for human suffering."[11] The ethical momentum of postcolonialism proceeds, to express it in explicitly theological terms, anamnetically and proleptically, "in the name of the suffering victims"[12] and for their restoration and healing. As David Theo Goldberg and Ato Quayson sum up, the ethical pre-text symbolizes "the idea that postcolonial criticism is itself an ethical enterprise."[13] It enables postcolonial practices of thought and life to advance the quest for justice and peace in ways that neither poststructuralism nor postmodernism would or could. Postcolonial critiques are aligned with the impetus which Gayatri Chakravorty Spivak has poetically described as the "joining of hands" between subaltern histories and literary criticism "in search of the ethical as it interrupts the epistemological."[14] Surely, given the pervasiveness of the unholy synergy of conquest, commerce, and Christ, ethics is equally indispensable to interrupt theology!

That being said, the ethical pre-text is not an exhaustively defined and codified rubric of postcolonial philosophy. Postcolonial theology is more specific here. According to Kang, we can rather speak of a methodological orientation that is actually rooted in the New Testament eschatological vision of the last judgment (Matt 25:31–46). In Jesus' parable of the last judgment, ethical discernment and action toward "the least of my sisters and brothers" could be recapitulated as a "hypersensitivity to the marginalized. . . colonized, imprisoned, and the poor."[15] The methodological comportment that Kang so perceptively describes as a hypersensitivity is not something accidental for postcolonial (and also feminist, in her assessment) theology. Instead, it is nonnegotiable. Although Kang does not use the fol-

11. Appiah, "Is the Post- in Postmodernism the Post- in Postcolonial?" 353.

12. Ibid.

13. David Theo Goldberg and Ato Quayson, "Introduction: Scale and Sensibility," xii. They emphasize that "all binary oppositions are value-laden, with the first term often implicitly assumed to have an ethical or conceptual, normative or indeed logical priority over the second," ibid.

14. Spivak, "In Memoriam: Edward W. Said," 7.

15. Kang, *Diasporic Feminist Theology*, 125.

lowing terminology, it involves nothing less than a biblically mandated metaphysical prolegomenon: "With a hypersensitivity to the marginalized, postcolonial and feminist theological discourses try to reinvent universals for and with the marginalized on various grounds. In this sense, what we need to do is think *with* and *beyond* the Euro-America characterized by a colonizing paradigm."[16]

Two additional analytical metaphors may be helpful for grasping the vital thrust here. First, the ethical pre-text functions somewhat like Wilson Harris' "fabric of imagination." According to Harris, the fabric of imagination is a living network, a rhythm of perception, an optic of reflection and numinous intuition, and finally also a style of relation and agency that is honed by and through the material and affective habitations in postcolony.[17] And the ongoing genesis of this fabric, as Harris warns, is "ceaselessly unfinished!"[18]

Second, the ethical pre-text is also akin to Raymond Williams' synthetic notion of "the structure of feeling." It adds the dimension of lived experience, practically expressed passion and affectivity to the postcolonial fabric of imagination that, as all imaginative concepts, can easily float into the disembodied realms of textuality and abstract theory. When it comes to the ethical pre-text of postcolonial critiques, staying firmly on the grounds of embodied reality is of paramount significance. According to Williams, structures of feeling or experience pertain to the "practical consciousness": they emerge, shape, and interact with "meanings and values as they are actively lived and felt."[19] Structures of feeling/experience are simultaneously individual and social. They are firm and yet delicate to the point of almost being intangible. The affective elements are specifically included, yet not juxtaposed to intellect: "not feeling against thought, but thought as felt and feeling as thought," and all of that in the process of emergence, with its peculiar connections, suppressions, and emphases, and, finally, all of that is happening "on the very edge of semantic availability."[20]

As a hypersensitivity, as a fabric of imagination, and as a structure of feeling, the postcolonial ethical pre-text is "underwriting" and driving forth the whole spectrum of various postcolonial endeavors well beyond

16. Ibid., 126. Italics in original.

17. Wilson Harris, "The Fabric of the Imagination," 175. Harris underscores the role of the intuitive and numinous elements of imagination even more evocatively in another essay also titled "The Fabric of Imagination" presented at the University of Cambridge on October 24, 1990, in *The Radical Imagination*, 69–79.

18. Ibid., 176.

19. Williams, *Marxism and Literature*, 132.

20. Ibid., 132–34.

the confines of ethics as a clearly demarcated discipline. Yet it also brings up the perpetual postcolonial misgivings toward universalism and foundationalism in philosophy, ideology, and religion. Such misgivings cannot be ignored.

POSTCOLONIAL UNIVERSALITY? THE ETHICAL NUANCE

During the present sunset of postmodernity, we are increasingly aware of expanding structures and networks of global economic, cultural, and ecological interdependence, for good and for ill. Globalized disenfranchisement, the upsurge in forced migration, intensification of chaoplexic violence, terrorism—and its Siamese twin, the endless "war on terror"—should be added to the networks of interdependence as one of their darkest undertows. In this context, a re-envisaged appeal to the ethical that is rooted in the recognition of the *universality* of human suffering and victimization, particularly of those who are the postcolonial "sinned against,"[21] does not necessarily resuscitate the stereotypical modern-*cum*-colonial trajectory of universalism or projected and imposed universalization. The appeal to a genuinely postcolonial/decolonial ethical universality can transcend the totalitarian impulse and memory of the colonial structures of belief, imagination, and action.

This kind of watchful universality is aptly perceived in Paul Gilroy's idea of planetary consciousness that is sensitized to recognize and honor suffering. Through such planetary consciousness and indeed, such planetary humanism, we are invited to entrain the capability "of comprehending the universality of our elemental vulnerability to the wrongs we visit upon each other."[22] Postcolonial universality here is a matter of intentionally seeking a translocal solidarity amid rapidly growing hyper-fragmentation of interests, ideologies, and allegiances, in the sense of discerning a comportment of solidarity which,

> might nurture the ability and the desire to live with difference on an increasingly divided but also convergent planet . . . We need to know what sorts of insight and reflection might actually

21. I am referring to Andrew Sung Park's term for the "experience of the powerless, the marginalized, and the voiceless in the world" and the "innocent who are caught in the wicked situation of helplessness" whose deep pain is routinely overlooked in the traditional Christian models of sin and salvation. See Sung Park, "The Bible and Han" in *The Other Side of Sin*, 46–47.

22. Gilroy, *Postcolonial Melancholia*, 4.

> help increasingly differentiated societies and anxious individuals to cope successfully with the challenges involved in dwelling comfortably in proximity to the unfamiliar without becoming fearful and hostile. We need to consider whether the scale upon which sameness and difference are calculated might be altered productively so that the strangeness of strangers goes out of focus and other dimensions of basic sameness can be acknowledged and made significant. We also need to consider how a deliberate engagement with the twentieth century's histories of suffering might furnish resources for the peaceful accommodation of otherness in relation to fundamental commonality.[23]

Postcolonial universality can emerge as a robustly historical "solidarity of others,"[24] to invoke the notion of the Korean-American liberation theologian Anselm Min. It emerges within the real world of sensible human embodiment precisely if and when the ethical appeal to recognize and respect the suffering of the multitudes of Frantz Fanon's *les damnés de la terrre*—the "wretched of the earth"—saturates the very hub of our planetary interdependence. Such suffering is poignantly characterized by the Asian notion of *han*: according to Andrew Sung Park, *han* is "deep agonizing pain" that develops as a "physical, mental, and spiritual repercussion to a terrible injustice done to a person, eliciting a deep ache, a wrenching of all the organs, an intense internalized or externalized rage, a vengeful obsession, and the sense of helplessness and hopelessness."[25] *Han* is not a mere consequence of abstract evil; it is also a corollary of interpersonal and intercultural sin. As a fabric of imagination and a structure of feeling, the quest for a postcolonial ethical universal originates from a concern much more ultimate and immediate—suffering, *han*—than mere intellectual routines of modern colonialism, totalitarian imagination, or their theoretical and disembodied opposites.

The postcolonial quest for an ethical universal does not need to preempt or negate particularity. Postcolonial universality gravitates around the quest for "a 'universalism' appropriate to a still conflictual world"—an "innovative and oppositional universalism that counters the restricted and monistic notion endemic to European thought."[26]At the core of such universality lies what Edward Said called the gravity of history: the postcolonial experience in all its existential and material dimensions of *han* but also the

23. Gilroy, *Postcolonial Melancholia*, 4.

24. Min, *The Solidarity of Others in a Divided World*.

25. Park, *The Other Side of Sin*, 48.

26. Ansell-Pearson et al, "Introduction: The Gravity of History," 12, 13.

somber exigency of a universalizing response to the manifold assortments of affliction and ongoing immiseration.

The appeal for a respectful and restorative wholeness for all, with all the differences, tensions, and particularities considered, does not equal totalitarianism. This is precisely what Édouard Glissant insists on when he deliberately foregrounded the notion of totality—but for him it is a preeminently relational totality. This is a planetary totality under the aegis of the "poetics of Relation." It is not something totalitarian, obvious, or transparent. It is rather an opaque kind of totality which "willingly renounces any claims to sum it up or to possess it."[27] The utmost focus here is on the planetary ecology of interdependence—"the relational interdependence of all lands, of the whole Earth."[28]

The postcolonial quest for an ethical universal is a quest that proactively honors the suffering of those sinned against precisely by taking seriously the tension that permeates such a quest. To draw once again from Min's analysis, the objective for a postcolonial ethical universality as a way of life, is not yet communion but solidarity. Communion implies an achievement of relational union, Min argues. Yet historically speaking, "communion is inadequate and misleading" insofar as our lived realities fall palpably short of such eschatological realization.[29] While teleologically retaining eschatological communion as the profoundest goal and significance of all historical solidarities, Min suggests that in the solidarity of others a universal imaginary emerges as a modest, down-to-earth, and yet steeply challenging aspiration amidst the manifold tensions of history. In this sense, solidarity is a "mode of interdependence of those who are other. . . a concrete universality or togetherness of others without totalization."[30] To sum up, the postcolonial quest for ethically constellated universality has more to do with

> a sense of wholeness, totality, connectedness, and solidarity regarding our human destiny, a sense of interdependence for all significant issues in a rapidly globalizing world which constitutes the common context for all struggles today. We should recover this sense of the whole, however, in a postcritical and a precritical way, that is, without in any way turning a deaf ear to

27. Glissant, *Poetics of Relation*, 21.

28. Ibid., 146.

29. Min, *The Solidarity of Others in a Divided World*, 141.

30. Ibid. Min's full argument underscores the tensions that permeate the decentering/recentering movements of solidarity inasmuch as the abolition of privileged perspectives is central for his proposal and how it relates to the problematic nature of the hierarchies of oppression, suffering, and victimhood. He does note, however, that solidarity does not abolish the "preferential option for the most oppressed," ibid.,142.

> the cry of the oppressed in all their particularity. I am not arguing for a simple, uncritical return to the deceptive universality of traditional, European theology.[31]

Within the horizon of the postcolonial search for wholeness, the ethical pre-text bears most powerfully—even though often obliquely—on the inherent "object relations referenced by the binary oppositions."[32] Ethically speaking, pre-texted postcolonialism strives to generate post-binary imagination and socio-political action not by abolishing difference but by calling into question the hierarchical inertias of dualism, especially when those are enthroned and projected onto all—including God—as "natural" and somehow self-evident. Despite trials and errors, it labors toward an ethically vigilant subjectivity, rationality, and spirituality.

At its best, postcolonial theology advances an imaginary of polyphonic universality and wholeness that is precisely the opposite of totalitarian universalism. The present fragmentation in virtually all arenas of life is overwhelmingly real. Hence the quest for postcolonial harmony is really, in the words of Gloria Anzaldúa, a quest for integration: "Torn between ways, we seek to find some sort of harmony amid the remolinos of multiple and conflictive worldviews; we must learn to integrate all these perspectives."[33] This imaginary of harmony unfolds in terms evocatively suggested by John Thatamanil in another context as:

> [a] vision of interrelatedness that is more fundamental than all the fragmentations that mark our age and the human heart. The tragic reality of rupture is not denied. . . [but] refuses to give to brokenness the final word. Instead, we're invited into a new and at once ancient harmony, one in which we move and live and have our being.[34]

The ethical fabric of imagination—or structure of feeling—engenders a trajectory of desire for a new intersubjective and intercultural space as "an arena where inequalities, imbalances and asymmetries could historicize

31. Min, *Paths to the Triune God*, 319.

32. Goldberg and Quayson "Introduction: Scale and Sensibility," xii. They point out the paradox involved in claiming a "foundational" role for the ethical pre-text in postcolonialism. Such an approach confronts the habitual suspicions directed toward any whiff of metanarrative within a generally post/anti-foundationalist theory. Postcolonialism, however, advocates for an ethical foundation, that is, the axiological point of departure, for critically interrogating the structures of dominance, hierarchy, and hegemony.

33. Anzaldúa, *Light in the Dark*, 17.

34. Thatamanil, "Front endorsement," in Newell, *A New Harmony*.

themselves 'relationally,' an arena where dominant historiographies could be made accountable to the ethico-political authority of emerging histories."[35] It is precisely the ethico-political thread, or the quest for non-totalitarian integration, that sustains postcolonial veracity and credibility as an invested and committed comportment among many other ways of theorizing and theologizing. In the words of Robert J.C. Young, postcolonialism entails a commitment toward the ideals of "transnational social justice."[36] This is where the very integrity of the whole postcolonial endeavor subsists.

Despite voluminous critiques and disappointments regarding the ability of postcolonial theoretical practices to generate original, effective, and clearly measurable changes in people's lifescapes and thoughtscapes throughout the global postcolony, the "visionary commitment to the end of all institutional suffering"[37] is still alive even as postcolonialism comes of age and continues to learn from its own occlusions and blunders. The appeal to the ethical universal might indeed be seen as one of the rare visionary, perhaps even utopian, tenets of the otherwise melancholic and deconstructive imaginary that abhors whitewashing afflictions, manipulating hopes, and exploiting vulnerabilities—yet again. But the times of relentless deconstructive resistance alone, oppositionality alone, and Marxist secularism alone have come and gone; even the times of routinely thinking about postcolonial theory and theology as the strangest of all bedfellows are finally going away. As the old routines wane, what remains steadfastly relevant is the imaginary and the praxis of a "truly equal and multilateral universality" that is "liberated from dominance and captive no more to the ventriloquism of the West"[38] or any other imperial formations of dominance.

RELATIONALITY AND POSTCOLONIAL ETHICS

Postcolonial engagement with ethics is not confined to specialized theoretical discourse. It is not confined within clearly demarcated disciplinary boundaries. Rather, the appeal to an ethical universal concerns the nature, the structures, and the power differentials of relationality among all levels of life within the totality of creation—within the realm of intersubjective and intercultural relations and all the way across the transontological divide into the realm of God's relation with the whole of created reality.

35. Radhakrishnan, "Postcoloniality and the Boundaries of Identity," 762.

36. Young, *Postcolonialism*, 58.

37. Gandhi, *Postcolonial Theory*, 137.

38. Radhakrishnan, "Postmodernism and the Rest of the World," 64.

Postcolonial ethics calls for a painstaking exploration and judicious scrutiny of the qualitative nature of the lived, remembered, and desired matrix of relationality with oneself, with one's local and global neighbors and their histories, hopes, wounds, and fears, and, in the end, all of the above in relation to their divine Other(s). Ultimately, it is relationality across the most asymmetrical terrains of life that constitutes the pivotal nexus of ethically pre-texted postcolonialism. And it is this nexus that organically overlaps our lived human *religio* with divine Other(ness) and our ways of reflecting upon this very relationality of *religio*—the ways we usually call theology.

It is the time now to ask pointedly and purposely: what is the specific constructive relation between an ethically pre-texted postcolonialism and theology? The pivotal issue here concerns the wholesomeness of God-world relationality as perceived and experienced from the postcolonial undersides. For ethics in postcolonialism is not a matter of theory; it is a matter of lived and often suffered relationality *par excellence*. In this sense, postcolonialism is a philosophy of life in which the question of *how* we as human beings are to relate to one another as individuals and as members of particular historical, political, cultural, racial, gendered, and socio-economic communities constitutes the throbbing heartbeat of just and life-affirming planetary conviviality. The postcolonial ethics of relationality is a quest for a reverential, life-giving, and dignifying relational reciprocity that takes seriously the glaringly obvious asymmetries of wellbeing, empowerment, and agency.

Simultaneously it is a quest for an analogous relational—and yet ever asymmetrical—reciprocity between the Creator and the creation in our present postcolonial condition. Hence the most vital postcolonial vocation today is to probe deeply and widely to search for ontologies and epistemologies of asymmetrical reciprocity that qualitatively transcend and transform the colonial imaginaries of hegemonic hierarchies, oppressive dualisms, and jealously competitive binaries. It is at this juncture, I submit, that there is a need for postcolonialism and theology to join hands ever tighter to create imaginative spaces and practices which labor together, in Bhabha's memorable words, to "entertain difference without an assumed or imposed hierarchy"[39] across all relational terrains of lived and hoped-for reality including the crucial spiritual dimensions of life.

39. Bhabha, *The Location of Culture*, 5.

ETHICS: A POSTCOLONIAL FUNDAMENTAL THEOLOGY

The ethical fabric of postcolonial imagination—even if oblique, elusive, and forlornly provisional—challenges and sharpens the theological quest for patterns of imagining and living justice. As Sugirtharajah points out in the context of biblical interpretation, the ethical structure of feeling in postcolonial criticism "provides openings for oppositional readings, uncovers suppressed voices and, more pertinently, has as its foremost concern victims and their plight."[40]

At the most profound and existential level these themes are as equally theological as they are ethical. This resonance constitutes a perichoretic interface: here theology kenotically and redemptively indwells ethics while ethics vigilantly seeps into every nook and cranny of theology with endless and stubborn perseverance as a different yet equal voice so that one is always in, with, under, and throughout the other. Herein resides the most radical, and arguably controversial, resonance between postcolonialism in its ethical and even "therapeutic" dimensions and the kind of Christian theology that ceaselessly toils to uphold, rejuvenate, and transform life so that all, but especially those sinned against by Occidental colonialism and the throngs of *les damnés de la terrre*, could at last live and thus glorify God by becoming fully alive. Namely, through this particular postcolonial lens, ethics, to invoke a gesture of Emmanuel Levinas, becomes a "first" theology or, as it were, a "fundamental" theology.

This vision of postcolonial theology resonates particularly with discourses such as liberation theology, feminist, womanist, *mujerista*, and other emancipatory fields of inquiry, all of which "spring from an ethical effort to do justice to human experience in all its diversity."[41] Like discourses of environmental studies and ecojustice, commitment to ethics is "an often unstated but constitutive element" of postcolonialism.[42] And it is here, I suggest, that an interesting and fruitful resonance with the contemporary work of "Transformation Theology" thinkers also comes to the forefront.

Taking the histories of colonialism and the ethical pre-text of postcolonialism seriously, the methodological center of gravity and veracity in theological inquiry ought to shift intentionally from dogma and doctrine to ethics. A similar suggestion, albeit not out of explicitly postcolonial concerns, has been recently expressed by "Transformation Theology." Drawing

40. Sugirtharajah, *Postcolonial Configurations*, 4.

41. De Jong-Kumru, *Postcolonial Feminist Theology*, 119

42. DeLoughrey, et al., "Introduction," *Global Ecologies and the Environmental Humanities*, 9.

from the provocative late work of Dietrich Bonhoeffer during the totalitarian nightmare of Nazism and the Holocaust, Paul Janz suggests that today

> theological orientation to the present reality of God in the world must be first and fundamentally to the will of God and not first to the "being" of God. . . It means that theology must be an *ethics* before it is a *dogmatics* or before it is doctrine. Or somewhat more accurately, it means that Christian dogmatics or Christian doctrine must be grounded foundationally in a "Christian ethics."[43]

The shift from the primacy or doctrine to the primacy of ethics is rooted in the generative primacy of revelation over doctrine. The ultimate challenge for Christian ethics, according to Bonhoeffer, is to discern the will of God (and not theorize who/what God is) and then to attend to the "making real" (*Wirklichwerdung*) of God's reality as revealed in Christ among God's creatures.[44] As Janz argues, this is the "essential 'from below' focus on Christian ethics" as it prioritizes the witnessing and the *imitatio Christi* vocation of Christians and their theology to embody "the *reality today* of the *righteousness* which comes from God, [and] the 'becoming real' of God's self revelation as such."[45] For Janz, ethics as the "making real" of divine revelation and righteousness in Christ for and in our world of sensible embodiment therefore takes the place of "fundamental" theology in which all doctrinal issues must be grounded.

The primacy of ethics is a primacy of the practical in the world of human agency and endeavor. It refers to the relational, sensible, intersubjective, participatory, and embodied "practical consciousness" in the practices of theology and spirituality.[46] In this sense, ethics means practicing Christ—implementing, witnessing, and embodying that extraordinary reconciliation and conviviality between God and the whole world in Christ (a pivotal Bonhoefferian theme!) which must be rendered real, present, and transformative within the terrain of sensible human experience and not just in intellectual or devotional dimensions. Hence:

> It is not first as discursive or intuitive 'participants' in the mind of God, or even first as discursive or intuitive 'hearers of the

43. Davies, et al., *Transformation Theology*, 108. Italics in the original.

44. Bonhoeffer, *Ethics*, 47, 49.

45. Davies, et al., *Transformation Theology*, 109. I am not following the full scope of Janz's historico-cultural argument regarding divine righteousness here but am rather sketching his methodological move for the sake of my constructive suggestion. Italics in the original.

46. Ibid., 111.

> word'—necessary and vital as these may be—that we become most fundamentally oriented to God as a present reality. It is rather much more as physically embodied "instruments of righteousness" that, as Oliver Davies says [. . .], the Spirit sets us today, through a "re-establishment" of the life of our senses, into a "new relation with the living body of Christ."[47]

The postcolonial endorsement of the methodological priority of ethics as fundamental theology presses beyond the late postmodern and post-Christendom Western perplexity about finding viable cosmologies and metaphysics for understanding the reality and presence of God. Postcolonialism goes further by adding a dimension of robust ethical depth and accountability that ought to permeate the whole theological enterprise—and not just the distinct and self-sufficient discipline of moral theology or Christian ethics.

The postcolonial priority of ethics foregrounds respect for the suffering of the sinned-against "wretched of the earth." In postcolonial analyses, a good deal of suffering for the colonial and postcolonial "wretched of the earth" originated precisely because the colonial(izing) Christians made horrifyingly real, no doubt in devilishly ironic ways, their arrogant, imperialistic, and genocidal ideas of Christ's dominance over the whole world.

Abuse and misuse of any ideas, theological or otherwise, cannot be prevented with watertight certainty as the genocidal twentieth century has shown even after the acknowledged horrors of the Holocaust and the fragile hopes of "never again." What can and must be done, particularly in the Occidental practices of Christian theology, is a judicious and kenotic scrutiny of images of God, sin, grace, love, and salvation. Such scrutiny must assess their historical performance and imaginative potential to condone and enable the violation of subaltern others and the sanctity of their lives prior to and above all other doctrinal, ecclesial, or liturgical spats. This is what the primacy of ethics as fundamental theology is all about from a methodological perspective.

To clarify once more with precision: postcolonial sensibilities highlight what David Ngong has called the "ethics of theology." Namely, in distinction from the discipline of Christian ethics, the ethics of theology "examines the ethics of theological discourses, focusing on how salutary a particular theological discourse might be to communities and individuals"[48] since "depending on how we do it, our theology may kill us or give us life."[49]

47. Ibid.

48. Ngong, *Theology as Construction of Piety*, xxi.

49. Ibid., xvii.

The postcolonial *examen* of theological conscience is akin to the course of reasoning that Jesus suggested while trying to discern false prophecies: "You will know them by their fruits. Are grapes gathered from thorns, or figs from thistles?" (Matt 7:16). Ngong's approach spells out precisely such a trajectory of self-critical interrogation of our theological efforts. Even though Ngong does not explicitly self-identify as a postcolonial theologian, his idea fittingly expresses the postcolonial exigencies as it "assesses the possible outcomes of the theological ideas that form Christians" and "only recognizes the *potential* of Christian worship to form Christian character in a salutary way rather than simply assuming [it] a priori. . ."[50] In fact, it "does not assume that all Christian theological ideas necessarily form and inform Christian lives for the better."[51] Rather, the ethics of theology mandates a scrutiny—in this context, through a postcolonial lens of discernment—"by asking what could be the possible outcomes of particular theological constructions" with a full recognition that "the actual outcome may be different from the imagined one."[52]

In sacramental and liturgical terms, the notion of *lex agendi* or *lex vivendi* (law of action or law of living) has been recently explored in a way that suggests a deep resonance with the ethical pretext in postcoloniality. Christianity as a lived and embodied religious imaginary of beliefs, values, behaviors, rites, and interpersonal commitments occurs at the "confluence of three distinct—yet essentially interdependent—liturgies: the 'liturgy of the world,' the 'liturgy of the church,' and the 'liturgy of the neighbor.'"[53] Drawing from the work of Louis-Marie Chauvet, the liturgical theologian Nathan Mitchell has pushed the envelope of liturgical conventions most vigorously—although without working out the full methodological and doctrinal impact of his innovative "confluence." While remaining (limited) within the framework of postmodern (and allegedly post-metaphysical)

50. Ibid., 25, 24. Italics in the original text. Underscoring that Christians do not hold a universal monopoly on truth, Ngong explains that "unlike the view of ethics which sees Christian beliefs and practices as inherently good, the ethics of theology questions the salutary character of the theological beliefs and practices that inform the Christian life. Christian beliefs and practices may be good but their goodness is not always obvious, especially to those who have been on the receiving end of some of the unsalutary effects of Christian formation," 26.

51. Ibid., 3. Ngong argues that "the unwillingness to extensively engage what the possible outcome of particular theological constructions might be may demonstrate a lack of desire to be accountable to the church for which theology is done, the society with which the church interacts, and the God in whom we live, move, and have our being," 2.

52. Ibid., 2.

53. Mitchell, *Meeting Mystery*, xiii.

rituality, Mitchell nonetheless boldly argues for an ethical "exteriority" as the criterion of sacramental-liturgical integrity and truthfulness:

> Christian worship, like its Jewish antecedent, is not—and can never be—*self*-verifying, *self*-authenticating. [. . .] Christian liturgy has to be verified outside itself, exteriorly, in what Emmanuel Levinas called "the liturgy of the neighbor" [. . .] The ethical action that flows from eucharist "gives body to God" and "gives privilege of place to the exercise of justice and mercy where we have recognized the 'liturgy of the neighbor' . . ." The ethics of "living-in-grace," primarily with regard to those whom humans have reduced to the state of slaves, is the place of verification . . . the *veritas* . . .[54]

The ethical exteriority of sacramental rites and rituals—with a striking Leviansian twist of ethical urgency and accountability as the foundational tenet of morally justifiable life—is where Mitchell relocates the risky and indeterminate crucible of genuinely Christian liturgical and sacramental truth. *Lex agendi/lex vivendi* is the safeguard and the terminus of genuine liturgy since "Christian liturgy begins as ritual practice but ends as ethical performance. Liturgy of the neighbor verifies liturgy of the church" so that "*lex agendi* breaks apart our comfortable 'faith and worship' duo. . . "[55]

Postmodern Western liturgical theologians like Mitchell do not talk about ethics as a fundamental theology. That language is too "metaphysical" for them. The terminological differences notwithstanding, Mitchell's *lex agendi*—or the ethical space in which otherness, divine and human, is encountered in and through sacramental liturgies—gestures in the same direction. Namely, the theo-ethical legitimacy of the church's public worship and its definitive revelatory truth can be verified "only through the 'liturgy of the neighbor,' only by passing through the face of the Other."[56] The ultimate truth of belief and prayer is ethical—or it is not truth at all.

The shift across the global theological mindscape toward ethics as fundamental and foundational for *theological* integrity and evangelic, i.e., gospel-sourced and gospel-vectored accountability, is nothing other than a somewhat belated fruition of penitential spiritual discernment within a religious tradition that had become addicted to violence, arrogance, and coercion. This manifested throughout the whole era of colonial modernity precisely as many Christians sailed and marched "onward as to war" across the globe to make Christ, so to say, perversely "real" and blasphemously

54. Ibid., 36–37. Italics in original.

55. Ibid., 38–39.

56. Ibid., 44.

"victorious" by conquest and subjugation. Today postcolonial theologies zoom their gritty ethico-historico-political gaze onto all things in relation to God and then again pivot back to the whole created reality as if in an unceasing vigil for those creatures of God whose lives, bodies, and souls have been violated and scandalized by the unholy colonial and imperialistic synergy of Christ, commerce, and conquest.

What might the implications of shifting to ethics as a postcolonial "fundamental" theology be? In Part III I will argue that such a shift can be envisioned as a critical and recuperative re-engagement with sacramental modes of theological imagination and praxis. However, before plunging fully into an explicitly constructive conversation between postcolonialism and sacramental discourse in Part III, a deeper look must be taken at a key postcolonial notion—hybridity. Hybridity and its visionary offspring—Third Space—is the postcolonial imaginary of faithful and vigilant remembrance of the quest for ethical transformation of power relations. As such, I submit, it can resonate most fruitfully with the most wide-ranging and far-reaching theological imaginary of relationality—sacramentality—which I will explore in Part III. For now, to the notion of postcolonial hybridity I turn.

2.2.

Postcolonial Hybridity

Elusive, Treacherous, and Potentially Liberating

Diversity needs the presence of peoples, no longer as objects to be swallowed up, but with the intention of creating a new relationship.
Sameness requires fixed Being, Diversity establishes Becoming.
As the Other is a source of Temptation of Sameness, Wholeness is the demand of Diversity.
Sameness is sublimated difference; Diversity is accepted difference.[1]

ÉDOUARD GLISSANT

. . .third space begins to seem something of a tease. It winks at us and draws us in; but as soon as we try to grasp it or map it, like the real itself, it begins to elude us.[2]

ROBERT J.C. YOUNG

WITHOUT CONTEST, HYBRIDITY TODAY is among the most popular analytical metaphors in the theoretical arsenal of postcolonialism. Hybridity has

1. Glissant, *Caribbean Discourse*, 98.
2. Young, "The Void of Misgiving," 81.

become the most "mainstream" buzzword among otherwise notoriously dense concepts and critical tools in postcolonial studies. Indeed, as some complain, it is "maddeningly elastic!"[3]

The distinctly postcolonial kind of hybridity is very resourceful, very nimble, and very messy. Before it congealed into a trendy scholarly concept, hybridity was and still is a lived experience—an existential actuality for millions of postcolonial individuals and communities. As lived experience, hybridity harbors a deeply felt ambivalence and restlessness throughout its creolized lifeworlds of invention and resilience. It lives and moves amid the chromatic harmonies of interrupted and displaced lives. And sometimes, as I already suggested in Part I, this sort of hybridity operates in the stealth mode of *sotto voce*—in a voice of modulation, diminutive, fragment, and nuance.[4] While certainly muddying the colonial wake of manipulative totalities and essentialisms, hybridity also represents a quest that challenges the fashionable Western postmodern "*doxa*"[5] of exaggerated and absolutized difference. Hybridity is an imaginary that emerges out of the postcolonial dynamics of survival, ambivalence, adaptation, and resistance—but also transformation!

HYBRIDITY: MADDENING AND TREACHEROUS

As there is an unruly plurality of postcolonialisms, there is also an equally unruly plurality of hybridities. Complaints about the malleability and vacuity of the term abound.[6] The broad imaginative scope of this concept, but

3. Kraidy, *Hybridity, or the Cultural Logic of Globalization*, 3.

4. Several postcolonial critics have lamented that hybridity as a subversive imaginary is insufficiently vigorous and too conciliatory about explicit resistance and opposition to imperialistic and colonial policies and practices. Benita Parry's work represents such critiques with substantial nuance and insight. See Parry, *Postcolonial Studies: A Materialist Critique.*

5. Rita Felski's expression "the doxa of difference" rightly draws attention to the disproportionate infatuation of postmodern critical theory with difference as an "unassailable value in itself" whereby "difference has become doxa, a magic word of theory and politics radiant with redemptive meanings," see "The Doxa of Difference," 1.

6. Critical and constructive appropriations of the notions of hybridity and diaspora involve dealing with the hazards of textual idealism. It often propels these notions into elitist theoretical abstractions and divorces them from historically specific experiences of hybridity where there is less triumph but more of the suffering of the displaced, the refugees, the migrants, etc. See, among others, Brah and Coombes' *Hybridity and Its Discontents*; Kraidy's, *Hybridity, or the Cultural Logic of Globalization*; Kalra et al., *Diaspora and Hybridity*; Prabhu's *Hybridity;* Moslund's, *Migration Literature and Hybridity,* and Acheraiou's, *Questioning Hybridity.*

even more so its unscrupulous usage, can make it available for appropriation in highly reactionary and exploitative causes of neo-colonial globalization.

In these situations, according to Marwan Kraidy, the notion of hybridity starts resembling nothing other than a triumphant "cultural logic of globalization."[7] As a result, the critical edge of specifically postcolonial hybridity may diminish precisely as its popular charm keeps expanding to the point of "annexation of hybridity discourse by neoliberal doxa."[8]

As with all and any human concept, the notion of hybridity is not infallible. R. Radhakrishnan observes the subtle yet crucial difference that needs to be remembered: "metropolitan hybridity" in its trendy "philosophic-bohemian sense" is "underwritten by the stable regime of western secular identity and the authenticity that goes with it, whereas post-colonial hybridity has no such guarantees: neither identity nor authenticity."[9] And Sabine Broeck rightly warns that,

> the celebration of hybridity always threatens to get stuck in an intellectual version of bastard chique, as one of the compensations white western intellectuals have, after the nomad, the homeless, the exiled, the stranger, the tourist, the bricoleur, and the margin dweller, paraded as New World paradigms to "bemoan the crisis, the fragmentation and loss of the Western subject or to re-vitalize its standing. . ."[10]

Do these merited critiques mean that hybridity is a useless and toothless analytical metaphor to be discarded as soon as possible? Not necessarily.

Hybridity is nowadays habitually used to *broadly* denote cultural syncretism or *métissage* due to migration and exile. It describes the process of fusion and mixture of cultural identities, knowledges, languages, spiritualities, traditions, races, and ethnicities. In this sense, hybridity is akin to what Mikhail Bakhtin termed unconscious, "organic," or unintentional hybridization.[11] In this comparatively generic sense, hybridity articulates

7. Kraidy, *Hybridity: The Cultural Logic of Globalization.*

8. Acheraiou, *Questioning Hybridity*, 180.

9. Radhakrishnan, "Postcoloniality and the Boundaries of Identity," 755.

10. Sabine Broeck, "White Fatigue," 53.

11. See Mikhail Bakhtin's work Вопросы литературы и эстетики, 170–73. It is known in the English-speaking world as *The Dialogic Imagination: Four Essays*, 358–59. For Bakhtin, the other type of hybridization, related yet distinct from the historically organic or dark hybridity, is the "intentional" or conscious "hybrid." That type of hybridity, theorized explicitly in literary contexts, entails not merely two voices or accents, but socio-linguistic consciousnesses and cultural epochs that have consciously come together and are struggling within the same literary utterance and implicitly also in socio-cultural settings, see Вопросы литературы и эстетики, 172.

a spectrum of cultural enmeshments and fusions that happen, to a varying degree of intensity, in virtually all cultures. It conveys with particular acuity the unceasing negotiations of difference and identity which underlie the experiences of translocality for migrants, exiles, refugees, displaced persons, and those who live in various borderzones. It applies even to those who encounter migrant people from the relative stability of their own more permanent abodes.

And yet: postcolonial hybridity is not simply "*any* given mixing of cultural materials, backgrounds, or identities, but [implies] a markedly unbalanced relationship."[12] Postcolonial hybridity is colored by a sustained historical and ethical attentiveness to what I called the postcoloniality "from below" in Part I and its "dangerous memories" (Metz)—its ethical pre-texts of *memoria passionis* of the vanquished, the useless, and the wretched of the earth. It does not whitewash the deeply ambivalent and inequitable interdependencies across the global postcolony in which, as Stuart Hall puts it, "differential temporalities and histories have been irrevocably and violently yoked together."[13] Relationality remains primordial here; yet it is a relationality shot through with a strong undertow of colonial and imperialistic *poétique forcée.*

In the world as we know it historically and experientially, all relations are always already inscribed with asymmetric power and capacity to act. The postcolonial optic is trained on the past and present carnages of abused power; hence its version of hybridity monitors the virtually omnipresent and often cruel asymmetries with particular attention.

In other words, postcolonial hybridity is not a paradisiacal image of consummated reconciliation, unspoiled revolutions, and ultimate harmonies of peace and justice. It is not a beatific state wherein all jaggedness of life and mind would be automatically resolved in a kind of elegiac sublimation that some postcolonial and postmodernist thinkers ascribe to it. It is not a camouflaged celebration of a new hierarchy of being and knowing, only this time privileging the impure, the migratory, the decentered, the postnational, the heterodox, and the uprooted. As the condition of in-betweenness and as an imaginary of relationality, it does not shy away from calling discordance and conflictuality for what they are. In Homi Bhabha's estimation, postcolonial hybridity does not equal "dialectical sublation" at all; instead "there is a contestation of the given symbols of authority that shift the terrains of antagonism" to still allow a "space in-between the rules of engagement."[14]

12. Kuortti and Nyman, "Introduction: Hybridity Today," 2. Italics added.

13. Hall, "When Was 'the Post-Colonial'?" 252.

14. Bahbha, *The Location of Culture*, 277.

HYBRIDITY AND ANAMNESIS: A RESONANCE OF PROLEPTIC REMEMBERING

As the key analytical metaphor, hybridity symbolically expresses the labyrinth of postcolonial survivorship, resistance, agency, and hope. It is attuned to relational plasticity, for good and for ill, as the elemental and ubiquitous matrix of planetary reality and our historical experience.

As an analytical metaphor, postcolonial hybridity functions as both a diagnosis and a catalyst for change. And for a correct diagnosis, a sound *anamnesis*—a witnessing interrogation and remembrance of the past—is indispensable. As diagnosis, it assesses the convoluted socio-cultural reality of life in the historical postcolony. According to Bhabha, it bears witness to the wounding asymmetries of power, welfare, authority, liberties, and agency speaking up from various positions of vulnerability:

> Postcolonial criticism bears witness to the unequal and uneven forces of cultural representation involved in the contest for political and social authority. . . postcolonial perspectives emerge from the colonial testimony of Third World countries and the discourses of 'minorities' within the geopolitical divisions. . . they intervene in those ideological discourses of modernity that attempt to give a hegemonic "normality" to the uneven development and the differential, often disadvantaged, histories of nations, races, communities, peoples.[15]

This hybridity is attentive to the lived experience of being on the receiving end of imperial hegemony, colonialist patriarchy, religious extremism, and a systemic disenfranchisement of human dignity and agency through coercion and exploitation. This is why, according to Bhabha, "it is from those who have suffered the sentence of history—subjugation, domination, diaspora, displacement—that we learn our most enduring lessons for living and thinking."[16] That being said, postcolonial hybridity "from below" or "subaltern" hybridity is not an automatically foolproof analytical metaphor or worldview; no critical or imaginative concept ever is.

But what it does accomplish is to epitomize what Radhakrishnan calls "the transformation of a lived reality into cognitive model."[17] According to Ien Ang, hybridity in its vigilant dimension of *anamnesis*,

15. Ibid., 245–46.
16. Ibid., 246.
17. Radhakrishnan, "Race and Double-Consciousness," 46.

> confronts and problematises boundaries, although it does not erase them. As such, hybridity always implies an unsettling of identities. It is precisely our encounters at the border . . . that make us realise how riven with potential miscommunication and intercultural conflict these encounters can be. This tells us that hybridity, the very condition of in-betweenness, can never be a question of simple shaking hands, of happy, harmonious merger and fusion. Hybridity is not the solution, but alerts us to the difficulty of living with differences, their ultimately irreducible resistance to complete dissolution.[18]

Ang's emphasis on "rivenness" is underwritten by concern for ethical veracity. When hybridity functions as a "sign of challenge and altercation, not of congenial amalgamation or merger,"[19] it does not gloss over the possibilities and actualities of conflict and contestation. In its anamnetic mode, hybridity prioritizes ethical vigilance and courageously highlights asymmetries, inequities, power games, blame games, and guilt trips that ravage the wounded relational interface of the postcolonial world.

Postcolonial hybridity has a certain aura of opacity around it. In this sense, it is the opacity of riven lives and jagged souls. Deep chasms of imperial, colonial, and totalitarian violence remain. Among those are the gaping wounds of ruefully unfulfilled human potential; stunted physical and emotional growth; abused hopes and trust; distorted lives of mind and self-worth; deliberately plundered gifts of nature; exploited labor; blasphemed divine revelations of love, justice, and compassion; monstrous idolatries of race, gender, sexuality, and religion; mocked values and traditions; ridiculed languages and wisdoms.

Without disavowing the jagged and riven opacity of traumatized psycho-spiritual genealogies and cultural memories, hybridity nevertheless acknowledges not just the lingering colonial traumas but also reclaims agency and modulates authority. It recuperates, reinvents and celebrates the human capacities to enact change and liberation, uneven and incomplete as those may be, for the disempowered, the subjugated, the demonized, and the victimized. Such agency may issue in vigorous and open opposition in the arenas of political liberation and cultural change, but that is not the only possible course. It does not rush into superficial forgiveness and reconciliation. Within the complex and "riven" relational terrains of postcolonial hybridity, all interactions and relationships—as jagged and as ugly as they may be—are nevertheless being disentangled from the dualism of pure tyranny

18. Ang, "Together-In-Difference,"149–50.

19. Ibid., 151.

versus pure impotence. While immersed in the postcolonial "rivenness" of history, this sort of hybridity nevertheless aches for rejuvenation, newness, and wholeness.

With the absolute privileges of both identity and difference relentlessly called into question, hybridity attempts a "strategic reversal of the process of domination;" it thrives on subverting, as Bhabha argued, "the production of discriminatory identities that secure the 'pure' and original identity of authority" while nudging forward the "deformation and displacement of all sites of discrimination and domination."[20]

A hybridized approach to the whole conundrum of authority, according to Gyan Prakash, allows repressed knowledges and subjects to reappear albeit "not as timeless traditional entities, but as figures to reclaim some ground to force a translation and transformation of power."[21] Young offers a helpful glimpse into how this dimension of hybridity functions:

> Hybridity . . . makes difference into sameness, and sameness into difference, but in a way that makes the same no longer the same, the different no longer simply different. In that sense, it operates according to the form of logic that Derrida isolates in the term "brisure," a breaking and joining at the same time, in the same place: difference and sameness in an apparently impossible simultaneity. Hybridity thus consists of a bizarre binate operation, in which each impulse is qualified against the other, forcing momentary forms of dislocation and displacement into complex economies of agonistic reticulation. This double logic . . . goes against the convention of rational either/or choices. . .[22]

The notion of postcolonial hybridity also signals a certain leaning forward and outward. It harbors a certain visionary and prophetic desire. It probes for a better and more equitable and peaceful version of itself. It lifts up the epiphanies of such better reality within itself and wherever else they may occur. Imaginatively and reflectively, hybridity epitomizes the diasporic pattern of trying to make the best out of whatever presents itself—or has been imposed upon us.

To transpose this crucial two-prongness of hybridity in more explicitly theological terms, postcolonial hybridity can be understood through the *liturgical* categories of *anamnesis* (meaningful, inspiring, and transformative remembrance) and *epiclesis* (invocation of and hope for transfiguration and redemption). As noted before, in its *anamnesis* mode, hybridity is always

20. Bhabha, *The Location of Culture*, 159.

21. Prakash, "Science between the Lines," 81–82.

22. Young, *Colonial Desire*, 26–27.

about remembering and living with, and suffering from, a hegemonic and depleting relational asymmetry. It is rooted in the remembrance of subjugated truths and lives. Echoing Walter Benjamin, Johann Baptist Metz's notion of "dangerous memory" resonates strongly with the thrust of the ethical pre-text of postcolonialism: "Every rebellion against suffering is fed by the subversive power of remembered suffering."[23] And a postcolonial *anamnesis* of history is indeed an anti-history—"an understanding of history in which the vanquished and destroyed alternatives would also be taken into account: an understanding of history *ex memoria passionis* as a history of the vanquished."[24]

At the same time, the notion of postcolonial hybridity also signals a resilient leaning forward, depthward, and outward. Like Metz's "dangerous memory" of Christ's passion and resurrection, postcolonial *anamnesis* also "intends the anticipation of a particular future of man (*sic*) as a future for the suffering, the hopeless, the oppressed, the injured and the useless of the earth."[25] It longs for an ethico-political and psychospiritual transformation. It harbors a certain visionary and prophetic desire. It probes for a better and more equitable and peaceful version of itself. It lifts up the epiphanies of such a better reality within itself and wherever else they may occur.

In its *epiclesis* mode, hybridity is an imaginary of hope, openness, and fecundity for transformative change. Clearly, hybridity is not a triumphant beatific vision of realized postcolonial eschatology! Yet it expresses and invokes desire for a genuine transfiguration of oppression, coercion, and immiseration. Postcolonial hybridity allows for "breaking" and "joining" in order to make life more livable not in spite of differences but amidst, around, and through them. This is where the contours of the *epiclesis* dimension of hybridity become more noticeable—experientially and imaginatively. It appears most unguardedly through the somewhat cryptic symbol of Third Space. Third Space is where the jaggedness and rivenness of hybrid bodies, minds, and spirits begin to shift and even transmigrate from wounds into visions—into another register of relationality. Wherever and whenever that desire coagulates beyond deconstructive critique and lament into the audacity to create new ways and means of living than those structured in dominance, a Third Space signals its gossamer advent.

23. Metz, "The Future in the Memory of Suffering," 15.

24. Ibid., 16.

25. Ibid., 24.

HYBRIDITY: AN EPICLESIS FOR THIRD SPACE

Now where might the *epiclesis* dimension of postcolonial hybridity dwell? As oblique and opaque as it often appears, there is a transformative thrust in hybridity that searches for a life-giving relational newness and integrity. Deconstructive *anamnesis does not exhaust the whole creative* continuum of hybridity. Hybridity resounds in another register, too. It has its own transformative and visionary, or some might call it utopian, timbre.

Utopia is no simple matter in postcolonial thought. Bill Ashcroft has recently observed that the utopian dimension of postcolonialism is not well-known or extensively theorized yet:

> The utopian direction of postcolonial thought, the irrepressible hope that characterized postcolonial literary writing in particular, is therefore the newest and most strategic direction . . . yet it remains vestigial . . . little has been written on this field. This may be due to an insistent and binary oppositionality in postcolonial studies, a binarism that overlooks the powerful transformative agency of postcolonial creative producers.[26]

History cannot be simply undone or turned into a theater of happiness overnight by imagination or will alone. It can only be lived within—but perhaps with a felt difference, with a stubborn hope, and a subtly percolating desire for transformation and wholeness. In this sense, the distinctive feature of postcolonial "utopian thinking is the importance of memory in the formation of utopian concepts of a liberated future."[27] Memory and re-membering, however, are not the terminus of the postcolonial pattern of utopian imagination. Rather, as Ralph Pordzik asserts, its vital objective is to "transmute the fragments of the past into new images of rebirth, intercourse, and creativity in which the disenfranchised and the silenced will find a new voice and enter into the dialogic continuity of community and place."[28]

The utopian dimension of postcolonial hybridity, or the subtle intimations of a certain Third Space within and yet beyond hybridity, gravitates around the "spirit of hope itself, the essence of desire for a better world."[29] The bond between the memory of colonialism and the hope for a transformed future embodies a sense of the sacred. Because of this sacred bond, the radically new is always embedded in the past. Therefore, in postcolonial societies and imaginaries, the intricate newness of transformation works

26. Ashcroft, "Introduction: Spaces of Utopia," 1.

27. Ibid., 2.

28. Pordzik, *The Quest for Postcolonial Utopia*, 172–73.

29. Ashcroft, "Introduction: Spaces of Utopia," 2,

"in very subtle ways, almost always driven by something we could call the energy of the sacred."[30]

Bhabha has written memorably about postcolonial hybridity not being simply "the third term that resolves tensions"[31] among histories, cultures, values, and authorities. The postcolonial suspicion of the language of resolution and reconciliation draws its simmering impetus from experiences of superficial and hypocritical settlements of colonial wrongdoing without real repentance, without real conversion, and without a genuine restitution for the sinned-against and dehumanized. Therefore it is not surprising that Bhabha and other postcolonial thinkers prefer only to hint—without too much determination and precision—at another possibility vectoring out of and yet somehow beyond postcolonial hybridity: a Third Space which "enables other positions to emerge"[32] beyond the binary logic, war, and the deep-seated compulsions of competitive dualism. Bhabha has intimated that,

> this third space displaces the histories that constitute it, and sets up new structures of authority, new political initiatives, which are inadequately understood through received wisdom . . . The process of cultural hybridity gives rise to something different, something new and unrecognisable, a new area of negotiation of meaning and representation.[33]

In Edward Soja's words, Third Space urges us "to set aside the demands to make either/or choice and contemplate instead the possibility of both/and logic" so that imagination can be expanded to encompass a "recombinational and radically open perspective" or indeed embrace a "multiplicity of perspectives that have heretofore been considered by the epistemological referees to be incompatible, uncombinable."[34]

The enigmatic metaphor of Third Space, I submit, ultimately conveys a tantalizing *epiclesis* of hope and longing for transformation. It is a landscape of interactive reciprocity and conviviality. Third Space is about transcending divisive and wounding dualisms. It does not remain chained to the painful, jagged, and riven opacity of hybridity although that opacity, like the scars on the resurrected body of Christ, are not forgotten or erased. All the jagged opacities notwithstanding, there is still a migration into a fecund kind of opacity—that of resilient resourcefulness that percolates *ex profundis* as

30. Ibid., 7.

31. Bhabha, *The Location of Culture*, 162,

32. Bhabha, "The Third Space," 211.

33. Ibid., 209.

34. Soja, "Thirdspace," 50.

it were, out of the depths of life and hope. It is as if the opacity of rivenness lifts its many veils of wounds to allow a birth of newness and at least a rudimentary wholeness emerging from in-between the hybrid layers of primal desolation and courageous anticipation. In this sense, Third Space exists as the "interval," as "a state of *alert in-betweenness and 'critical' non-knowingness*"[35] without the hegemony of transparency and control. This is why Young concludes, with a certain exasperation, that Third Space functions like an apophatic tease: "It winks at us and draws us in; but as soon as we try to grasp it or map it, like the real itself, it begins to elude us."[36]

But is this Third Space just a dream? In his more recent reflections on Third Space, Bhabha describes this dialogical reality through parable-like analogies with Truth Commissions, the Southall Black Sisters women's movement, and the Rwandan Gacaca Courts. Third Space is comprised of hybrid dialogical sites for postcolonial "political transition and ethical transformation in societies made wretched by violence and retribution."[37] He continues:

> The *gacaca* is not simply a neutral area of confession, nor is it principally a space of confrontation and guilt. It is a place and a time that exists in-between the violent and the violated, the accused and the accuser, allegation and admission. And that site of in-betweeness becomes the ground of discussion, dispute, confession, apology, and negotiation through which Tutsis and Hutus together confront the inequities and asymmetries of societal trauma not as a "common people," but as a people with a common cause.[38]

The historico-political instances of Third Space such as the Gacaca Courts are fragile. Precariousness notwithstanding, Third Space is "where one can move beyond the existing borders. It is also a place of marginal women and men, where old connections can be disturbed and new ones emerge. A Thirdspace consciousness is the precondition to building a community of resistance to all forms of hegemonic power."[39]

Third Space it is not an all-or-nothing theater of action and imagination. It emerges, as it were, as a "catholic" preference for a "both/and" tonality of reasoning, imagining, feeling, and acting. In Third Space mode, hybridity is a sensibility and an imaginary that bears the potential—in a

35. Trinh, *When the Moon Waxes Red*, 234. Italics in original.

36. Young, "The Void of Misgiving," 81.

37. Bhabha, "Preface: In the Cave of Making," x.

38. Ibid.

39. Soja, "Thirdspace," 56.

practical, unsystematic, irregular, rudimentary, and perhaps a bit bizarre way—to elude the habitual and dualistic "politics of polarity"[40] and its routinely coercive practices. It eludes being boxed in perennial negations and unmitigated suspicions. It desires a fertile space for new alliances, new conviviality, and liberated reciprocity. Ultimately, "*everything* comes together in Thirdspace"[41] and there everything longs for and invokes (*epiclesis!*) a consequential transformation.

To transpose this enigmatic notion into a theological framework, I can say that Third Space is an imaginary of an eschatological character and an apophatic provenance. The postcolonial imaginary of Third Space indwells precisely the enigma of straddling two temporalities: it is anamnetically inscribed in the historical postcolony and its jagged hybridities while it is also epicletically longing for what cannot yet be realized historically. But besides the eschatological aspect, Third Space is also an apophatic imaginary. A somber awareness of the actual historical molestations of utopian imagination under the false pretenses of Marxism, Communism, or neoliberal capitalism rightfully warrants caution around any optimistic exuberance of activism in culture, politics, and spirituality. Hence, the visionary utopianism of postcolonial Third Space is permeated precisely by "a longing that cannot be uttered."[42] It is rooted in the apophatic tonality of Theodor Adorno's iconoclastic approach so clearly sourced from the Jewish spiritual tradition: "Insofar as we are not allowed to cast the picture of utopia . . . insofar as we do not know what the correct thing would be, we know exactly. . . what the false thing is . . . [since] the true thing determines itself via the false thing."[43]

FROM HYBRIDITY TO THEOLOGICAL IMAGINATION

What are the crucially challenging markers of this postcolonial kind of hybridity that, as I will argue in Part III, can be fruitful for emerging postcolonial constellations of sacramental imaginary?

Postcolonial imaginaries of hybridity and Third Space are attempts to reconceive difference as intrinsically relational while operating with a visceral and cognitive awareness that the world of historical postcolony "remains structured in dominance."[44] This imaginary distinguishes vigilantly

40. Bhabha, *The Location of Culture*, 56.

41. Soja, "Thirdspace," 54. Italics in original.

42. Jacoby, *Picture Imperfect*, 113.

43. Theodor W. Adorno, quoted in Jacoby, *Picture Imperfect*, 147.

44. Radhakrishnan, *Theory in an Uneven World*, 93

between what was and is, what might have been, and what ought to be. The latter dimension is where hybridity opens up to Third Space: that is, it opens up to its own liberative transsignification, to its own transubstantiation on the path of healing and the quest for wholeness.

On the one hand, hybridity unflinchingly—anamnetically—maps the distorted and jagged terrain of inequitable relations. It captures the palpably "fallen" and unredeemed aspects of life that continue to be suffered by millions under the global regimes of neocolonialism, neoimperialism, and increasingly, religious extremism.

On the other hand, hybridity charts the instinctual, natal, and vital energies of survival and ingenuity, the indwelling capacity and desire for "joining" even amidst and after the most cruel "breaking." It betrays a watchful if anxious desire for empowerment and dignity. It whispers for mutuality and shared resourcefulness in the most cunning ways of mimicry if more decorous forms of gaining recognition, healing, and confidence are not yet available.

As anamnetic and epicletic, the postcolonial imaginary of hybridity dethrones the rationale of binarity or dualism wherein absolute contrasts reign supreme not only in epistemological imagination but also in the perception of human (and divine!) agency socially, culturally, politically, ethically, and religiously. Hybridity does not have to devalue resistance to oppression and liberative dissent (*pace* Acheraiou and some other critics who blame hybridity for its "impeachment" of the logic of binarity).[45] But it does contest and dilute the habitual dualisms of zero-sum juxtapositions. As a result, it is not surprising at all that hybridity also carries a certain "paranoid threat" as Bhabha observed. It is the threat to "the symmetry and duality of self/other, inside/outside"[46] which are routinely imposed on life and thought by the colonial cosmologies of divinity, humanity, value, goodness, and beauty. Might hybridity be precisely the sort of constructive "threat" that theology could benefit from?

Margaret Miles' observations in the context of the Western theological tradition are helpful to gain some inkling as to how creatively mutinous the "threat" aspect of hybridity might turn out to be . Her historical analysis helps appreciate the persistent quandary of dualism that saturates the whole Western ontological imaginary. Miles remarks that "where there are two or more entities, Western thinkers inevitably place them in hierarchical value."[47] For example, the penchant for hierarchical zero-sum view of dif-

45. Acheraiou, *Questioning Hybridity,* 150–62.

46. Bhabha, *The Location of Culture,* 165.

47. Miles, "The Resurrection of the Body," 45.

ference "provides the rationale for identifying 'man' with rationality, and 'woman' with body and emotion. Christian authors repeatedly instructed readers that mind must firmly control and/or ignore the body at all times."[48]

The correlate of such dualistic imaginary in the Western tradition is the presupposition that there is always a chasm between different entities. From such a perspective, relationality is all about bridging ontologically preordained chasms. No wonder, then, that to imagine relationality is to already "assume and emphasize distance" rather than connection from the outset![49] Miles' observations, however, put a spotlight on the ironic fact that the Western dualistic imaginary grinds against the theologically pivotal vector of the incarnation. It also grinds against every gospel-sourced spiritual insight that depends on the incarnational, i.e., fleshy visions of integrated wholeness such as, for example, the case of Christ's resurrection. The haunting consequences of such competitive dualism are deeply problematic across the whole spectrum of Christian theological tradition, including sacramental imagination:

> Christianity, it seems, *must have* two entities in order to transcend and unite them. Spirit and matter; divinity and humanity; soul and body. Christian doctrines and practices assume spirit and matter in order to achieve the *frisson* of bringing them as close as together as possible, yet without mixing them, for accompanying these dualities was the horror of mixture. The contents of the Roman sewer were called "*mixtus*." Thus, conceptualizing an intimate blending of soul and body, spirit and matter, that produces a "third thing," was not tolerated. Yet surely this is what Christians claim to believe in and hope for in the resurrection body, an intelligent body in which . . . soul and body will be utterly fused."[50]

The mischievous "threat" dimension of hybridity emerges most clearly when it challenges the deep-seated inertias of hierarchical and competitive logic of binarity. Instead of dualistic juxtapositions and deeply ingrained structural and hierarchical competitiveness, hybridity celebrates life precisely by saluting its diversity, entanglements, and interdependencies in the name of a more charitable, bountiful, and reciprocal conviviality.

48. Ibid.

49. Ibid., 46.

50. Ibid., 51. Italics in the original.

IN LIEU OF CONCLUSION

As in Part I, my goal here is not to claim that the postcolonial vision of reality and relationality constitutes the next triumphant meta-grasp on truth, virtue, justice, or beauty. It is also not to argue that hybrid models of living, relating, thinking, and imagining are or should be viewed as the final word for overcoming social and political affliction with comprehensively guaranteed and salvific consequences. There is no primordial omniscience in the current postcolonial lore. Postcolonialism, like any human endeavor, is not automatically immune from false theoretical, political, or theological messianism. What remains, however, is the "endless and yet ethical critique operating with neither intellectual guarantee nor political piety."[51] But even here a corrective caveat is necessary. Namely, deconstructive critique alone is not life-giving. Constructive and creative rearticulations of what is found wanting are equally important. Far from being a vision solely entrenched in the negative dialectic of critique, but rather as an ethical commitment to transformation, postcolonialism engenders an "intervention in the general scheme of things" and is a "matter for general concern and awareness and not the mere resentment of a ghetto."[52]

The transformative intervention of postcolonialism for the renewal of Christian theology consists in its potential for re-orchestrating the most problematic patterns and imaginaries of relationality and power. That includes relations among sources, traditions, norms, methods, temperaments, and authorities within theological reflection as it ponders all things in relation to God in the deeply disjointed world of ecological degradation, polarizing diversity, unhealed wounds, and unremitting violence. To explore how postcolonial notions of hybridity and Third Space can resonate most fruitfully with theological imagination and how these mutually challenging resonances could reinvigorate sacramental theology in particular will be my constructive aspiration in Part III.

To proceed with that aspiration, I will first invite a key postcolonial voice into this conversation in order to voyage further and deeper into the crevices of hybridity and the elusive Third Space. This voice is, perhaps surprisingly, the late Edward W. Said. I will specifically focus on Said's musically saturated notion of postcolonial contrapuntality. My engagement with Said here is a theologically hushed reading of his work. That is, I will not attempt to conjure a theologian out of Said who would undoubtedly protest as vehemently as possible. My engagement with Said is a constructive one as I

51. Krishna, *Globalization and Postcolonialism*, 172.

52. Radhakrishnan, "Postcoloniality and the Boundaries of Identity," 767.

retrieve some useful facets from a seminal postcolonial thinker whose work expressed deep suspicion toward theology as a discourse of (presumed) closure and authoritarianism, and has hitherto gone unnoticed by most postcolonial theologies. In what follows I will embark on the diasporic mischief of "poaching": that is, according to Michel de Certeau, to the wandering "across lands belonging to someone else, like nomads poaching their way across fields. . . ."[53]

53. De Certeau, *Practice of Everyday Life*, 174.

2.3.

Voyaging into the Third Space of Contrapuntality with Edward Said

. . . la musique est une trace qui se dépasse . . .[1]

Édouard Glissant

. . .the essence of counterpoint is simultaneity of voices, preternatural control of resources, apparently endless inventiveness.[2]

Edward W. Said

What does postcolonial hybridity have to do with the modern European musical notion of counterpoint? And what does hybridity have to do with the seminal—if ambiguously reluctant[3]—postcolonial thinker Edward W. Said? After all, hybridity and Third Space do not appear among the most popular indexed terms that populate the pages of the most senior among the so-called "holy trinity" of postcolonial thinkers' (that is, Said

1. Glissant, *Tout-monde*, 280.

2. Said, *Music at the Limit*, 5.

3. See the excellent overview of Said's fraught relationship with the field of postcolonial studies that he, ironically, launched according to many genealogies of postcolonialism in Young's "Edward Said: Opponent of Postcolonial Theory," 23–43.

himself, Homi Bhabha, and Gayatri Spivak[4]) prolific writings. Where do the hidden connections reside and why are they useful in the context of a theological project?

To sketch the itinerary of this chapter, I must start with a disclaimer: it is beyond the scope and beside the goal of this project to delve into the complexities of Said's conflictual yet foundational standing in postcolonial studies and its internal theoretical and ideological battles. Moreover, it is also beyond the scope and objective of this study to dissect Said's ever so complicated relationship with all and any things religious and theological. His profound suspicion about religion as an agent of subjugation and authoritarian closure of critical inquiry is well-known and represents one of the more reductionist and dated elements of his work.[5] Fortunately, the most fruitful features of Said's postcolonial vision are found elsewhere—and to these features and ideas I will turn in this chapter.

My goal here is to develop a somewhat transgressive constructive trajectory of interpretation of Said's arguably best known analytical metaphor—contrapuntality—as an indirect, yet particularly fecund, elaboration on the pivotal postcolonial theme of hybridity. Now it is time for contrapuntality to start emerging from the motivistic background and be phrased into a theme that serves as the contextual and methodological *basso continuo* of this project.

The theme of contrapuntality entails two aspects: first, Edward Said's elaborations on the musical notion of counterpoint expand and nuance the relational ecology of postcolonial hybridity particularly fruitfully as they nudge us beyond the experiential, conceptual, and imaginative limitations of exaggerated and insular (obsession with) textuality. This sort of textuality has mired postcolonial imagination in a most constrictive way. No wonder that Said was among the loudest critics of such poststructuralist entrapment of postcolonial endeavors! Bringing the aesthetic modality of music to bear on postcolonial epistemology and postcolonial politics is among his most innovative and unique contributions to the field.[6]

4. As memorably suggested by Young, *Colonial Desire*, 163.

5. The recent work of Wietske de Jong-Kumru is among the few theological texts engaging Said's thought in a more than cursory way. See her analysis of Said's preference for "worldly" and "secular" as categories of liberation and empowerment in the context of this criticism of religion and theology, in de Jong-Kumru, *Postcolonial Feminist Theology*, 62–67, 164–68.

6. For example, consider the famous West-Easter Divan youth orchestra that Said founded in collaboration with the famous conductor Daniel Barenboim to bring together Israeli, Palestinian, Lebanese and other young musicians from countries and cultures that are at war or suspended in deep cultural and religious conflict today. See www.west-eastern-divan.org.

Secondly, I will suggest that a Saidian imaginary of postcolonial counterpoint brings out the facets of hybridity in their most fruitful visionary mode—the epicletic or Third Space mode. Contrapuntality, I suggest, articulates the relational ecology of Third Space as a profoundly reciprocal, interdependent, and non-reductive imaginary. The contrapuntal Third Space emerges out of conflicts and tensions, yet does not valorize them. It bursts forth out of postcolonial asymmetries, ambivalences, and oppositions yet does not remain deferentially captive to desolate and grinding dialectic juxtapositions, no matter how theoretically seductive those might appear. In the end, I will suggest that the contrapuntal hybridity of Third Space facilitates a uniquely dynamic resonance between postcolonial hybridity and sacramentality. The latter resonance, however, will have to wait for a fuller elaboration until Part III. For now, the stealthy resonance between hybridity and Said's imaginary of counterpoint deserves closer attention.

A SURREPTITIOUS RESONANCE: EDWARD SAID AND HYBRIDITY

Edward W. Said (1935–2003) was a one of the most remarkable diasporic scholars of postcolonial literature and cultural criticism. Said, who straddled many disciplines, methodologies, and canons was of Arab-Christian Palestinian origins. He lived most of his intellectually productive life in the USA as, in his own estimation, an exile. Disappointment over the ongoing gridlock of the Palestinian crisis surfaced ever more poignantly in Said's "late style" writings in the early twenty-first century before his untimely death. In a sense, for the reluctant "founder" of postcolonial studies, a distinctly postcolonial moment never arrived as far as the cause of his own exilic experience as a Palestinian was concerned. Despite his reservations and his disappointments about "high" postcolonial theory, Said's intellectual fingerprints are all over postcolonial studies. Arguably, it was Said's *Orientalism* (1978) that played the most decisive role in inaugurating the very discipline of postcolonial studies.

As many exiles and migrants do, Said did see his life experience in terms of hybridity ("I am . . . a sort of hybrid"[7]). Even though he did recognize the complexity and relevance of Bhabha's work on hybridity, Said did not pursue the subsequent and prevalent Bhabhian pattern of articulation. The use of terminology alone, however, does not exhaust the theme itself. The theme—of in-betweenness, of being more-than-one-thing,

7. An interview with Said, quoted in Karavanta and Morgan, *Edward Said and Jacques Derrida*, 3.

of intertwinement, of exilic displacement and its contrapuntal "mind of winter"[8]—features prominently in Said's work albeit through different vocabulary. It was precisely his exilic displacement and his diasporic awareness of being constantly "out of place"[9] that shaped the inimitable existential actuality of Said's life and work. And it was his carefully examined experience of postcolonial migrancy that prompted Said to repeatedly claim his non-belonging to any singular culture.[10] Being "out of place" nudged Said to seek and privilege connections.

Alongside his vigorous performance of cultural and disciplinary border thinking, Said grounded the hybridity of human imagination, self-understanding, self-expression, and interpersonal action in the reality of "worldliness." Worldliness, too, is ultimately about connections and accountability. It is not a simplistic synonym of "secularism" vis-à-vis "religion." It describes critical practices and habits of mind that are consciously and deliberately grounded in lived reality. Worldliness, for Said, is about a robustly historical self-consciousness—"a knowing and unafraid attitude toward exploring the world we live in."[11]

Said memorably argued that "because of empire, all cultures are involved in one another; none is single and pure, all are hybrid, heterogeneous, extraordinarily differentiated, and unmonolithic."[12] That being said, the exilic lifeworld, through its experiential and theoretical expressions, remained for Said a figure of particularly acute and hyper-self-aware intensification of lived hybridity. It is hardly surprising, then, that Said often troped the diasporic imaginary originating out of experiences of displacement and migrancy through the notion of counterpoint, beginning with his 1984 reflections on exile: "Most people are principally aware of one culture, one setting, one home; exiles are aware of at least two, and this plurality of vision gives rise to an awareness of simultaneous dimensions, an awareness that—to borrow a phrase from music—is *contrapuntal*."[13]

In Said's hands, counterpoint turned out to be the most stimulating analytical metaphor. It highlights intense relational simultaneity. Out of this complex simultaneity sprouts an appreciation of "contrapuntal juxtapositions that diminish orthodox judgment and elevate appreciative sympathy."[14]

8. Said, *Reflections on Exile*, 186.

9. It is noteworthy that Said chose this self-description as the title of his autobiography, *Out of Place: A Memoir.*

10. Said, *Culture and Imperialism*, xxvi; *Reflections on Exile*, 557.

11. Said, *Reflections on Exile*, 565.

12. Ibid., xxix.

13. Said, *Reflections on Exile*, 186. Italics in original.

14. Ibid., 186.

Eventually the notion of counterpoint migrated beyond the existential actualities and narrations of exile in Said's work. He enlarged the contrapuntal consciousness of exile to denote—rather generically and, occasionally, even a bit presumptuously—the consciousness of intellectuals in a "metaphorical" and even "metaphysical" sense.[15] Gradually, a whole imaginary of contrapuntality becomes discernible in Said's work. It simultaneously unpacks, fine-tunes, and qualifies the common postcolonial notion of hybridity as "tying together of multiple voices in a kind of disciplined whole" while underscoring that such a "tying together" is by no means a "simple reconciliation."[16]

FROM HYBRIDITY TO CONTRAPUNTALITY

Musically speaking, counterpoint is a specification of polyphony, a *simultaneous* and *dynamic* multi-voicedness. As an exile, Said finds in contrapuntal polyphony a model of "multiple identity" that fits the lived experience of hybridity and migrancy with the amount of least distortion and reduction. It also allowed him to form a potentially emancipatory model of politics, art, and social life. For one who belongs and non-belongs multiply, there are things that "can't be reduced to homophony. That can't be reduced to a kind of simple reconciliation."[17] Instead, in contrapuntal polyphony "many voices play . . . off against each other, without, as I say, the need to reconcile them, just to hold them together . . . [this] is what my work is all about. [. . .] It's basic instinct [for me]."[18]

Musically speaking, counterpoint is a polyphonic audioscape of interplay, interdependence, and reciprocity. Counterpoint stretches beyond the various aesthetic models of visuality precisely when it comes to such relational business as simultaneity, interaction, and reciprocity. Counterpoint, above all, is a sonorous imaginary of simultaneity, overlap, and intertwinement with virtually limitless accommodation of difference, imitation, and variation. Counterpoint is the unique musical capacity to sound two or more voices comprehensibly and simultaneously. It facilitates "the coherent combination of distinct melodic lines in music, and the quality

15. Said, *The Edward Said Reader*, 373–79. This is one of the rare times when Said actually uses the notion of metaphysics in a constructive way. A similar line of reasoning appears in *Culture and Imperialism*, 332–33.

16. Said, "Criticism, Culture and Performance," 26.

17. Viswahathan, *Power, Politics, and Culture*, 99.

18. Ibid.

that bestfulfils the aesthetic principle of unity in diversity."[19] Contrapuntal music is structured as a "balance between independence and interdependence, and this is as true of a canon by Webern as of a fugue by Bach."[20] The sonorous incarnations of counterpoint may be as simple as a canon (based on relatively simple repetitions and imitations of the same "voice") or as maddeningly complex as a fugue that can accommodate and sustain a multiplicity of different and interacting "voices"—be they vocal or instrumental, individual or collective.

It is virtually impossible to grasp the full stretch of Said's notion of contrapuntality apart from understanding his own musical background. In addition to being a brilliant scholar of literature, Said was also a Julliard-trained classical pianist with an intricate knowledge of music. By his own admission, Said's relationship to music was exceptional: music is "a particularly rich, and for me, unique branch of aesthetic experience."[21] According to his friend and collaborator in the unique West-Easter Divan Youth orchestra project, Daniel Barenboim, Said "was one of those rare people who sought and recognized the connections between different and seemingly disparate disciplines."[22] "In music," Barenboim summarizes, "there are no independent elements."[23]

The contemporary British composer David Matthews describes it as a particular kind of interactive and responsible/answerable audioscape:

> Counterpoint is a conversation; it acknowledges the presence and participation of the other. Two independent voices may be played by the same musician, on a keyboard for instance, but they are more often given to two players, who must listen to each other. It is significant that counterpoint grew to maturity in Europe where the concept of democracy was born. [. . .]But try whistling a Bach fugue. After the first few bars where the main subject is announced unaccompanied, the music divides into two parts, then three, then possibly four, or even five or six. The contrapuntal discourse is continued throughout the duration of the piece. How can you hear all these lines at once? Most of us probably don't. The experience of listening to a fugue is stimulating yet at the same time forbidding. This is the most intellectual music that has been devised. But it is also capable

19. "Counterpoint," *Grove Dictionary of Music*. Oxford Music Online: www.oxfordmusiconline.com:80/subscriber/article/oprt114/e1670.

20. Ibid.

21. Said, *Reflections on Exile*, xxxii.

22. Barenboim, "Foreword," vii.

23. Ibid., ix.

> of expressing emotion on the highest level, and where intellect and emotion are in perfect balance, the result can be sublime.[24]

The relational interplay among the "voices"—and each of the can be a complex amalgam in its own right—in counterpoint may engender more than just augmented and ever more complexified harmonies or textures. New voices can emerge in the acoustic process due to the contrapuntal ability and requirement to respond:

> Because of this "ability to respond," the voices may be perceived as transforming each other continuously. Through their harmonic interference, they elicit sonorous aspects in each other that one could not hear if the voices were sung or played separately. The listener may even become aware of *new* voices that are not performed as such. [. . .] This perception of new voices may also happen when voices cross each other in pitch position (*Stimmtausch*), thereby causing them to temporarily lose their original identity (that is how they sound separately). In the latter instance, fresh melodic formations may be perceived, arising out of fragments of these crossing voices.[25]

The characteristic mark of contrapuntality is therefore a complex sonorous texture that practically cannot be cognitively exhausted. Finally, in the immediate context of Said's appropriations of counterpoint as a critical strategy and "emancipatory model," the musicologist Rokus de Groot rightly argues that contrapuntal polyphony incarnates "respect for difference without domination within a shared harmonic system."[26] Out of a whole spectrum of musical styles and techniques, "if one had to choose the musical texture most likely to defy a single authoritative listening, polyphony would be a convincing candidate."[27]

A POSTCOLONIAL COUNTERPOINT: TRACING A SAIDIAN MELODY

Said sought connections and concurrences in all things and found them in more places than cultural and intellectual inertias would fathom. He could not help but be fascinated by "forms in which many things go on simultaneously" even if he had to put up with Italian opera![28]

24. Matthews, "The Art of Fugue."
25. Ibid., 210. Italics in original.
26. De Groot, "Edward Said and Polyphony," 217.
27. Ibid., 213.
28. Viswahathan, *Power, Politics, and Culture*, 184.

But contrapuntality here does not equal a generic polyphony. Counterpoint facilitates an acoustic partnership and reciprocity wherein the "voices" live and move in relief against and with each other as they enter into complex relations depending on their relative and provisional importance. The focus is on interaction, overlapping, intertwining, interpenetration, the hide-and-seek, the movements of flee-and-chase (fugue!), and all of that happening simultaneously—in other words, in concurrent "playing off each other" as Said has put it:

> in the counterpoint of Western classical music, various themes play off one another, with only a provisional privilege being given to any particular one; yet in the resulting polyphony there is concert and order, an organized interplay that derives from the themes, not from a rigorous melodic or formal principle outside the work.[29]

The fascination of counterpoint resides in its complexity and orientation to non-reductive integration and unity amidst diversity. In the influential essay "The Music Itself: Glenn Gould's Contrapuntal Vision" Said argues that "the essence of counterpoint is simultaneity of voices, preternatural control of resources," and in this simultaneity the voices always continue "to sound against, as well as with, all the others."[30] The value of counterpoint can be seen here as the concurrence of two or more orientationally distinctive, yet somehow interactive and mutually augmenting, themes that participate in the same acoustic chronotope without absolute dominance.

The contrapuntal wholeness consists precisely of "various themes playing off one another"—never separately, never absolutely sovereignly, and never incarcerated in their singularity of difference. The point here is precisely to maintain connections in the pattern of contrapuntal fugue: "A fugue can contain two, three, four, or five voices: they're all part of the same composition, but they're each distinct. They operate together, and it's a question of how you conceive of the togetherness: if you think it's got to be this *or* that, then you're paralyzed. . ."[31]

Furthermore, a harmonious (vertical) nonalignment or irreconcilability is also possible here despite more or less transitory harmonious co-sonorities that may emerge in the acoustic framework of counterpoint.

29. Said, *Culture and Imperialism*, 51.

30. Said, *Music at the Limits*, 5. Said's reflections on counterpoint here mainly invoke the music of J. S. Bach—preeminently as performed by Glenn Gould—as the actual point of departure for the elaborations on the supra-audible meanings of contrapuntal music without, however, being limited to J. S. Bach.

31. Said, *Power, Politics, and Culture*, 91. Italics in original.

In this regard, counterpoint is the embodiment of musical imaginary that challenges the impetus of "working toward domination and sovereignty."[32]

What stands out in Said's elaborations on counterpoint is his sustained attraction to the interplay of independent, unassimilable "voices." As Ben Etherington has pointed out, what is at stake here is really postcolonial ethics. Said's musically colored postcolonial ethics seeks a way beyond structural coercion and its combative and dominative pattern of relationality. Counterpoint here functions both as "a strategy of anti-colonial opposition" but also as "an idealistic aperture in his criticism"—even "an idealised 'post-imperial' condition of consciousness."[33]

Counterpoint is an acoustic configuration of both interdependence and autonomy. It is not entirely post-hierarchic, in the final analysis. Yet the acoustic hierarchies and asymmetries are impermanent, shifting, variational, and relative throughout the meandering musical process. The flipside of this aural regime is that autonomy is also not absolute but relative. Within this echoic configuration of relationality, nimble and dynamic reciprocity is a foundational principle. Counterpoint allows for similarity and yet dissimilarity; imitation and innovation; repetition and digression; austerity and ornamentation. Contrapuntality can accommodate symmetrical as well as asymmetrical reciprocity among various "voices" without forcing them into an "either/or" competitive dialectic.

Furthermore, in Said's "late style" in particular, an emphasis on the "irreconcilabilities" which transgress the apparitions of pre-containment of conflictuality comes prominently to the fore.[34] At the end of his life while battling terminal illness, Said clearly seemed to be drawn toward a radically dissonant harmonic version of contrapuntality in his own late style. The term "oppositionality" appears very often in Said's works. Oppositionality, however, is a means to an end—not the end in itself. In Said's usage, oppositionality is not a metaphysically intransigent theoretical gesture on automatic repeat function but rather a practice of ethical vigilance to honor and transform the suffering of the disinherited, the disempowered, and the disenfranchised peoples. Hence Said insists that the sonorous topography of postcolonial counterpoint can indeed resound as an "atonal ensemble."[35]

32. Said, *Musical Elaborations*, xxi.

33. Etherington, "Said, Grainger and the Ethics of Polyphony," 221, 227.

34. See, for example, "An Interview with Edward W. Said," *The Edward Said Reader*, 427, 437. Typically, when discussing "irreconcilabilities" Said engages the thought of Theodor Adorno as this interview—among other publications—demonstrates. Said's interest in "late style" was sparked by Adorno's work on Beethoven. This is where the theme of irreconcilable elements and tensions in life and art blossomed into a major topic of exploration for Said, see also his *Freud and the Non-European*, 28–31, 54–55.

35. Said, *Culture and Imperialism*, 318.

And atonality, of course, is a sign of harmonic dissonance. In other words, this contrapuntal method is extraordinarily accountable to the jaggedness of postcolonial life with all its devastating asymmetries of power, agency, value, and authority—impermanent as they hopefully will be from a visionary standpoint.

Staying true to the ethical exigencies of postcolonial *anamnesis*, Said honored the irreconcilabilities of our jagged postcolonial experiences in their throbbing historical truths of affliction and ambivalence. But it is important to highlight that the tensions that these irreconcilabilities express are not valorized by Said. Rather, he sees them as tragic. The irreconcilabilities are historical, i.e., they are empirically real, yet contingent—and therefore potentially transformable. The "irreconcilabilities are always experiential; they are not metaphysical."[36]

The implications here are worthwhile to tease out. While answerable to the ethical exigencies of postcolony, the contrapuntal approach is neither imaginatively nor ontologically incarcerated in its hybrid historical jaggedness. The irreconcilabilities of postcolonial hybridity, with all its predatory asymmetries and hierarchies, are no metaphysical necessities. Nor are they providentially ordered for some esoteric and manipulative teleology of progress (like Hegel's *List der Vernunft*), salvation, providence, or revelation. They are, rather, historical and psychospiritual consequences of colonial cruelty and injustice which can and ought to be transformed. In this sense the contrapuntal imaginary aims to overcome romanticized lures of grinding dialectic and competitive detraction according to the extreme patterns of "either/or" which, for Said, entail simply "an ultimately uninteresting alternation of presence and absence."[37] Contrapuntality is after something else entirely.

RELATIONALITY BEYOND COERCION AND DOMINATION: A CONTRAPUNTAL THIRD SPACE

Charles Forsdick has aptly suggested that the epistemological thrust of Said's notion of counterpoint is a (largely unfulfilled in his opinion) quest for "anti-Manichean middle course;" it emerged as a "response to and a *potential* movement beyond restrictive binary versions of the colonial encounter."[38]

36. Said, *The Edward Said Reader*, 437.
37. Said, *Reflections on Exile*, 379.
38. Forsdick, "Edward Said After Theory," 193, 194.

It is here that the cautiously utopian[39] slant of Saidian counterpoint inconspicuously transgresses over into Third Space.

The visionary dimension of Said's postcolonial counterpoint intimates hope for a future "grounded in, but not imprisoned by memory."[40] Thus, in its Third Space register, Said's contrapuntality comes across as a cautiously epicletic imaginary of hope. The aspiration here is to realize "a shared, bilaterally constructed totality"[41]—or better yet, a multi-laterally relational totality. The contrapuntal imaginary is a trajectory of desire, a most existentially urgent and spiritually restorative homing desire for a victory of justice and wholeness for all "voices" in our planetary polyphony. As Radhakrishnan summarizes,

> Said is insistent that connections need to be made across discrepant experiences and that existent asymmetries need to be bridged and transcended in the name of a common and relational humanity in search of a universality to come. It is in this context that contrapuntal reading or analysis finds its mandate.[42]

Said's contrapuntality is a sounding image of laborious effort: remembering the old, but striving toward new alignments of identity, difference, and most importantly, qualitatively new and life-giving relationships. It is a quest for a post-imperial universality beyond the colonial dialectic of domination, hegemony, and dualism.

Ultimately, it is a quest for Third Space—such social, cultural, and spiritual models of human cohabitation that would preserve "human distinction and concreteness" through "non-dominative and non-coercive modes of life and knowledge as essential components of the desired future."[43] That being said, Said does not present contrapuntality as the triumphant cadenza of some final historical victory, despite charges about his alleged "aesthetic pre-containment of antagonism."[44] Even in its utopian register, contrapuntality is not a space of *realized* eschatology. For Said contrapun-

39. Said explicitly linked the power of music with utopian imagination: "music thus becomes an art not primarily or exclusively about authorial power and social authority, but a mode of thinking through and thinking with the integral variety of human cultural practices, generously, non-coercively, and, yes, in a utopian cast, if by utopian we mean worldly, possible, attainable, knowable," *Musical Elaborations*, 105.

40. Ashcroft, "Introduction: Spaces of Utopia," 10.

41. Radhakrishnan, *A Said Dictionary*, 24.

42. Ibid., 26.

43. Said, *Reflections on Exile*, 172. See also 214.

44. Radhakrishnan, "Derivative Discourses and the Problem of Signification," 784. See also his *A Said Dictionary*, 28.

tality is an imaginary of hope—but also of effort. Harmonic consonance can happen but it is not always already preordained. On the other hand, historical irreconcilabilities are not preordained metaphysical necessities or fixed universals either.

In the end, the contrapuntal conviviality of Third Space is about the desire for, and the possibility of, harmonic consonance—the possibility of non-coercive, non-hegemonic, and reciprocal love and life. It allows Said's vision to blossom though transdisciplinary elaborations far beyond of what he might have envisioned.

BETWIXT AND BETWEEN ORTHODOXIES: CAN ANYTHING GOOD COME FROM EUROPE?

There is one nagging question that carries a particular gravity in the post-colonial milieu: Why counterpoint? Why, since "counterpoint is a European domain and achievement?"[45] Why, on earth, use a quintessentially European musical technique that blossomed precisely during the "golden era" of colonial modernity to develop a postcolonial hermeneutic and even a visionary postcolonial imaginary of conviviality? Unsurprisingly, Edward Said has been criticized for treating modern European art music as an allegedly unquestioned norm.[46] Another fixture of critique is to rail against Said's allegedly "mandarin" and "elite" aesthetic preferences in music similarly to the unceasing complaints about Adorno's use of music in critical theory.[47] The paradox of Said is that he was and remains too conservative for some while at the same time being too iconoclastic for others! He is a theoretical maverick, a walking intellectual prototype of living and thinking betwixt and between canons, orthodoxies, and allegiances.

But the truly relevant question here is not about a scholar's supposedly "mandarin" musical tastes. Rather, it is about the postcolonial legitimacy of a European audioscape. Can anything genuinely transformative come from Europe without the typical "Eurocentric" arrogance to show, yet again, the

45. Honold, "The Art of Counterpoint," 197.

46. Derek B. Scott provides a good overview of this perennial critique of Said's work, in "Edward Said and the Interplay of Music, History and Ideology," 104–23. Obviously, I beg to differ with simplistic and often musically challenged assessments of Said's musical analysis but this is neither the place nor the time to delve into these arguments at length.

47. Benita Parry expressed the oft-repeated (yet ultimately essentializing, I submit) rebuke of Said's musical affinities: "Like Adorno, Said was a mandarin exiled from his milieu by the untimeliness of his own elite tastes and by contempt for the hegemonic ethos," in Parry, "Countercurrents and Tensions in Said's Critical Practice," 509.

indispensability and superiority of Occidental cultural accomplishments?[48] Said's migratory experience and hermeneutics offer a nuanced (alas, for some it may be too nuanced to count as pristinely and ideologically "orthodox" postcolonialism) affirmation that there are recuperable, valuable, and life-giving elements in all cultures. To search for a fully accountable postcolonial method of analysis which would be potent enough to imaginatively embody a homing desire for a truly transformative Third Space, or for a genuine "beyond" *vis-à-vis* the logic of coloniality and imperiality, Said very daringly reached into both the crevices of the inner sanctum of European art (let alone a very churchly art form[49]) as well as into the abyss of postcolonial wounds. This transgressive and insubordinate move, so vintage Saidian in its adherence to the migratory sensibility of "both/and," exemplifies his life-long "search for an alternative to both radical and conservative orthodoxies."[50]

I find it exceptionally inspiring that, for Said, no culture is *a priori* predestined for eternal damnation regardless of how obnoxious its historical track record may have been so far. Whatever affirms humanistic fields of coexistence and sharing, whatever fosters peace based upon fully recognized equality of all participating voices, is very much worth saving regardless of where the trailblazing ideas for such fields of coexistence originate. Said's approach articulates precisely what Gayatri Spivak so memorably described as trying to "see" if "the magisterial texts can now be our servants, as the new magisterium constructs itself in the name of the Other."[51]

I have already alluded to the strangely democratic undertow of counterpoint as it paradoxically matured during the era of absolute monarchies and full-fledged Western colonial escapades. Some European composers curiously linked contrapuntal compositional techniques with the quest for philosophical and even scientific alternatives to the modern Cartesian mechanistic worldview by exploring the perceived analogies between counterpoint and alchemy![52] Karen Painter has traced the interpretations of counterpoint as containing "limitless individualization and democratization

48. Just consider this: Encyclopedia Britannica blatantly explains the notion of counterpoint through the "Western spectacle" by describing it as "the most characteristic element in Western music and a major distinguishing feature between the music of the West and that of the Orient and of primitive peoples," see "Counterpoint," *Encyclopædia Britannica Online*. http://search.eb.com/eb/article-9110126.

49. On the postcolonial ambivalence about Christianity, see Kathryn Lachman, "The Allure of Counterpoint," 162–86.

50. Kennedy, *Edward Said*, 97.

51. Spivak, *A Critique of Postcolonial Reason*, 7.

52. Yearsley, "Alchemy and Counterpoint in an Age of Reason," 201–43.

of voices" since contrapuntality was perceived as enormously threatening by reactionary political and anti-Semitic ideologies in early twentieth-century Western Europe.[53]

Contrary to the dualistic colonial vision of either/or that conquers, invalidates, and shames perceived or fabricated otherness, Said heard in contrapuntal music an alternative, indeed, an internally dissenting and transcending counter-tradition to the dominant colonialist imaginary during the colonial modernity. Perhaps others would disagree with this appreciative—and for him, life-giving—recuperation. But a Saidian approach recognizes that a work of art is paradoxically always "within" (immanent) and yet "without" (transcendent) the culture of its origin. Music indeed, as Glissant mused, is a trace that transcends itself. For Said, music was always more than a purely aesthetic experience alone. Music is always embedded in a cultural milieu which it more or less reflects, but also critiques and challenges in a unique way.[54] Music, "for all its irreducible individuality, is nevertheless a part—or, paradoxically, not a part—of the era in which it was produced and appeared."[55] It always crosses over from the aesthetic realm of life and interacts with social, philosophical, and cultural realities. In this sense, musical conjectures of power, development, mastery of time, and the administration of relational patterns among different musical subjects can express and celebrate their socio-cultural setting. Moreover, precisely the opposite can happen, too: music can function as an avenue of resistance, as "an indictment of the political. . . a stark contrast, forcefully made, to inhumanity, to injustice."[56]

Counterpoint, according to Said, is a quest for alternatives to dominant cultural imaginaries.[57] Even though his theoretical elaborations did

53. Painter, "Contested Counterpoint," 210.

54. Interestingly, de Groot argues that to assume that the West owns polyphonic music—of which counterpoint is a distinct developmental specification—is just an Occidentalist fiction: "If the West has developed a high art of polyphony, it does not hold exclusive claim to it," "Said and Polyphony," 210–11.

55. Said, *On Late Style*, 134.

56. Said and Barenboim, *Parallels and Paradoxes*, 168.

57. Obviously, not everyone agrees with Said's approach. D. R. M. Irving argues, for instance, that early modern European counterpoint is a form of sonic intransigence and control and hence a "formidable agent of colonialism" that, together with colonialism itself, represents nothing else than pure hegemony, *Colonial Counterpoint*, 3, 5. Irving argues that "strict counterpoint" symbolizes the totalizing rationality of European colonial imperialism that, as a power structure, controls and governs all colonial relationships (5). Irving argues that counterpoint was "a manipulative form" of European colonialism and a "tool of imperial heteronomy" (236). Hence counterpoint "mirrors the objectives of empire" and is a means of "conquering, subduing, and 'rationalizing' other societies" (237). However, Irving affirms and uses "Said's contrapuntal

focus prominently on modern European music, his perspective was "more attuned to Arab aesthetics than to a Western classical one" with his preference for variational, exfoliating, digressional, and contemplative aural regimes *vis-à-vis*, say, the dominant and hierarchical sonata form of modern composition.[58] The musical countertradition of variations and contrapuntal polyphony functions as an "antidote to the more overtly administrative and executive authority contained in . . . classical sonata form."[59] Ultimately, Said remained convinced that even in the Western context "not all music can be experienced as working toward domination and sovereignty, just as not all music follows the awesomely invigorating patterns of sonata form."[60]

Said's contrapuntal imaginary is not an exercise in conservative nostalgia. Nor is it a pitiful symptom of some postcolonial "Stockholm syndrome"—the humiliating cultural and theoretical derivativeness (Partha Chatterjee), unoriginality (Derek Walcott), or dreadful secondariness (Said) that gets routinely ascribed to postcolonial creative endeavors. On the contrary: it embodies a visionary itinerary for sustainable and ethically accountable conviviality amidst desperate asymmetries and disparities in a way that is uniquely nuanced, complex, and hard to ideologically pigeonhole. Saidian counterpoint invokes the best of postcolonial utopia—"no longer a place but the spirit of hope itself, the essence of desire for a better world;" as an *epiclesis* for "the reality of liberation, in the possibility of justice and equality;" and ultimately as a migrant desire for a "home that we have all sensed but have never experienced or known."[61] These are the qualities that make contrapuntal Third Space a particularly meaningful imaginary for diasporic versions of postcolonialism.

---

analysis" more or less similarly to Benita Parry's interpretation except Irving juxtaposes counterpoint (colonialism) to contrapuntal analysis (postcolonialism) (6). Irving's understanding of counterpoint is patterned upon the "strict counterpoint" tradition of compositional rules. Irving pivots the theoretical analysis on the idea that in counterpoint each note is opposed (231) by another note (*punctum contra punctum*) and thus they cannot exist otherwise than antitheses or opposites rather than differences in a more continuous and dynamic texture of the contrapuntal "voices." Of course, the varieties of contrapuntal techniques are open to interpretation in more than one way and it seems that here two different musicological approaches offer entirely different judgments about the same musical phenomena.

58. De Groot, "Said and Polyphony," 211–12. See Said's famous passage on the above contrasts in *Musical Elaborations*, 102. Said found profound resonances between the Arab musical tradition exemplified by Umm Kulthum, the variation style of European contrapuntal compositions, and the nonnarrative aesthetics and compositional style of Olivier Messiaen.

59. Said, *Musical Elaborations*, 102.

60. Ibid., xvii.

61. Ashcroft, "Introduction: Spaces of Utopia," 2, 5.

To sum up: contrapuntality engenders the visionary ecology of postcolonial hybridity that is, all things considered, a quest for a radically relational, radically reciprocal, and radically life-affirming Third Space. The contrapuntal Third Space is a space of postcolonial liberation and wholeness. Taking Said's insights into consideration, perhaps it would be right to say that it is a space where wounds can at least become scars—wounds acknowledged and honored in their painful truth yet transformed from sheer affliction into a mysterious, albeit scarred, interface of transformation. Perhaps it is indeed a space of resurrection—not eschatologically triumphant yet nevertheless, proleptically, at least gestational? And then, perhaps, it might also be a subtle and somewhat shy quest for love and reconciliation since Jonathan Arac suggests that "oppositional criticism is aggressive: it cuts. Contrapuntal criticism is loving: it joins."[62]

On that note, it is now time to transgress disciplinary boundaries yet again in order to voyage ahead with constructive explorations of sacramentality through the prism of diasporic imaginary as well as postcolonial histories and hybridities. Part III will offer one constructive variation—among many other possible and probable variations—on how the triple fugue of postcolonialism, diaspora, and sacramentality might resound together.

62. Arac, "Criticism between Opposition and Counterpoint," 57.

PART III

Contemplating the Sacramental Pluriverse

Unscrambling the Watermarks of Coloniality Through a Postcolonial Diasporic Imaginary

3.1.

Revisiting Colonized Baptismal Waters

Sacraments under the Gaze of Postcolonial Vigilance

Intellectual honesty is one of the supreme goals of philosophy of religion, just as self-deception is the chief source of corruption in religious thinking, more deadly than error. Hypocrisy rather than heresy is the cause of spiritual decay.[1]

Abraham Heschel

All geography, after all, is history.[2]

Susan Abraham

The historical imagination aims not only to reconstitute the past, but also to release the past so that the present is livable. Memory is a powerful tool in resisting institutionally sanctioned forgetfulness.[3]

Kwok Pui-lan

1. Heschel, *God in Search of Man*, 10–11.
2. Abraham, "Queering the Pitch," 43.
3. Kwok, *Postcolonial Imagination*, 37.

SACRAMENTAL THEOLOGIANS—AND THAT INCLUDES a great many liturgical scholars in the Western academy—have so far showed remarkably little interest in postcolonial modes of critical analysis and imagination. Postcolonial studies have returned the compliment with a corresponding vacuum of interest in sacramental discourse or with very sporadic ethnographic inquiries in the field of liturgical and ritual studies. The reasons for such a mutual distancing are rather complex—but by no means should they thwart more vigorous conversations in the future. In Part I, I offered a thick description of postcolonial diasporic imaginaries. In Part II, I sketched the contours of several particularly salient postcolonial themes such as hybridity and contrapuntality for theological engagement. Here, in Part III, I will flesh out the interplay of how these pivotal postcolonial themes can enter into an interlogue with some vital facets of sacramental imagination in Christian theology.

An earnest postcolonial and diasporic *ressourcement* of sacramentality cannot happen without an awareness of the historical and contextual powerscapes of Christian sacramental traditions. Namely, it cannot naively ignore the powerscapes' institutional inertias, their (often unwritten) metaphysical underpinnings, and fixtures of ecclesiastical traditionalism in the variety of forms that they manifest in diverse cultural contexts. It cannot fail to appreciate the challenges posed to the desire for a sacramental, as it were, re-enchantment of Christianity by its most intimate nemesis—"Christianity subjected to the pathologies of power."[4] This is why these powerscapes continue to be spiritual, ethical, and doctrinal minefields.

It is not feasible nor is it the purpose of this study to offer a comprehensive survey of these minefields. Nevertheless, a watchful awareness of the impact these powerscapes continue to yield is especially relevant for postcolonial theology since it intentionally listens to the voices of those who find themselves exiled to the margins of dominant dynamics of gender, race, and sexuality as well as the institutionally sanctioned manifestations of "proper" (i.e., Occidental) liturgical "inculturation."[5]

The objective of this opening chapter is to deepen and sharpen the historical contextualization of my diasporic and postcolonial locus of

4. Boff, *Christianity in a Nutshell*, 97.

5. So-called "inculturation" is an extremely complex issue. The very term "*in*culturation" as such is deeply problematic for postcolonialism due to the authoritarian, unilateral, and unidirectional undertones. Inculturation remains a highly relevant and yet highly contentious topic among African and Asian theologians. On the contemporary neocolonial and anti-authoritarian issues surrounding inculturation in the African and Asian liturgical contexts, see for example, Kekong Bisong, "A Postmodern Response to Sacramental Presence," 40–64, and Aloysius Pieris, "A Liturgical Anticipation of a Domination-free Church."

enunciation (Part I) from an explicitly postcolonial *theo-historical* perspective. I begin again with a brief *compositio loci*: a historical reflection on the imperial and colonial imbroglios of Christian sacramental practices as they appear from the context of Baltic postcoloniality that I continue to inhabit diasporically.

RESISTING SACRAMENTAL NATIVISM

Geography is indeed history; my geography is my history. It is not just a line of demographic statistics but rather a rich, and sometimes very convoluted, wellspring of insight. And so with history I must begin by "reexcavating and recharting the past from a postcolonial point of view, thereby erecting a new postimperial space."[6]

The most organic way to start charting the contours of postcolonial sacramentality is to intentionally embed critical and constructive inquiry in what Edward Said referred to as the gravity of history. Postcolonial retrievals of sacramentality will be credible and accountable only if they remain mindful of historical as well as moral conundrums bequeathed to us by the previous generations of sacramental theology. Such a retrieval and re-envisagement cannot begin with a ritualistically saturated intraliturgical idealism if it aspires to remain accountable to the ethical exigencies in global postcolony. Like any other modality of Christian theology, the sacramental approach does not offer us the luxury of tapping into a pristine stream of theological creativity and spirituality that would be absolutely uncontaminated by so palpably unredeemed life and the unrelenting vicissitudes of history. There is simply no such thing as a golden age or golden form of sacramental theology to which a postcolonial theologian could credulously return with any remaining shreds of integrity. Historically speaking, postcolonial sacramental theology is always already overshadowed by what Tissa Balasuriya called "the tragedy of the Eucharist":

> The tragedy of the subordination of Christianity to European power politics was also the tragedy of the Eucharist. As the priests and monks went hand in hand with the colonialists, the Eucharist was desecrated in the service of empire. The Eucharist was (one hopes unconsciously) perverted in the close alliance between imperialism and the church. [. . .] Hence we must not be so naïve as to accept as "faith" whatever beliefs or practices prevail at any given time concerning the Eucharist. We must not think that the so-called simple faith of the people is innocent

6. Said, "Invention, Memory, and Place," 247.

> in itself. It has been evolved alongside the world's worst exploitation and did not contest it or, rather, it tended to justify the status quo.[7]

In the course of this chapter I will explore how one version of this sacramental tragedy played out through the medieval Baltic crusades and their long and ambivalent aftermath in my own postcolonial backyard of Latvia. In fact, most postcolonial and diasporic theological conclusions would hardly make sense without recognizing their embeddedness in the histories, cultural memories, and spiritual legacies that remain, as if watermarked by colonialism and imperialism, in a multitude of uncanny but very lively ways.

The Latvian memory of conquest is long and resilient. It is specific but by no means entirely unique in the global context of the so-called era of "Discovery." Considering the instrumental role of sacramental practices in the Christian crusades and conquests of "pagans," "savages," and "infidels," it needs to be underscored right away that these discourses and practices are imbricated in a habitual undertow of violence.[8] The typical Western European Renaissance and modern violence of conversion, conquest, and Christianization is not limited to the postcolonial locations of the former European transmarine colonies in Africa, South America, and Asia. Before it was unleashed on the Native Americans after 1492, the unholy alliance was already well-rehearsed across the intra-European frontiers and colonies that were produced by the Northern crusades (1147–1500s) and its "monastic war machine"[9] on the south-eastern Baltic littoral. In this context, Baltic history signals rather clearly that the field of sacramental theology carries its own, though rarely known or acknowledged, colonial baggage.

The better known recollections of the medieval Spanish crusades against the Muslims, the coerced baptisms of the Jews under the hegemony of post-*Reconquista* Spain, or medieval and early modern anti-Semitic pogroms in Western and Central Europe ought to temper premature triumphalism and naiveté in historically informed sacramental discourse. Similarly, riding the ecstatic wave of the twentieth-century Western liturgical renewal should not blind one to the twisted histories of how Christian

7. Balasuriya, *The Eucharist and Human Liberation*, 37.

8. Concise summary of the entanglement between medieval Latin Christianity and military violence as it played out in the Baltics, see Eric Christiansen, *The Northern Crusades*, 50–59. Also see the Latvian historian Eva Eihmane's work which explores the ordinariness of the violence that accompanied medieval Latin perceptions of mission and conversion, for example, "Christianisation of the Local Peoples of Livonia: Cultivation of God's Vineyard or Brutal Subjugation under the Cover of Religion," 9–28.

9. Christiansen, *The Northern Crusades*, 73–92.

liturgies and sacraments again and again proved malleable to the vicious logic of coloniality and imperiality. Instead of communicating salvation and the sacramental transformation of all creation through the power of divine love, on numerous occasions they readily facilitated cultural imperialism, political oppression, and economic exploitation.

Worst of all, sacramental practices, especially baptism, accommodated deeply destructive psychospiritual abuse of the "barbarians" conscripted into Christendom by "fire and sword"[10] through forced, or commercially transacted, conversions as well as zealously implemented strategies to "extirpate idolatry." All of it indeed may have happened a long time ago; yet, lest we forget, its pneumato-psycho-somatic memory dilly-dallies on, even in the peripheries of Europe.

REVISITING THE HISTORICAL GHOSTS OF COLONIZED BAPTISMAL WATERS

The actual crusades to the Baltic region started with pope Eugenius III's call for converting the non-Christian Slavs (the "Wendish crusade") within the framework of the Second Crusade in 1147. The territories of today's Latvia, Estonia, and Lithuania comprised "the last pagan corner of Europe"[11] and their tribal peoples were the last official European pagans. But that was to change soon and change dramatically. It is not that the Baltic peoples were totally isolated in their hilltop fortresses; commerce was ongoing between German, Danish, and Russian merchants in the late twelfth century. Eventually, in what is today's Latvia, merchants were joined by German monastic missionaries from the 1180s onwards. This was by no means the indigenous locals' first interaction with Christianity. The Baltic tribes of *Līvi* and *Kurši (Curonians)* already had had sporadic contacts with Danish Christians in the eleventh century but without any conclusive religious implications. A similar situation developed in the territories of *Latgaļi* (*Latgalians*) in the northeastern Latvia.

All this changed radically when the more sustained German missionary offensive took off. It was spearheaded by missionary priests like the

10. This expression captures the customary Latvian critique of the violent ("ar uguni un zobenu") process of Christianization of Baltic tribal lands and peoples that constitute contemporary Latvia.

11. Plakans, *A Concise History of the Baltic States*, 54. It also needs to be noted that the subsequent centuries of Western European hegemony in the Baltics worked out rather differently for Lithuanians. They aligned with the Poles during the Middle Ages and early modernity in contrast to Latvians and Estonians who were unable to develop sustainable political formations until after World War I.

Augustinian St. Meinhard von Segeberg and the Cistercian Berthold. Despite some initial success, and particularly Meinhard's initially non-violent approach, the Germans soon experienced indigenous pushback. It is important to remember that St. Meinhard's peaceful missionary ideology did not last long. Even Meinhard "was ready to organize military activities when he realized that his missionary attempts had failed; only death put a stop to his project."[12] Meinhard's death notwithstanding, the mission morphed into a full-blown crusade under Berthold and the entrepreneurial Bishop Albert von Buxhoevden from 1199 onward. Resistance, apostasy, sporadic rebellions, internal indigenous rivalries or not, a radically brave new world had marched in for good across the eastern Baltic littoral.[13]

Amid increasingly systematic efforts of colonization-*cum*-Christianization by the Germanic crusaders, some of the Baltic tribes' idea of buying time for resistance was to undergo baptism more or less willingly. There is historical evidence that some individuals, such as the tribal chieftain Kaupo, were actually baptized due to their religious convictions and stuck to their conversion. For the most part, however, undergoing baptism seemed to offer a chance to maneuver through and survive not only German but also Russian and Danish efforts to control their lands and socio-economic structures during the "long twelfth century."[14] It is notable that, judging from the available sources, the Baltic tribes tended to undergo the sacrament of baptism "after military defeats of the pagan side, which leaves open the question of how thorough such conversions were."[15] As Eva Eihmane summarizes, for the conquerors "religious motives were intertwined with material ones and did not conflict with each other;" rather, "following the Christian tradition of the causal relationship between success and faith (deriving from the Old Testament where victories and prosperity go to pious rulers) . . . the material gains of Christians [were seen] as a just reward, granted by God in return for worship or for serving His purpose."[16] And so, whatever else baptismal grace might have brought for the indigenous tribes in Livonia, it came with political, military, and economic costs:

> Often the result of military defeat, the formal act of conversion was inevitably accompanied by political subjugation and the imposition of new administrative measures such as tithes. Rebellions were the expressions of the disappointment of the converts

12. Andris Šnē, "The Emergence of Livonia," 55.
13. Ibid., 33–76.
14. Blomkvist, *The Discovery of the Baltic*.
15. Plakans, *A Concise History of the Baltic States*, 39–40.
16. Eihmane, "The Baltic Crusades," 42.

> at the material burdens that were brought by baptism, or at their general standing under the new circumstances. [. . .] Behind individual Christian armies stood all of Christendom, its religious zeal intertwined with material interests pushing inexorably into Livonia. [. . .] The further history of Livonia was less and less in harmony with Christian ideals. . .[17]

Maybe this is why—simultaneously sensing the power and also the commercial malleability of the religion of love—the late twelfth century Baltic indigenous tribe of Līvi (Livs) rather willingly, but not without some crafty survivalist calculation, went through the baptisms administered by Latin Christian merchant priests and monastic missionaries without a deeper understanding, or even desire for, the salvation it was supposed to offer. Indeed some of them, alongside their neighboring Latgaļi (Latgalians), might have already been baptized by the Germans' and Danes' equally eager expansionist rivals from Russian Orthodox Novgorod, Polotsk, and Pskov.

However, the acceptance of baptism and incorporation in the Christian sacramental system, often only after military defeats at the hands of technologically superior Western Christians, has constantly raised questions about the nature of such conversions and how they are understood today by the contemporary descendants of the converts. It helps to keep in mind that under the auspices of medieval and early modern missionary strategies these conversions were imagined not just as religious incorporation into the triumphant Body of Christ and its exclusive promise of eternal life, but equally as a cultural and socio-economic conquest of whole territories, cultures, and ethnic groups into the political world system of Christendom. Amid the crusaders' political rivalries, "baptism [was] clearly a symbolic act of confirming the power of a particular [ethnic crusader] group over a particular territory."[18] In these circumstances sacraments practically served as ideological tools of political and economic conquest.

A pattern of constant frontier squabbles over land, feudal seniority, ports, as well as civil and spiritual authority intensified throughout the *senlatvieši*,[19] or the Ur-Latvian micronations' lands, and newly built crusader and merchant cities in the thirteenth century. The main participants

17. Ibid., 50, 51.

18. Kala, "Rural Society and Religious Innovation," 181.

19. I am using the linguistically hybrid abbreviation "Ur-Latvians" to convey the historical dimension of the term *senlatvieši*. The prefix "*sen*" is derived from an adjective for ancient history, indeed, pre-history, hence *Ur*. The specific term usually describes the pre-colonial indigenous Baltic tribes, the ancestors of the present nation of ethnic Latvians. Some historians call the Baltic tribes *maztautas* "micronations" while others use terms like "indigenous peoples."

in the frontier wars were Western European merchants, missionary bishops, monastics, and various motley crews of crusade recruits from across Europe, mostly Germany and Denmark. All these interest groups were vying for control of Baltic territories alongside several popes who tried to establish a papal state in Livonia under the direct rule of the monarchical papacy and the Roman curia. In the early thirteenth century the Order of Swordbrothers (*Fratres Militiae Christi Livoniae)* became a major force with a particularly voracious appetite for colonial spoils.[20]

Meanwhile, the neighboring Russian Orthodox principalities also did not sit idly by as passive observers. In historians' estimation, the Russian princes were more pragmatic in their missionary efforts: the point was to impose a system of tributes and levies upon the Baltic peoples in exchange for alleged protection and trade privileges without a formal requirement of conversion and baptism.[21] Nevertheless, it seems that a number of *Latgaļi* ended up baptized into Russian Orthodoxy during the late twelfth century before the Western Catholic crusades picked up speed.

These facts do not, however, imply that Russian Orthodox princedoms did not entertain military and political interests around the highly profitable trade routes along the river Daugava just like the Germans and Danes did. The Russians did not shy away from using military force and a system of tributes and levies to keep economic and spiritual control over the *Latgaļi* whenever and wherever they could.[22] The Russian quest for Baltic lands and profits was militarily and technologically arrested, albeit temporarily, by the German superiority in the "long twelfth century." Yet there are no grounds to assert that their quest was somehow more spiritually motivated than that of Western Latin Christians from German lands and Scandinavia.

And the rest, as they say, is a "proper" (by Occidental standards, anyway) history. Later Livonian wars and subsequent re-colonization of Latvian, Estonian, and Lithuanian lands by the Russian empire tell a story that is not at all different from the colonial objectives and strategies of German crusaders or trans-European business elites. Ultimately, whether these early Orthodox conversions were spiritually fruitful or just a matter of cultural convenience and survival tactics without deeper spiritual meaning remains a very open question indeed.[23] What is clear is that in the 12th—13th centu-

20. For example, see Roberts Feldmanis, *Latvijas baznīcas vēsture*; Arnolds Spekke, *Latvijas vēsture*; Ilgvars Butulis and Antonijs Zunda, *Latvijas Vēsture*; see also Eihmane, "The Baltic Crusades," 37–51.

21. Zemītis reflects the consensus on this issue in "*Kultūru saskarsme un komunikācija*,"172–94.

22. Strods, *Latvijas katoļu baznīcas vēsture,* 66.

23. The Latvian Orthodox theologian Jānis Kalniņš has recently challenged the

ries Baltic lands and peoples became a battlefield in the military, economic, and ideological war between the Western Latin and Eastern Orthodox civilization in which both sides allegedly wanted to claim the Baltic for Christ but mostly, really, for themselves.[24]

ON THE EXISTENTIAL CLEVERNESS OF WEARING COLONIZED GRACE LIGHTLY

On the "Western front" of Christianization-*cum*-colonization, the sacrament of baptism certainly served as an instrument of subjugation, increasing economic exploitation, and genocidal violence. As Benjamin Lieberman argues, the forging of medieval Christendom was underwritten by an exclusivist "genocidal impulse." The "genocidal impulse" is above all a religious category in the context of medieval Christian conquests with the goal to eradicate non-Christian religious practices—and their practitioners if they declined to convert. Thus, "genocidal thinking in this sense complemented missionary activity"[25] including the deliberate activities of cultural genocide.

Under these crusading circumstances, sacramental rites played a wicked role as building blocks for the developing socio-political system of two tier identity politics and, eventually, serfdom and apartheid that in some Latvian lands lasted into the nineteenth century. The baptismal "grace" of conquest did not bring peace where there had been war and violence before. Often it was neither desired nor understood, despite growing familiarity with the technicalities of this liturgical ritual. Most of the time it seems not to have qualitatively changed anything at all—neither in those who baptized nor in those who were baptized. The whole south-eastern Baltic region remained mired in decades of violence.

historical consensus about Russian Orthodox motivations for, and methods of, Christianizing mission among the Baltic tribes in what is today's Latvia. His work aptly underscores the still under-interrogated colonial aspects of cultural and religious violation of the Balts during the crusades by Latin Christianity and its spiritual legacies in Latvian spirituality and culture. But his arguments that there was a large, genuinely meaningful, and successful pre-Latin Orthodox mission offer little reliable evidence and so are not entirely persuasive. Nor is his cliché-rich and supercilious confessional polemic against both Roman Catholicism and Lutheranism. The title of the book is telling: "The Latvian Way of the Cross" or "The Latvian *Via Dolorosa*." See Kalniņš, *Latvju Krusta Ceļš*. Most Latvian historians agree that Orthodox Christianity's impact on the Ur-Latvians was far more superficial than that of Latin Catholicism, see Zemītis, "Kultūru saskarsme un komunikācija," 190.

24. Ibid., 172–94.

25. Lieberman, *Remaking Identities*, 81.

On the spiritual plane, the earliest Latin chronicle of the era of crusades, the *Heinrici Cronicon Lyvoniae*, garishly reported that the newly minted Baltic converts routinely used to return to the ancestral spiritual practices "like a dog to its vomit."[26] Nevertheless, such minor heretical glitches aside, the crusader chronicles presented the history of crusade as "the inevitable unfolding of God's will, with a few flattering observations about the military prowess of the pagans" since "the triumphalist chronicles saw the hand of God at work and on that basis portrayed the victories of the crusaders as inevitable."[27]

But of course, there were insurrections. An interesting early manifestation of indigenous resistance and survival strategy was to "wash off" their baptisms in the river Daugava amidst constant skirmishes with the Western crusaders. It is not exactly clear what the theological objectives of such counter-sacramental rites were. However, considering the spiritual valence of the Daugava—effectively a Latvian equivalent of spiritual symbolism akin to the river Jordan in Judaism—these counter-sacramental actions convey intentional spiritual resistance. These counter-sacramental actions were deployed, in Silvio Torres-Saillant's words, as a "technology of existential cleverness" in order to "cope with a challenging history."[28] A spiritual *metanoia* was hardly achieved—or even sought—by what preaching and catechesis of the gospel that there actually was amidst the fast and furious *Drang nach Osten*. From a theological perspective, the outcome was spiritually dubious despite the routine theo-political justifications for violent subjugation in the context of Medieval Latin Christendom:

> it was the continued apostasy of the Livonians which eventually led Berthold to seek permission from the pope to use force against the Livonians [. . .] Returning to Livonia with an army, Berthold began to use force to subjugate the Livonians and bring them to the faith, stating . . . that he took this step because the Livonians "had returned too often from faith to paganism." [. . .] The idea to employ crusaders—presumably in defence of the Christians and to force apostates back into the fold—thus appears to have originated with the missionary bishops rather than in the curia. [. . .] As for the justification for allowing the use of force against the Livonians . . . the missionary bishops argued that they needed help to fight the apostasy among the Livonians and that the just cause brought forward by the popes

26. *Indriķa Livonijas hronika*, II, 5.

27. Plakans, *A Concise History of the Baltic States*, 42, 39.

28. Torres-Saillant, *An Intellectual History of the Caribbean*, 161.

> was the Livonians' apostasy which, as a rebellion against the Church, posed a serious threat to the Church.[29]

As the Rome-endorsed "Northern" or "Livonian" crusade unfolded in all its bloody "penitential" glory, the *Līvi* stepped into the river Daugava to defy the conquerors and their God by "washing off" the sacrament of baptism, no longer as a merely strange and incomprehensible Latin ritual that might have temporarily saved their physical lives and served as a tool of negotiation, but as an affliction and a sign of betrayal and suffering. They also made it clear to the missionary Bishop Berthold, as reported in the *Heinrici Cronicon Lyvoniae*, that he should "make those who have accepted the faith to stick to it but invite others to accept it by persuasion, not blows."[30]

The political resistance was growing, too, as the missionary offensive grew more militarized and oppressive. Eventually the German Cistercian Bishop Berthold who brought the pope-sanctioned military force to the Baltic lands was expelled from Salaspils and finally killed in a battle between the crusaders and the *Līvi* in 1198. Another German Cistercian, Theodorich, was instrumental in organizing the Swordbrothers' Order and subsequently facilitating the Baltic crusades in collaboration with popes Celestine III and Innocent III. His militant efforts were not to be forgotten. As a bishop in Estonia, Theodorich met his end in battle at the hands of the enraged Estonians while serving as the local envoy of yet another major contender for gold and glory in the crusades—the Danish king—in 1219.

In spite of regular and increasingly desperate insurrections and even a few short-lived military successes against the Swordbrothers and the Livonian Order, the Ur-Latvian peoples were (at least formally) Christianized and Europeanized by the end of the thirteenth century. The last non-Christian region in the medieval Europe was finally baptized and confirmed into Christendom and simultaneously into the peculiar intra-European colonial system. It was, as Nils Blomkvist succinctly puts, a small scale "dress rehearsal" for what was to come on a global and even bloodier scale after 1492 worldwide.[31] Lieberman agrees and emphasizes that,

> making Europe Christian marked both an end and a beginning. With conquests, conversion, and colonization in frontier zones, Europeans pioneered many of the techniques later used elsewhere to move frontiers and press people to adopt a new identity. In their experiences of colonization and holy war, parts

29. Fonnesberg-Schmidt, *The Popes and the Baltic Crusades*, 70, 74–75.
30. *Indriķa Livonijas hronika,* II, 5.
31. Blomkvist, *Discovery of the Baltic,* 704–5.

> of Europe functioned almost as a first America when it came to finding ways to create Christians.[32]

The colonized baptismal waters may have led the Ur-Latvians into a violently imposed and otherworldly redemption, but in this world they were marched through these waters toward losing political and economic rights already in the thirteenth century. And that trajectory only expanded all the way into a comprehensive system of serfdom and apartheid that, curiously, peaked precisely during the glorious Age of European Enlightenment.

Ultimately, the conquered Ur-Latvians and their hybrid offspring could savor the fruits of the multitasking crusade for the centuries to come: after all, we were finally "discovered" and incorporated into Europe, right? And, we were effectively conquered not only into eternal salvation but finally also into "proper," i.e., Western, "History!"[33] This colonial "voyage in" is hard to miss, as Eric Christiansen summarizes:

> the lands the crusaders conquered had changed almost out of recognition—in population, speech, culture, economy, government. [. . .] For seven centuries these east-Baltic countries were colonial societies, bearing the mark left by their medieval conquerors whatever outside power tried to annex or change them. If ever the crusades had any lasting effect, it was here, and in Spain.[34]

But what about the spiritual and theological consequences, so stealthy yet so pervasive and so persistent as that peculiar postcolonial "sense that the past endures, that it remains unresolved"[35] not only in the Caribbean but also in Eastern Europe?

CHRISTIAN HISTORY AND ITS COLONIAL WATERMARKS: BEYOND EMBARRASSMENT?

The idealization of the medieval Baltic tribes in their erratic efforts to resist the tide of Christianization was not a particular pastime of the colonial Germano-Baltic historians. Nor is it something that the postsoviet/postcolonial Latvian historians enjoy doing albeit for substantially different reasons. Today's historians are very content to leave any romanticizing attempts in the past. The early indigenous Latvian National Romantic poets did embark on

32. Lieberman, *Remaking Identities*, 81.
33. Plakans, *The Concise History of the Baltic States*, 45–47.
34. Christiansen, *The Northern Crusades*, 1–2, 3.
35. Torres-Saillant, *An Intellectual History of the Caribbean*, 165.

a very predictable nationalist course of inventing a mobilizing and nativist, even if not quite entirely golden, past in the nineteenth century.[36] But that time is long gone.

To swing the pendulum in the opposite direction, some twentieth-century Latvian church historians have openly expressed a sense of embarrassment over the perceived backwardness and primitiveness of Baltic indigenous religions vis-à-vis the assumed (West-Euro-centric, of course) religious superiority of Western Christianity. Roberts Feldmanis was arguably the most outspoken on this topic:

> According to our oral tradition, neither temples nor priests are mentioned there. There was some sort of peculiar religion among these tribes. . . very similar to the ancient Prussians, who were, on the one hand extremely hospitable but on the other hand, extremely intolerant if someone else tried to learn more about their magic practices. The Latvian religion is summed up in practices of magic, wizardry, and superstition. . . there are no temples, no holy places, no priesthood. [. . .] If we look at the quality of their [Baltic tribal] religiosity—there was not much to offend and not much to defend."[37]

What is most glaringly obvious in such theological interpretations of Christianization is the lack of what Edward Said would call a contrapuntal interpretive strategy. Namely, there are no sustained attempts to interpret the traditions, voices, texts, beliefs, and religious practices of both Christian colonizers and indigenous non-Christian cultures together, and to let them play off one another with an acknowledgment that both, the dominant and the subjugated, have a right to speak for themselves, if possible, and to be noticed and heard. The historically postcolonial yet un-decolonized imagination—or in Achille Mbembe's words, the "internalized authoritarian epistemology"[38]—often manifests precisely as an internalized, indeed

36. Aldis Purs exemplifies this perspective by arguing that nineteenth-twentieth-century nationalist historians chose to "vilify German conquest. Estonian and Latvian nationalists portrayed the actions and plans of German knights and priests as duplicitous and inhumane, with one ultimate goal: to conquer and rule the lands of the eastern Baltic littoral." Without explicitly naming it as such, Purs emphasizes the serfdom of the modern colonial period rather than the era of medieval crusades as the most detrimental for the Baltic nations: "The travails of war and the exactions of great, centralizing kings between the sixteenth and the eighteenth century likely scarred and oppressed the peoples of Estonia, Latvia, and Lithuania more than did the arrival of German and Danish Christians in the twelfth to the fourteenth century," *Baltic Facades*, 30–31.

37. Feldmanis, *Latvijas baznīcas vēsture*, 20–21.

38. Lartey, *Postcolonizing God*, xii. Lartey's lament that in the historical postcolony, "European hegemony reigns supreme in African theology" might sound like a strange

"learned" embarrassment about the ancestral history that, clearly, does not and cannot measure up to either ancient Greco-Roman or Hebrew standards of religious development, let alone modern Western Euro-Atlantic standards. That probably explains why postcolonial/postsoviet Latvian church historians and theologians remain overall reluctant to further critically interrogate the ominous connections between the core Christian doctrines of salvation and the logic of monotheism as such that has proved so malleable to imperialistic cooptation and very profitable colonial abuse.[39]

There is yet no sustained critical trajectory of interrogation in the Baltic postcolonial milieu which would plumb the deepest entanglements between the historical manifestations of Christianity and "the theo-and egopolitics that has sustained the global imperial designs."[40] Nor is attention typically given by Baltic historians to a regionally specific critical analysis of the global Doctrine of Discovery[41] and how it advanced across the Baltic littoral in the larger context of the emerging global dominance of Western Christian civilization which reached its peak during the era of colonial Euro-Atlantic modernity. The local becomes incomprehensible, at least theologically, if the global is overlooked because Christianity was the "first global design of the modern/colonial world system and, consequently, the anchor of Occidentalism and the coloniality of power drawing the external borders as the colonial difference" and as such, a part of the "hegemonic project for managing the planet."[42] Top-down globalization was not invented only a couple of decades ago by the neoliberal market ideology or Google but by the colonial system of Euromodernity. In this framework, inescapably, "the majority of local histories on the planet have had to deal, in the past five hundred years, with an increasing spread of *imperial* global

thing to invoke in the Latvian context but it, ironically, it does capture a common facet of postcolonial dynamic at play also in the margins of Europe.

39. The work of Regina Mara Schwartz and Laurel Schneider calls attention to the hegemonic and totalizing lacunae of monotheistic religions in a commendable way. See Schwartz's *The Curse of Cain* and Schneider's *Beyond Monotheism*.

40. Tlostanova and Mignolo, *Learning to Unlearn*, 77.

41. The so-called "Doctrine of Discovery" does not seem to be prominent on the radar screen of postsoviet/postcolonial Latvian historians and theologians despite the relevant resonances between the Christian conquests of indigenous peoples elsewhere. The World Council of Churches summarizes the doctrine as "the idea that Christians enjoy a moral and legal right based solely on their religious identity to invade and seize indigenous lands and to dominate Indigenous Peoples." Brief theological analysis of the doctrine and its historical and contemporary implications is available from the World Council of Churches. Online: http://www.oikoumene.org/en/resources/documents/executive-committee/2012-02/statement-on-the-doctrine-of-discovery-and-its-enduring-impact-on-indigenous-peoples.

42. Mignolo, *Local Histories/Global Designs*, 21.

designs of all kinds: religious, political, economic, linguistic and epistemic, and cultural."[43] To ignore these connections, postcolonially speaking, is short-sighted.

A (EASTERN EUROPEAN) CASE OF POSTCOLONIAL HYPERMNESIA

But theories and historiographies, be they ecclesiastical or political, tell only a partial story. Meanwhile, like it or lump it, a few things are writ so large in the Latvian memoryscape that they call for a theological analysis beyond what some might dismiss as mere regional idiosyncrasies. Among them is the enduring felt sense of virtually uninterrupted and overwhelming colonial and imperialistic violence. Despite the lamentations of educators that younger generations are becoming scandalously ignorant in history or the perennial fears that Russian imperialistic historiography is spread around the world by ruthlessly executed media campaigns of cyber-warfare, there is, at the same time, a strong culture of postcolonial remembrance that gravitates around the ambiguity of Christianization.

And here again, an insight from the postcolonial Caribbean can help to understand the presence of the past that remains unresolved. This postcolonial culture of remembrance can be described as "hypermnesia." In the postcolonial context, hypermnesia is, as Silvio Torres-Saillant has argued

> a condition, dramatically opposed to amnesia, that exacerbates the memory of the past, producing a state of compulsive remembering that could be deemed clinical were it not for its inevitability and its salutary function as a mechanism for coping with the devastating events that have taken place in the region since the start of the colonial transaction.[44]

Although it may seem weird, particularly to the widely exported North American future-oriented cultural imaginary, cultural and psychospiritual memoryscapes stretch long, far, and deep in the Baltic ethos, including its diasporas. The Latvian-British cultural anthropologist Vieda Skultans underscores, that "history and culture combine to shape the memory of individual experience. Indeed, history and memory are difficult to prise apart in Latvia."[45] After all, historical narratives are always already "interplays of past worlds and times with the present."[46]

43. Tlostanova and Mignolo, *Learning to Unlearn*, 77.

44. Torres-Sailant, *The Intellectual History of the Caribbean*, 150.

45. Skultans, "Theorizing Latvian Lives," 763.

46. Ibid., 777.

It is beyond denial that the pre-crusade Eastern Baltic region was no paradise of peace as the nineteenth century emancipatory movement of Latvian National Romanticism occasionally tried to paint it. It is also indisputable that all the main players in the Baltic colonial theater of war, from the Germans and Danes to the *Līvi, Latgaļi, Sēļi* (*Selonians*), *Kurši, Zemgaļi* (*Semgalians*), Lithuanians, and the Russians fought brutally, fought one another, and fought often.[47] As Andrejs Plakans argues, "it would be a mistake to think of indigenous violence as purely defensive or retaliatory; indeed, it seems to have been a standard part of everyday life in the littoral."[48] That being said, there is a widely shared public consensus that such a state of affairs could not justify and ought not ever to be invoked by Christians to legitimize a theopolitics of military and sacramental conquest.[49]

As psychoanalytical lore suggests, the organizing principle of human memory is not chained to strict chronology but is open to sequences of associations that travel between various temporalities. For example, the outcome of the mutinous era of conquest and Europeanization of the Baltic was—and still is—a pervasive and enduring ambivalence toward organized Christianity as an established institution. Secondly, it is common knowledge that Latvian popular spirituality, religious practices, and the whole cultural space continue to be persistently colored by syncretism.[50]

47. The work of the late Latvian-American medievalist Indriķis Šterns demonstrates a strong challenge to some pre-World War II nativistic tendencies in Latvian historiography during the early postcolonial period and its methodological and ideological pushback to the previously reigning Germano-Baltic colonialist historiography. See particularly Šterns' *Latvijas Vēsture* 1180–1290: *Krustakari*. Strods also argues against nativist "romanticization" of the pre-crusade indigenous forms of life while voicing the present pragmatic (or the pragmatically disguised West(Euro)centrist?) consensus that the "geopolitical situation of the Baltics in between the West and the East was such that it had to be incorporated into one or the other structure," see Strods, *Latvijas katoļu baznīcas vēsture*, 64. This political consensus of historians, however, does not even start to address the *theological* conundrums of the Baltic crusades and the missionary-colonial ideology that underpinned them.

48. Plakans, *A Concise History of the Baltic States*, 33–34.

49. The Latvian historians Ilgvars Butulis and Antonijs Zunda summarize the currently and widely shared consensus regarding the process of Christianization in the following way: "Without idealizing the local tribes, it must be pointed out that the very process of baptizing the pagans was extremely far from the Christian principles and was related to constant violence, robberies, betrayals, slave trade," see Butulis and Zunda, *Latvijas Vēsture*, 20.

50. Strods provides a helpful summary of indigenous Ur-Latvian religious practices and beliefs in his *Latvijas katoļu baznīcas vēsture*, 47–61. He notes that "under the influence of the Christian faith, Ur-Latvian beliefs significantly changed and resisted the social, political, and spiritual change that Christianity effected in Latvia thus obtaining an opportunity for their continued existence," 59.

Meanwhile the ambivalence, mimicry, and syncretism that emerged from under the constrictions of political and spiritual apartheid continue to surface as traces of the still unhealed colonial trauma of Christianization. These traces are present in the postcolonial/postsoviet homeland as well as in diasporic spirituality. They flicker through contemporary Latvian popular spirituality, sacramental practices, and underlying perceptions of cultural and psychological identity in homeland and diaspora.

Virtually every religious and church-related matter of public relevance in the postcolonial and postsoviet space sooner or later loops back to the cultural memory of the violation of ancestral land and culture in the name of the Christian God of love. This process happens in the homeland as well as in diaspora; in scholarly discussions and in pastoral conversations; in cafes and on social media. Agita Misāne's summary illustrates the contentious situation very well:

> It seems that there are few questions in the history of Latvia about which there is so much wrangling as about the reception of Christianity in the history of our nation as well as today. Whenever there is a discussion about things like the constitution of the European Union and the possible reference to the Christian heritage in it, or about the erection of a monument for Bishop Albert in Riga, or the election of a new pope in the Vatican, or about the church treaties with the state or about any regular church holidays in the liturgical calendar, this question is actualized.[51]

What is amply demonstrated here is Edward Said's observation about how past events and present exigencies individuate and co-create a particular postcolonial history. For history, precisely as "collective memory, is not an inert and passive thing but a field of activity in which past events are selected, reconstructed, maintained, modified and endowed with political meaning."[52] History is never a "neutral exercise in facts and basic truths"

51. Agita Misāne, "Latvijas kristianizācija." Online resource, no pages. In addition, Christiansen accurately remarks that "the issues involved are by no means all dead ones, and that contentiousness remains a dominant characteristic in the field of medieval Baltic history;" see Christiansen, *The Northern Crusades*, 4. Moreover, having become a seemingly tranquil political backwater under the Soviet empire, the cost of this Baltic "tranquility was an implacable grievance among the millions who have left, and a continuing series of wrongs done to the millions who stayed put. In such a climate, old wounds do not heal, and old quarrels are not forgotten, even by historians. The interpretation of conflicts between Christianity and paganism, between Western Catholicism and Eastern Orthodoxy, between German, Balt and Slav, still rouses passion after the ending of the Cold War," Christiansen, *The Northern Crusades*, 4, 5.

52. Said, "Invention, Memory, Place," 251.

since "memory and its representations touch very significantly upon questions of identity, of nationalism, or power and authority" that is needed to construct "a desirable loyalty to and insider's understanding of one's country, tradition, and faith."[53]

How does the history and legacy of internalized violence, mimicry, and ambivalence fare today? On a deeper level, the accumulated psychic legacy of having been spiritually—and not just politically, culturally, and economically—"sinned against" stubbornly keeps resurfacing in situations of felt threat as well as in real or perceived confrontations with today's neocolonial empires, be they of political, economic, military, cultural, or religious nature. This, arguably, underlies overanxious postcolonial wrestling with issues of cultural and spiritual identity and belonging (In Europe? Which Europe? In the West? Or not? Then where exactly?).

The majority of contemporary postcolonial-*cum*-postsoviet Latvian society is tenaciously anticlerical and religiously undemonstrative apart from the dedicated minorities that form the devotionally active "inner circles" of the major faith denominations or, on the opposite end of the religious spectrum, indigenous wisdom groups like *Dievturi*. With the characteristic reserve and hands-off disposition towards institutionalized Christianity, Latvia increasingly fits the profile of the "spiritual but not religious" orientation in its own unique postcolonial-*cum*-postsoviet way. But just how far and how deeply the ambivalence toward the Christian religion will run in the postcolonial milieu will likely remain a relentlessly contested issue in the foreseeable future, especially when the next big political upheaval rolls around.

TOWARD A POST-CHRISTENDOM THEOLOGICAL SENSIBILITY: A POSTSOVIET VARIATION

At this point I can already sense the shrug: Why bother with allegedly irrelevant and "peripheral" fringe histories in an inquiry pertaining to something so seemingly rarified as sacramental theology? What do medieval European crusades have to do with postsoviet religiosity and postcolonial sacramentality? Where, then, does this leave a postcolonial theologian and why do these observations matter beyond the Baltics?

Without idealizing any historical analysis—or its ironies—they highlight the histories of the Baltic crusades as yet another instance of a broader, indeed paradigmatic, theo-ethical challenge that Christendom's colonial escapades continue to pose for theological imagination today. Facing these

53. Ibid., 242.

histories in their ominous multiplicity of cruelty and oppressive longevity is imperative for a postcolonial World Christianity that is committed to moving beyond theological imperialism, albeit now in a relatively de-institutionalized, post-Christendom style.

Diasporic modes of theological inquiry can be particularly fruitful here. A promising place to start is to consciously experiment with a mindset of "minor transnationalism" to "provincialize" and creatively modulate seemingly indisputable epistemological and doctrinal constructs in historiography, cultural studies, and theology.[54] That entails entering into multiple interlogues with other postcolonial margins and imperial undersides to cultivate a willingness to question, deconstruct, and reconstruct the images of God, Christ, salvation, heaven, hell, sacraments, and liturgies—in short, all those theological constructs "that easily lend support to any forms of political and cultural imperialism" since "the militaristic and triumphant character of Christ during the Crusades and Western expansion demonstrates how easily a religious symbol can be coopted for political purposes" that ultimately "justified Western political domination."[55]

In this sense, Eastern European theological lacunae are symptomatic of a much more widespread bewilderment about the decolonization of Christian theological imaginary, including its sacramental discourses, both "from above" and "from below." Disorienting as it may be, there is no pre-colonial sacramental golden age to invoke and mine for the pure gold of insights, precedents, and answers for today's theological needs and ethical pressures. On the other hand, the historical postcolonies "from below," be they in Africa or Eastern Europe, are not necessarily immaculate enclaves of pristine theological "authenticity" and liberating liturgical renewal—nor are the (neo)colonial metropoles "from above!" Neither should be exoticized or idealized.

Both the "highs" and the "lows" of the historical postcolony are genuinely messy and deeply asymmetrical spaces. In these messy spaces the stolid colonial fixtures of theological imagination, ecclesial traditions, and liturgical practices scrape against nascent, hybrid, and rhizomatic efforts to discern and model fresh and non-hegemonic ways of relating to God, other human beings, and the whole non-human creation. Nevertheless, all these paths of discernment for newness are always already colored by their location on the postcolonial spectrum of "from below"/"from above." This crucial asymmetry must not be ignored by those who embark on intentionally post-imperial and counter-hegemonic quests for spiritual renewal.

54. Lionnet and Shih, "Introduction," 5–13.

55. Kwok, *Introducing Asian Feminist Theology*, 91.

The vector toward true decolonizing, toward a true epistemological and ethical *metanoia* of theological imagination and liturgical practices, frequently points in a similar direction regardless of where one starts—closer to the "from below" or the "from above." At the same time, it is also clear that the paths from "below" and "above" will have their own unique, and different, courses precisely because the point of departure is not the same. Each will encounter its own, genuinely different, roadblocks to wrestle with for a long time to come. The final chapters in this study will chart the course of one such possible path, originating in the diasporic *nepantla* land of "in-between" the "from above" North America and the quirky Latvian postcolony "from below." Before that, however, a few additional remarks must be made about theology and theopolitics.

3.2.

On the Postcolonial Theopolitics of Sacramentality

Christian theology suffers from an imperial condition. Shall we start there, with that proposition, but as a theological proposition?[1]

Catherine Keller

The vision of God is a moral act. This optics is an ethics.
The ethical order does not prepare us for the Divinity; it is the very accession to the Divinity.
All the rest is a dream.[2]

Emmanuel Levinas

Postcolonial sacramental theology—however else it might be described—is a "worldly" endeavor. It is "worldly" in the sense that for this mode of Christian theology, matter really matters. Contrary to what some unfortunate preconceptions of sacramental theology might suggest, it is—or at least should be—the most this-worldly of all theological modalities, equally concerned with the movement of God in the life of flesh and blood

1. Keller, *God and Power*, 113.

2. Levinas, *Difficult Freedom*, 275, 102.

as it is with the life of spirit and soul. In the words of Kevin Irwin, "sacramentality is a worldview that invites us to be immersed fully in the here and now, on this good earth, and not to shun matter or avoid the challenges that such earthiness will require of us. . ."[3]

Yet postcolonial sacramental theology is also "worldly" in the Saidian sense, as already mentioned in the Third Prelude: namely, it happens in the world in which beauty, love, justice, and wholesomeness struggle for sheer survival amid structures of hegemonic dominance and inertias of competitive egoism that often prove incapable of "comprehending the universality of our elemental vulnerability to the wrongs we visit upon each other."[4]

Edward Said's notion of "worldliness" denotes a methodological sensibility that all humanly produced texts, concepts, symbols, theories, and imaginaries are "influenced by the historical, political and social circumstances their authors found themselves in."[5] To further unfold and nuance Said's comportment of robust methodological sensuality—in distinction, for example, from a Derridean kind of hypertextual idealism—"worldliness" insists on acknowledging the radically embodied and profoundly contextual nature of all creative human endeavors, including theological imagination, semiotic production, and ritual practices alike.

From a "worldly" perspective, any and all theological reflection cannot but take place precisely in this "worldly" world of tumultuous and ambiguous history. In fact, theological imagination is manipulated, often far more deeply and far more strongly than many dare to admit, by the functional dark sides and even neurotic blindspots within our sociocultural, political, and religious imaginaries.

And yet: the tragic betrayals and blindspots notwithstanding, I am nevertheless arguing in the present study that certain Christian sacramental and liturgical traditions are potent and compelling enough to nurture vital and generous treasures for postcolonial transformations of mindscapes and lifeworlds. These treasures exceed the legacies of their ideological cooptations. Their depths are not exhausted by ethical blasphemies even as these frequently punctuate the history of imperial Christendoms, Western and Eastern alike. No matter how often overpowered and obscured by the manipulations of imperial orthodoxies, these pearls of divine wisdom are yet to be fully retrieved in order to empower the unmasking and subverting of the scripts and conquests of imperial Christendom.

3. Irwin, *The Sacraments*, 210.

4. Gilroy, *Postcolonial Melancholia*, 4.

5. De Jong-Kumru, *Postcolonial Feminist Theology*, 66.

A postcolonial approach in sacramental theology undoubtedly calls for an optics of self-critical honesty. Yet it simultaneously calls for a hermeneutics of bold generosity that is willing to risk a much more complex, nuanced, messy, and where necessary, also a contesting engagement, indeed an intentionally hybrid engagement (remember Bakhtin?) with the Christian sacramental tradition. Such an intentionally hybrid engagement seems far more preferable than an ideological *a priori* dismissal of religion and theology (*pace* Edward Said and many other postcolonial thinkers) as hopelessly reactionary discipline.

HISTORY MATTERS IN SACRAMENTAL MATTERS: QUESTIONING THE CHRISTIAN "EGO CONQUIRO"

The postcolonial historical paradigm—and the theological paradigm, for that matter—does not hide its axiological inflection and its fundamental hermeneutical prism of ethics. Why? Simply because no historical inquiry lives in an axiological vacuum even if it furiously denies such inscriptions as impingements on its aspirational (myth of) zero-point objectivity. Postcolonialism cannot shun the axiological facets of analysis, implicit or explicit as they may be and as loaded as they always already are, when it embarks on the long journey of interrogating the dominant constructions of truth, goodness, and beauty without at the same time abdicating its integrity.

Hence, in the postcolonial context, the summons to scrutinize the Christian past is not just a matter of historical accuracy but precisely a theological, theopolitical, and theoethical exigency. It is a matter of the "ethics of theology"—matter of integrity in theological enterprise. What is the historical, theopolitical, spiritual, and cultural *Wirkungsgeschichte* of colonial and imperial legacies of Christendom in contemporary postcolonies and their spiritual ecology? Tissa Balasuriya has put his finger on the underlying fundamental need to candidly scrutinize imperialistic conceptions of salvation and the sacraments: "The theory of salvation then was such that the Eucharist could be offered in the morning and soldiers could then go to battle to kill the natives and aborigines . . . especially if they refused to be baptized."[6] Obviously, not many Christian theologians would advocate such an understanding of salvation today. At the same time, have the underlying doctrinal perceptions and liturgical images of the redemptive exclusivity of the ecclesial Body of Christ been sufficiently examined in the Occidental metropolitan mainstreams of conventional sacramental theology? Have the existential consequences of sacramental and liturgical

6. Balasuriya, *The Eucharist and Human Liberation*, 36.

concepts and images been sufficiently scrutinized under the penetrating light of what David Ngong aptly described as the "ethics of theology" and what Namsoon Kang called "hypersensitivity to the marginalized" (Part II, Ch. 1)?

Looking back at the Latvian case of Christianization-*cum*-Europeanization, local indigenous religious practices, or even their practices of intertribal violence, cannot and may not be deployed to rationalize, objectivize, and ultimately justify theologically underwritten Christian violence—even if they could be historically proven to have been more vicious than what the Latin Western Christians routinely unleashed onto the non-Christian peoples. They cannot be disregarded or made to appear so rare and so exceptional as to somehow legitimize the ruthlessly effective enmeshment of imperial conquest with sacramental imagination and practices, even if it really was an unconscious perversion, pure and simple, of revelatory truth and Christ's command to "go and make disciples of all nations" (Matt 28:19).

From a postcolonial perspective, imperialistic histories of sacramental performances and the ease with which Christian sacramental imagination colluded, in many forms and in many locations, with the global colonial designs of racism, Eurocentrism, and patriarchy carry far more than just a historical burden that mandates a politically correct footnote in church history textbooks. As far as the ethics of theology is concerned, these histories of sacramental abuse and misuse ought to condition the comportment of watchful theological accountability precisely in terms of how sacramentality and sacraments are defined, how they are endowed with ecclesiastical, doctrinal, and ritual authority and; ultimately, how they are performed in today's increasingly multipolar and fragmented planetary community.

Pretending that these genealogies of aggression, exclusion, and coercion are no longer relevant for sacramental discourse today amounts to not just a self-indulgent oblivion but to an ideological mockery akin to claiming that World War I was a genuine effort "to end all wars." Conversion by imposition of hegemonic force, be it an end in itself or merely a convenient religious auxiliary for political and economic imperialism, is the most grievous spiritual and theological failure of Christianity in its two thousand year history. Sarah Travis is right to remind Christian theologians that,

> while some of us might argue vehemently that Jesus Christ sought to challenge and overturn the prevailing empires, history has taught us that the Christian church has been implicated in modern colonialism/imperialism by active choice, passive collusion, or pure accident. Theologians committed to a postcolonial perspective are anxious to overcome reluctance on part of the

> church and the field of theology to acknowledge the profound relation between Christianity and empire.[7]

The short excursus on Latvian church history simply serves as a reminder that the most profound and ominous nemesis of the Christian vision of God and reality is nothing other than itself. This nemesis is Christianity's own idolatrous, yet repressed and disavowed, *eqo conquiro*.[8] Nelson Maldonado-Torres has elaborated on Enrique Dussel's notion of the colonialist *alter ego*, or the shadow of the Cartesian *ego cogito*, i.e., the will to power—the phenomenology of "I conquer." Maldonado-Torres shows how *ego conquiro* emerged during participation in colonial conquest under God—and for God. Gradually it metamorphosed into a "warring subjectivity when it assumes the role of God"[9] and a quasi-divine feeling of superiority and chosenness. As modernity marched on, *ego conquiro* gradually came to exhibit a new sense of independence and even "a peculiar ambiguity toward God that comes from recognizing him as Lord but at the same time knowing that new earthly lordship does not ultimately rely on His authority."[10] Internal Western confessional differences notwithstanding, if one looks from the dark undersides of colonial Euromodernity, then the hegemonic status of theology was, in Walter Mignolo's critical assessment, the "common ground on which Catholics and Protestants played out their differences. The Theo-logical politics of knowledge and understanding was, then, the platform for the control of knowledge and subjectivity"[11] across various colonized locations and cultures.

Of course, modernity was also the era of transition from colonial/imperial theopolitics of knowledge, being, and authority to a more secularized, yet no less colonial/imperial egopolitics of knowledge, being, and authority. The colonial matrix of power, knowledge, and being suffered no substantial loss of potency and reach. This is why conventionally postmodern theological critiques of secularism, and especially the modern sacramental disenchantment, ought to take note of Walter Mignolo and Madina Tlostanova's

7. Travis, *Decolonizing Preaching*, 77.

8. Maldonado-Torres, *Against War*, 213.

9. Ibid., 213–15.

10. Ibid., 215.

11. Mignolo, "Delinking," 459–60. He adds that, the "very historical foundation of the modern/colonial world in America (and I am using foundation here with careful awareness and not endorsing fundamentalisms), is characterized by the 'pulling out (extirpation) or removal of 'idolatry' which tells the story of the genocidal and epistemic violence of theology (e.g., 'extirpation' of knowledges and beliefs among the indigenous population that Spanish missionaries believed, or at least said, were the work of the Devil)," 462.

helpful reminder to those of us in theological disciplines of some inconvenient continuities:

> Both Christian theology and secular philosophy and science are grounded in the Rationality of Ego rather than in the Wisdom of God. By so doing, the [modern Occidental] zero point epistemology posited itself not just as the right way of knowing but as the only way. Whatever did not fit the demands of theological and egological principles was relegated to the world of barbarians, the not quite yet or those who maybe, some day will. Both, Christian theology and secular philosophy and Western science shaped Western imperial expansion throughout the last five centuries.[12]

Theologically speaking, the ever present nemesis that postcolonial theology must wrestle with is Christianity's unredeemed hegemonic fixation to dominate and to universalize in an imperialistic and monological way—the very opposite of the kenotic and relational Holy Mystery of triune Love that Christians are called to proclaim as the true evangel, the true "good news," of differences playing off one another in perichoretic conviviality. This nemesis, the unconverted *ego conquiro*, was the spiritual progenitor of the Doctrine of Discovery. It played out with genocidal consequences not only in America, Africa, and Asia, but also in Europe. It underwrote a whole corpus of sensibilities, attitudes, civilizations, and legislative traditions that have been incarnating not so much Christ, I submit, but rather the colonial logic of certain Christians.

In this context, it behooves us to remember, for example, how near and dear to Christian liturgical and sacramental theology is the understanding of the church as one of the extensions/prolongations of no less than the Word/Wisdom incarnate itself in historical time and space—the sacramental image of the church as the Body of Christ. Colonial histories and postcolonial legacies mandate an extreme caution precisely at this, nowadays very popular, interface between Christology, ecclesiology, and sacramental imagination. From a postcolonial perspective, ironically, it is precisely the church that is the sinful "cross on which Christ is crucified" again and again as William Cavanaugh pointed out while pondering over Romano Guardini's poignant observations that "the imperfections of the Church are the Cross of Christ."[13]

A case in point: any theological conceptualizations that emphasize, for example, the idea of the Church as the basic or foundational sacrament

12. Tlostanova and Mignolo, *Learning to Unlearn*, 64.

13. Cavanaugh, *Migrations of the Holy*, 163.

(*Grundsakrament* in the Rahnerian parlance) must acknowledge and face the profoundly ambivalent historical connotations of Christ's "presence" as embodied in and by the Church that has been deeply steeped in cultural and religious imperialism and even in genocidal violence. And, as such, this ambivalence remains a (often conventionally overlooked) challenge for all and any ecclesio-centric sacramental imaginaries particularly in the post-modern Western theology. This is particularly true for those approaches which assign a sacramental "rank" of grounding primacy or foundationality to the Christian Church, or even just one particular historical expression of Christianity such as Roman Catholicism.[14]

That being said, I share Tissa Balasuriya's position that the imperialistic perversions of sacramental grace in the colonial history of Christianity do not exhaust its redemptive thrust and healing potential. It is clear that no matter how often Christians loved to invoke the adage of being "in the world but not of the world," their only too solid a footing "in the world" and "in" its violent, prideful, and greedy ways has often remained a secret only for themselves. This is why I share Balasuriya's hope while simultaneously highlighting the haunting historical ambiguity and the precariousness of theological enterprise. Beyond doubt, both colonial histories and postcolonial legacies strongly caution that the well-heeded assumptions that Christian sacraments and liturgies can self-reform and self-correct were and still are significantly overestimated. And yet this study proceeds with a vigorous conviction that a sacramental "counter-imperial ecology of love"[15] nonetheless remains possible. Otherwise, it seems to me, it would be incongruous to remain a practicing Christian let alone to continue as a theologian and member of Lutheran clergy.

SACRAMENTS AND POSTCOLONIAL THEOPOLITICS

While it is pivotal for postcolonial sacramental thought to heed the critical and ethical exigencies of Saidian "worldliness," it is equally important to distinguish this kind of "worldly" comportment from another kind of "worldliness." The colonial histories of Christianization from the Baltics to the Caribbean bear an uncomfortable witness to what Aloysius Pieris identifies as the "imperialistic worldliness" of organized political Christianity whereby "sacraments gradually became the remote-control apparatus of a clerical caste (that is, of ministers who 'put on' Christ's priesthood without

14. A useful critical analysis, from a Western perspective, of this concept is offered by Osborne, *Christian Sacraments in a Postmodern World*, 133–36.

15. Keller, *God and Power*, 116.

sharing in his victimhood). . ."[16] If functionally magisterial theologians, wherever they may come from, learn nothing else from the colonial histories of Christianity, then at least the prudent insights which are borne out of centuries of useless suffering should set the tone for the criteria of theological faithfulness and integrity in contemporary sacramental and liturgical theology.

To come to grips with the intricacies of the unholy alliance between the symbolic universe of Christian doctrine and spirituality on the one hand, and political and cultural imperialism on the other, remains a paramount task for postcolonial critiques. And it is not a sole province of church history or, more narrowly, missionary history alone! As important as these specialized areas of study are, it is even more decisive in the present milieu of World Christianity to engage the doctrinal traditions in their full un-whitewashed stretch through the lenses of postcoloniality in systematic theology as well as in liturgical and sacramental studies. A vibrant and life-giving World Christianity—postcolonial, post-Western, and post-Christendom—is possible, accountable, and sustainable only on the foundation of a nuanced and unflinching *anamnesis* of its own incarnational roots in the life, death, resurrection, and ascension of Christ as well as the churches' historical blasphemies of the very Gospel they were summoned to embody for the life of the whole creation. In a universe understood to live and move under the redemptive scope of incarnation (*ex convenientia incarnationis*, as Thomas Aquinas would perhaps say), both history and religion have always belonged, for good and for ill, in the hybrid public spheres of theopolitics and geopolitics even if it was always somehow more profitable to ignore it.

Doctrines, spirituality, and especially sacramental liturgies often seem—and sometimes are purposefully mystified to appear—so metaphysically remote, so ritually apolitical, so ethically ahistorical, and so generally uncontaminated by the mundane skirmishes of the unceasing cultural and political turf wars and psychological conditioning of those who invent and authorize these staple articulations of Christianity. Yet these appearances are at best naïve illusions and at worst aestheticizing fabrications. To resist the lure of such smoke-and-mirrors fetishiziation of theological concepts, practices, and historical precedents, post-Holocaust and postcolonial historical awareness requires a mindful grasp that sacramental theologies and practices are part and parcel of the Christian symbolic universe of imagination, relation, and action. As such sacramental imagination and performances are not exempt from crusading and colonizing metastases and continue to "suffer from an imperial condition."[17]

16. Pieris, *An Asian Theology of Liberation*, 7.

17. Keller, *God and Power*, 113.

Precisely in this context, postcolonial engagements with sacramental discourses cannot do otherwise than insist on what Hans Frei (of all theologians!) has summarized so concisely: namely, "there is no such thing as a Christian theology which is not together with other things also a political theology."[18] Or, as Catherine Keller puts it with even more precision, "theology always means—whatever else it means—theopolitics."[19] What we have to work with today is an internally diverse and non-linear sacramental imaginary that manifests itself through multiple strands of theological imagination and liturgical practice and that harbors an exceptional liberative and transformative potential.

To reiterate: Christian sacramental and liturgical theology is embedded in a faith tradition that has vigorously accommodated the carnage of crusades, "discoveries," and colonial conquests. In the most recent times, it is also a tradition which has, oftentimes, been remarkably accommodating toward the postmodern neocolonialism of predatory globalization. This historical hangover cannot be undone by reactionary mystification of sacramentality or simply written off in order to move on and live happily ever after in the presumed innocence of ignorance. Rather, it must be judiciously discerned again and again while contemporary Christians keep walking the path of a genuine spiritual, cultural, imaginative, ethico-political, and epistemological *metanoia*. Postcolonial efforts, and indeed all worthwhile efforts in Christian sacramental theology will inescapably and urgently need to discern how to constructively balance meaningful reverence for the "pearls of great value" in the Christian tradition without slipping into a defensive fetishization of this tradition. John Thatamanil captures the task at hand remarkably accurately and is therefore worth quoting at length:

> Human beings are historical creatures, creatures of context and culture . . . If knowledge of ultimate reality or the real as such is to be had, it will be had only by means of thick instrumentalities made possible by religious traditions. Even traditions that hold to the possibility of unmediated encounter with ultimate reality understand themselves to be custodians of just those practices that make such encounter possible. Hence, reverence for tradition is indispensable to religious life. But such reverence need not amount to fetishization. Religious traditions must be understood as complex sign systems and networks of practices that enable persons to rightly engage the relevant features of ultimate reality. They are not themselves that ultimate reality and so are unworthy of idolatrous attachment. They are means to an end

18. Cited in Higton, "A Carefully Circumscribed Progressive Politics," 55.

19. Keller, *God and Power*, 135.

> and not that end itself. Making that truth plain to adherents is a central task for theologians and religious teachers if adherents are to participate in the public square as articulate and passionate but also generous, self-critical, and humble advocates of the traditions to which they belong.[20]

For a fruitful theological imagination to body forth, a theologian's task is always a Janus-faced endeavor within the Christian tradition. On the one hand, it is vital for the sake of theological integrity and unpretentious accountability that the sapiential treasure troves of tradition are mined. On the other hand, its painful legacies must also be acknowledged and mended. And that can be accomplished by nothing less than a whole-hearted commitment to humble and courageous vigilance to probe the deviations of all those "thick instrumentalities" of messy evolutionary history to learn from the past in order to guard against the sneaky tendencies of self-serving theological inertias to reoffend.

NAVIGATING THE MINEFIELDS OF THE PAST IN THE PRESENT

Looking back at the colonial history of Christianity in the Baltics—similarly to, say, large swaths of South America or Africa—it is often very tricky to distinguish between the situations where sacramental liturgies were misused to legitimate conquest and cultural imperialism through a blatant perversion of their symbolic agency vis-à-vis the situations where their theological semiotics in fact fueled the collective Christian *ego conquiro* under the guise of allegedly divine "mission."[21] Was the unholy synergy of Christ, conquest, and commerce indeed an unambiguous perversion of Christianity? Was it indeed a genuinely unwitting repetition of the current political and cultural conventions—and thus unavoidable? Was it just an "organic" consequence of post-Constantinian theopolitics springing forth from the doctrine that there is no salvation outside the church (i.e., a church fitting the respective standards of established imperial orthodoxy)?

Or was there something even subtler, much messier, and more ominous at play to facilitate such efficient fusions of the Good News and the imperial power structures? Should we probe further into the particular slant of monotheistic exclusivism and its distinctive synthesis with Christian revelation which, according to Catherine Keller, is itself a "syncretism of a

20. Thatamanil, "How Not to Be a Religion," 64.

21. Maldonado-Torres, *Against War*, 213–15.

colonized Judaism with a colonizing Hellenism" that "absorbed the imperial metaphysics?"[22] These questions, precisely as *theological* and *not merely historical* questions, are still in their critical puberty in Occidental as well as Eastern Orthodox Christianity.

This line of questioning calls for contemporary sacramental-liturgical theology to engage in judicious explorations of what Leonardo Boff has described as the "diabolic movement" of sacramentality with more urgency. Viewing the perversions and distortions of sacramental practices from a liberationist perspective, Boff calls attention to the distortions of sacraments into "mere sacramentalism," something akin to what Alexander Schmemann always lamented as liturgical nominalism. Seduced under this sort of diabolic thrust, sacramental liturgies coalesce into a sheer ideology of subjugation. Those who preside over such liturgies live with an illusion of faithfulness while in reality "their concrete lives embody values that are opposed to the faith: for example, the exploitation of human beings and the greedy quest for more and more wealth."[23]

Moreover, postcolonial theology cannot do otherwise than take Paul Tillich's warning regarding the "demonization" of sacraments with utmost seriousness. As all religious signs and symbols, sacraments are susceptible to idolatry: "In all sacramental activities of religion, in all holy objects, holy books, holy doctrines, holy rites, you find this danger which we will call 'demonization.' They become demonic at the moment in which they become elevated to the unconditional and ultimate character of the Holy itself."[24]

Whatever else they are, sacraments are signs, Boff carefully reminds us. And as such they "invariably share the ambiguity of any and every sign" and as such "they can be misused, abused, and turned into signs of condemnation because they have been entrusted to human beings."[25] When—and not if—perverted, liturgies and sacraments become toxic "countersigns"[26] that perpetuate wounding lies about both humanity and divinity. The task

22. Keller, *God and Power*, 114.

23. Boff, *Sacraments of Life*, 85.

24. Tillich, "The Nature of Religious Language," 50–51. Idolatry, in this context, is the "absolutizing of symbols of the Holy, and making them identical with the Holy itself," 50.

25. Ibid., 86–87.

26. In addition to Boff's use of "countersign," here I am also invoking George Lindbeck's term that he uses to describe the church—often viewed as a sacrament of salvation if not always necessarily the primary, the basic, or *Grundsakrament*—when it has been derailed from its genuine vocation of being the sign of redemption. In such cases, Lindbeck argues, "the church becomes not a sign but a countersign, a contributor to that human confusion which is the opposite of God's design," see, *The Church in a Postliberal Age*, 159.

of critical exploration is to expose the workings of imperial and patriarchal metaphysics in sacramental imagination and liturgical practices—regardless of wherever such workings present, in "developed" first world "metropoles," in the "developing" "peripheries" of the two-thirds world, in the "West," in the "Rest," or "in between" all of the above.

SACRAMENTAL LITURGIES: SOME EMERGING POSTCOLONIAL INKLINGS

The troubling of imperial metaphysics is precisely what some recent interventions, some explicitly and some rather implicitly postcolonial, have started to initiate in sacramental and liturgical discourse. The work of Michael Jagessar and Stephen Burns in liturgical theology charts several hitherto unexplored constructive and transcultural avenues for Christian liturgical practice from a sustained postcolonial perspective.[27] The initial naming of these postcolonial avenues invites further elaborations by liturgical and sacramental theologians.[28] Alas, scarce attention has been so far given to the questions of sacraments and sacramentality on the level of doctrine and theological methodology in order to build a stimulating momentum and contribute to the monumental task of re-envisioning a genuinely post-Christendom World Christianity.

At the same time, a number of theological perspectives from Africa, South America, Asia and their diasporas percolate with diverse, often implicit yet very real, very vibrant, and sometimes very controversial (just recall that horrifying ghost of "syncretism" roaming the "pure" Occidental edifices of doctrinal orthodoxies!) sacramental threads of theological imagination—let alone on the level of actual spiritual practices. These threads crisscross the whole gamut of theological disciplines, from biblical scholarship and systematic theology to pastoral theology and worship. Thus, recently Agbonkhianmeghe Orobator, S.J. has mischievously, yet with brilliant acuity wondered about the true scope and institutionally camouflaged

27. Jagessar and Burns, *Christian Worship: Postcolonial Perspectives*.

28. The recent interfaith essay collection edited by Claudio Carvalhaes, *Only One is Holy* (Palgrave, 2015) strives to ameliorate the dearth of explicitly postcolonial inquiry in this area. In North America, the North American Academy of Liturgy (NAAL) Critical Theories and Liturgical Seminar gathers established and emerging scholars from across the world even though the majority of participants are located in North America. For the last few years the discussions and presentations have consistently included postcolonial perspectives.

reasons for the Occidental sacramental crisis: "I am tempted to ask: crisis? What crisis?"[29]

JOINING HANDS WITH THE FELLOW TRAVELERS ON THE ROAD TO TRANSFORMATIVE JUSTICE

At the intersection of these critical trajectories, emerging postcolonial sacramental discourse does not need to travel entirely alone. It can join hands not only with various global strands of liberation theology but also with the feminist liturgical and sacramental explorations.

Explicit conversations about sacraments have so far played a relatively minor role—or have been strategically evaded altogether—in many whitefeminist and womanist theologies and their visions of liberation and transformation. Without question, there are many contextual, disciplinary, and linguistic reasons within and outside church communities that have contributed to the widespread ambivlance about sacraments among women theologians. Susan Roll captures the mood by observing that even in more recent times "sacraments are not high on the list of well-cultivated fields of feminist theological investigation."[30] One obvious reason is that until the relatively recent practice of ordaining women in many Western Protestant denominations, most of the time "sacraments were 'done to' women, never 'done by' women."[31] This continues to be the case in several dominant Christian denominations across the world.

Whitefeminist sacramental theologians recognize that this is a worrisome situation, albeit an unsurprising one, for those who are familiar with church history.[32] Although things are starting to shift, feminist sacramental theologies are still, ironically, often a "misnomer" as Susan Ross noted some years ago.[33] There is more than one reason as to why this state of affairs goes on. In the Roman Catholic context, in spite of its overt sacramental predilections, it is clearly related to the fact that "sacramental and liturgical theology's support for, or, at best, lack of concern about, women's official exclusion and invisibility, many women have not found in these disciplines the potential for inclusion, much less transformation."[34]

29. Orobator, "A Global Sign of Outward Grace," 15.

30. Roll, "Sacraments as Energy," 259.

31. Ibid., 260.

32. Teresa Berger provides an excellent recent overview of the field in her "Spying in the Promised Land," 28–41.

33. Ross, *Extravagant Affections*, 27.

34. Ibid.

A similar challenge persists for those women and men who live and worship on the margins of normative heterosexuality, in Roman Catholic, Protestant, Eastern Orthodox, and Pentecostal contexts, despite the emerging disposition of hospitality toward people who manifest sexual otherness amidst their communities of faith—at least in some communities in the Euro-Atlantic spiritual milieu. Without doubt, normative heterosexuality is a far more contested issue than it is in the Euro-Atlantic West throughout virtually all locations that variously inhabit the global postcolony "from below"—from Africa to Eastern Europe to Pakistan.

Protestant confessional contexts carry their own peculiar mix of tensions. As Elizabeth Stuart argues, Western whitefeminism has woefully conceded sacramental modes of theology in a move that repeats the oversights and weaknesses of modern liberal Protestantism. Stuart believes that "European and North American Christian feminist theology has largely conceded the mystery, the invisible, the sacramental to patriarchy when there was absolutely no need for it to do so and indeed good theological and political reasons exist to resist such a concession."[35] Instead, Stuart argues, it is worth reclaiming sacramentality from the historical stranglehold of patriarchy since "the liturgy, particularly the Eucharist, is a space beyond patriarchy although patriarchy has attempted to colonise it and feminism has largely retreated before it."[36] The transformative potential of sacramentality is simply too fecund of salvific possibilities to be ignored, all ironies notwithstanding, as a field of spiritual practice and theological imagination:

> The mistake of feminist theology has been to concede to men and in particular those men who consciously invest in the most patriarchal mis-constructions of Christianity, the liturgical space because it is in that space in which the divine and the human co-operate in the work of redemption, the space of the magical, the space in which gender along with the rest of the material world is taken into the divine, transfigured and poured back out to warm and nurture the world with the first light of dawn.[37]

Experiences of sacramental marginalization and exclusion are not something that only whitefeminists are concerned about. Women liberation theologians in South America, diasporic *mujerista* theologians in North America and African and Asian theologians raise similar questions even if they don't explicitly work out of a whitefeminist or even postcolonial

35. Stuart, "Exploding Mystery," 228.

36. Ibid., 235.

37. Ibid., 233.

perspective. After all, gender injustice remains injustice regardless of whether it is a Western colonial import, an indigenous socio-spiritual convention, or a hybrid product of inculturated patriarchal "African-religio-culture."[38]

The broadly defined field of feminist critique has inspired the important cluster of questions concerning whether the modern Occidental notion of sacraments might have already become too dualistic. This is particularly important if "sacraments" are understood to be fleeting, narrowly defined, hyper-ritualized, and ecclesially policed incursions of the sacred divine reality into the otherwise vast ocean of profane worldliness. Can such sacramental signs, and even notions of such signs, reeking of competitive dualism, still play a genuinely transformative role when it comes to race, culture, ethnicity, other religions, nature, and grace?[39] If the fundamental ontological divide between the sacred and the profane is made overly rigid, as quite a few conventional (modern and postmodern) sacramental imaginaries continue to presuppose, then the "question of who or what is qualified to mediate 'officially' turns quickly into one of power and control" while completely ignoring the fact that God is free to act outside the institutionalized system of ecclesial sacramental rites.[40] No wonder, then, that liberation, as well as feminist theologies, warn that the "doctrinal category 'sacrament' as it is presently constructed is actually incompatible with the doctrinal desire that it serve an ethic of justice."[41]

POSTCOLONIAL RIDDLE: WHOSE SACRAMENTALITY? WHOSE DEFINITIONS?

Taking the globalized realities of World Christianity seriously, it behooves nascent postcolonial sensibilities in sacramental imagination to carefully discern the constructive ways of moving forward by appraising the unhealthy inadequacies and unrealized potential of genuinely transformational and planetary wisdom. Such wisdom is certainly to be found in the major Occidental sacramental traditions in Christianity. At the same time, this discernment entails a responsibility to highlight the sort of critical

38. Mutambara, "African Women Theologies Critique Inculturation," 173–91. Mutambara provides a helpful overview of the African women's reflection on the issues of inculturation, colonization, and patriarchal structures.

39. Ross has raised alarm about this underlying difficulty for feminist, and frankly, any type of incarnational sacramental theology in her trailblazing *Extravagant Affections*, 39–40; 54–57.

40. Ibid., 261.

41. Garrigan, *Beyond Ritual*, 26.

assessment of Occidental epistemological and ontological presuppositions which originate from the undersides of colonial modernity. Why? Because these presuppositions as a rule continue to serve as the presumptive philosophical and theological foundations for the doctrinally (in some denominational cases, even canonically and magisterially) binding expressions of sacramentality in general as well as various sacramental rites in particular. But here's the important wrinkle: they continue to be binding not just for Christians in the West, but all over the globe wherever the Occidental theological traditions have been exported or have migrated to, and by now taken hybridized root—and today that means almost everywhere on the planet.

Small wonder, then, that tensions have been duly noticed in the historical postcolonies "from below" between conventional Occidental sacramental ontologies of colonial modernity vis-à-vis the exponentially more relational and wholistic imaginaries about the nature of reality in sociocultural contexts such as Africa and Asia. African lifeworlds have viscerally resisted imposed/imported Western dualism while affirming and living with the inseparability of the "sacred" and "secular" planes of the universe. Musa Dube points out that "for most Africans the presence of the Divine is obvious" and "therefore the sacred vis-à-vis the secular realm does not exist."[42] That puts the Occidental sacramental crisis mindset into a much more complex perspective, even though it does not automatically solve the lingering conundrums of colonial Christianity and its cultural imperialism. Even in light of sacramentally-friendly Western theological postmodernity, African theologians assert the ongoing need to "transcend Western cultural hegemony" including its "restricted versions of reality" amidst the ever-convoluted process of "inculturation."[43]

Sacramental discourses are part and parcel of Western cultural hegemony—and of its internalized versions of mimicry elsewhere in the world. Such a state of affairs is increasingly in question. For instance, Kekong Bisong argues, "sacramentology is not Western scholarly prerogative" and thus "must not necessarily be dependent on the hegemony of Western metaphysical constraints."[44] Instead of intellectualized compliance to imported orthodoxies and the corrupt aloofness of local postcolonial elites toward the deep suffering in Africa, the sacramental thrust for redemptive renewal manifests in a theopolitical and theo-ethical "quest for wholeness."[45]

42. Dube, "Postcolonial Feminist Perspectives on African Religions," 127.

43. Bisong, "A Postmodern Response to Sacramental Presence," 47.

44. Ibid., 62–63.

45. Ngong, "Christianity in Africa," 208–19.

This quest absolutely does not require a return to some romanticized indigenous nativism in the Two-Thirds world—as if that would be even possible—or a naïve and escapist exoticization of such nativist fabrications in the Euro-Atlantic West to alleviate its own sacramental anguish. What is relevant and useful, in a constructive sense, to all Christian theological endeavors is rather the recognition that the prolific cultural and religious diversity in Africa can assist in generating an imaginary in which sacramental sensibilities permeate a robustly embodied spirituality. And this spirituality is ultimately and vitally concerned about life as a whole since the Divine is seen to inclusively interpenetrate everything from cosmology to everyday life events.[46]

Transformative sacramental imaginaries also resonate with the search for a multidimensional and open wholeness in the tremendously diverse religious and cultural landscape of Asia. The Indian theologian Jacob Parappally calls for a sacramental imagination that is not constrained by either excessive theocentrism or excessive anthropocentrism but rather for a post-Hellenistic affirmation of "an integral and liberating understanding of this world" wherein "creation is not subordinated to the theme of redemption" nor subjected to "exclusivistic interpretations about the sacramentality of Christ."[47] Instead of these dualistic imaginaries, cosmotheandric sacramentality opens up a path toward genuinely relational wholeness on cosmological and intersubjective levels. The Christ-event—the "perfect sacrament"—constitutes a uniquely sacramental revelation that the whole creation is "the radical interrelationship between God, humans and the world."[48]

Another Indian theologian, the Jesuit Francis D'Sa, underscores the liberative nature of authentic sacramentality as rooted in the mystery of wholeness, not the mastery of absolute instrumentalization. For D'Sa, a genuine discovery of sacramentality is the discovery of the Divine through "a holistic . . . search for wholeness" which is nothing other than "to discern and make known the operative presence of the divine mystery in our times."[49] From this perspective, sacramentality is not limited to ardent resurgence of rituals, religious fundamentalism, or emotionalism. Rather, D'Sa argues, a new way of being human is currently being birthed; a new "sacra-mentality" is emerging through the "struggle for wholeness [that] ultimately derives

46. Louw, "Sacramental Presence within and African Context," 202–6.

47. Parappally, "The World, God's Primary Sacrament," 88, 92–93.

48. Ibid., 95. He uses the term "cosmotheandric," coined by Raimon Panikkar, S.J., to describe a radically and essentially interpenetrating and interdependent structure of God-world relationship.

49. D'Sa, "The World as Sacrament," 37.

from the divine alone."[50] Hence to rediscover sacramentality is to rediscover the Divine as well as the world and the human being in the flux of ongoing revelatory transformation:

> Wholeness, harmony, integration, justice, etc. are not just new names for the divine; they are new revelations of the divine. Gradually but surely these will replace the reified, ossified and fundamentalist religious traditions and institutions of human history. As the process gathers momentum they too will slowly start generating their own beliefs and rituals and symbols. But if they allow themselves to be reified and instrumentalized they too will be discredited.[51]

These visions of passionately wholistic, indeed advaitic (nondual), retrievals of sacramentality are bold and far-reaching. I will engage them in a more detailed way in the upcoming chapters. Here suffice it to note that the creative potential of reclaiming trans-Occidental visions of the intrinsic and constitutive relationality of cosmology, ontology, and epistemology as well as their growing emphasis on justice generates a tremendously exciting momentum for Christian theology and spiritual practice. The quest for sacramental wholeness resonates with a common thirst and shared poignancy in both the "from below" and "from above" locations of the global postcolony—arguably in a way that nothing else currently does considering political, economic, and cultural differences. It resonates across chasms of suffering and disillusionment that the colonial logic of dualism and ongoing imperial liturgies of political dominance, economic exploitation, and cultural hegemony have branded into our postcolonial soulscapes, bodyscapes, powerscapes, and mindscapes—albeit with variable power differentials—from Asia and Africa to Euro-Atlantic postmodernity.[52] Drawing these sacramental threads into a common conversation bears the potential to modulate and hybridize the imperialistic unilateriality of Christian imaginary far beyond the paternalistic inculturation models of the Occidental habitus.

50. Ibid., 36–37.

51. Ibid., 37.

52. One of the leading voices in postmodern sacramental theology, Kenan Osborne, recently called for Euro-American sacramental theology to sit, as it were, at the feet of the Asian imaginary of radical interrelationality such as is offered by the relational equilibrium of *yin* and *yang* so that it can be delivered of its insular scruples about juridical validity and dualistic fixations on form/matter dichotomies. See "Euro-American Sacramental Theology—It's Need for Asian Help."

POSTCOLONIAL SACRAMENTS: JUSTICE SACRAMENTALIZED

Postcolonial sacramental inquiry cannot proceed otherwise than insisting—with a Levinasian perseverance—that our conceptions of sacramentality always already represent a certain *theopolitics* and nothing less significant than a *theoethical* vision of God and all things in a *theoethical* relation to this God. Sacramental images, symbolic universes, and ritual practices do not belong in the adiaphora compartment of inconsequential "arts and crafts." Hence, today perhaps more than ever, it pays to challenge the modern Western stereotype that the lifeworld of sacraments and liturgies is a mostly benign, sometimes entertainingly exotic, yet ultimately obsolete side-show, only fitting for the fanciful exploits of niche theological lightweights. Heavyweight, serious theology that really matters, this perception suggests, happens in systematic and fundamental theology, ethics, or biblical disciplines. Despite the resilience of this misleading modern cliché in increasingly unchurched Western societies, it is imperative to remember that sacramento-liturgical theology represents, mediates, and indoctrinates an effective powerscape, for good and for ill. It is far from being a sort of ornamental backdrop of theological aesthetics behind the center stage action of the presumed heavyweights of scripture, church history, systematic theology, or ethics.

In other words, what happens—or does not happen—in the sacramento-liturgical lifeworlds of Christian communities and their theological imaginaries matters in lived experience of faith andalso in the common public sphere when individual Christians live out their faith. Whatever pathologies of power afflict Christian sacramental imagination and practice sooner or later end up afflicting the human spirit and flesh in a way that warps the lives and souls of individuals and whole societies. Indeed, in times past and present, not just concepts and doctrines but real human lives have been not only formed and transformed, but also ferociously malformed by the power of sacramental imagination and liturgical rites.

Today, many lament (and "vote" with their feet and wallets) that for them the supposedly salvific terrain of sacramentality and its ecclesial manifestations have turned out to be minefields of profound longing, but also pain, injustice, trauma, and alienation. Theological maturity is needed in order to recognize that, as James White summarizes, "just as they can witness to and reinforce the full human worth of all, so unquestionably the sacraments frequently are used to deny that same human worth to many."[53]

53. White, *Sacraments as God's Self Giving*, 119. White dedicates Ch. 5 to an analysis of the interplay of sacramental justice and injustice. His overview is one of the most

The wretched outcome, attested only too graphically by Christendom's colonial histories of chauvinistic religious supremacy, racism, and patriarchy, is that sacraments have been vehicles of precisely such self-righteous denials of justice and dignity. Indeed, it is still the case that, as Siobhan Garrigan argues, "most sacramental theology is written from a white, middle class, North Atlantic perspective" and this socio-cultural location often remains invisible to proliferate a "tendency to be oblivious to a sacrament's ability to exclude, alienate and oppress."[54] Postcolonial retrievals cannot ignore such historical limitations, such lingering memories, and such still festering wounds. When it comes to honoring and mending the ongoing wounds, not only economic, gender, and sexual justice come to the fore but also ecojustice—an escalating concern on a truly foundational planetary scale.

It is a relief to emphasize that postcolonial sacramental explorations do not have to travel alone but seek further opportunities to interlogue with Western postmodern sacramental inquiries. As Garrigan observes, "the relationship between sacrament and ethics . . .can be seen as the second most significant development in contemporary [Western] sacramental theology, after the 'turn to language.'"[55] Again, despite the (ironically disembodied) turn to linguistic idealism that Garrigan accurately flags as the tenor of postmodern Occidental sacramentology, the postmodern turn to ethics is a much more embodied, relational, and historically consequential avenue—and hence more conductive for the holistically oriented postcolonial purposes of psychospiritual, cultural, and political empowerment.

It is at this juncture that there emerges a methodological consubstantiality between Western postmodern, whitefeminist, womanist, *mujerista*, Latina feminist, *minjung*, liberation, ecological and postcolonial comportments in sacramental theology. Namely, as Kekong Bisong and Mathai Kadavil summarize, "in postmodernity ethics rather than doctrine is central to the task of sacramental presence; consequently doctrine emerges from ethics rather than ethics from doctrine" with the dangerous (in the Metzian sense) effects that sources of such theological imagination will "come not from the top and center but from the bottom and edges."[56]

To conclude: the perils of the colonial past and the predicaments of the postmodern neocolonial present and their sneaky neoimperial imaginaries

judicious, systematic, comprehensive, and clearheaded assessments of the injustice aspects of sacramental practice apart from feminist liturgical critiques.

54. Garrigan, *Beyond Ritual*, 26.

55. Ibid., 22.

56. Bisong and Kadavil, "Introduction," 9–10.

require patience to sort through in the seemingly endless ambivalence of spiritual postcolony. Crucially, it requires us to sort through the track record of how the perceptions of sacramentality and sacramental rites have functioned and are still functioning today. And they function indeed: the definitions of sacraments and their purposes "function" similarly to how, in the classic formulation of Elizabeth Johnson, the symbol of God "functions." Neither the images of God nor the conceptions of sacraments are "abstract in content [or] neutral in [their] effect."[57] All theological constructs "function" with real consequences not just in the life of an individual mind, soul, and spirit but also in embodied social and power relations as well as in ongoing cultural negotiations with otherness and newness.

It requires stamina to acknowledge and honor the historical and spiritual gravity of the mutilated sacramental tradition in Christianity, and yet keep looking for the melodies and ecologies of non-hegemonic love. Postcolonial Christian theology cannot simply wash off the *poétique forcée* of its imperial and colonial baptismal (dis)graces like my ancestors attempted to do in the river Daugava during the medieval Northern crusades. Unsettling, unglamorous, and even painful as it may be, such comportment of patience, stamina, and courageous hope makes the postcolonial sacramental *ressourcement* viable, meaningful, and life-giving. For ultimately, sacraments are truly sacramental only if and when they are as Walter Burghardt puts it, the events of "justice sacramentalized."[58]

57. Johnson, *She Who Is*, 4.

58. Burghardt, *Justice*, 107.

3.3.

Sacraments and Postcolonial Planetarity

Pursuing a Nascent Resonance

Our original sin, so it seems, lies in our prideful refusal to receive the world as gift of reconciliation, humbly to regard the world as a sacrament of communion. At a time when we have polluted the air that we breathe and the water that we drink, we are called to restore within ourselves the sense of awe and delight, to respond to matter as to a mystery of ever-increasing connections.[1]

John Cryssavgis

When one defines nonhuman nature as 'the other' that has been colonized by the human species in the anthropocentric worldview, it becomes clear that decolonization of nature is necessary in our era. As Gayatri Spivak suggests, today's subaltern must be rethought.[2]

Jea Sophia Oh

It is time that we took sacraments, signs that give grace, out of the churches and into the open air and public spaces.[3]

David Toolan, S.J.

1. Chryssavgis, *Light Through Darkness*, 112.
2. Oh, *A Postcolonial Theology of Life*, 2.
3. Toolan, "The Voice of the Hurricane," 99.

If sacramentality is about how justice plays out in a sacramental mode—as divine "justice sacramentalized" (Walter Burghardt)—then what can postcolonial and diasporic thought contribute to a transformative *ressourcement* of sacramentality in contemporary theology? The answer, however preliminary at this stage of nascent postcolonial sacramental theology, concerns the conundrum of power. Namely, how can divine power and agency be transformatively reimagined in the context of the created world, precisely as always already potentially sacramental—yet also fully aware that they must "work" in the world that remains woefully structured in racial, economic, cultural, and gender dominance? How can sacramental relationality between the Uncreated and the created—and then, by analogy, also among everything and everyone that lives and moves in this all-encompassing theological galaxy of God-world relationality—be conceived and lived beyond the coloniality of power, being, and knowledge?

The conundrum of power—political, economic, cultural, and religious—is absolutely central in postcolonial discourse. In theology, postcolonial critiques focus not just on a world that is enduringly structured in dominance but also, increasingly, on certain prominent Christian theological perceptions of divine transcendence and divine agency as hegemonic, imperialistic, unduly unilateral, non-relational, and non-reciprocal (overpowering instead of empowering). Such models of divine power are, for all practical purposes, reflective of colonial power. They valorize and authorize colonial imaginaries of being, knowing, and acting. They legitimate colonial cosmologies of power which, in turn, condone and enable violent and victimizing practices of power relations in social, cultural, gender, racial, and ecological arenas. Sacramental doctrines and sacramental liturgies are often deeply imbricated in such colonial cosmologies and hegemonic configurations of divine agency. This trajectory of critique goes far beyond the discussion about the historical uses (misuses?) of sacraments and liturgies in conquests, crusades, and the cultural imperialism of Christian missionary endeavors.

The pivotal issue at the level of postcolonial *theology*—and not just postcolonial historiography—is the underlying conception of divine transcendence, divine power, and divine agency vis-à-vis created reality and our agency. Typically, these conceptions also structure the very meaning of sacramentality, the shape of sacramental liturgies, and our epistemological perceptions of how sacraments signify, effect change, convey meaning, authorize values, legitimate behaviors, and negotiate power relations. In other words, sacraments "function" not just in theologians' heads or liturgical manuals for clergy. Most importantly, they "function" existentially—spiritually, emotionally, socially, economically, politically, and culturally in our flesh-and-blood historical lifeworlds. They shape and are, in turn, shaped by our culturally contextualized imaginaries of reality.

Like liberation theologies, postcolonial imagination intentionally "places the concern for right relations with other human beings at the center of the doctrinal discussion, refusing the disjunction between theology and ethics."[4] Postcolonial imagination certainly does not dismiss or discount transcendence. In fact, quite the opposite is increasingly the case as postcolonial theological inquiry voyages beyond ethnographic, sociological, and strictly historiographical approaches into the inner sanctum of theology—doctrines, creedal traditions, and confessional beliefs. The point of departure here is the conviction that however divine transcendence and its relation to creation might be re-envisioned, such reimaging of transcendence ought not to be held captive to the conventional "Western imaginary" which continues to "retain the versions of the disembodied controlling power that theism commonly associates with transcendence."[5]

Two sacramental *loci* seem to present particularly fascinating avenues for exploring sacramental dynamics as power dynamics of transcendence from a postcolonial point of view. First, the idea of the created world as the original/primordial/primary sacrament in the context of our planetary ecological crisis and secondly, the eucharistic dynamic of transformative change. In the chapters that follow, my goal is not to present a comprehensive treatment of both *loci* since it is simply impossible in the format of this exploratory study. The present chapter will offer some reflections on the emerging resonance between the growing awareness of planetary environmental degradation in both sacramental theology and postcolonialism.

ECODEGRADATION: THE GLOBAL(IZED) SACRAMENTAL EMERGENCY

There is a growing ecumenical recognition that the mounting ecological emergency is not merely a crisis of economy, national security, or politics. Evidently, it is all of those things. Yet at its deepest roots, as I, among others, have argued elsewhere, it is a peculiarly sacramental calamity.[6] Whatever else it may entail—culturally, politically, technologically, and economically—the environmental crisis is a profoundly spiritual crisis.[7] But even

4. Rivera, *The Touch of Transcendence*, 3.

5. Ibid., 5.

6. Suna-Koro, "Postcolonially Bittersweet in America," 1–47.

7. See, for example, Matthew T. Eggemeier, *A Sacramental-Prophetic Vision* for a concise recent analysis of the pervasive anthropocentrism and the market imaginary,

though it is a spiritual crisis, it is not a generically spiritual, but an explicitly sacramental, tragedy.

Genealogically, the ecological crisis is predominantly Western and modern in its spiritual, epistemological, and cultural origin. It is modern in the sense that Western colonial modernity is marked by a dissolution of the sacramental view of reality. What came instead of the participatory ontology that undergirds, in one way or another, a sacramental worldview was a serial march of distancing and separation:

> Western modernity has involved the first kind of distancing: from the organic to the mechanic; from the corporate to the individual; from hierarchy to equality; from an understanding of reality in which everything resonates with everything else (or, more radically, in which everything is present in everything: the medieval mystical formula *quodlibet in quodlibet*), to one built around precision and the increasing differentiation of domains. . .[8]

But to be clear, as things now stand in the globalized world, the dualistic and fragmentary worldview is no longer and not merely Western. By now it is cosmopolitan or Occidental in the imperialized, instrumentalized, and globally internalized sense of this term. It is Occidental, and colonial, and modern all at the same time in the sense of promoting a competitively dualistic and hegemonic attitude toward non-human otherness—in other words, it promotes instrumentalized and greedy subalternization of the non-human reality.

This worldview did indeed peak in the modern geopolitical Euro-Atlantic West but has been since disseminated worldwide. Lest we forget: the habits and routines of instrumentalized reason were colonially exported with abandon as part of the civilizing-*cum*-Christian mission. As Ashis Nandy has emblematically summarized, "this colonialism colonises minds in addition to bodies and it releases forces within colonised societies to alter their cultural priorities once and for all . . . The West is now everywhere, within the West and outside, in structures and in minds."[9]

Modern Western epistemologies and cosmologies were successfully implanted throughout the colonies of the modern empires, by hegemonic force, by persuasion, and through tactical mimicry. It seems to be obvious that at the beginning of the twenty-first century they have sprouted deep

---

and the ways these attitudes embody the spiritual crisis as the root cause of environmental degradation.

8. Benavides, "Modernity," 190.

9. Nandy, *The Intimate Enemy*, xi.

and hybrid roots throughout the global postcolony from China to Brazil. It is noteworthy that Asian, South American, and African theologians are pleading for ecojustice among their own faith communities and societies in ways that are remarkably similar to the Western approaches despite all the postcolonial differences. Regardless of the origins, the patterns and habits of pure economic reason are now intimately present and operative in consumerist societies worldwide, both metropolitan and subaltern.

The Occidental crises of sacramentality and ecology are intimately interrelated, albeit in a sinister way. The planetary scope of the accelerating environmental emergency urges us to seek for a more profound and wide-ranging sacramental response. That includes, but also goes beyond, liturgical renewal by fostering "active participation" and "inculturation" in ecclesiastical rituals by modifying the rites themselves to make them more ecologically conscious and better understandable in various cultural contexts. But such ritual modifications comprise only the tip of the iceberg.

A more consequential theological intervention must dig deeper and address the reduction and bureaucratization of sacramentality into narrowly demarcated and zealously policed sacramental rituals that have, for all practical purposes, rendered the world unrecognizable as the original/primary sacrament of God. The globally functional result of such theological attitudes is the habitual reflex to encapsulate sacramentality in "sacred" rituals while leaving the "profane" world behind to be conquered and lorded over by pure economic reason. The modern dualistic and mechanistic imaginaries of the universe are still very much alive, if perhaps more camouflaged, in face of increasing demands for an efficient technological and scientific change as if that alone will be able to relieve a problem that far surpasses its instrumental expressions.

Furthermore, a certain kind of naïve oppositionality between the "West" versus "the Rest" must also be resisted. The underlying dualistic imaginaries of the disenchanted *Zweckrationalität* have become fully globalized. Today they operate with an equally "native" or "inculturated" efficiency in both so-called "One Third" and "Two Thirds" worlds. The pervasive metaphysical presence and the cosmopolitan economic efficacy of these imaginaries propel us all, together, ever closer to a planetary environmental disaster as sacramental ecotheologies from various continents convey with such frightening lucidity. Africa, Asia, the Caribbean, and even Eastern Europe are far from being innocent wonderlands of ecological or spiritual purity where disillusioned Westerners can go on an exotic soul searching safari of penitence alongside local nativists. Such romanticization of allegedly pure and unspoiled non-Western primitive societies amounts to nothing less than a "green orientalism."[10]

At this point in history, the Occidental theo-ontological dualism clearly borders on idolatry. It has carved itself deeply, to the point of being sedimented into the common sense of Christian imagination all over the planet. Hence the focus on eco-friendly liturgical rites alone without a deeper retrieval of certain sacramental ontology or a sacramental "chamber metaphysics" will not suffice to facilitate a sustainable and effective transformation of spiritual or cultural imaginary, let alone political and economic praxis. Here a dialogue with postcolonial perspectives can be of particular value since "ecological crisis is a fundamental concern for postcolonial criticism, one that reveals the breadth and depth of destruction caused by human practices promoted by today's empires."[11] As Mayra Rivera argues, an "earthy postcolonial theology" must be fully aware of its vocation and mission as an ecologically committed theopolitics; it is urged to rediscover "the inextricable connections between political, theological, and ecological: deepening its reading strategies and critiques of empire to denounce the mutilation of the elemental bonds of our world and attuning itself to traditions of reverence toward fire, water, air, and earth."[12]

ARE THE "TURNS" TO (HUMAN) RITUAL AND (HUMAN) LANGUAGE ENOUGH?

What does postcolonial involvement in ecocriticism and emphasis on planetarity as a new and alternative imaginary of empowerment have to do with the theological notion of the world as the primary/original/primordial sacrament? Looking at the Christian sacramental landscape through the lens of postcolonial planetarity can yield some interesting insights.

A particularly fruitful arena for engagement between postcolonialism and sacramental discourse, I submit, is emerging due to the shared concerns about the global ecological crisis. Overdue questions have recently been raised about the limits and liabilities of the anthropocentric focus that has underwritten much of the sacramental imagination stemming forward from the Liturgical Movement, especially after Vatican II. Without doubt, the lineages of thought that conceptualize Christ and the Church as foundational sacraments have invigorated the sacramental discourse immensely. The revitalization of the ritual dimensions of sacramental liturgies

10. See George Handley's *Postcolonial Ecologies*.

11. Rivera, "Elemental Bonds," 348.

12. Ibid., 358.

in conjunction with postmodern critiques of "ontotheology" through the "turn to language" have also admirably broadened the fragmented terrain of modern sacramentality. Indeed, these approaches have offered a salutary corrective to truncated and dualistic inertias.

But given the dominant anthropocentric, linguistic, and ecclesiocentric slants, have these praiseworthy attempts gone far enough? Are they integrative enough to engage not just the pluralistic multireligious world of global postcolony, but even the challenges for many Western Christians of the new cosmological visions? Is the Christomonism of many late modern sacramentologies not too reductive in a Trinitarian context? Aren't both, anthropocentrism in general and Christomonism in particular, actually unhelpful if there is a genuine desire to keep the two vectors of creation and salvation in a contrapuntal interaction and unity instead of automatically privileging the habitual Western preoccupation with substitutionary and sacrificial atonement models of salvation? Ultimately, is the underlying anthropocentrism of postmodern sacramentality spacious enough and hospitable enough to engage the present existential exigencies of life on this planet as a whole—and not just human beings—as an interdependent global ecosystem of the whole creation in relation to God?

This is the juncture at which some theological voices have begun to call for a more expansive, inclusive, holistic, and indeed planetary sacramental imaginary. An ecumenical and translocal momentum is building for what Mathai Kadavil calls the "sacramentality of Creation as a new paradigm in contemporary sacramentology."[13] This emerging paradigm has manifold manifestations even in these early stages. It frequently involves creative *ressourcement* of certain Western pre-medieval as well as non-Western modes of imagination. More often than not it promotes a constructive *aggiornamento* in conversation with critical theories, ecofeminist discourses, and environmental studies.

According to this emerging paradigm, the world is understood as a sacrament. To say that the world is a sacrament is not to squabble about a parochial niche concern in one rather marginalized subdiscipline of Christian theology, especially as things stand in Protestant theological circles. What is at stake here is the question of how we ensure a sound doctrinal equilibrium of Christian theological enterprise between creation and salvation. As the Indian Roman Catholic theologian Jacob Parappally observes, creation-centered theologies reexamine the whole triad of theocentric, anthropocentric, and cosmocentric dimensions in Christian imagination and call for a more even modulation:

13. Kadavil, *The World as Sacrament*, 304–5.

> The creation is not subordinated to the theme of redemption which in the past was the central theme in theological discourses. Going beyond the anthropocentric understanding of redemption from the "fallen" world, efforts are made to understand the goodness of God-created world which itself is the revelation of God, his sacrament.[14]

Consequently, when the three-pronged relational nexus of God, humanity, and cosmos becomes lopsided in theological enterprise, consequences go far beyond doctrinal technicalities:

> A cosmological Nestorianism can lead to disastrous consequences both for the world and humans. Likewise a cosmological Monophysitism can lead to naïve natural mysticism that does not promote the eschatological movement of the creation for its final liberation. Both attitudes are dangerous for the well-being of the entire creation.[15]

More theological voices are starting to urge contemporary theological inquiry to re-examine and re-imagine presently dominant ideas of sacramentality at their very roots. Namely, they invite us to consider the idea of this world as the primary/original/primordial sacrament—or as *Ursakrament.* This trajectory highlights the previously downplayed (Overlooked? Fully unrecognized? Ignored? Formalized?) cosmocentric dimension of sacramentality in addition to theocentric, Christocentric, anthropocentric, (i.e., ritual) dimensions.

POSTCOLONIALISM GOES PLANETARY

Now what about postcolonialism? Might there be any meaningful connections between these emerging explorations of sacramentality and postcolonial discourse? Indeed, there are. In recent years a new subfield of postcolonial ecocriticism and postcolonial ecojustice has appeared. Voices from this field call for a rigorous reassessment of the deep-seated anthropocentrism of postcolonial studies. The trademark of postcolonialism is sociohistorical and geocultural modes of critical analysis. Today, in the circumstances of environmental crisis, these worthy but limited modes of critique can no longer suffice if the commitment of postcolonialism still remains to foster transformation toward global access to justice and empowerment.

14. Parappally, "The World, God's Primary Sacrament," 92.

15. Ibid., 94.

Postcolonialism is speedily catching up its contributions to environmental humanities. Graham Huggan and Helen Tiffin speak for most postcolonial sensibilities when they argue that the growing ecological crisis,

> requires a broader *ecological* conception of natural-cultural relations on several different levels—including the planetary level—than has tended to be the case in much ecocriticism until now. Postcolonial approaches remain helpful here in ensuring that the ongoing struggle for global environmental justice is pursued; that cultural differences are taken into account in building bioregional models of sustainability and resilience; and that new ways of thinking about human—also thinking *beyond* the human—are developed that recognize the imbrication of social and ecological factors in what Rob Nixon calls today's "high age of neo-liberalism": an age characterized by conspicuously uneven distribution of natural resources, the forced displacement of animals and people, and the routine abuses of transnational corporate power.[16]

The sheer scope of ecojustice problems mandates a methodological and material expansion of the postcolonial analytical toolbox beyond pervasive anthropocentrism to be able to meaningfully unmask the overlapping dynamics of ongoing exploitation of human and non-human subalterns—the wretched of the earth, the disinherited, the sinned against.

In this context, Paul Gilroy has called for a new "planetary consciousness." When perceived through the prism of planetary consciousness,

> the world becomes not a limitless globe, but a small, fragile and finite place, one planet among others with strictly limited resources that are allocated unequally. This is not the globalized mindset of the fortunate, unrestricted traveler or some other unexpected fruit of heavily insulated postscarcity and indifferent overdevelopment. It is a critical orientation and oppositional mood triggered by comprehension of the simple fact that environmental and medical crises do not stop at national boundaries and by a feeling that the sustainability of our species is itself in question.[17]

Gilroy insists on keeping the ecological and socio-political aspects of life closely intertwined as we search for a new postcolonial relationship with the non-human world. Planetary consciousness is a consciousness of the "tragedy, fragility, and brevity of indivisible human existence that is all the

16. Huggan and Tiffin, *Postcolonial Ecocriticism*, viii. Italics in original.

17. Gilroy, *Postcolonial Melancholia*, 75.

more valuable as a result of its openness to the damage done by racisms."[18] It "supports an appreciation of nature as a common condition of our imperiled existence, resistant to commodification. . ."[19]

Gayatri Chakravorty Spivak has advocated the notion of planetarity—an alternative imaginary to the globalized world which remains spitefully structured in neo-colonial dominance, coercive homogenization of cultures and lifeworlds, and in exploitative competition. The turn to planetarity conveys substantial self-criticism within postcolonial studies since the imaginary of planetarity disrupts the habitual anthropocentrism of postcolonial analyses. It situates all of them within a transcendence which, in itself, is an immensely interrelated and interdependent complexity surrounding and conditioning all forms of life. Planetarity is the transcendent meta-context of life. As Spivak argues, "the planet is in the species of alterity, belonging to another system; and yet we inhabit it, on loan."[20] Spivak highlights the urgency of the "turn to planet" by calling for a postcolonial self-scrutiny: "To globalize is to think a manageable world. To think of ourselves as planetary is to remember that if we live a hundred years, even a devastated planet lives a billion, without us."[21] Realizing we are "planetary creatures" also means the recognition that our planet's "alterity remains underived from us," and, very importantly, "it is not our dialectical negation."[22]

The turn to planetarity is not a betrayal or dissipation of the critical focus on the machinations of hegemonic and exploitative power in the globalized postcolony. Rather, it makes it sharper and more adequate for the pursuit of decolonial justice and post-imperial flourishing of life:

> Postcolonial ecocriticism has offered important new perspectives of how environmental change is entwined with the narratives, histories, and material practices of colonialism and globalization. Postcolonial approaches emphasize how experiences of environmental violence, rupture, and displacement are central ecological challenges across the Global South while at the same time identifying possibilities for imaginative recuperation that are compatible with anticolonial politics.[23]

After all, the history of colonialism and imperialism is integral to understanding contemporary environmental predicaments. It is time to

18. Ibid.
19. Ibid.
20. Spivak, *Death of a Discipline*, 72.
21. Spivak, "Reply," 247.
22. Spivak, *Death of a Discipline*, 73.
23. DeLoughrey, et al., "Introduction," 2.

acknowledge, according to Spivak, that "postcolonialism remained caught in mere nationalism over against colonialism. . . today it is planetarity that we are called to imagine" since "we are dealing with heterogeneity on a different scale and related to imperialisms on another model."[24]

The turn to planetarity in postcolonialism has allowed it to explore the environmental crisis through the prism of postcolonial power dynamics. Our planet, the natural world, is now recognized as a subaltern other:

> Postcolonial thought criticizes the modern versions of a dualistic hierarchy, deconstructing various oppositional differences, while opening a new space of hybridity for the colonized other. When one defines nonhuman nature as "the other" that has been colonized by the human species in the anthropocentric worldview, it becomes clear that decolonization of nature is necessary in our era. As Gayatri Spivak suggests, today's subaltern must be rethought.[25]

Jea Sophia Oh argues that the Earth is "the new subaltern in the anthropocentric world" and that Spivak's classical analysis of postcolonial women's subalternity now "can be applied to nature as subaltern which has been alienated from an anthropocentric world."[26] The planetary modulation of subalternity opens up new avenues to critically challenge the operations of hegemonic power and the logic of dualistic dominance on a most inclusive scale. As Oh summarizes, subalternization "is a process related to the general psycho-social mechanism of 'othering'" and the time is ripe for rethinking "postcolonial/colonial subalternization of nature as similar to the subaltern woman as the 'othered subject,' nature (nonhuman/more than human) is the 'othered subject' in the subalternization of nature as objects of discursive management and control."[27]

Even though "there is not yet a full version of a postcolonial ecotheology, there have been recent and more sustained attempts to bring postcolonialism and ecology into dialogue outside of the theological field that shape a 'postcolonial ecocriticism' or 'green postcolonialism.'"[28] As Whitney Bauman argues, postcolonialism has (finally) recognized that "religions help to co-create the worlds in which we live, and for better and/or worse help to make up the planet on which we all (humans and non) live."[29] Susan Abra-

24. Spivak, *Death of a Discipline*, 81, 85.

25. Oh, *A Postcolonial Theology of Life*, 2.

26. Ibid.

27. Ibid., 10.

28. Ibid., 8.

29. Bauman, "Opening the Language of Religion and Ecology," 95.

ham has pointed out that "planetarity is a 'peculiar mindset' that challenges the exploitative dualisms of colonial and postcolonial power."[30] And this is precisely where a genuinely fruitful conversation between postcolonialism and sacramental theology can materialize. Namely, it is a conversation through dialogic explorations of how divine and human power, as well as divine and human agency, function within and across the planetary sacramental interface of God-world relationality.

On top of that, if the world is seen as the primordial/original/primary sacrament—or *Ursakrament*—then at some point, quite inevitably, it also becomes a conversation about how divine and ecclesiastical powers function in a sacramental universe that aspires to move beyond anthropocentric and ecclesiocentric sacramental systems and instead gesture toward a more postcolonial mode of sacramentality—say, something akin to the idea of a sacramental pluriverse/multiverse which I will explore in more detail in Part III, Chapter 4.

Obviously, entertaining the idea of the created world as the primordial sacrament cannot proceed through a straightforward reading of a distinct and particular liturgical rite and the history of its performative manifestations. There is no approved liturgical rite to celebrate the world as the primordial sacrament in a way that would be analogous to the rites of Baptism or Eucharist. Perhaps there can never be such a rite since the *Ursakrament* always already has its, as it were, diasporic traces in, with, under, and through all other sacramental mysteries, no matter how many and however structured they may be. That opens up the broadest possible theological vistas to consider as sources of sacramental elaborations, including, but not limited to, liturgical studies.

One thing, however, seems to be inevitable: the notion of world as the original/primary sacrament does bring up the "numbers game" for critical reexamination. Virtually all Western Christian traditions still play according to the rules of the conventional "numbers game" to a greater or lesser extent, regardless of how charmingly full of twists and turns the "numbers game" has become with the broad endorsement of ideas such as seeing Christ as the *Ursakrament* and the Church as the *Grundsakrament*. In recent decades

the sacramental landscape has grown even messier—and more fascinating. Creative retrievals of premodern cosmological and sacramental insights in conversation with the so-called new cosmology, environmental studies, and critical socio-historical analyses have emerged to suggest that the cosmos itself deserves to be recognized as the *Ursakrament*. But to grasp what a radical modulation of sacramental imagination, at least in

30. Abraham, "The Pterodactyl in the Margins," 80.

Occidental modes of theological inquiry, is at stake here, a quick look at the history of the ever tempting "numbers game" is necessary.

SACRAMENTS: A BRIEF EXCURSUS THROUGH THE NUMBERS GAME

When it comes to the actual practice of liturgical sacraments, most Western Catholics, Western Protestants and the Eastern Orthodox live and move within the limits of an institutionalized sacramental system—however differently structured it may be across the historical spectrum of Christian traditions. And this system, in Kevin Irwin's words, is comprised of "the church's agreed-upon and time-tested signs, symbols, gestures, words, and the context in which these are enacted, all of which comprise what sacraments are and do. Words will always fail to describe adequately and fully what sacraments are and do."[31]

Indeed, words will always fall short of conceptualizing the sacramental mysteries of creation and salvation. The agreements about which words and which images fit best, have a very long, complex, and often divisive genealogy not only among various denominations but also inside those same denominations. On some issues—such as the nature of eucharistic conversion and the numbering of the officially sanctioned ecclesiastical sacraments—there are no comprehensive agreements at all, despite the many gallant efforts of the ecumenical movement.

As far as Western incarnations of Christianity are concerned, all the so-called liturgical traditions share a common intellectual, spiritual, and cultural genealogy—both its splendor and its perils.[32] Regardless of how many liturgical rites are officially defined as "sacraments" (seven or two), both Roman Catholics and mainstream (the so-called "liturgical") Protestants, such as Lutherans, Anglicans, Methodists and Presbyterians, are

31. Irwin, *The Sacraments*, 2.

32. Hans Boersma has insightfully assessed the present sacramental predicaments across the Western ecumenical spectrum as follows: "the recovery of a sacramental ontology is incumbent not only on Protestants but also on Catholics. They owe their common task to a shared intellectual history that has caused problems on both sides of the ecclesiastical divide. Protestants may be characterized by a rational mindset more than by a sacramental imagination. But the argument of the *ressourcement* theologians was that a sacramental ontology had been declining also in Catholicism. Their *ressourcement* of patristic and medieval theology implied a negative evaluation of later theological approaches [. . .] Sixteenth-century Protestants and Catholics were both heirs to the problematic ramifications of the decline of mystery," *Nouvelle Théologie and Sacramental Ontology*, 15.

heirs, in more or less enthusiastic ways, to the medieval Latin sacramental imaginary.[33]

During the medieval period, this sacramental imaginary, multifaceted and multilayered as it was, embarked on a progressively accelerating course toward greater theological refinement. Yet it was also a movement toward a consolidation of institutional "validity" and increasingly centralized clerical control over the signs, actions, and interactions that were to be recognized as "properly" and legitimately sacramental:

> Before the number seven was finally settled upon during the medieval period (at Lyons II in 1274, at Florence in 1439, and at Trent in 1547), the Church lived through its entire first millennium and then some without ever having settled upon even a final definition of *sacrament*, let alone their precise number. On the contrary, there were literally hundreds of sacred rites (what we call today "sacramental") which were simply referred to as "sacraments." These included Sacred Scripture, the mysteries of faith, cultic rites, and even allegory and typology.[34]

It was already during this period (and not singularly due to the later revolutionary upheavals of the sixteenth century European Reformations in Western Christianity) that a profound sacramental compartmentalization gained traction. The trademark of the modern cultural and spiritual outlook—disenchantment/*Entzauberung*—has its roots already in the medieval permutations of sacramental, i.e., ontological, sensibilities.

Furthermore, after some sporadic preludes in the late Middle Ages, the sixteenth century exploded with sacramental iconoclasm resulting in theological and liturgical austerity, especially among the Reformed and Radical versions of the Protestant Reformation. At the same time, the sacramental trajectory of Catholic Reformation underwent a considerable institutionalization. The development of more centralized ecclesiastical control mechanisms overlapped with a general tendency toward an ever greater

33. Even though the number of seven sacraments started appearing in the works of influential Western theologians since Peter Lombard (c. 1100–c.1160), it was only at the Second Council of Lyons in 1274 and the Council of Florence in 1439 that the Latin Catholic Church officially defined that there were seven sacraments without, however, specifically naming what they were. Eventually the Council of Trent (1545–1563) clarified it decisively for Roman Catholics by defining the seven sacraments in the order that remains authoritative today. On the Protestant side, documents dating back to the same eventful sixteenth century such as, for example, the Augsburg Confession for Lutherans and The Thirty Nine Articles for Anglicans, explicitly state that only two dominical sacraments—Baptism and the Eucharist—are recognized as proper sacraments.

34. McBrien, *Catholicism*, 800.

uniformity and streamlining of liturgical practice not only in Europe, but also worldwide through the colonial missions.

Eventually, even the Roman Catholic sacramental and liturgical tradition was not left entirely untouched by a ritual and theological austerity of its own kind.[35] As the movement of *nouvelle théologie* revealed in the twentieth century, the nominalist fragmentation of sacramental ontology had penetrated deeply into both Protestant and Roman Catholic worldviews during colonial Western modernity. Hence, the project of re-envisioning sacramental ontology and epistemology remains a challenge for all Christian imagination steeped in the promises and perils of Occidental colonial modernity.

Starting with the great changes of the eleventh century and reaching its culmination in the sixteenth century, the numbers of the official ecclesiastical sacraments were slowly but surely reduced, narrowed down, defined, refined, demarcated, enclosed, and fixed. Among some movements emerging from the Radical Reformations, the sacraments were done away with almost completely. That trajectory is alive and well today among many Evangelical assemblies worldwide, even though liturgical creativity never sits still.[36] Numerous sacramental actions and signs that theologians like Augustine of Hippo and Hugh of St. Victor counted among the sacraments ended up, as it were, on the second tier of the institutionalized sacramental edifice—the "sacramentals" for Roman Catholics and "ordinances" or "occasional services" for numerous mainstream/magisterial Protestants.

The most pertinent historical observation, however, is this: there is a clearly discernible trajectory toward reducing and systematizing the intricate panorama of sacramental images and practices under the ever tighter control of institutional ecclesiocentrism and, in particular, patriarchal clericalism. Yet the momentum of this trajectory only emerged in the second millennium Latin West. It was only in the middle of the tweflth century that theologians like Peter Lombard felt compelled and justified to begin systematizing and, in a sense, flattening the still fluid landscapes of sacramental precepts and practices into seven privileged, singled-out, compressed modes of encounter with God under increasingly centralized control. Overall, the history of Christian sacramental theology in the West presents a frighteningly clear case of what John Thatamanil has recently called attention to as the religionization and reification of spiritual traditions. Namely, "the reification of a religious tradition refers to the processes by which historically malleable and porous traditions come to be constructed as fixed,

35. Macy, "The Medieval Inheritance," 37.

36. See, for example, Ross, *Evangelical Versus Liturgical?*

transhistorically static, tightly integrated and bounded conceptual systems (possessed of a single dominant metanarrative or an internally consistent transtemporal deep grammar)."[37]

With the advent of Western colonial modernity at the dawn of the sixteenth century, the fragmentation of the neo-platonic sacramental worldview (which, in the eyes of many, remained very much wedded to slowly fading ecclesiastical power structures which modern sensibilities viewed with apprehension) gradually picked up speed. During the heyday of colonial modernity, sacramental imaginary had to compete—and almost always lost the battle—with rationalism, empiricism, skepticism, and the scientific penchant for dualistic and mechanistic perceptions of reality. In the theological division of labor, liturgical and sacramental studies became an eccentric footnote to the power discourses of systematic theology, biblical disciplines, and moral theology until the Liturgical Movement started to gain ecumenical traction in the second half of the twentieth century.

But now, at the beginning of the third millennium, the Western dualistic impasse is only slowly starting to fade away as the "new cosmology," the changing paradigms in quantum physics, neuroscience, and evolutionary biology are slowly but surely dethroning the rigidly mechanistic worldview. Occidental sacramental theology is also starting, if only at a turtle's pace, to tune into the theological voices from the Majority, or the Two-Thirds World, even though the input from those regions and cultural sensibilities still mostly stops at an ethnographic "context" level. All these phenomena together are cracking open quite a few doors for further exploration to tease out new terrains for sacramental renewal.

BEYOND THE NUMBERS GAME: *QUO VADIS*?

Meanwhile Eastern Orthodoxy has tried very hard to stay above the fray of the much criticized Western reductionism and juridical formalism by resisting the reductive closure of the sacramental universe—at least on a theological level. John Cryssavgis explains:

> Orthodox Christians in fact prefer to speak of "mystery" rather than a "sacrament," the latter of which tends to imply the acquisition of something "objective." Traditionally, it is said that there are seven mysteries or sacraments. Yet this categorization is neither completely true nor always helpful. The Orthodox Church has never limited itself to seven sacraments, preferring to speak of every moment and aspect of life as being sacramental—from

37. Thatamanil, "How Not to Be a Religion," 61.

> birth through death. Indeed, the funeral service was once also classified as a sacrament in Orthodox liturgical practice. So the sacraments do not work in some magical manner; rather, they function "mystically," silently permeating the hearts and lives of those who choose to be open to the possibility of encounter with God—like the flow of blood in the human body.[38]

In comparison with the Western traditions, the Eastern Orthodox approach is the most fluid and open-ended, at least from the point of view of the institutional memory that has shaped the lives and practices of faithful individuals and communities. When it comes to understanding the world as sacrament, the (panentheistic) Eastern Orthodox can arguably ease into such an imaginary with the least amount of friction as the influential work of Alexander Schmemann demonstrates.[39]

Occidental modes of theologizing, which Schmemann criticized often and at times not entirely judiciously, do present a more entrenched methodological rigidity. Already in the 1960s Schmemann boldly challenged these Occidental conventions of sacramental imagination and practice precisely by calling for a wholesale reevaluation of the dualistic ontologies and epistemologies that have wreaked havoc in sacramental theology. Instead of focusing on grace which was sacramentally "measured out in small doses," he proposed an imaginary of "holy materialism" that affirms the world as nothing less than a sacrament and reasserts the sacramental character in the whole of life.[40] Hence Schmemann laments:

> In all our various Christian traditions, we are taught to think of the sacramental as existing first and primarily in the form of a particular and fixed numbers of *sacraments*, these being conceived as more or less isolated acts of the Church, and concerned principally with the personal needs of the individual Christian. [. . .] Unfortunately, this kind of concern with the sacraments, valid and indeed necessary as it has been, has tended to be self-defeating. Theorizing about isolated sacramental acts, we lost the sacramental sense in general. The number of these acts, their institution, the conditions of their validity and so on—we asked

38. Chryssavgis, "A New Heaven and a New Earth," 160.

39. See Schmemann, *Church, World, Mission*, 217–27. Chryssavgis' essay referenced above is just one concise example among many of how organic such an approach appears to be in the context of Eastern Orthodox theology. See also, for example, Kallistos Ware's "Through Creation to the Creator," 86–105.

40. Schmemann, *Church, World, Mission*, 225, 218.

> these questions in too narrow and concentrated a fashion, so that everything else became nonsacramental.[41]

Appreciating the creative imaginative potential of Eastern Orthodox sacramental theology, it is uplifting to note that the notion of the world as sacrament is not an absolute stranger alsoin the Occidental lineage of sacramental imagination. Inspired by "green" and ecofeminist movements, a few recent Western attempts to work with the notion of the world as sacrament have emerged. Such ideas still mostly occur on the margins of broader projects in ethics, systematic and comparative theology—but not, with very few exceptions, in sacramental and liturgical theology.[42] But at least they are starting to show up!

There are a few vectors of inquiry to consider. For example, if Christian theology (at least in some of its soundest expressions) is indeed serious about its recurrent claims that the ontological makeup of this creation is sacramental, then how must our methodological imagination be modulated to attempt a more consequential and meaningful engagement with this—ever ancient and ever new—mystical insight about matter being a sacramental "mystery of ever-increasing connections?"[43] How might Christian sacramentality be conceived and performed if the full imaginative and performative potential of what Maximus the Confessor envisioned as the "cosmic liturgy" would indeed be recognized as the "interdependence of all persons and all things?"[44]

The sacramental counterpart to the postcolonial idea of planetarity—the idea of the world as *Ursakrament*—highlights the methodological exigencies that contemporary Christian sacramental theology will have to address sooner rather than later, and not only in its postcolonial expressions. Some Western theologians, like Kenan Osborne, have expressed reservations about the need to name any sacrament, even the humanity of Christ, as primordial or original by inquiring "whether any finite sacrament . . . can be called primordial" since "sacramental primordiality must remain, it would seem, totally with the action of God, a God who is infinitely and freely beyond all revelation."[45] It is beyond the scope of this study to delve into Osborne's challenge. Be that as it may, Osborne is right to observe that to "say the world is a sacrament of God is not in any way self-evident"—at

41. Ibid., 220. Italics in the original.

42. The work of the ethicist John Hart presents a case in point here, see his *Sacramental Commons*.

43. Chryssavgis, *Light Through Darkness*, 112.

44. Ibid., 113.

45. Osborne, *Christian Sacraments in a Postmodern World*, 83. See also 109.

least in Occidental mainstream conventions of sacramental theology—and "involves an enormous reformulation of the sphere of discourse."[46] This sort of methodological shift is clearly not limited to postcolonial perspectives on sacramentality even though postcolonial approaches can certainly make a constructive contribution to fostering such a visionary shift. For now, I turn to a sampling of inklings from the emerging sacramental wisdom—and an attendant emerging methodological shift—that glimmer through the planetary prism of looking at the world as *Ursakrament*.

IMAGINING THE WORLD AS URSAKRAMENT: TUNING INTO FOUR VOICES

Speaking of the world as the *Ursakrament* within an imaginary of sacramental pluriverse, I would like to begin with highlighting four diverse theological voices from North America and India (Theodore Runyon, Elizabeth A. Johnson, C.S.J., Dorothy C. McDougall, and Francis X. D'Sa, S.J.) which offer a creative challenge to the edifice of the Occidental methodological mindset of sacramental "number games." My working presupposition here is that to conceive of the created world as *Ursakrament* does not necessarily require one to marginalize Jesus Christ, as some theologians worry. Even though the discussion about how to best reimagine Christ's vital position precisely as a sacrament of the triune God is absolutely riveting, it is not feasible to address this issue at length here.[47] I will, however, propose some postcolonial ways of envisioning the pivotal purpose of Christ as the crescendo of sacramentality in the upcoming Chapter 5.

The Cosmic Sacrament: Theodore Runyon

First, shifting the methodological focus in sacramental theology from the exclusive concentration on the anthropocentric and androcentric model of redemption through the atonement, the American Methodist theologian Theodore Runyon, argues that,

46. Ibid., 83.

47. For example, Therese B. DeLisio presents a critical analysis of Dorothy McDougall's argument for the earth as the primary sacrament which captures the main issues at stake in this context. For the main tenets of this type of critique see DeLisio, "Considering the Cosmos as Primary Sacrament," 160–84. Appreciating the merits of DeLisio's analysis, it is still possible, I submit, to have a viable, sound, and thoroughly Trinitarian sacramental imaginary where both creation and Christ—among other sacraments of various levels of intensity and opacity—co-exist with their unique salvific purpose and relevance. But that is a conversation quickly extending beyond the scope of this study.

> too often the church has been unaware of the larger meaning and cosmic implications of the sacrament, and has fostered a timid, truncated, narrowly ecclesiastical understanding, content to settle for religious practices in a sacred corner of the world where it controls the sacramental keys to heaven—yet has lost the keys of the kingdom and its world-transforming power.[48]

Taking the wider ecological, indeed cosmic, context seriously, the movement here is "from kingdom to creation."[49] To reclaim the world-transforming power of sacramentality, Runyon suggests that "in the hands of the Creator, the world itself serves as the *first sacrament*, the first and most basic use of the material to communicate and facilitate the divine-human relationship."[50] To attend to the fullness of revelation, the theology of creation must coexist in an equilibrium with the theology of redemption. Hence, "the gift to humanity of the world entrusted to our care is therefore the most fundamental sacramental act. In and through it are mediated those interrelationships which are basic to human existence. . ."[51]

Runyon's approach begins with the Eucharist as a crossroads of the "three basic forms of reality: the divine, the material world, and humankind."[52] Yet, upon a closer analysis, it is obvious that the world is habitually marginalized into invisibility or irrelevance within this triple helix of sacramental imaginary. It is becoming to ask, then, what is the "most fundamental sacramental phenomenon in which all of the particular sacraments are rooted"[53] including both Jesus Christ and the church as *Ursakrament* and *Grundsakrament*, to use Rahnerian language, respectively. The subalternization of the world within the sacramental triple helix can be ameliorated by considering the world as the "original sacrament." Why so? Like Apostle Paul and a slew of Eastern Orthodox theologians, Runyon argues that the ultimate object of salvation is not humanity alone but rather the whole creation. If so, then "this world is the object of God's redeeming

48. Runyon, "The Sacraments," 216.

49. Ibid., 214.

50. Ibid.

51. Ibid., 215.

52. Runyon, "The World as the Original Sacrament," 495.

53. Ibid., 496. Runyon argues that the exaggerated Christological bias of Western sacramental theology has overshadowed the cosmic themes of the Pauline and Johannine traditions while "the world has been silently subsumed under the human as fellow creature, but seldom has it been addressed explicitly, with the result that the world Jesus came to reconcile has been understood as restricted to the anthropocentric world of human sin and corruption," 495–96.

and transforming activity; and christology, the Church, and sacraments, must all be seen within the context of this overarching purpose."[54]

On this account, there remains a lot to discern and reevaluate in both the Roman Catholic and Protestant versions of Western Christianity. Keeping postcolonial planetarity in mind, Runyon's critique is multi-pronged, far-reaching, and remains urgent in more than one cultural context of Christian practice and doctrine:

> The problem with most traditional eucharistic theologies, Protestant or Catholic, is that their horizons do not extend far enough. They stretch neither to the eschaton nor to creation [. . .] and they have encouraged what I would call incomplete or *truncated* versions of eucharistic interpretation and practice. They interrupt the divine intention short of its ultimate goal. The Protestant truncation typically has reduced the sacrament to an occasion for repentance and the receiving of divine forgiveness [. . .] The Catholic truncation has been to see the purpose of Christ's coming as the founding of an institution to provide the means of grace and a safe passage to the other shore [. . .] But even in some of the best Catholic thought. . .the understanding of the significance of the Eucharist seems to begin and end with the personal and interpersonal—and miss its final purpose.[55]

To remedy these widespread truncations, Runyon argues that it is precisely the eschatological vector of the real presence of Christ in the Eucharist that positions us to "look back from the *eschaton* to the *proton*, from kingdom to creation, and to look at the creation with new eyes."[56] While Christ "remains the sacramental means to reconcile a fallen humanity,"[57] the created world is the original sacrament in the sense that it constitutes the overarching planetary, indeed, cosmic horizon, within which all creative, redemptive, sanctifying, and transforming actions unfold. Thus, "the original sacrament is not the Church. . . and not even Christ, important as the sacramental nature of Christ and of the Church are for Christian faith and practice. But the original, visible, sign of God's grace is the world he entrusts to our care."[58]

Runyon's notion of original sacrament broadens the horizon of sacramental interface in planetary terms. Such a move decenters, even though

54. Ibid., 498.
55. Runyon, "The World as the Original Sacrament," 510–11. Italics in the original.
56. Ibid., 500.
57. Ibid.
58. Ibid., 501.

without hierarchical subalternization, the anthropocentric fixations of salvation. Such a move also performs a much needed correction of the narcissistic temptation of the Church "to be fascinated and preoccupied by its own institutional life" so that, disabused of such preoccupations, the Church can then interpret the true original sacrament "through the Word given it in Christ."[59]

The Primordiality of Intracosmic Communio: Elizabeth A. Johnson

The American Catholic feminist theologian Elizabeth Johnson has been calling for a "turn to the cosmos"[60] before anything ecological or postcolonial even registered as a blip on most theologians' radar screens. Johnson not only rekindled the idea of the world as sacrament but also proposed a methodological shift toward constructively re-appropriating the conception of the created world as a sacrament precisely as an inclusive hermeneutical horizon for the Christian theological enterprise.[61] Moreover, Johnson has elaborated that the created world ought to be seen as the "primordial sacrament that reflects the glory of God and that speaks a revelatory word."[62]

For Johnson, the natural world as the primordial sacrament denotes a revelatory and, what often gets sidetracked in typical Western definitions of sacrament, also an inherently pneumatological interface:

> Pervaded and empowered by the Creator Spirit, the natural world itself has a sacred character. It is revelatory of the beauty, wisdom, and power of God. It is a primordial sacrament which communicates the presence of God. To say that the *communio sanctorum* includes the sacred gifts of air, water, land, and the myriad species that share the planet with human beings is to give this phrase a theological interpretation replete with ecological significance [. . .] Everything exists, lives, and moves with others and for others in the cosmic community of creation in the Spirit. This many-faceted community, which includes human beings but not limited to them, is the primordial *communio*

59. Ibid., 503.

60. Johnson, "Presidential Address," 53–69.

61. Ibid. On the world as sacrament see, for example, Johnson, *Women, Earth, and Creator Spirit,* 64.

62. Johnson, *Friends of God and Prophets,* 223.

sanctorum, or communion of holy ones, engendered by the power of the Spirit.[63]

Johnson's notion of creation as a primordial sacrament is exquisitely attentive to the planetary dimensions of our ecological predicaments. Her sacramental elaboration of *communio sanctorum* certainly expands and enriches both the semiotic, that is, the revelatory *signum*, dimension of the sacramental structure of reality, as well as a truly comprehensive and holistic sacramental solidarity throughout the whole creation. But relating to the created world as the primordial sacrament also entails an interactive, indeed, causative dimension (the *causa* or the dynamic efficacy aspect in traditional sacramental parlance). What this means is that creation as primordial sacrament is not about soteriological closure and the finality of "mission accomplished" in a grandly expanded, and supersized, way or even in an exceptionally transparent way that precludes further evolution in creation and revelation.

Instead of making such preemptive and triumphant claims, Johnson points not just to the fully fledged *communio* aspect but also to the intricate *unio* aspect that this cosmic sacramental interface makes possible and invites us into as a path—an unfinished process in progress—toward union with the Divine. We, humans, are not "lost in expansion" or somehow unduly marginalized in the now cosmic warp of space and time. Rather, quite the opposite obtains: this unitive trajectory opens up new vistas of transformative intimacy with the Divine under the auspices of the world as the primordial sacrament, "for the universe itself is the primordial sacrament through which we *participate in* and *communicate with* divine mystery."[64]

Additionally, Johnson's pneumatological amplification of the idea of primordial sacrament to reflect the scope of the universe also affirms an ethical aspect which "reveals its prophetic edge" and "calls forth an ecological ethic of restraint of human greed and promotion of care for the earth."[65] In postcolonial parlance, what the idea of the world as the primordial sacrament critiques and attempts to modulate in Johnson's argument is precisely that imperialistic subalternization of non-human creation in the cosmology of divine and human power which postcolonial critical metaphors such as planetarity also try to undermine. Namely, they try to undermine, and eventually transmute, dualistic and hegemonic power as dominance which inscribes its cruel zero-sum logic into every nook and cranny of human relationships and into the very texture of wider earthly reality wherever hu-

63. Johnson, *Abounding in Kindness*, 284–85.

64. Johnson, "Community on Earth as in Heaven," 13. Italics added.

65. Ibid.

mans can make our presence and agency felt. And this leads me to the third brief example—the idea of cosmos as the "primary sacrament" by Dorothy McDougall.

World as the Primary Sacrament: Dorothy C. McDougall

The Canadian Roman Catholic ecofeminist Dorothy McDougall takes on the anthropological implications of the "turn to subject" in modern and postmodern sacramental theology by appropriating a critical ecofeminist cosmology to apply the ecofeminist analysis of domination "to overcome the anthropocentric and androcentric bias that undergirds and propels the socio-ecological crisis."[66] Drawing inspiration from Thomas Berry's work, McDougall seeks to modulate the dominance of a totalizing Christocentrism (i.e., a glorified version of anthropocentrism) and ecclesiocentrism of mainstream (mostly Catholic) sacramental theology by calling into question the popular notion of Jesus as the primordial sacrament since it "undermines [that] priority, both in regards to evolutionary time and to the efficaciousness of God's relationship in the whole of cosmic history."[67] The ecological crisis mandates a serious reexamination of the anthropocentrism "that is inherent in the exclusive attention to human history that is endemic in sacramental theology."[68]

As we find ourselves in the midst of ecological degradation, McDougall argues that shifting precedence—yet not exclusivity or dominance—to the cosmos as the primary context of sacramental liturgy has several advantages. First, the understanding of cosmos as the primary sacrament aids the commitment to prioritize the intrinsic connection between creation and salvation which is theoretically highly esteemed in Christian theology yet frequently only paid lip service to in modern and postmodern Western thought.[69] Secondly, it fosters not only a more holistic approach beyond anthropocentrism but also a more open-ended theological method in relation to interreligious dialogue:

> The cosmos is the primary event in which humanity is drawn into and participates in God's creative redeeming love (along with the rest of creation). The Christian liturgy is an efficacious moment but it is not the only moment nor the only mode of expressing eschatological hope and fulfillment. Such perspective

66. McDougall, *The Cosmos as the Primary Sacrament*, 159.

67. McDougall, "The Cosmos as Primary Sacrament," 237.

68. Ibid., 235.

69. Ibid., 237–40.

> not only tends toward undercutting the anthropocentrism inherent in contemporary sacramental theology, but also creates a context for a postmodern approach to inter-faith dialogue.[70]

Thirdly, the idea of the world as the primary sacrament signals a shift away from an exclusivist and inward-looking orientation in sacramental theology. McDougall proposes that it "acknowledges the contingency of the Christian narrative within the framework of the larger narrative of the universe."[71] Furthermore, in a way that is particularly resonant with the recent postcolonial emphasis on planetarity, McDougall underscores that seeing cosmos as the primary sacrament "recognizes the contingency of all cultural narratives" and precludes the approach in theology "that limits divine involvement in the world to humanity or to its Christian ecclesial expression."[72]

On top of that, fourthly, like other sacramental theologians who entertain the idea of the world as primary/primordial/original sacrament, McDougall observes that it "challenges the limitations imposed on the sacramental life by the ecclesial assertion regarding the primacy of *seven* sacraments" while aspiring to "reclaim the number seven's original meaning of plenitude and perfection and to affirm the myriad ways the church may give witness to the divine presence in the world."[73] In a specifically eucharistic context, "the cosmos as primary sacrament affirms that the paschal mystery is embedded in the earth's struggle towards life, and that the divine promise is revealed in the beauty and fecund aliveness of the universe itself."[74]

Last but not least: what is clearly overdue not only in sacramental theology but in Christian theology in general, McDougall argues, is a divestment from coupled anthropocentric and androcentric bias. The joined bias functions throughout patriarchal and dualistic worldviews. It "has been not only historically reflected in ecclesial governance" but also "continues to be promoted as divinely ordained."[75] Such a divestment, however, must also "go beyond a symbolic understanding of the sacramentality of the natural

70. Ibid., 236.

71. McDougall, *The Cosmos as the Primary Sacrament*, 117. To preempt the anticipated critique, McDougall immediately adds: "At the same time, it recognizes a universal relevance in the particularity of Jesus' life, death, and resurrection as another paradigm 'in which God's presence and action are felt'. It contextualizes the Christian story as one of the many places in which God's presence is revelatory and operative as creative, redeeming love," 117.

72. Ibid., 162.

73. Ibid., 163. Italics in the original.

74. Ibid., 164.

75. Ibid., 160.

world" so that it can "articulate the principle that the universe is comprised of community of subjects who are active participants in the divine activity—cosmogenesis."[76] McDougall invites a reconsideration of the alienating juxtaposition of nature (everyday life, sheer materiality) versus culture (objectified symbols, disconnected ritual action) which sacramental theology, at least potentially, should be particularly well-suited to engage in a creative way.

McDougall's concept of the world as the primary sacrament engages constructively with the same concerns that mark the postcolonial notion of planetarity and postcolonial ecocriticism in general. These concerns gravitate around the imaginaries and practices of power that continue to inscribe our lived reality in dominance, hegemony, injustice, and pain.

From a planetary view, the quest for justice and the flourishing of life simultaneously traverses many terrains of reality. It underscores the interdependence of justice and the holistic well-being of all creation. The persistent realities of sociohistorical colonialism, geopolitical imperialism, anthropocentrism, sexism, oblivious utilitarianism, and racism—to name just the most widespread operational constructs of empowerment and disempowerment—can only be understood, and their pernicious impact duly appreciated, through an intersectional, multidimensional, and indeed a "catholic," approach. In the early twenty-first century, both sacramental theology and postcolonial studies have arrived at a juncture where this sort of planetary intersectionality or such "catholicity" of critical and constructive efforts is becoming, in my estimation, the most responsible and the most fitting theoretical sensibility in the world of globalized postcoloniality.

Sacramentum Mundi of Liberation and Wholeness: Francis X. D'Sa

Finally, I would like to briefly address the work of Francis X. D'Sa, an Indian Jesuit theologian, who straddles the cultural and historical interval between the Latin roots of Roman Catholicism and postcolonial India. In contrast to many postmodern sacramental conventions, D'Sa proposes a constructive Ignatian vision of sacramentality where the created world, not Jesus or the church, is conceived as *sacramentum mundi*, and as such it completes the cosmotheandric structure of reality.[77]

As is immediately obvious from the terminology alone, D'Sa's work is influenced by another Jesuit, Raimon Panikkar, and his vigorous promotion

76. Ibid.

77. D'Sa, "Sacramentum Mundi," 239–93.

of "theantropocosmism": the three-pronged constellation of lived reality—God, cosmos, and humanity. These are the three primordial adjectives for both Pannikar and D'Sa—"the Cosmic, the Human, and the Divine, which describe Reality" on three interrelated and communitarian, yet also irreducibly unique, levels.[78] From this perspective, sacraments are really sacraments—that is, "fully liberative relationships" beyond anthropocentric individualism—only if and when their texture is "woven from the warp of the human community and the woof of the cosmic community so that both are opened up to the realization of their full potential."[79]

D'Sa never identifies himself as a postcolonial theologian. Yet his sacramental theology is rooted in the postcolonial and religiously plural context of India. Hindu spiritual traditions provide a comparative context for D'Sa's constructive sacramental vision, as does Ignatian spirituality. In the present context, however, it is the notion of the world as *sacramentum mundi*, or as "the primordial sacrament, the Ursakrament"[80] that I would like to focus on in these brief reflections.

The sacramental interface of reality, according to D'Sa, is characterized by what postcolonials would call ethics/the ethical pre-text. Sacrament, D'Sa argues, "is whatever functions as a liberative symbol in the experience of a people."[81] What distinguishes sacrament from a generic symbol is precisely the "liberative dynamics" that is "thematically stressed."[82] Consequently, "a liberative symbol is one that leads a community to wholeness; it is symbolic of wholeness that frees from all alienation and bondage. This is precisely what a sacrament intends; it is symbolic of wholeness and total freedom."[83]

According to D'Sa, the world as primordial sacrament does not function exclusively or competitively among all other sacraments. Rather, its particular kind of sacramentality is akin to being the ground that underpins all other sacramental relations and events:

> To neglect this aspect is to neglect the foundation of all sacramental theology, as the history of most of our sacramental

78. Ibid., 245. D'Sa quotes Panikkar to explain: "The times begin to be ripe now to gather again the broken pieces of these partial insights into a new wholistic vision: there is no matter without spirit and no spirit without matter, no World without Man, no God without the Universe, etc. God, Man and World are three artificially substantivized forms of the three primordial adjectives which describe Reality," 245. Panikkar's use of "Man" is not an expression of blunt patriarchal sensibilities as D'Sa carefully explains.

79. Ibid., 253.

80. Ibid., 249.

81. Ibid., 248.

82. Ibid., 249.

83. Ibid.

> theologies sadly testifies. It is rare that we find a theology of sacraments that takes the world seriously. The source of the "otherworldly" character of today's sacramental praxis is to be located here. That is why there is urgent need to work out the base of all sacramental theology, namely, the sacramentality of the universe.[84]
>
> The world alone is the sacrament of reality. Whatever is real has a perceptible aspect. There is nothing that we can experience, understand and judge which does not have some perceptible dimension. . . The world as the perceptible aspect is the meeting point of the cosmic, the human and the divine. This makes the world alone the sacrament of reality. The world alone is the place where humans can encounter one another as well as the divine. [. . .] If the world as the sum total of reality's perceptibility is a sacrament then every thing in the world shares in the sacramentality of the world. [. . .] This of course does not imply that all these beings participate in it the same manner. Water is a sacrament but not in the way that Jesus is a sacrament. . . Ultimately, all sacraments are grounded in the one and only the sacrament of reality, namely, the world.[85]

Despite the ambiguity and precariousness of all sacramental interactions,[86] and despite the growing number of people for whom God has become functionally meaningless and inconsequential,[87] D'Sa insists on the urgency of retrieving the reality of wholeness that sacraments reveal, model, perform, and effect. Engaging with environmental and feminist discourses, D'Sa argues that the "sense of the divine seems to express itself in a holistic manner . . . in the search for wholeness and fullness."[88] The re-envisagement of sacramentality focuses on the retrieval of the wholeness of reality for all—for humanity as well as for the overarching ecosystem of the whole planet in the context of the even more spacious created universe—and goes hand in hand with an emphasis on ethics through transformative liberation.

Sacraments, starting with the cosmos as the *Ursakrament*, embody the potential to derail and then re-rout the edifices of dominance, including

84. Ibid., 249.

85. Ibid., 258–59.

86. Ibid., 255.

87. Ibid., 261–62. What is not meant here is lack of religiousness or fundamentalist fervor but rather the observation that "God and religion have lost all credibility in the eyes of people of good will. God and religion are taken to be the refuge of the gullible and the dogmatic, not of the critical and the committed," 262.

88. Ibid., 265.

patriarchal ecclesiastical dominance as well as wholesale anthropocentric dominance, according to D'Sa. Again the resonance with postcolonial visions of emancipatory transformation is quite remarkable. Instead of the hegemonic exercise of competitive self-empowerment through the disempowerment of others and the effective subalternization of the natural world, or women, or indigenous peoples, or the poor, the sacramental mode of divine power functions from within as the "operative presence of the divine mystery in all things and at all times."[89] At the end of the day, according to D'Sa, the very integrity of sacraments hinges on ethics:

> Our sacraments have been privatized, individualized and, to a great extent, psychologized and ritualized; their efficacy, if at all, is at work only within the precincts of the church. This is indeed a far cry from the sacramental intentionality of liberating the world from the demons of instrumentalization and retrieving the originary wholeness of reality. But such a retrieval is difficult because the church's sacraments are in the main juridically anchored and ritualistically preoccupied.[90]
>
> Only the realization that a sacrament is first and last a sacrament of liberation can bring about a radical change in our approach to sacraments. It is this that has to inform all ritual celebration. Indeed the importance of ritual (in contradistinction to ritualism) cannot be underestimated but it derives from the fact that the ritual is not for itself but precisely for focusing on the specific function of sacraments. This consists in the retrieval of the wholeness of reality.[91]

The pivotal mark that determines the very sacramental quality of a sacrament, its truthfulness and legitimacy—a sacrament being always an interactive and relational event, always a situation and not merely a thing—is what the postcolonial ethos would describe as ethical intentionality and ethical efficacy. In the words of D'Sa, "a genuine sacrament is always a sacrament of liberation"—it "intends liberation" and it "promotes liberation" toward bringing wholeness to fruition in the entire created reality.[92] There can hardly be a more postcolonial, and indeed a more decolonial, way of perceiving the planetary and cosmic purpose as well as the salvific vocation of sacraments.

89. Ibid., 265–66.

90. Ibid., 269.

91. Ibid.

92. Ibid.

3.4.

Toward a Sacramental Pluriverse

On Sacraments as the Ethical Ciphers of Postcolonial Transcendence

To think that we Christians are moving into the third millennium with a serene sacramental theology is a Pollyanna dream.[1]

KENAN B. OSBORNE, O.F.M.

The notion of sacramentality is subject to historical change.[2]

GEORGES DE SCHRIJVER, S.J.

God-talk is enmeshed in and affects the sociopolitical realm, but this does not reduce God to an incidental product of the collective imagination.[3]

MAYRA RIVERA

1. Osborne, *Christian Sacraments in a Postmodern World*, 40.
2. De Schrijver, "Experiencing the Sacramental Character of Existence," 12.
3. Rivera, "God and Difference," 32.

This chapter offers a constructive sketch—indeed only one sketch or one variation on the theme among many possible others—of how the postcolonial idea of planetarity might resonate in a sacramental framework of theology as an imaginary of sacramental pluriverse. Putting insights about the world as the primary sacramental mystery, *Ursakrament*, in conversation with postcolonial sensibilities that are rooted in its "ethical pre-text" and emphasis on planetarity, I will share some constructive suggestions about how sacraments and the whole pluriverse of sacramentality might be re-envisioned beyond the conventional and numerically "closed" sacramental systems. The conventional Occidental approaches today seem to bring up more theological and ethical frustrations than spiritually life-giving momentum for healing old confessional antagonisms among various Christian groups, let alone adequate responses to the unprecedented planetary challenge of environmental crisis in the early twenty-first century. The time is ripe to seek for more revitalizing sacramental imaginaries in the present era of postmodernity, postcoloniality, and the emerging perplexities of posthumanism.

POSTCOLONIAL SACRAMENTALITY: A HYBRID INTERFACE OF LIBERATION AND TRANSFORMATION

How can sacraments start to be conceived from within the postcolonial acoustics of imagination? How do they signify, how do they relate, how do they communicate—and how do they effect change, indeed effect a transformative and liberative change? At this juncture some more systematic elaborations are finally in order.

Considering how foundational relationality is—all reciprocal asymmetries considered—for postcolonial and diasporic imaginaries, it is only pertinent to underscore relationality again. Fortunately, in this regard, there is an instinctive affinity between postcolonial, diasporic, and sacramental discourses. Sacraments also are relational, embodied, intersubjective, and interactive events—actions, occasions, happenings, proceedings, situations. In sacraments we are encountered by the Divine but that does not happen in a disembodied nowhere-land. It does happen through that one irreducible *Ursakrament*, the initial and earliest sacrament: the creation. Across the interface of sacramentality we encounter Divinity, again and again, through that one irrevocable planetary horizon of meaning, agency, and efficacy that alone renders such transontological encounters possible—our planet, our common sacramental home, our *Ursakrament* within the broader cosmic constellation of creation.

Sacraments are relationally dynamic, polyvalent, multi-mediated, and multidirectional mysteries. They are efficacious—and yet they are opaque. They are not static objects or immutable rites trapped into what Edward Said would describe as an ultimately uninteresting competitive dialectic of presence and absence.[4] They are not limited or even exhausted by rituals and images that have been hijacked by—or have tamely surrendered to—pathologies of colonial empires past and present. At the most basic level of understanding, a sacrament, as I already intimated in Prelude III following Jean-Jacques von Allmen, is not a "thing" (*une chose*) but a "'situation' *(une situation*): it is where our world is visited, or better: it is inhabited and transformed by the presence of the future eon."[5]

Sacraments are not "the remote-control apparatus of a clerical caste."[6] Rather, as interactive mysteries, they embody and render experientially meaningful that underlying relational interface which unceasingly flares forth within the Trinitarian *creatio continua* in which creation can never be segregated away from the salvific *theosis* of cosmic transfiguration through the Incarnate Word and Wisdom and in the movement of the Holy Spirit. And what might that underlying, all-embracing, all-grounding, and in a sense "basic" yet absolutely mysterious, interface be? Sacramentality is that interface. Sacramentality is indeed, before anything else and above all else, and whatever else it might mean, an interface—but not in a sense of being amere boundary or border. Rather, in this context, interface is what the language of computer science describes as the "platform" or a boundary space, or a circuit of interaction between various programs, systems, applications, and devices.

To speak of sacramentality is not a neutral enterprise. The notion of sacramentality entails a certain metaphysics, a metaphysics of particular relationality, even if such terminology is staunchly avoided in postmodern circles. For, to speak of sacramentality is to speak not only epistemologically, or in terms of sheer rituality, but also, and even primarily, ontologically. Sacramentality as the relational interface among the Divine, humanity, and non-human and cosmic creation is the very space of creation, in which what Eastern Orthodox theologians usually call God's "energies" (in Greek, *energeiai*, or Godself in relational action) interabide and interact with the creation. Sacramentality as an ontological and epistemological interface describes the distinctive constitutional terrain of this unique God-world relationality.

4. Said, *Reflections on Exile*, 379.

5. Von Allmen, *Prophétisme sacramentel*, 13.

6. Pieris, *An Asian Theology of Liberation*, 7.

The notion of sacramentality articulates dynamic and hybrid entanglement: the worldwardness of God and the godwardness of the world on the journey of continuous creation and salvation. It conveys the mysterious interactivity in which our human bodies, senses, intellects, relationships, and wills live and move, and have their being, all of them in relation to the Divine—no matter how opaquely in the present dispensation of chaos, injustice, poverty, and strife. Sacramentality describes a relational ontology in which a cosmovisionary scope and a gossamer microcosmic intimacy holds together, indeed, plays off one another in a shared panentheistic hybridity of asymmetrical reciprocity.[7] In this sense, sacramentality is a name for a transontological borderscape where the Uncreated encounters the created through a pluriverse of sacramental refractions—the sacraments—to revitalize, to liberate, to reconcile, and to make whole already here and now, in the thick of messy history, in an inexhaustible multitude of ways and places. Once more with feeling: sacramental interface comes to life only in the density and opacity of human embodiment in history. And sacramentality as an interface of relationality is radically hybrid—and opaque.

What exactly might sacramentality really have to do with hybridity? Actually quite a lot. As already noted in Part II Ch. 2, postcolonial hybridity is not a figure of realized eschatology. Hybridity is an imaginary of radical, deep-rooted and irrevocable relationality of existence—and so is sacramentality. Both hybridity and sacramentality are convivial imaginaries of differences concurring, interacting, and confronting one another. But postcolonial hybridity bears a vigilant witness not only to the intricacies of organic and intentional relations but equally to the wounding asymmetries of power, welfare, authority, liberty, and agency that color all and every relation in this world. Hybridity articulates the dynamic of "breaking and joining" and of making difference into sameness and sameness into difference (to use Robert J.C. Young's language) to engender the concurrence of difference and sameness in an apparently impossible simultaneity that eschews the either/or and zero-sum logic of dualism.[8]

Postcolonial hybridity certainly entails the *anamnesis* of the wretched of the earth and "the universality of our elemental vulnerability to the

7. My approach here is somewhat similar to the pansacramental vision of the world, though without the Hegelian overtones, that Hans Gustafson has proposed in his recent study *Finding All Things in God: Pansacramentalism and Doing Theology Interreligiously*. Even though my approach has originated independently from Gustafson's fascinating proposal, I share a similar panentheistic theo-philosophical comportment which puts a premium on exploring "how the divine is in all things, how all things reveal the divine, and how all things have their existence in the divine," 245.

8. See Part II, Ch. 2.

wrongs we visit upon each other."[9] On the other hand, it also bodies forth an *epiclesis* for the Third Space that is radically open for transformation, liberation, and wholeness. The notion of hybridity holds anamnesis and epiclesis together, letting them play off one another with all the intricacy of, as Edward Said would say, contrapuntality. Isn't something similar to a certain counterpoint—not identical, but analogous—playing out across the sacramental interface of God-world relation?

To begin with, sacramentality is a "worldly" concept that describes the "worldly" state of affairs on this planet and in this cosmos of evolutionary emergence with all the natural and interpersonal realities of evil, inadequacy, failure, limitation, sin, and suffering. Namely, sacramentality is not an imaginary of a fully realized eschatological fulfillment. As easy as it is for liturgical minds to forget, sacramentality articulates a state of affairs *in via*, and not *in patria*. Despite claims and desires for panoptical transparency, sacramentality does not denote the consummation of the beatific vision and *theosis*. Sacramental performances and sacramental imagination are as malleable as everything and anything in creation: they can mediate healing, yet they have often fallen prey to the pathologies of sinful power; they can embody liberation for the whole creation to become fully alive, yet they have also been "worldly" in the demonic sense to effectively become countersigns against divine grace and spiritual liberation; they can be marvelously Reign-of-God-centric, but also humanly, oh, too humanly, egocentric.

Thus sacramentality is a truly contrapuntal imaginary as I articulated such an imaginary in conversation with Edward Said in Part II. It is simultaneously kataphatic and apophatic, an imaginary of "already, but not yet." It is also an imaginary of the irrevocable and the true, good, and beautiful interabiding of the Uncreated and the created—yet such an interabiding cannot be responsibly described otherwise than veiled: namely, fragile, fragmentary, and fleeting. The God who reveals and relates sacramentally is always already, in the words of Louis-Marie Chauvet, "at the mercy of the body."[10]

Sacramental veracity, theologically speaking, resides precisely in the contrapuntal capacity to be an interface and an imaginary of both the redemptive *anamnesis* of the Christ event, including Jesus' crucifixion, and as an eschatological *epiclesis* for and *epektasis* toward the "new heaven and new earth." But sacramental veracity, historically and epistemologically speaking, also resides in an non-triumphant critical realism that postcolonial sacramental theology would do well to keep in mind and that David Bentley Hart has so insightfully summarized:

9. Gilroy, *Postcolonial Melancholia*, 4.

10. Chauvet, *The Sacraments*.

> Our longing for transcendence is inextinguishable in us, and the appeal of the transcendent to our deepest natures will always be audible and visible to us in some form "first and finally in the form of beauty" and will continue to waken in us both wonder and an often inexpressible unhappiness. But in an age such as ours, within the picture of the world that now prevails, that beauty must seem more ambiguous, more beleaguered, and the call of transcendence more elusive of interpretation, like a voice heard in a dream. In the absence of that scale of shining mediations that once seemed seamlessly to unite the immanent and the transcendent, the earthly and the heavenly, nature and supernature, we are nevertheless still open to the same summons issued in every age to every soul; but it must for now come to us as something more mysterious, tragic, and terrible than it once was.[11]

To avoid unwarranted triumphalism, it is worth repeating once more that sacramental interface does not equal (a presumptuous) angelic transparency or (a premature) eschatological resolution of ambiguity, limitations, and suffering that permeate human life and the whole creation as we know it today. Hence sacramentality in postcolonial perspectives cannot lose the awareness of the opacity which postcolonial hybridity expresses. Sacraments, as the first two chapters in Part III reiterated, live and move in the "worldly" world that is structured in dominance and in which the pathologies of power, knowledge, and will so often wreak havoc on our bodies, souls, environments, societies, and churches. The evolutionary emergence of life is replete not only with beauty and creativity, but also with cruelty, folly, and waste. But of course, there is also a dimension of *epiclesis* in hybridity. Hence sacraments, if we see them as hybrid interfaces, vector toward the Third Space of redemptive transformation even in their "worldly" opacity—outward, inward, upward, backward, downward, depth-ward, onward, forward—and as they interface countless pathways and profound intuitions of the presence and action of the triune Mystery that ultimately undergirds all that is.

It is always so tempting to claim a simple and uncomplicated transparency of presence and purpose in sacramental matters. But what marks all sacramental events and situations is precisely opacity. More will be said about sacramental opacity in the upcoming Chapter 5 in relation to Christ's presence in the Eucharist. Here is it imperative to note that opacity does not mean a lack of truth or lack of reality. It conveys precisely the exquisite complexity of the truth about reality that eludes superficiality and the seductive

11. Hart, "The Gnostic Turn." Para.13–14.

grasp of manipulative human schemes about ourselves, God, and the world that we, humans, share with the dazzling and bewildering multitudes of animal and plant life.

POSTCOLONIAL SACRAMENTS AS ETHICAL CIPHERS

But what about the postcolonial ethical pre-text, the postcolonial *articulus stantis et cadentis*, the sensibility upon which postcolonialism stands or falls? How does the postcolonial hypersensitivity toward the suffering of those marginalized, disinherited, and sinned against voyage into this sacramental imaginary? What role would those nonnegotiable ethical comportments play in this sacramental galaxy of relations and revelations?

As I already signaled in the previous chapter in a Levinasian spirit, sacraments do not belong to the order of "dreams"—disconnected aesthetic neverlands of self-indulgence in which the decadence of the pious interiority of those who find themselves fortunate in this world can run amok. Instead, like Emmanuel Levinas, postcolonial sensibilities prioritize ethics before not only ontology and epistemology, but also before the history of dogmatic expressions. If so, then a postcolonial vision of sacramentality indeed cannot be a neutral imaginary that can smoothly fit into whatever profitable mold is in need of spiritual(ized) legitimation.

The question that really matters in postcolonial sacramental imaginary is this: all things considered, is sacramental relationality a characteristically ethical relationality? I submit that it can be conceived as such despite all the pathologies of power that any particular sacramental manifestation has been and is subjected to. The next chapter on the Eucharist will offer further elaborations as to why it can be conceived as such. Here, suffice it to say, sacramentality is an interface of a primordial relationality that is embedded, in potentiality and divine intentionality, in a distinct qualitative pattern or an axiological structure. Perhaps it could be said that sacramentality as a relational interface refers to certain ethical ground rules, the ethical "how" that shapes the makeup of reality the more it becomes Godward, divinized, transfigured, and fulfilled.

A sacrament—if and when it is "genuine," as Francis D'Sa would say—is what happens when the Uncreated and the created agencies, energies, and intentionalities intersect, intertwine, interact and interabide non-coercively, non-reductively, and non-hegemonically. Sacrament expresses an imaginary of relationality characterized by reciprocity, albeit an asymmetrical reciprocity. Sacramental interface of the God-world relationality is asymmetrical—and thus also subject to the apophatic proviso of *dissimilitudo semper maior*, even amidst the layers, mirrors, fractal patterns, and analogical intervals that infuse the sacramental interface in so many evolving ways. Here, however, the asymmetry between the Creator and creation models something very different from the overwhelmingly unidirectional master-slave relationship that colonialism always strived to embody. This sort of reciprocal and synergistic asymmetry between the Creator and the created reality allows for more than just the tired and dualistic zero-sum kind of dominance and subservience when it comes to empowerment and agency.

Why? At its best, Christian theology has vigorously affirmed that Uncreated grace does not obliterate, devalue, or displace creation. Rather, in Thomas Aquinas' classic expression, grace—or God's "energies," to use a more Eastern expression,[12] permeating creation in a non-competitive way—perfects nature which is always *in via* toward decisive fruition, yet very palpably not *in patria* yet. Perfecting in this context means not only a progressive transformation but also a deep decontamination, as it were, or a deep decolonization of being, relating, knowing, and acting. Therefore, properly speaking, sacramentality is about those encounters which enable (that is, cause, effect, empower, facilitate, and sustain) a salvific transformation of awakening, reconciliation, renewal, healing, and whole-making through a fitting relational reciprocity and synergy, asymmetrical as it may be, among God, humanity, and the rest of creation. Such encounters are ultimately sourced in the perichoretic triune love of the Holy Mystery in whom we all live, and move, and have our being (Acts 17:28).

As all great mysteries of life, anything to do with love is perhaps best described with apophatic reverence. Hence the most fitting postcolonial elaboration of how sacraments signify and effect transformative change can be summarized, taking a cue from Chalcedon, within an apophatic horizon: the melodies of the sacraments unfold without coercion, without competition, without intimidation, without cruelty, without manipulation, without deceit, without avarice, and without violating the integrity of all sentient beings and the whole material universe. Because, as James White has put it so succinctly, sacraments are about nothing less than God's gift of self: "ultimately sacraments reflect our understanding of how God works in this world."[13]

12. McGuckin summarizes the concept of uncreated divine energies as follows: "God's energies [are] God's outreach to the world (the force of creation and creative sustenance of all being, the force of grace that deifies and saves humankind and reveals the Godhead to the disciple. . ." and "as divine energies they are not just external operations of God, but the Presence itself in its active saving role," McGuckin, "Gregory Palamas," 142.

13. White, *Sacraments as God's Self Giving*, 143.

CONSIDERING POSTCOLONIAL SACRAMENTAL TRANSCENDENCE: AN INSIDE JOB

A postcolonial vision of sacramentality speaks of an interface across which a decidedly non-imperialistic divine transcendence interacts with every nook and cranny of created immanence through a "nonconfining embrace" in such a way that it "refuses the 'hard boundary' between divine and the created."[14] Mayra Rivera is right: there is a good reason to resist reductionist understandings of creation and instead envision a "broad cosmic sacramentality that embraces the interhuman encounters and the nonhuman world" since our conceptions of sacramentality shape our understanding of God—and the way God acts.[15]

Furthermore, postcolonial envisagement of divine transcendence as relational and as sacramental is indeed, in a very important sense, what Rivera also describes as "internal" transcendence. Namely, according to Rivera's notion of "broadly sacramental transcendence," it "transcends *in* and not as something that transcends *away* from; as something that physically impels to more but not by taking out of; as something that *pushes* forward, but at the same time *retains*."[16] Transcendence here "pushes forward and retains;" thus "the future emerges from within the matrices of relations that characterize created life, which include sociopolitical relations as well as the organic energies that sustain life and evolution in the cosmos."[17]

Here postcolonial vision joins hands with liberation theology. Leonardo Boff makes a similar point: the sacramental interface, which he idiosyncratically calls "transparency" is a borderland, an in-between space, or a third dimension which escapes being pigeonholed, as it were, in either transcendence or immanence. Rather, sacramentality can be perceived as a hybrid reality that "emerges through the world itself" and thus cannot be fully exhausted by the conventional dualistic "polarity of transcendence-immanence."[18] Even though I would be much more reticent to give prominence to ontological and epistemological "transparency" as victoriously as Boff does, it foreshadows a certain third space in which the entanglement of "mutual presence means that simple transcendence and simple immanence are overcome. There emerges an intermediate category, transparency, which is precisely the presence of transcendence within immanence."[19]

14. Rivera, *The Touch of Transcendence*, 135, 133.
15. Rivera, "God and Difference," 38.
16. Ibid., 39.
17. Ibid.
18. Boff, *Die Kirche als Sakrament*, 125–26.
19. Boff, *Cry of the Earth*, 153.

God continuously creates and saves not through extrinsic interventions but through "complexity, interiority, and connectedness."[20] Despite the haste of "transparency," it is nevertheless Boff's emphasis on complexity and connectedness that brings us right to the crux of postcolonial concerns.

Postcolonial visions of sacramental transcendence foreground "an image of development that evokes the organic rhythms of nature or the subtle modulations of history" while in the mainstream Occidental (both modern and postmodern) sacramentality is "frequently overshadowed by the (more phallic) imagery of something 'breaking in' from the outside."[21]

The postcolonial point, ultimately, is to develop a sacramental cosmo-ontology "in which transcendence flows through reality as the sap through the branches of a tree. Transcendence moves in the world, with its material and vital forces in their relation to human freedom, producing transformations that follow the nonlinear patterns of biological time."[22] The ethical "how" of sacramental relationality remains a matter of utmost concern because it is often very profitable to ignore that all theological images—of God, of salvation, of sacraments—"function." How we relate to the transcendent God, Rivera rightly argues, cannot but influence how we relate to other human and nonhuman creatures:

> Our images of divine transcendence inform our constructions of interhuman otherness. Ideas about the divine Other are always related to our perceptions of and relationships with the human Other [. . .] theologically God's transcendence is inseparable from theological anthropology [. . .] Interhuman transcendence takes place in and contributes to cosmic co-creation. The interhuman, the cosmic, and the social converge.[23]

How should it feel to be on the receiving end of genuinely sacramental encounters with the transcendent Divine? Most likely somewhat like this: God works in each of us "by invitation and by stealth. . .never by coercion, drawing us with mercy and patience toward the way of peace, truth, and nonviolence."[24] Sacramentality is the interface that mediates a transcosmic reality and a divinely empowering agency which is, as Georges de Schrijver puts it, "internally active in cosmic reality" and to which we are invited to attune and harmonize with:

20. Ibid.,150.

21. Rivera, *The Touch of Transcendence*, 51.

22. Ibid., 53.

23. Ibid., 128, 129.

24. Pramuk, *At Play in Creation*, 38.

> In the sacramental view, one . . . takes notice of a light "in" and "behind" beings and through which these beings take on a fluid transparency that makes them manifest the strange light. But what we can describe here as a process of becoming fluid, in my opinion, can just as well be called "self-harmonization" of the beings to the power of the holy intangible origin, which discloses itself in them.[25]

But let's not forget where the postcolonial rub is, namely, the ethical emphasis on preserving the integrity of creation in the sacramental encounter. De Schrijver's subtle modulation of the interplay between activity and passivity, empowerment and receptivity can serve the synergistic postcolonial imaginary well:

> this harmonization to divine empowerment, a harmonization that can be perceived through a sacramental way of seeing, is also—in spite of the receptivity that it presupposes—an activity, that is, neither pure passivity nor a destruction of one's own being. The transparency of finite things toward the living God always presumes the powerful activation of the being of these things.[26]

In the long run, sacramentality is as much about creation as it is about salvation. But whose salvation? Postcolonial planetary consciousness calls for an affirmation that no lesser or narrower salvation is worthy of the transformative intentionality, as Spivak would say, than "teleiopoiesis"[27]—salvation precisely as *soteria*, as *salus*, as transformative healing and fruition of all creation. By happy concurrence, there are strands of Christian cosmology and sacramentology, past and emerging, that embrace this planetary resonance. Of paramount importance now, and for the sacramental imagination yet to body forth, is to hold fast to the interconnection and interdependence that is most aptly expressed—at least in the current moment—by the notion of our created planetary home as the *Ursakrament* of the whole sacramental pluriverse we indwell.

As creatures, we are sacramentally inscribed into an utterly relational, interdependent, and hybrid entanglement of time and eternity. Sacramentally speaking, "we are impregnated with the universe just as the universe is

25. De Schrijver, "Experiencing the Sacramental Character of Existence," 14.

26. Ibid., 14.

27. As already mentioned in the Introduction, Gayatri Spivak refers to "teleiopoiesis" as those conscious imaginative and performative structures that interrupt the past in the name of a liberated and transformative future beyond the competitive and dualistic dialectic of colonial imaginary, in Spivak, *An Aesthetic Education*, 302.

impregnated with us. And in this mutual presence of universe and humanity, the numinous presence lights up from the one who is the most internal of all, 'God, creator of heaven and earth.'"[28]

In other words, the sacramental *opus Dei* that signifies, effects, conveys, and "deeply" incarnates the transcendent, yet intimately transformative, hybrid space of "grace" laboring together with "nature" and within "nature" for the salvation of the world in a myriad ways and in countless places through countless interactive events (i.e., sacraments) of liberation and whole-making, is an inside job—at least postcolonially speaking. The eschatological vector of this sacramental synergy of whole-making liberation weaves through the life of Jesus Christ, the mystery of the Divine Word/Wisdom incarnate. It weaves itself through Jesus Christ who is for Christians the crucial cipher signifying and effecting precisely that proleptic Third Space in which the sacramental counterpoint of hybridity becomes an ever more thorough counterpoint of peace. Of course, more needs and will be said about this proposition in the next chapter. At this juncture, a few remarks must be made about the notion of sacramental pluriverse.

SACRAMENTALITY: A PLURIVERSE OF RELATIONS AND REVELATIONS

How might this hybrid imaginary of sacramentality be conceived as a vibrant pluriverse of relations and revelations? On the one hand, the postcolonial notion of sacramentality in this context articulates an interface of reciprocal, interactive, and non-coercive relations between 1) God, the Uncreated relational Mystery that underlies all that is and is internally active in all that is, and 2) the whole created reality as far as we can even fathom its depth and breadth at this point in evolutionary cosmic history. On the other hand, the notion of sacramentality also refers to the whole interrelated and interdependent web of particular, historical, and contextual events, those relational and revelatory "situations," those transformative mysteries which are by no means mere lifeless "things," which the Christian tradition calls sacraments.

Yet in contrast to closed Occidental sacramental systems and the particular "numbers games" that engender various confessional identity politics and their ecclesiastical boundaries, the postcolonial sacramental pluriverse suggests a space—indeed, a hybrid space on its far-from-finished journey toward an *eschatologically* victorious Third Space—in which many worlds can coexist. Pluriverse is, almost needless to say, multipolar and polyvocal. It is marked not by compartmentalized agencies, sealed boundaries,

28. De Schrijver, "Experiencing the Sacramental Character of Existence," 26.

and clear divisions of labor, but by omnidirectional—though not always, and not necessarily, symmetrical—relationships of mutuality. As Walter Mignolo suggests, a pluri-or multiverse in which many worlds coexist is a "convivial, dialogical, and plurilogical" imaginary.[29]

Taking into account the actual historical developments in various Christian traditions of theology and worship, it would be fair to say that, at the level of empirically observable historical and cultural reality, there already exists a certain sacramental pluriverse. Like it or lump it, several sacramental systems—Orthodox, Oriental, Roman Catholic, Lutheran, Reformed, Anglican, and certain Evangelical varieties—have already coexisted rubbed off one another for centuries despite ongoing quarrels about whose system and whose lineage is the most authentic, most magisterial, most traditional, or most scripturally grounded. For some, this kind of empirical pluriverse is a sign of ecumenical failure. It is sometimes seen as a sign of metaphysical division and ecclesiastically entrenched antagonism that continues to haunt the ever jumpstarting, and yet stalling, ecumenical efforts. On top of it all, there are theological sentiments, shared across the denominations, continents, and cultures that cannot interpret such sacramental plurality otherwise than in the competitively dialectical terms of heresy.

But then there are alsogrowing numbers of the faithful who find themselves questioning the very meaningfulness as well as the exclusivity, insularity, and injustice of these seemingly competitive and contradictory sacramental systems. For example, as noted before, feminist liturgical and sacramental discourses call into question the androcentric clericalism that permeates the very structural framework of certain sacramental systems. In such systems, some sacraments indeed "function" precisely as institutionalized gateways of exclusion and marginalization. Such sacramental systems actually demonstrate how, to reverse the dictum of Walter Burghardt, injustice can also be "sacramentalized." The result is a pernicious, indeed an idolatrous, tendency to erect and uphold closed sacramental edifices which are dominated by a hegemonic logic of dualism—be it primarily racial, sexual, ethnic, political, or cultural. What then obtains is an unholy state of affairs, or what James White called "the Church's power for injustice."[30] White's analysis remains pertinent today and across the globe. No historic ecclesial communion is *a priori* immune to the logic of coloniality and its power differentials which are embodied above all by defensive patriarchy and the seemingly endless mutations of racism that continue to scar the empirical Christian pluriverse of sacramentality:

29. Mignolo, "On Pluriversality."

30. White, *Sacraments as God's Self Giving*, 119.

> it is no secret that the Church frequently is involved in injustices within its own doors. The Church's power for injustice is intertwined with an ambiguity; the power of injustice is also present in a community pledged to justice. The sacraments share this ambiguity, too. Since the sacraments are so fully human, they can also be diverted to serve purposes far less beneficial than divine self giving. Just as they can witness to and reinforce the full human worth of all, so unquestionably the sacraments frequently are used to deny that same human worth to many.[31]

Furthermore, it is important not to downplay the ironic ethical ambiguity that overshadows the strange contradictions that frequently play out in the fragmentation between social justice and ecclesial justice as White so aptly summarizes:

> One is confronted with the difficulty the Church has in promoting social justice when it often fails to obtain ecclesial justice. . . How, then can the Church witness for justice in society if it cannot act justly within itself? Yet, every time the Church denies justice to a majority of its members (e.g., women) or to a minority (e.g., blacks), it vitiates its own power to witness to the world. Much of this denial of justice is carried out, albeit unwittingly, through the sacraments.[32]

It is only fair to note that the empirical and historical diversity of sacramental imagination and practice is by no means a paradise of realized eschatology even for ecumenical optimists. But, I submit, frustration is certainly not limited to the elusive lack of visible Christian unity (uniformity?) that many ecumenically minded Christians decry and lament especially in the context of the divided eucharistic celebrations. Ecumenical work is ongoing and, for it to be fruitful and enduring, a more nuanced understanding of unity will be needed in the future—and that will require courage and hard work. For now, however, it is particularly frustrating to observe the widespread scarcity of institutional, that is, doctrinal and in some cases magisterial, willingness to genuinely dialogue not only with the present longings of those driven away from the churches by the cultural inertias of institutions, but also with widely shared early Christian traditions. Many earlier, pre-modern, sacramental traditions harbor theological and liturgical precedents of a much more sinuous and much more roomy patterns of sacramentality with fluid borderlands between various groupings, even hierarchies, of sacramental mysteries. Why not explore those in order to

31. Ibid.

32. Ibid.

retrieve wisdom that could rejuvenate the stagnating sacramental systems of imagination and practice?

As already noted in the previous chapter, the numerical rigidity of the (particularly) Occidental sacramental imagination is neither historically indisputable, nor theologically normative as at least the first thousand years of Christian history attest. At the present time, the historically diverse sacramental pluriverse—somewhat like the global postcolony—is a pluriverse of jagged hybridity. It is, to borrow Mignolo's words, a "world entangled through and by the colonial matrix of power"[33] that manifests across liturgical diversity and within the dynamic hierarchies of race, gender, and class that color all liturgical spaces and all theological traditions. Meanwhile, acknowledging socio-historical pathologies and genealogies of power that continue to tempt and trouble the historical and empirically observable pluriverse of sacramental theologies and practices, what might the *theological* vision of the postcolonial sacramental pluriverse be? Here are some theological—not merely sociohistorical—conjectures.

The postcolonial sacramental pluriverse is like a roomy galaxy with manifold borderlands which contrapuntally play off one another as they incessantly hybridize one another while being poised in the creative tide of divine generosity and sustained by the plenitude of the triune fountainhead of the Holy Mystery that underlies all that exists, visible and invisible. This sacramental pluriverse is lively, earthy, fleshy, messy, polyphonic, and eschatologically open-ended. It is a web of interconnected fractal patterns signifying, mediating, and effecting divine grace in history.

Now, it might sound like a totally chaotic space in theological freefall. But that is not necessarily so. The pivotal hermeneutical cipher of this sacramental pluriverse is Christ. Its paradigmatic wellspring is the Word and Wisdom in whom all things are created (John 1:3) and who, crucially, became the sacramental crescendo of incarnate divine life while becoming human with us, for us, for our salvation, and for the life of the world (John 1:14)—indeed, indwelling into the deepest tissues of material creation.[34] Yes, that is right: the divine Word/ Wisdom did not just become a human person let alone "man." The Word/Wisdom became flesh, *sarks* (John 1:14). In other words, "in Jesus Christ the entire matrix of materiality is assumed

33. Mignolo, "On Pluriversality."

34. I am referring here to what Niels Henrik Gregersen calls the "deep incarnation": namely, "in Christ, God is conjoining all creatures and enters into the biological tissue of creation itself in order to share the fate of biological existence. God becomes Jesus, and in him God becomes human, and (by implication) foxes and sparrows, grass and soil," see Gregersen, "Deep Incarnation," 82.

in his blood and body" only to be similarly invited into the cosmic "deep resurrection."[35]

The presence and action of the sacramental pluriverse can be felt in liberating liturgies, transformative encounters, experienced blessings, challenging revelations, and unexpected mercies that all work together to body forth the redemptive wholeness of life. This sacramental pluriverse can certainly beckon inside specially designed sanctuaries and during specially designated times of worship. But it also encounters us amid the everyday liturgies of life, and it does so powerfully and meaningfully. And sometimes it glimmers there even more profoundly, and with a more compelling momentum of liberation, than in spaces set apart for the ecclesiastically administered and ritualized sacramental incursions of the Divine. After all, God is love and God is freedom in their fullest plenitude beyond human imagination and historically circumscribed human institutions.

In addition to the historically contingent and culturally circumscribed genealogies of the sacramental "numbers game," these "games" can never, theologically speaking, engender any binding regulatory authority over the creative and transgressive limitlessness with which the Spirit brooded in, with, over, under, and throughout the innovative origins and depths of creation (Gen 1:2–3) and remains unbound in a manner most interiorly akin to breath and in a manner most exteriorly akin to wind (John 3:8)—and everything in between. Nor can—or should—such historically circumscribed "games" ultimately exercise unchallenged hegemony over the pattern of sacramental performative efficacy of Jesus of Nazareth, the God-with-us, the Wholemaker, the Truthteller, the Peacemaker, and the Border-Crosser, who healed on the Sabbath and ate together with all the "wrong" sorts of people at the "wrong" times and in the "wrong" places.

The sacramental pluriverse percolates throughout a creation that is unfinished and opaque. Its goodness is far from perfected. The depths of its complexity and coherence are far from comprehended. The pluriverse of sacraments vibrates amid this unfinished symphony of creation and salvation. The multiple sacramental melodies play off one another and weave in and out of this incredibly multifarious cosmic fugue of visible and invisible realities, materialities, and energies. In this world, which is always a "work in progress" sacramental melodies often reverberate as if through a veil of static noise, as if slightly out of tune. Thus the sacramental melodies can resound, feel, and appear opaque, hardly discernible, perplexing, uncertain, unpredictable, and perhaps even frightening. And yet within and throughout all these painful fissures of the unfinished symphony of *creatio continua*,

35. Gregersen, "Deep Incarnation and Kenosis," 252.

the sacramental pluriverse stealthily scores its rhythms and melodies into our lifeworlds to invite us, creatures, into the raw and intimate borderland where the triune Mystery, which underlies all that is, is tirelessly migrating toward us and where we, creatures, can be empowered to embark on our own holy migration into the divine life.

SACRAMENTAL PLURIVERSE: THREE RHYTHMS, MANY MELODIES

Perhaps a musical analogy might serve as the most fitting framework for the postcolonial sacramental pluriverse. This pluriverse, I propose, can be perceived as resonant in three rhythms and multiple melodies.

The *first rhythm* is that of the sacraments of creation. The world, our planet, the mystery of creation, is the all-embracing context or the *Ursakrament* of the divine *fiat*. It is the irreducible and irrevocable planetary context of our existence. In a sense, it is transcendent vis-à-vis us: it is underived from us, human creatures. It predates us—hence the German prefix *Ur*—primeval, primordial—and it might outlive us. To use Spivak's words, this *Ursakrament* "is not our dialectical negation"—and yet its "alterity remains underived from us."[36] From this *Ursakrament* emerges a whole rhizomatic web of the sacraments of creation—like marriages, like funerals, like friendships. . . like so many culturally specific rites of passage that may fit into the inclusive rhythm of creation. This rhythm is played out in manifold sacramental melodies of time and place.

The *second rhythm* is that of the sacraments of salvation. Christ as the Word and Wisdom incarnate is the key, the unique efflorescence, and the proleptic crescendo of this rhythm of sacramental existence. Christ is the sacrament of union and peace symbolized as the paradigmatic Third Space of a perfected transontological hybridity. The diverse churches, or the convocations of discipleship called together by and sustained in the Holy Spirit, are the "members" or components of the ecclesial body of Christ. Thus they can be said to be sacraments of *communio*. They are sacraments of the ecclesial body of Christ in the eschatologically and apophatically qualified sense of being historical, embodied, "real," experiential, political, and intersubjective signs of encountering the Divine even through their present condition of opacity, be it ontological, epistemological, or moral. And the Eucharist, that profoundest mystery of salvific transformation, can be perceived as the mystical body of Christ—as the consummate sacramental melody of unitive transformation toward *theosis* playing out in this particular rhythm of

36. Spivak, *Death of a Discipline*, 73.

sacramentality.[37] Obviously, "mystical" is not competitively or dialectically juxtaposed to "true" or "political"—that simplification must be resisted as vigorously as possible. Both the Eucharist, the mystery of communion and (often ironically, at least from a historical perspective) unity, as well as the sacraments of churches (i.e., the convocations of embodied faith), no matter how tiny or gigantic they may be, embody and reflect pivotal unitive and relational facets among the mysteries of salvation.[38]

Baptism can be conceived as the sacramental melody of awakening, initiation, and new beginning in the communion with God. Scripture can be understood as a sacramental melody that resounds ever anew as it stirs and nourishes truthful discipleship, and challenges it to grow ever deeper. Preaching of the Gospel is a sacramental melody that rejuvenates the life of the spirit and constantly attunes it to the "dangerous memory," as Johann Baptist Metz would say, of Christ's life, death, and resurrection.

The *third rhythm* is that of the sacraments of discipleship or *askesis*.[39] Reconciliation, as well as various traditions of anointing, can be conceived among the sacramental melodies of healing and renewal. Sustained spiritual practice and spiritual direction can be seen as sacramental melodies of spiritual maturation that require courageous, often countercultural, and indeed, even effortful ascetic perseverance of body and mind over long periods of

37. Here I am referring to the historically earlier understanding of the dynamic multiplicity—and hybridity!—of Christ's Body using the sacramental insights predating the dominant Occidental pattern of understanding the Eucharist as the true Body of Christ versus the Church as the mystical Body of Christ as explored by Henri de Lubac in his *Corpus Mysticum*, particularly 221–62.

38. The postcolonial idea of sacramental pluriverse indeed decentralizes the notion of the church as the foundational or basic sacrament that is very popular in some Christian traditions. In the postcolonial context, Kenan Osborne's reservations are entirely relevant on this topic: "The gathering, called church, is finite in respect to all other finite gatherings; is limited in respect to all other limited gatherings; is relative to all other relative gatherings" since "no one finite entity can claim an exclusivity for sacramentality"—and therefore, "Christians, of and by themselves, have nothing that can be called foundational and unsurpassable," *Christian Sacraments in a Postmodern World*, 135. Additionally, Anselm Min's resolutely historical proposal to understand the church as the "flesh" of Christ rather than the body of Christ is noteworthy in the postcolonial context. Min argues that the church is the flesh of Christ since flesh "refers not only to the basic materiality, sexuality, sociality, and historicity of human existence, but also to all of these in their fragility, vulnerability, mortality, and sinfulness. It captures the resistance of unredeemed human nature and creation to the reconciling work of the Holy Spirit by dominating, exploiting, dividing, and destroying. It stands for fall humanity and fallen creation and their need for redemption and reconciliation," in "The Church as the Flesh of Christ Crucified," 97.

39. I take *askesis* to mean "the kinds of practices one needs to perform so as to make oneself available to God's love" and "to remove what gets in the way of experiencing what is readily available [i.e., divine love]," Papanikolaou, *The Mystical as Political*, 3.

time. Sacraments of time and place—the celebration of Sunday, daily office, and pilgrimages to name just a few—are among the resounding melodies in this rhythm. Of course, ordinations, professions of vows, and various other occasions that mark dedicated commitments to discipleship that manifests in faithful and prophetic action inside and outside of the communities of faith are sacramental melodies that play out not just in the spaces of ritual celebrations but equally so, as the Eastern Orthodox sometimes say, in the manifold "liturgies after liturgy."

No doubt, there can be many more sacramental melodies resounding the rhythm of discipleship! To further explore the numerous avenues for sacramental manifestation of the Divine a whole other study would be necessary. The point to be highlighted here is simply that sacramentality blooms forth in multiple rhythms and multiple melodies that do not need to be automatically perceived as numerically and ritually limited just because such an approach was considered desirable or optimal by some Christians in some historical and cultural contexts in the past or present. In the long run, the polyphony of the sacramental pluriverse challenges the logic of dominance and competition.

Fortunately, the constructive imaginary of postcolonial sacramental pluriverse can dialogue not just with the Eastern Orthodox sacramental tradition—which feels restless when it comes to limiting the sacramental encounters to a set number, be it seven or two, or whatever other "numbers game"—but also with the Occidental traditions.[40] Some voices from the Western Christian milieu, such as Michael Himes, have boldly invited a process of far-reaching sacramental re-envisagement. It is with voices like Himes' that emerging postcolonial sacramental theology will want to join hands in further explorations. After all, as Himes suggests, the sacraments are in their deepest and most liberating sense all those

> occasions when grace is made effectively present for us . . . by sacrament I mean any person, place, thing, or event, any sight, sound, taste, touch, or smell, that causes us to notice the love which supports all that exists, that undergirds your being and mine and the being of everything about us. How many such sacraments are there? The number is virtually infinite, as many as there are things in the universe. There is nothing that cannot be a sacrament, absolutely nothing.[41]

40. No wonder that the Orthodox sometimes prefer to talk about "greater and lesser mysteries," see McGuckin, *The Orthodox Church*, 277–82.

41. Himes, "'Finding God in All Things,'" 99. Himes' approach to sacraments as well as my proposal of the sacramental pluriverse here again resonates with Hans Gustafson's framework of panentheistic pansacramentality within which an infinite number of sacraments is possible, see Gustafson, *Finding All Things in God*, 15–18.

ETHICS:A POSTCOLONIAL SACRAMENTAL ORTHODOXY: AN ETHICAL POLYDOXY?

The trajectory of constructive sacramental imagination engenders a re-orchestration of sacramental power and agency away from the limiting and, sometimes, even outright reductive conventions of numerically closed and institutionally controlled sacramental systems that various Christian ecclesial dispensations continue to operate in today. No doubt, early Western postmodern ideas of Christ as *Ursakrament* and the church as *Grundsakrament* expanded—or rather messed up, depending on whom you ask—the solidified juridical sacramental edifices of colonial modernity and its churches from the middle of the twentieth century onward. And now, the intensely anthropocentric/androcentric focus of modern, and even postmodern, sacramental imagination, is being transposed again. Re-envisioned in a postcolonial key, sacramentality will no longer be about closed systems with vigilantly policed ritual and juridical borders, but about an emancipatory analogical imagination seeing sacraments as fractal patterns of revelation and relation across the plurality of scales, intensities, and expressions.

Sacramental imagination is becoming dilated and fine-tuned. It is opening up and becoming sensitized to what Gayatri Spivak alluded to as planetarity. A planetary theoretical sensibility is liquefying. It crosses the borders of ecclesiastical insularity. And planetarity in a sacramental sense is precisely what is being suggested by the notions of the world as the primary/primordial/original sacrament. The most urgent aspiration of an intentionally postcolonial sacramental theology might as well be a sustained elaboration of the planetary approach to sacramentality as such.

What I have sketched so far are some improvising articulations of polyphonic counterpoint of sacramental melodies which all together shape the constellation of the sacramental pluriverse. This pluriverse, resonating analogically with the ultimate triune Mystery of mutually indwelling Love, can be perceived as something akin to a contrapuntal fugue.[42] This fugal pluriverse is an open-ended multitude of melodies that intertwine, interact, cross-pollinate, and ultimately, as Edward Said would argue, "play off one another." It engenders a concerted polyphony that emerges from within this dynamic simultaneity of voices in which there is no absolute dominance of only one voice over others in zero-sum dialectic.

42. I gratefully acknowledge my indebtedness to Robert W. Jenson who planted the most exciting idea about the Trinity as a fugue: "this evocationof God's being, beyond which there is no more to say: God is a great fugue. There is nothing so capacious as a fugue," *Systematic Theology. Vol. 1*, 236.

As I noted before, the Saidian approach (Part II, Ch. 3) affirms a contrapuntal wholeness of constantly transformed and resolutely hybrid textures of reality in which imitation, elaboration, repetition (but with a difference), and, finally reciprocal (sometimes inescapably asymmetrical, yet not necessarily hegemonic) integration resist a combative and dominative pattern of relationality. It is sometimes virtually impossible to "hear" the full melodic and rhythmic span of the composition from one's individual location—just ask symphony orchestra musicians what and how they actually hear in their seats while performing a complex work such as, say, Olivier Messiaen's *Turangalîla-Symphonie*!

Evidently there are multiple ways of perceiving, performing, and envisioning sacramentality. What is particularly relevant from a postcolonial point of view is that this contrapuntal, fugal pluriverse of sacramentality is an open, dynamic, convivial, reciprocal, and non-hegemonic imaginary. It does not glorify impermeable boundaries between ever more narrowly defined "insides" and "outsides" that measure out sacramental grace in stingily controlled doses. Postcolonial sacramental pluriversality pursues a different acoustics of imagination. It seeks to move—spiritually, epistemologically, doctrinally, pastorally, culturally, aesthetically, and even institutionally—beyond the power games of imperial orthodoxy which, as history shows only too often, can stifle the life of the spirit into the procrustean beds of racist hierarchies, institutional hegemony, cultural colonialism, and patriarchal subalternization.

From a postcolonial perspective, it is counterproductive to cling to any, as it were, padlocked "numbers game" in sacramental theology. Can we really impose a limit on how many melodies of redemptive mystery can signify, effect, and convey the revelatory and transformative encounters with the Holy Mystery of the triune Love? Most certainly, not all of these melodies are as equally intense, luminous, resonant, transparent, or harmonious—at least not yet, or no longer—to midwife the existential transformations of life that God engenders so inimitably through the incarnate Word/Wisdom and in the movement of the Holy Spirit. Not all of them are equally elaborate, recognizable, or meaningful for everyone everywhere on this planet or everyone in every historical moment. Each sacramental melody has its own pitch and timbre. Indeed, some sacramental mysteries are "greater" and some "lesser," to borrow the Orthodox parlance. Yet each sacramental melody can, has been, and is being modulated from culture to culture, from historical era to historical era. The Spirit, the unoverlordable "wind" and "breath" of God, does not stand still, and neither does the swirl of planetary history.

The planetary turn in postcolonialism is a turn toward decolonization of sacramental ontology or our sacramental "outlook on reality."[43] And this is where the postcolonial commitment to the ethical pre-text needs to be emphasized again. What the new "planetary turn" in both postcolonial studies and sacramental theology gestures toward is the liberation of sacraments so that they can mediate, on a new level of intimacy and efficacy, divine liberation for us, with us, in us, and through us. By "us," I mean the whole creation, not just the human persons as we know ourselves at this moment in evolutionary history.

Postcolonial sacramental imaginaries cannot bind themselves to a nostalgic mimicry of the past, particularly the imperial and colonial past and its pathologies of power which are woven far more deeply into the very historical texture of the Christian tradition than many Christians are ready and willing to recognize.

Obviously, no theological endeavor is bulletproof against ever lurking temptations of idolatry and self-righteousness. The actual and living sacramental interface between the Divine and our human *sensus divinitatis* is always in excess of what historically hemmed in concepts, signs, rites, or institutions can aspire to express, let alone idolatrously monopolize. As D'Sa points out, "the credentials of symbolic [i.e., sacramental] relationships are to be gauged in the depth and breadth of their liberating effect" so that all involved "can be taken up by the fullness or wholeness of reality."[44]

Most importantly,, the earth itself, which human beings are rendering more and more wretched, must be now included among Fanon's *les damnés* . Postcolonial sacramental vision cannot uphold orthodoxies more attuned to the routines of dominance then the spirit of Jesus, "the border-crosser and the dweller at the margins."[45] Rather, a new postcolonial "magisterium" ought to be vectored toward the intentional *kenosis* of dominance and hegemony.[46] Its springboard is the hope that is "vigilant, standing on tiptoe, a

43. I am using here Hans Boersma's definition of ontology without any specific metaphysical thematizations, *Heavenly Participation*, 10.

44. Ibid., 247. D'Sa explains that one must steer clear of both the reification and mystification of the sacraments and their effective outcomes. Using the Ignatian framework, D'Sa explains that "there are no 'scientific' criteria which guarantee the authenticity of a sacrament. Like elsewhere here too we know the good spirit is at work only from its fruits. The fruits of the cosmotheandric spirit are not only internal freedom and abiding peace in the community members, but in an equal measure commitment of the community to the welfare of all beings" as they "search for justice for all," 255–56.

45. Phan, "Embracing, Protecting, and Loving the Stranger," 101.

46. I refer to Gayatri Spivak's adage that "the magisterial texts can now be our servants, as the new magisterium constructs itself in the name of the Other," *A Critique of Postcolonial Reason*, 7.

longing expectation, a leaning forward into the future, and above all, hope in embodied actions to bring about, or at least prepare for and anticipate, the coming of the reality that is hoped for."[47]

47. Phan, "Embracing, Protecting, and Loving the Stranger," 104.

3.5.

Toward a Sacramental Third Space

Christ and the Contrapuntal Hybridity of Peace

The most hybridized concept in the Christian tradition
is that of Jesus/Christ.[1]

Kwok, Pui-lan

Christianity, after all, offers as its central doctrine the symbol of a
divine/human hybrid, at once mimicking and scandalizing the operative
metaphysical binaries of the time.[2]

Catherine Keller, Michael Nausner, and Mayra Rivera

The postcolonially colored notions of the world as *Ursakrament* and the sacramental pluriverse push deep into the inner sanctum of Christian theological imagination. Ideas like these both signify and effect a certain postcolonial shift, this time in explicitly sacramental terms, in how divine transcendence, divine power, and divine agency are conceptualized. Given the ethical pre-text in postcolonialism, the ethical makeup of what counts as genuinely sacramental, or genuinely revelatory, needs to be discerned with

1. Kwok, *Postcolonial Imagination,* 171.
2. Keller et al., *Postcolonial Theologies*, 13.

utmost care. Such care can be exercised by paying attention precisely to the sociohistorical and environmental fruits—or what David Ngong called the "ethics of theology"—that sacramental images and concepts have already produced. In light of enduring (neo)colonial and (neo)imperial histories, it is not difficult to see why the moment is opportune to seek more accountable, more faithful, more liberative, and ultimately more life-giving sacramental imaginaries to empower all those routinely pushed to the margins of life. Now it is time to delve deeper into the ethical ecology that exemplifies the sacramental interface of relationality, liberative empowerment, and transformative change.

And so, which facets of power mark the sacramental mysteries as ethical in postcolonial imagination? What—or who—might be the ethical root note or tonic key, to use musical analogies, for discerning genuinely life-giving and transformational patterns in sacramental relations and revelations? Where might we discern a pattern of relationally empowered and liberative transformation that can be realized in, through, with, under, and around the sacramental mysteries? My itinerary of constructive reflection first leads to a conversation between postcolonial perspectives on power and the incarnational constellation of Christ, interpreted precisely as an inimitable hybridity *par excellence* and thus the paradigmatic Third Space (as I articulated it in Part II, Ch. 2) of the hypostatic conviviality of divinity and humanity.

It almost goes without saying that much, much more can be said about Christology through the prism of hybridity than will be feasible to say in this chapter. All necessary limitations of scope considered, I am offering here only one, and inescapably partial, itinerary of reflection on these topics of boundless theological significance. Considering the horizon of Chalcedonian Christology—which also has been and remains an influential yet far from unanimous Christological perspective[3]—my itinerary will focus on the negotiation of power in the hypostatic hybridity of Christ as the root note, or tonic key, for sacramental empowerment and conviviality that finds its further expression, transposed across the interval of analogy, in the way that Christ's presence can be perceived in the Eucharist precisely as a sacramental mystery of and for planetary transformation.

3. For a more detailed analysis of Chalcedon in the context of postcolonial World Christianity see the fine contribution of K. K. Yeo, "Biblical Christologies of the Global Church," 162–79. Diarmaid MacCulloch argues that from a perspective of communal divisions and made even more so by the conquests of Christian communities in the Middle East by Islam, the imperially mandated compromise of Chalcedon "should be seen as one of the great disasters in Christian history, not one of its triumphs," *Silence*, 193.

POSTCOLONIALISM, SACRAMENTALITY, AND POWER RELATIONS

Power is the ever troubled and elusive contestant of all things postcolonial. Yet power is never something static, insulated, exclusive, or predestined in postcolonial imagination. In the world as we know it, power plays out across the dynamic entanglements of empowerment and disempowerment. Some of these entanglements tend to come across as timeless, unassailable, and impassable, and never seem to miss a chance to impose themselves as such with a messianic self-indulgence. Yet the entanglements of empowerment and disempowerment are nevertheless open-ended. They live and move in the unsettled, at least on this side of the beatific vision, space where both narcissistic and profitable self-fossilization is as possible as is a creative agency in response to the *kairos* for emancipative modulation. In other words, a jealously dualistic, unilateral, and ultimately competitive perception of power—and all of that enshrined in timeless legitimation be it of political, racial, cultural, social, and above all, religious nature—is only one possible constellation of power relations no matter how ubiquitous and victorious it seems.

Granted, this dualistic and competitive constellation of power has been historically naturalized. Even though Western colonial modernity engenders, arguably, the globalized prime of this understanding of power, it pre-dates colonialism and imperialism. This sort of power was brought to maturity precisely in the operational imaginaries of power during the "high colonialism" of Western modernity and made to appear virtually self-evident, absolute, and transcendentally immutable. Jan Nedervesen Pieterse and Bhikhu Parekh summarize: "Conquest and domination may have been perennial in human history, but Western imperialism differs from other episodes of domination in that it involved a different mode of production (capitalism) and technology (industrialism), and took on a virtually global scope."[4]

The imperial constellation of power as hegemonic domination is suffused with the "effect of power" that "has been built into the notions of race, progress, evolution, modernity and development as hierarchies extending in time and space."[5] And this colonial/imperial constellation of power, or domination in short, is not a matter of the historical or conceptual past: it endures, and continues to mutate in the fertile progeny of, Western and otherwise, neocolonial cosmologies of power. Most importantly, many

4. Pieterse and Parekh, "Shifting Imaginaries," 1.

5. Ibid.

Christian cosmologies of absolute divine power and agency still reflect—or are reflected in—precisely such neocolonial and neoimperial constructs of hegemonic dominance. Alas, this image of divine power "functions" with stubborn resilience. Its presence is no stranger in quite a few constructs of Occidental sacramental theology. The aspiration of postcolonial theology is to question such constructs of sacramental power and to suggest other acoustics of imagination.

Like it or lump it (or pretend not to notice), power *is* always already relational—for good or for ill. The specific and pivotal nexus between post-colonialism and various imaginaries of power resides precisely in the spaces where we imagine and practice *relationality*—epistemologically, socially, politically, ethically, culturally and sexually, but also trans-ontologically, within the relational space where the worldly encounters the Divine. As Robert Young has observed, "much of postcolonial theory is not so much about static ideas and practices, as about the relations between ideas and practices: relations of harmony, relations of conflict, generative relations between different peoples and their cultures."[6]

If so, then this is where a postcolonization of, or decolonization of, theological imagination must also factor in: "What is at issue in decolonizing the imagination is the relationship between power and culture, domination and the imaginary."[7] Since our cultural and theological imaginaries are constitutive (i.e., they "function) of value judgments and behaviors on individual, communal, societal, and planetary levels, "the imaginary of power is concerned with the ways in which images, regardless of whether they are true of false, are constitutive of social relations and realities [. . .] images function as signals and markers in constituting boundaries between self and other, us and them, normal and abnormal. . ."[8]

Sacramentality—the dynamic, creative, interactive, and potentially salvific interface of relationality among the Uncreated and the created, —is not a neutral interface in terms of power. Whatever the notions of God, divine transcendence, and divine power might be, it is these notions that "function" to form the conception of what the sacraments are and what they do. And the sacraments, in turn, then "function" as a performative and imaginative pluriverse of these operational notions of God in the lives of individuals, societies, and cultures—but they can also modulate these underlying notions in return. This is the open-ended and interactive circle of functional imaginative efficacy which postcolonial sacramental theology

6. Young, *Postcolonialism: A Very Short Introduction*, 7.

7. Pieterse and Parekh, "Shifting Imaginaries," 4.

8. Ibid., 5.

must enter to enkindle a creative shift. To begin with, where might we look for a galvanizing revelation of divine power? Unsurprisingly, toward Jesus Christ, the tonic key and the root note of revelation, relation, and salvific transformation. More specifically (and more surprisingly perhaps), we might look to the horizon of the Chalcedonian vision of Christ.

POSTCOLONIZING CHRIST: FROM A HYBRID HYPOSTASIS TO THE THIRD SPACE OF PEACE

What exactly does the *dense* postcolonial notion of hybridity, let alone Third Space, have to do with seemingly impenetrably arcane Chalcedonian Christology (except, perhaps, sharing an aura of impenetrability)? Quite a lot, I submit. Let's start with the obvious: both are imaginaries of relationality, indeed asymmetrical relationality. Both are also discourses that highlight the "how" of relationality: particularly, the "how" of boundaries, identities, and relational asymmetries that are contested, destabilized, subverted, and rendered fluid—yet not simply annihilated.

Suggestions about the incarnation of Jesus Christ as the supreme instantiation of hybridity have already surfaced in recent postcolonial theology. The connection with the "high" Christology of Nicea and Chalcedon is particularly interesting. What else can match the imbrication of the Chalcedonian "definition" in the power games of Roman imperial orthodoxy and culturally contingent Greco-Roman metaphysics trying to impose itself as universal?[9] Kwok Pui-lan (among others) noted not that long ago that the Hellenist ontological and epistemological imagination is unproductively substantialist. As far as Christological normativity is concerned, she argued that "the church worldwide is still much under the yoke of the Chalcedonian captivity and Eurocentric theological formulations based on Western heritages."[10]

Far from dismissing the legitimacy of such concerns, I am inclined to think that Chalcedonian imaginary can also kick up a sandstorm of conceptual iconoclasm when it comes to the Hellenist metaphysics of substance. It mimics and scandalizes, intentionally or not, the metaphysical binaries

9. For the wide spectrum of approaches of these contentious issues see, for example, Thomas Cattoi, "What Has Chalcedon to Do with Lhasa," Victor Ifeanyi Ezigbo and Reggie L. Williams, "Converting a Colonialist Christ: Toward an African Postcolonial Christology," and the essay collection *Jesus Without Borders*, edited by Genre L. Greene.

10. Kwok, "Ecology and Christology," 118. A differently shaped, yet nevertheless similarly reticent stance toward the theological fecundity of Chalcedonian Christology from a "whitefeminist" perspective is classically expressed by Elizabeth Johnson in *She Who Is*, 164.

of its cultural context. Chalcedonian Christology makes piecemeal use of the Hellenist epistemological imagination while refusing, as Lai Pan-chiu maintains, "to be bounded by the straitjacket of the Greek philosophical framework."[11] Indeed, Chalcedonian imaginary, with its robust "high" Christology, can offer a powerful critique of what Laurel Schneider calls the "monologic of noncontradiction" by precisely underscoring the "promiscuity" of the incarnation. Namely, in Schneider's words, the "coming to flesh of divinity completely disrupts the smooth otherness of the divine, its separateness from the changeable stuff of the earth, its abhorrence of rot, its innocence of death, and its ignorance of life or desire."[12] The "promiscuity" at play in the incarnation is a "quality of distinctly impure hybridity" which "stands in opposition to divinity understood as the pinnacle and epitome of purity and immutability. In incarnation God chooses to entrust the Divine desire for whole-making self-actualization to the warp and woof of the finite realm."[13]

The decidedly non-Occidental ambivalence of postcolonialism toward Chalcedon notwithstanding, Kwok—herself one of the most rigorous postcolonial trailblazers in theology—nevertheless asserts that,

> . . .the most hybridized concept in the Christian tradition is that of Jesus/Christ. The space between Jesus and Christ is unsettling and fluid, resisting easy categorization and closure. It is the "contact zone" or "borderland" between the human and the divine, the one and the many, the historical and the cosmological, the Jewish and the Hellenistic, the prophetic and the sacramental, the God of conquerors and the God of the meek and the lowly. . .[14]

In a similar vein, the editors of *Postcolonial Theologies: Divinity and Empire* noted in their Introduction that "Christianity. . . offers as its central doctrine the symbol of a divine/human hybrid, at once mimicking and scandalizing the operative metaphysical binaries of the time."[15]

11. Lai, "A Mahāyāna Reading of Chalcedon Christology," 222. Lai argues that the Chalcedonian notion of hypostatic union between two natures entails precisely a "challenge to the Hellenistic philosophical hypothesis that contrary attributes could not possibly coexist within the same subject at the same time," 222.

12. Schneider, "Promiscuous Incarnation," 232.

13. Ibid., 239. Schneider adds that the doctrine of incarnation "directly dismantles the purity, immutability, and simplicity of divinity, undoing both its oneness and its innocence of complex flesh. Incarnation is therefore the principle of promiscuity, in divine terms at least," 239.

14. Kwok, *Postcolonial Imagination and Feminist Theology*, 171.

15. Keller et al., *Postcolonial Theologies: Divinity and Empire*, 13.

Jesus Christ is the hybrid *par excellence*: but what kind/mode of relationality between divinity and humanity could this be? As explored in this study, the notion of postcolonial hybridity as a critical and constructive notion is above all an analytical metaphor, indeed an imaginary, sourced from the hybrid lifeworlds of postcolony and diaspora. It is a figure of interactive, reciprocal, overlapping, entangled, multidirectional, and polyphonic relationality—often jaggedly and in a riven and unsettling way—which is nevertheless inscribed in the asymmetrical power grids of the global postcolony.

As described in more detail in Parts I and II, postcolonial hybridity is about "polluted" identities. It articulates porous and leaky boundaries of identity flaring forth across whole spectrum of "organic" and "intentional" intertwinement of races, cultures, languages, religions, genders, abilities, knowledges, and memories. Through its dimension of postcolonial *anamnesis*, hybridity is above all a challenge to homogenized identities and essentialized differences, especially when those are locked into habitually warring zero-sum juxtapositions of dignity, empowerment, and agency. With an eye on the "wretched of the earth," hybridity transgresses into what opens up beyond the gridlock of hierarchically construed binary couplings of identities, races, cultures, orthodoxies, values, and allegiances.

On the other hand, through its *epiclesis* dimension, hybridity also articulates an *epektasis* toward a Third Space—a relational interface. Across this interface, the unidirectional architectonic of power modulates into the multidirectional and reciprocal re-orchestration of identities and integrities touching one another and being touched by one another in transformative—commendable rather than intrusive—ways. It is impossible to resist a theological transposition here: there is indeed something perichoretic about this utopian register of hybridity. The hybridity of Third Space is no longer primarily inscribed in the jaggedness, ambivalence and ambiguity that watermark the lived reality of the global postcolony. Rather, Third Space leans into an imaginary of peace wherein difference—especially difference that is virtually by default branded as competitive, antagonistic, mutually exclusive and necessarily contradictory—is unseated from the absolute privilege that hierarchical dualism assigns it. Third Space intimates the seemingly impossible simultaneity of intertwinement of identities and integrities in which their boundaries are mutually challenged even as they are reciprocally enriched to a lesser or greater degree.

Third Space opens up the preferential option for the possibility of a relational concurrence and conviviality without necessity, without compulsion, without fatalistic guarantees—within a contrapuntal conviviality that is non-reductive, non-depleting, non-wounding, and non-coercive. This, I suggest, is what the relation between Divinity and humanity in Jesus Christ, true Divine Word/Wisdom "deeply incarnate" in flesh and true human being, could fruitfully imply as the unmatched Third Space hybrid. And this is what the Chalcedonian definition, or rather as Sarah Coakley has persuasively argued, the Chalcedonian "apophatic horizon,"[16] seems to encourage. Christ, according to the Chalcedonian hermeneutical horizon, is,

> truly God and truly man . . . consubstantial with the Father according to the Godhead, and consubstantial with us according to the Humanity . . . One and the same Christ, Son, Lord, Only-begotten, to be acknowledged in two natures, without confusion, without change, without division, without separation; the difference of the natures being by no means taken away by the union, but rather the property of each nature being preserved, and [both] concurring in one person and one subsistence, not separated or divided into two persons, but one and the same Son and only-begotten, God the Word, our Lord Jesus Christ . . .[17]

There is a complex semantic and doctrinal history behind each word, if not each syllable, of this formula. It is beyond the scope and purpose of this chapter to delve into these fascinating intricacies of late antique theological mindscapes. What matters in the present context, is to notice the conceptual struggle to articulate an interface that prioritizes intrinsically relational, yet unviolated and inviolable, integrity. What is expressed in the apophatic terms of Chalcedon is a theological walk on the razor's edge to intimate through the notion of the hypostatic union a particular fabric of imagination which is needed to fathom an interface of relationality that obtains only if *both* divinity and humanity concur in non-coercive and non-detractive hybridity. The ethical ecology of this conviviality is neither accidental nor soteriologically and sacramentally neutral.

The conviviality of the hypostatic union is not a relationship suspended in some cosmic—or intimate—competition. Rather, it is a concurrence and synergy of two natures and two incommensurable integrities in Christ—cohabiting, intertwining, interpenetrating almost to the point of confusion,

16. Sarah Coakley, "What Does Chalcedon Solve and What Does it Not," 161. According to Coakley, Chalcedon "leaves us" precisely at a boundary—or at a horizon—that resists incarcerating precision vis-à-vis what ultimately remains a mystery of the most ineffable proportions by "presenting a 'riddle' of negatives by means of which a greater (though undefined) reality may be intimated," 161. Coakley's essay is arguably the finest Occidental postmodern contribution to offer a methodological insight into how to constructively retrieve the imaginative potential of the Chalcedonian vision.

17. I am using here my own translation with addition of more inclusive language that I believe the original Greek does not strictly contradict.

and yet resistant to complete dissolution into a dialectical sublation wherein the winner "takes it all" and hegemonically overwrites all differences. The term *syntrechouses* expresses concurrence as it comes from the verb *syntrecho*. It denotes coalescing, coinciding, concurring, and running together. The presence of this term in the Chalcedonian "horizon" signals a resistance against both the coercive and passive annihilation of human integrity (the weaker, the less empowered partner of the relationship) as well as against a pantheistic meltdown of divine transcendence.

This kind of concurrence, or synergy, asymmetrical as it remains in the Christological context, presupposes interactive *perichoresis* without annihilation of the weakest. This is not a dialectic of pure power versus pure impotence, idealized or actual. The Chalcedonian "concurrence" comes mesmerizingly close to accomplish theologically what hybridity aspires to do in cultural and socio-political contexts—to problematize boundaries without erasure, to unseat the dualistic logic of difference as mutually exclusive, to break and join at the same time, and to engender an existential sonority of both/and in an apparently impossible simultaneity. But this is a Third Space of reconciled relationality, a borderland in between a suffocating union of absorption and a grinding tension of allergic difference. Jesus Christ embodies the hybrid Third Space in which Divinity gives without forcing to take, and assumes to transfigure, not assimilate without residue or consent.

This Third Space is emancipatory, in a contrapuntal way, for creation: humanity and the whole creation can remain true to itself even as it is changed, by consent and not by passive absorption; not by being raped into salvation, but through a synergistic participation in the divine life empowered, energized, nurtured by the Holy Spirit. In this kind of Third Space the uncreated divine energies interact with the whole gamut of created reality. In this hybrid conviviality contrasts coexist, and to various degrees of harmonic attunement with the Divine, also participate in the ongoing planetary movement of co-creation in which humanity is particularly called to consciously collaborate with God.

Last but not least: the hypostatic conviviality of Third Space in Christ is the configuration of relationality that is, creedally, speaking, "for us and for our salvation." The hypostatic hybridity of Christ as Third Space is not soteriologically exclusive but rather soteriologically extensive. It reaches into the furthest planetary crevices of "flesh" as part and parcel of the "deep incarnation." In other words, this particular incarnate Third Space of hybridity in Christ is not held hostage by Christ and for Christ alone, not "something to be exploited" (Phil 2:6). Rather, it is generously shared, mediated, enabled, communicated, and emulated on all levels of being, feeling, knowing, sensing, and acting—at least potentially.[18]

CHRIST AND SACRAMENTS: CHRIST THE CRESCENDO

Now how do the sacraments—and two among them in particular—relate to Christ, or in other words, to the soteriologically hybrid contrapuntality of hypostatic Third Space? Is Christ indeed a sacrament—even if he is not, as one might already suspect after reading the previous chapters, the *Ursakrament* of God?

The crucial presupposition for all that follows is that for *all* things *as related* to God according to a sacramental imaginary, Christ is the hermeneutical root note or tonic key. For the sacramental imaginary, Christ is, to use Slavoj Žižek's expression, "the knot which holds the texture of reality together."[19] In other words, Christ is the hybrid (indeed, braided, as it were, into a knot) ontological, epistemological, imaginative, and behavioral key to discern the "already but not yet" nature of God-world relationality. In another context, Kathryn Tanner has summarized what is really at stake here:

> As the culmination and completion of what is true generally of God's interactions with us, Christ is the key. . . to what God is doing everywhere. Christ clarifies and specifies the nature, aim, and trustworthiness of all God's dealings with us because Christ is where those dealings with us come to ultimate fruition [. . .] The whole of who God is for us as creator and redeemer, which in its varied complexity might simply overwhelm and mystify us, is found in concentrated compass in Christ. Christ . . . provides . . . a clue to the pattern or structure that organizes the whole even while God's ways remain ultimately beyond our grasp.[20]

If so, then Christ is by no means extrinsic to, or in any way competing with, other sacraments. There is no need to worry about using the language of sacramentality regarding Christ (be it as *Ursakrament*, primordial sacrament, or whatever other notions might be used) as if it might somehow mess

18. Here I am falling back on Karl Rahner's argument that what we claim is true in the context of the Incarnation must also be true for the all-embracing relational interface between God and creation: "if in the Incarnation the Logos enters into relationship with a creature, then it is obvious that the ultimate formal determinations of the Creator-creature relationship must also hold in this particular relationship"—and vice versa. Rahner, *Theological Investigations*, Vol.1, 163.

19. Žižek and Milbank, *The Monstrosity of Christ*, 80.

20. Tanner, *Christ the Key*, viii.

up the sacramental system or even eclipse or marginalize other sacraments or divine transcendence.[21] Granted, conceiving Christ as sacrament certainly messes up the time honored "numbers game"—but for a very laudable reason. Instead of competition or impingement on divine transcendence, Christ, precisely as the incarnation of the hybrid hypostatic union of Third Space, is the crescendo of sacramentality.

Consequently, the whole sacramental pluriverse crescendos in the incarnation, life, death, resurrection, and ascension of Christ—and even beyond that, all the way through the ever more effusive and ever more hybrid Pentecostal indwelling of the Spirit. Incarnation does not annihilate, displace, subjugate, or detract from the sacramental structure of creation which, as tradition asserts, was created through the Word/Wisdom of God (John 1:3) and ever remains vitally indwelt by the Spirit. To say that Christ is the crescendo of sacramentality is to say that the sacramental structure of creation swells to its fruition, its efflorescence, and its "high deepness"[22] in the hybrid Third Space of Christ. Christ is the crest, vertex, or blooming and fertile *anthesis* of sacramentality. From an eschatological perspective, it is indeed apt to call the hypostatic union, or the hybrid Third Space in Christ—precisely as a relational nexus and not just a fixed human nature—the "perfect sacrament of God, humans, and the world."[23]

A THEOPOLITICS OF SACRAMENTAL CRESCENDO: SOLIDARITY AND HARMONY IN THE BORDERLANDS

Christ, as the hybrid hypostatic union of Third Space, is also a theopolitics incarnate and sacramentalized. In this sense, postcolonial sacramental theology can build on the Korean-American theologian Anselm Min's proposal that the hypostatic union in Christ is not just the sacrament of God—primordial, perfect, crescendoing, or otherwise—but precisely the sacrament of divine solidarity. Min argues that, far from being a merely obsolete and parochial doctrinal conundrum, the notion of the hypostatic union has far-reaching social and political implications in the world replete with suffering and injustice: "The connection between politics and theology is precisely the ontology of participation provided by the hypostatic union."[24] Christ challenges the logic of hegemonic and unilateral dominance since Christ is,

21. For those concerns, see Irwin, "Liturgical Actio," 111–23, and Osborne, *Christian Sacraments*, Ch. 4.

22. Julian of Norwich, *Showing of Love*, 84.

23. Parappally, "The World, God's Primary Sacrament," 92.

24. Min, "The Church as the Flesh of Christ Crucified," 95.

> the sacrament of the solidarity of humanity among all peoples, the solidarity of humanity and nature, and all of these in the prevenient ontological solidarity or communion of all creation with the Father produced by the Holy Spirit. Theologically, this solidarity of all humanity and creation in Christ the Son is the most profound reality that relativizes all the divisive human distinctions based on gender, nationality, class, culture, and even religion.[25]

The Third Space of hypostatic union reveals—and invites all creatures to synergistically effect by participating in the ongoing planetary and cosmic solidarity of God with all creation amidst the omnipresent struggle for dignity, wholeness, and justice. The Third Space of the hypostatic union is a participatory interface of the non-hegemonic praxis of planetary solidarity across which new, liberating and transformative, relations among humanity and the whole creation can sacramentalize—that is, can be not only imagined but then also embodied, experienced, and enacted. Postcolonially speaking, Christ is both the sacrament of transontological and transcosmic solidarity while also being the sacrament of interhuman and intracosmic solidarity.

But what about the gravity of history in the sacramental Third Space of hypostatic union? Where does the Chalcedonian riddle of apophatic metaphysics hit the rough road of the coloniality of power, being, knowledge, and agency? Does it at all? No doubt, in the imperial context of Chalcedon, quite a few things remained wittingly or unwittingly unrecognized and as if invisible. The Chalcedonian horizon is notably short on historical detail. Yet, the sacramental crescendo of hypostatic union does not, indeed cannot, refer to some kind of generic and ahistorical incarnation. It is meaningless without the scandalous historical particularity of Jesus of Nazareth. The sort of incarnation that Christianity proclaims is theopolitically invested, indeed geopolitically subalternized, as it crescendoed precisely within the borderlands of empire and through the undersides of colonial subjugation. The redemptive veracity of sacramental efflorescence bodies forth precisely from the hybrid backwaters of imperial power.

Postcolonial sacramental theology does not have to choose between the false dichotomies of metaphysics or history, or of aesthetics or politics. The sacramental crescendo of Christ is always already inscribed in all of them and it would be artificial to segregate and compartmentalize all these dimensions of life. For incarnation is precisely a migration and a crossing of borders, bringing and holding together and letting to play off one another of

25. Ibid. 93–94.

what is routinely seen as isolated, oppositional, contradictory, competitive, and even mutually exclusive. Out of this sacramental migration of God deep into the "flesh" of creation, a new hybridity, a pivotal Third Space emerges through a marginal Jew. It is here that postcolonial sacramental reflection can build on the diasporic theology of *Deus Migrator* by the Vietnamese-American theologian Peter Phan.

To begin with, postcolonial imagination resonates strongly with Phan's theology of incarnation as God's migration: Jesus Christ is "the Border-Crosser" and "the Dweller at the Margins." The historical incarnation of the Word and Wisdom of God in Jesus is the culmination of the initial divine migration—creation itself:

> The mystery of the Word of God made flesh in Jesus can certainly be viewed as an act of border crossing. Essentially, it is the culmination of that primordial border crossing by which the triune God steps out of self and eternity and crosses into the *other*, namely, the world of space and time, which God brings into existence by this very act of crossing. In the Incarnation, the border that was crossed is not only that which separates the eternal and the temporal, the invisible and the visible, spirit and matter, but more specifically, the divine and the human, with the latter's reality of soul and body.[26]

The incarnation is the genuine *telos* of creation and not an emergency plan under the frivolous aegis of *felix culpa*, the allegedly "happy fault" of human sin that requires a divine savior. Nevertheless, the incarnation proceeds precisely as God's migration into the dark undersides of history to heal, restore, embolden, and transform. Thus Phan emphasizes:

> In this migration into history as a Jew in the land of Palestine, God, like a human migrant, entered a far country where God, as part of a colonized nation, encounters people of different racial, ethnic, and national backgrounds, with strange languages, unfamiliar customs, and foreign cultures, among whom God, again like a migrant after a life-threatening journey, "pitched the tent" or "tabernacled" (John 1:14).[27]

The life of Christ is ultimately the hybrid life of a migrant, Phan argues, since Christ as "truly divine and truly human, the incarnated Logos, like the migrant, dwelt betwixt-and-between two worlds"[28] living out a hybrid

26. Phan, *In Our Own Tongues*, 147.

27. Phan, "Embracing, Protecting, and Loving the Stranger," 100.

28. Ibid.

identity and agency. And Christ is not frozen in time but rather is unceasing hybridity in action:

> Consequently, the traditional doctrine of *unio hypostatica* in Jesus . . . should not be taken to mean a kind of static joining of two opposite ontological states but a dynamic movement back and forth between them, just as the migrant has to move and "mediate" constantly between the two existential conditions of being this-and-that.[29]

Reading Phan's migratory Christology with a sacramental spin, it can be said that while dynamically indwelling the hybrid borderlands of divisions and separations, Jesus Christ signifies and effects a sacramental transformation of those transontological and intersubjective borders that isolate, segregate, compete, and antagonize. In the nonviolent and noncoercive hypostatic union, a new hybridity of Third Space bodies forth in which borders, as Phan suggests, can become frontiers for change:

> Thus, in the Incarnation as border crossing, the boundaries are preserved as identity markers, but at the same time they are overcome as barriers and transformed into frontiers from which a totally new reality, a *mestizaje*, emerges: the divine and human reconciled and harmonized with each other into one single reality.[30]

Ultimately, the new incarnational hybridity of Third Space opens up a sacramental interface for reconciliation, liberation, and wholeness. Here the gravity of history and the jagged, riven, and seemingly irreconcilable hybridities of postcolony are met by the deeply incarnate One who suffers these burdens in solidarity to finally die as an outcast, "hung between heaven and earth, at the margins of both worlds" to become the "sacrament of new harmony."[31]

Drawing from Asian wisdom traditions that highlight harmony as a web of peaceful relations, Phan foregrounds the idea of harmony precisely by emphasizing "ethics as 'the ethic and aesthetic of right relationships.'"[32] Harmony, from this perspective, is not a mere nostalgia for the superficial

29. Ibid.

30. Phan, *In Our Own Tongues*, 148. Phan adds that "even in death Jesus did not remain within the boundaries of what death means: failure, defeat, destruction. By his resurrection he crossed the borders of death into a new life. . . in this way the borders of death become frontiers to life in abundance," 149.

31. Ibid., 149, 144.

32. Ibid., 144.

armistice of ignored suffering, suppressed insurgencies, and camouflaged injustices. Nor is it a romantic desire for cheap settlement instead of the slow painstaking labor—indeed, the contrapuntal effort—of healing, restoration, reconciliation, and liberation. Christ the hybrid Third Space is the sacrament of harmony—but a complex harmony, a contrapuntal harmony in which Edward Said's "irreconcilabilities" of life are recognized and honored, and in which dissonant and non-serene tensions are not rushed to a premature and hegemonic resolution. Rather, Christ as the contrapuntal sacrament of new harmony is the eschatological "already," the utopian Third Space, which reveals and models the extravagant counterpoint of peace without, however, imposing it across all present dissonances and atonalities of history. After all, harmony is an option, a hope, and longing—not fate or conscription. Harmony is contrapuntal, that is, it is worked out over a laborious and polyphonic stretch of interaction in search of a curative, restorative, and ultimately sustainable conviviality and thriving consonance—with no one and nothing being absorbed in an imperialistic monophony of the strongest voice alone.

Christ, the hybrid and contrapuntal Third Space, does not equal a hegemonic and reductive synthesis since the hypostatic union, like counterpoint, privileges neither a militant dialectic, nor a fetishized difference, nor an automatic and slick fusion. For those in the postcolonial camp who would always love to err on the side of irreconcilability, it might be helpful to keep in mind that dissonance is not the universal and preemptive condition of truth. Ultimately, as the sacrament of solidarity and new harmony, Christ is the abundant counterpoint of peace. Christ's hypostatic hybridity is a decolonial Third Space because it is a countersign to the colonial paradigm of making war, conflict, dualistic antagonism, and competitive dialectic as these are normalized, legitimized, and domesticated into the structures of everyday life.

Christ as the sacrament of solidarity and new harmony challenges what Nelson Maldonado-Torres calls the imperialist "paradigm of war."[33] The paradigm of war is the ontology of conflict and tension. It stretches back to Greek philosophy and permeates the whole Western social and cultural imaginary. It is "deeply connected with the production of race and colonialism as well as by the perpetuation, expansion, and transformation of patriarchy" as the cosmology of war continues to promote the "naturalization of the death ethic of war through colonialism, race, and particular modalities of gender differentiation."[34] The paradigm of war naturalizes the

33. Maldonado-Torres, *Against War*, 3–4, 100.

34. Ibid., 4.

dialectics of lordship and bondage in both a transcendent dimension (the transontologically imperial God of the master who reigns by mastering) and an immanent dimension (disinheriting the "wretched of the earth" into a subontological existence). As a result, "in an imperial context"—politically, culturally, but most importantly, *theologically*—"one never finds God, but rather the God of the master or the God of the slave." And thus, as Maldonado-Torres shows with frightening clarity, a colonialist idol of God is produced through projection of "imperial man" across the transontological difference between the Uncreated and thus idolatrously "making God a most fundamental structural piece in the sustenance of empire."[35]

It is this dialectic of war and this ontology of imperial power and agency that postcolonial sacramental theology is called to challenge and to constructively modulate into oblivion. As the sacramental Third Space of peace, Christ is the hybrid interface of an altogether different chamber metaphysics—a postcolonial chamber metaphysics of solidarity, of contrapuntal harmony, and of peace. As such, Christ as the crescendo of the whole sacramental pluriverse resounds in a poignantly eschatological key—already but not yet, for in the world as we know it today, "of peace there can be only an eschatology."[36]

35. Ibid., 113.

36. Levinas, *Totality and Infinity*, 24.

3.6.

Sacramental Transformation and the Ethical Powerscapes of Postcolonial Eucharist

When does memory become redemptive?[1]

Ivana Noble

It is only within . . . reciprocal transcendence and the ethical obligation that it entails that the question of freedom can even begin to be posed contrapuntally against the reality of objectification.[2]

R. Radhakrishnan

It goes without saying that much, much more can be said about Christology through the prism of hybridity than was feasible to address in the previous chapter. Exactly the same is true regarding the ever fascinating and never settled issue of how Christ is present in the Eucharist and what some eucharistic theologies really mean when they affirm that a certain change, "conversion," happens in the Eucharist. All those unavoidable limitations considered, my aim in the present chapter is to explore how the Eucharist,

1. Noble, *Theological Interpretation of Culture in Post-Communist Context*, 139.
2. Radhakrishnan, *Theory in an Uneven World*, 104.

which is the paradigmatic sacramental mystery of transformation, can, by an analogical resonance with Christ's hypostatic Third Space conviviality, model a synergistic imaginary of sacramental power, empowerment, and agency for liberative change—a certain kind of "transubstantiation."

THE EUCHARISTIC BODY OF CHRIST: ON THE OPACITY OF SACRAMENTAL CONVIVIALITY

If the hybrid hypostatic union—the Third Space of Christ—is indeed the key and crescendo of sacramentality, then Christ must be an efficacious semiotic "situation" that conveys something profoundly and intimately true about God and about us, the creation. But what is it? And what exactly is sacramental in Christ—is it Christ's humanity as the convention goes? And how might the hypostatic, i.e., the sacramental structure of the hybrid Third Space of Christ, presage the style, or the "how," of salvific communion and transformation in and through the Eucharist?

To begin with, the historically circumscribed *humanity* of Christ alone is not—*pace* most sacramental discourses that vigorously promote the primordial sacramentality of Christ—the reason why Jesus Christ can be understood as a sacrament, let alone the crescendo of sacramentality.[3] Instead, I submit, it is the relational pattern in Christ's hypostatic union as the hybrid Third Space—an interactive union of uncreated Divinity and created humanity synergistically concurring together, contrapuntally, without violence, reduction, hegemony, separation, absorption, displacement, or even annihilation. All mysteries in the sacramental pluriverse—but above all, the Eucharist—signify and effect this relational pattern and this synergistic hybridity of hypostatic Third Space to varying degrees of intensity and harmony. This hybrid pattern of relationality is what sacramentality is really all about—not a nature, nor a substance, nor anything static or self-sufficient at all, be it uncreated or created. As Yngve Brilioth has put it so succinctly, "there is no greater mystery than the communion of [humans] with God, however mediated."[4]

In this sense, Christ as the crescendo of the sacramental pluriverse is indeed not only the sacrament of God or the sacrament of humanity but, as Jacob Parappally argues, the "sacrament of the inter-relationship of God,

3. See Osborne's analysis and critique of the popular Occidental tradition in sacramental theology which asserts that it is precisely the *humanity* of Christ that, presumably hypostatically, functions as the primordial sacrament of God, *Christian Sacraments in a Postmodern World*, 84–111 and 196–98.

4. Brilioth, *Eucharistic Faith and Practice*, 285.

humans, and the world."[5] Across the sacramental interface, neither divinity nor creation, nor more specifically humanity, is required to execute or undergo any detraction, diminishment, invasion, or assimilatory conquest. This mode of relationality is sacramental precisely because it does not obliterate differences in order to unite most intricately and intimately. Sacramental relation invites, models, and accommodates a hybrid conviviality of transformatively engaged, yet unviolated, realities. In short, relationality perceived as sacramental "is not a thunderous clap from the beyond that flattens the listener into shock," but rather it instigates an interaction, an interplay, a synergy, which always remains a "conversation, not a devastation, and not the kind of overwhelming ravishing that crushes."[6]

Now the mystery of the Eucharist as the efficacious extension of Christ, indeed a radically disseminated and proliferated embodiment of Christ ever and forevermore "deeper" into the crevices of planetary history, signifies and effects—as far and as deep as our worldly aptitude currently is able to negotiate—precisely this sacramental pattern of hybrid relationality. At the end of the day, in this sense, sacramentality is nothing less than "constitutive of revelation."[7] In this sense, sacramentality grounds and expresses what in postcolonial imaginary would be seen as a robustly ethical ontology as well as an equally robust theopolitics and cosmopolitics in search of a lifeworld beyond war, beyond the competitive logic of binarity, and beyond the imperial agency of domination.

How might this constitutive sacramental pattern of revelation and relation play out in postcolonial conceptions of Christ's presence and action in the Eucharist? Here I am drawn to my own Lutheran tradition or, to be more precise, the eucharistic theology of Martin Luther.

First of all, the Eucharist entails a "whole economy," not an isolated cultic moment.[8] The question of the presence, arrival, and action of Christ as the incarnate Word/Wisdom in the Eucharist is, among other tricky things, a question of how divine and, sometimes even more so, ecclesial-*cum*-clerical power functions in the economy of salvation. Against the background of Chalcedon, a certain parallax view of the mysteries of the incarnation and the Eucharist can emerge such as the one advocated by Martin Luther as the idea of *unio sacramentalis*:

5. Parappally, "The World, God's Primary Sacrament," 89. Consequently, "the Christ-event cannot be seen only in its specific relation to the sacraments of the Church and the Church as sacrament. What is revealed through the Christ-event is the radical inter-relationship between God, humans and the world," 95.

6. Schwartz, *Sacramental Poetics at the Dawn of Secularism*, 131.

7. Ross, *Extravagant Affections*, 35.

8. Lathrop, *Holy People*, 16.

> Thus, what is true in regard to Christ is also true in regard to the sacrament. In order for the divine nature to dwell in him bodily [Col. 2:9], it is not necessary for the human nature to be transubstantiated and the divine nature contained under the accidents of the human nature. Both natures are simply there in their entirety. . . In like manner, it is not necessary in the sacrament that the bread and wine be transubstantiated and that Christ be contained under their accidents in order that the real body and real blood may be present. But both remain there at the same time. . .[9]

Luther's point, a rather uncharacteristic one considering his penchant for grinding dialectical tensions, is to insist on the analogical resonance among the two mysteries of salvation and to affirm nonhegemonic and noncompetitive conviviality even between the greatest possible ontological and epistemological contrasts. This is the vision which grounds the broad-spectrum Lutheran approach of *unio sacramentalis*. Keeping the spotlight on the indispensable analogical interval between the hypostatic union and sacramentality, the Formula of Concord presents this vision of eucharistic hybridity:

> Just as in Christ two distinct, unaltered natures are inseparably united, so in the Holy Supper two essences, the natural bread and the true natural body of Christ, are present together here on earth in the action of the sacrament . . . This union of Christ's body and blood with the bread and wine, however, is not a personal union, as in the case with the two natures of Christ. Rather . . . it is a "*sacramentalis unio*" (that is, a sacramental union).[10]

Historically speaking, this is not a sheer novelty since there are clear resonances with some versions of both Eastern and Western medieval concepts of "consubstantiation" or "coexistence" of the bread/wine with the body/blood of Christ in the Eucharist after consecration.[11] Here again, the

9. Luther, "The Babylonian Captivity of the Church," 37. The important issue of interpreting transubstantiation will be addressed in the last section of this chapter. Here, suffice it to note, Luther critiques a particular historical and theological interpretation of sacramental change which he deemed inadequate while the issue of sacramental change is a much broader one that Luther does not engage in a meaningful way in this text.

10. "Formula of Concord," Article VII, 599.

11. Gary Macy's writings provide a good overview of this controversial topic; Macy's chapters "The Medieval Inheritance" and his "Theology of the Eucharist in the High Middle Ages" offer very helpful resources. Edward Kilmartin's, *The Eucharist in the West*, especially Ch. 5, offers a nuanced treatment of the struggle to conceptualize the eucharistic presence of Christ and the theological battles that characterize Western

Eastern Orthodox have, at least on the level of binding doctrinal pronouncements, refused to be tied down to a single articulation of sacramental change such as the medieval western European idea of transubstantiation. Eastern Orthodoxy ordinarily distances itself from the quasi-Aristotelian language of transubstantiation while preferring non-technical terms for change like *metastoicheiosis* or simply *metabole*. Additionally, even these Greek terms are deliberately left vague.

Be that as it may, the contrast between *unio sacramentalis* and the more dualistic and dialectical versions of transubstantiation is rather clear, particularly regarding the insinuations of displacement and annihilation of material reality vis-à-vis the divine reality in the Eucharist. The Lutheran approach is crystallized in the *Formula of Concord* which points to "the sacramental union of the unchanged essence of the bread and the body of Christ."[12] Christ's presence *in pane, sub pane, cum pane* is analogous to how the divine and human nature concur in the person of Jesus Christ through the Third Space of hypostatic union. The *Formula* ventures that in Christ "the divine essence is not transformed into the human nature, but that the two unaltered natures are personally united."[13]

To emphasize the archetypal role of the Eucharist—itself a modulation, or a parallax resonance, of the hybrid Third Space of hypostatic union—for conceptualizing the whole interface of God-world relationality, I turn again to the quite unconventional Lutheran voice from Sweden, Yngve Brilioth. In a way that few Lutherans have cared (or dared?) to explore, Brilioth points out the sweeping ontological, epistemological, and soteriological implications of our eucharistic imaginaries. In a neo-Irenaean fashion, Brilioth argues that "the central secret of genuinely Christian theology is the holding in combination of the two contrasted opposites of God's Transcendence and Immanence; and precisely at this point the eucharist is the surest safeguard of a sound theology."[14] Indeed, the Eucharist is "a meeting-point on which

---

medieval and early modern theology. Edward Yarnold presents a concise summary of the Tridentine position on transubstantiation along with an analysis of the contemporary critical issues in his "Transubstantiation."

12. "Formula of Concord," Article VII, 599.

13. Ibid.

14. Brilioth, *Eucharistic Faith and Practice*, 274. One of the earliest expressions of what could be called, somewhat anachronistically, a eucharistic method in theology is arguably best summarized by this adage by Irenaeus of Lyons: "But our opinion is in accordance with the Eucharist, and the Eucharist in turn establishes our opinion. For we offer to Him His own, announcing consistently the fellowship and union of the flesh and Spirit . . .the bread, which is produced from the earth, when it receives the invocation of God, is no longer common bread, but the Eucharist, consisting of two realities, earthly and heavenly. . ." *Against Heresies*, Book IV, 18:5.

all the issues of theology converge."[15] As such, the Eucharist represents a whole imaginary of hybrid relationality that is resolutely structured as non-hegemonic, non-reductive, and non-allergic conviviality of difference, even transontological difference. This convivial hybridity originates far deeper and stretches far beyond the ritual and cultic occasions of the Lord's Supper/Mass/Holy Communion/Divine Liturgy or however else the Eucharist might be named in the worship traditions of various Christian denominations.

The hybrid *unio sacramentalis* affirms both divinity and humanity, transcendence and immanence, together—opaquely, yet truly and fully—in the space of an interactive plenitude of asymmetrical reciprocity. In contrast to many sacramental visions that promote transparency as the central element of sacramental relationality, the hybrid *unio sacramentalis* rather underscores the dimension of opacity. This opacity has little to do with the hair-splitting terminological dance around highly contested basic terms of sacramental discourse during the theological battles of early Western modernity: sign, symbol, reality, sacrament, essence, and substance. Eucharistic hybridity is opaque in the sense of being mighty complex—intricate, ambiguous, multidirectional, multivalent, and multilayered. Furthermore, the revelatory and salvific signification here is really fleshy, which means it is not pure, nor automatic, nor exclusive, nor total, nor universal, nor absolute. It is irrevocably mediated—refracted and modulated—by histories, cultures, identities, traditions, rituals, languages, and experiences that do not always translate cleanly from one context to another. As Kevin Irwin has underscored, through sacramentality "God is both revealed and yet also remains hidden" since "all sacramentality both reveals and hides the complete reality of God."[16]

A myriad of angles and themes could be further explored in the context of eucharistic communion, relationality, and interaction. Space does not permit me to delve into these fascinating questions here. What

15. Brilioth, *Eucharistic Faith and Practice*, 1. Brilioth appears to hint, in an understated manner, at something akin to what many years later was proposed by Louis-Marie Chauvet as "a fundamental theology of sacramentality which would permit a global reinterpretation of Christian existence" through the articulation of "a sort of law of the symbolic order, which is valid over the entire territory we propose to cross," *Symbol and Sacrament*, 548, 2. For Brilioth, the Eucharist is "the content of the whole Christian faith of the revelation of the Creator who is also the Redeemer is focused with unique intensity, and proclaimed with uniquely eloquent brevity," 283. Ultimately, "the eucharist sums up the Christian faith and the Christian religion with a fullness which verbal definitions can never adequately express," 54. I think that Brilioth's argument is consonant with Luther's early reflections on the role and significance of the Eucharist as the "testament" or the "short summary of all God's wonders and grace, fulfilled in Christ," see Martin Luther, "A Treatise On the New Testament," 84.

16. Irwin, "A Sacramental World," 202.

is nevertheless of paramount importance from a postcolonial perspective is that the eucharistic structure of "in, under, with" is a model of relational hybridity that cannot be pinned down to the operations of the imperial logic of rigid borders, clarity, and control. Postcolonial eucharistic hybridity is an eschatological sign of liberative, non-totalitarian wholeness into which no one and nothing is conscripted, conquered, or merely annihilated.

While the both/and hybridity of the Uncreated and created is vigorously affirmed, the exact "how" of *unio sacramentalis* remains opaque and irrevocably under an apophatic proviso—"the reality is joined to the symbols in such a way that Christ's body is even now present on earth in some invisible and incomprehensible way."[17]

It is here that Édouard Glissant's postcolonial meditations on opacity (*opacité*) are helpful. The "in, under, with" vision of sacramental hybridity was described as "invisible" and "incomprehensible." But to transpose that language into postcolonial parlance, this sort of invisibility and incomprehensibility is a discourse of ambiguity and opacity. Again, postcolonially speaking, "ambiguity is not always a sign of some shortcoming."[18] Relentless pursuit of clarity, univocity, and transparency, according to Glissant (and many other postcolonial thinkers), is a peculiarly Western strategy of tackling all sorts of challenging otherness since "Western thought has led us to believe that a work must always put itself constantly *at our disposal*. . ."[19]

To chase after transparency at the expense of life's rightful opacities is to create alienation and endorse a self-absorbed domestication and reduction of otherness. Such an attitude culminates, according to Glissant, in an imposition of oppressive totality.[20] Opacity, however, is the fecund matrix of freedom and wholeness that honors one's integrity and celebrates the ineffable dimension of depth in life, be it human or divine. Opacity is neither coercive appropriation of the incomprehensible otherness nor what Glissant terms as arrogant "autism."[21] It is positively and hope-fully "distracting:"

> The thought of opacity distracts me from absolute truths whose guardian I might believe myself to be. Far from cornering me within futility and inactivity, by making me sensitive to the limits of every method, it relativizes every possibility of every action within me (. . .) the thought of opacity saves me from unequivocal courses (*des voies univoques*) and irreversible choices.[22]

17. "Formula of Concord," Article VII, 594.
18. Glissant, *Caribbean Discourse*, 93.
19. Ibid., 107. Italics in the original.
20. Ibid., 155. Also see Glissant, *Poetics of Relation*, 190–91.
21. Glissant, *Poetics of Relation*, 190, 192.
22. Ibid., 192.

To preempt a misunderstanding, I must hasten to reiterate that, on this side of eschatological fulfillment, opacity does not equal postmodern absence. Postcolonial hybridity and postcolonial opacity are cognitive and imaginative tools that help to sacramentally articulate the complexity of life. Opacity does not valorize pure absence, endless rupture, sterile displacement, or hegemonic sublation. Rather, it gestures to an aptitude or virtue to recognize and live with more than just immediately visible, classifiable, and assessable outcomes and without the compulsion to conquer, dichotomize, simplify, and reduce.

To sum up: according to postcolonial visions, uniquely sacramental hybridity as signified and effected by the Eucharist does not operate according to the logic of displacement, detraction, substitution, and coercive supersession. Like the Lutheran notion of the eucharistic *unio sacramentalis*, it does not afford—*pace* many Western postmodern claims—any soteriological priority to what Edward Said described as the ultimately uninteresting competitive dialectic of presence and absence.[23]

Nor does it privilege the imaginary of rupture and endless deferral. The recent fascination with rupture/disruption/interruption/trauma[24] in Western postmodernism betrays its embeddedness in socio-cultural position of privilege, dominance, comfort, and insulating wealth that indeed might benefit from some kind of a purifying interruption from its self-absorption and introspection. But such metropolitan embeddedness, mostly native only to those in the dominant racial and gender strata who are sheltered in metropolitan privilege, is a luxury that postcolonial lifeworlds "from below" rarely participate in. Being disrupted and traumatized—note the passive voice here—is often a tediously recurrent and pernicious reality in the global postcolony "from below." It is not a matter of ascetic choice. And there is nothing inherently liberating or healing about trauma, interruption, and disruption. Thus glorifying the metaphors of violent in-breaking, disruption, and even trauma in sacramental discourse ought to be used with an abundance of hermeneutical and ethical caution unless the imagery of rupture is explicitly held accountable to the mutilated lives and souls of the "wretched of the earth." Or, better yet, discerning alternative images of empowerment, wholeness, and curative change that prioritize mending what is already being traumatized and interrupted might be a more fruitful and pastorally responsible avenue of theological creativity in the global postcolony.

23. Said, *Reflections on Exile*, 379.

24. See, for example, Marcus Pound, "Eucharist and Trauma" among other works in the postmodern paradigm.

ON EARTH AS IT IS IN HEAVEN: THE EUCHARISTIC CHANGE GOES PLANETARY

The second sacramental *locus* which is of paramount theological importance from a postcolonial perspective is the ever-so-fascinating (and ever so convoluted!) issue of change in the Eucharist. Since the Eucharist is also a *signum prognosticum*, and not just a *signum rememorativum* and *signum exhibitivum*,[25] it is also a question with profound eschatological implications. Space does not permit me to go into the details of these presuppositions. Suffice it to say that my point of departure is the conviction, in Herbert McCabe's words, that the most adequate Christian "account of heaven" is found in the sacraments. Specifically, "the Eucharist has an intrinsic relationship to the next world, so much so that the next world is best defined as what the Eucharist realizes and shows forth."[26]

If the Eucharist functions as a foretaste of the transfigured, divinized reality or the Reign of God, then it indeed matters what kind of God-world relationality is signified and effected in this sacramental mystery. How is this relational interface revealed and effected? By what agency and by what power dynamic? Because, ultimately, the Eucharist is not just about what happens to some bread and some wine, or even what happens to and in the people who receive these mysteries of faith in a particular ritual context. The Eucharist has a cosmic reach, a planetary scope as an eschatological *exemplum* that models a transfigured future for the whole creation.[27]

Working from an evolutionary paradigm—which in this case highlights and builds upon an ancient insight—John Haught rightly reminds

25. I am using the well-known terminology of Thomas Aquinas to indicate the polyvalence of eucharistic signification from *Summa Theologiae*, Tertia Pars, 79.1 and 73.4.

26. McCabe, *New Creation*, 137. McCabe is aware, of course, of the analogical—and therefore apophatic—nature of such comparisons: "Of course heaven is not present to us in the sacraments as it will be after the resurrection. It is, as we say, present in the sacrament in mystery, available to us only in faith—present to us through being symbolized, but none the less present in reality. . .," 137.

27. These theological assumptions are rooted in the Eastern Orthodox thought of understanding the whole universe as the "matter" of the cosmic Eucharist as Alexander Schmemann has argued in *For the Life of the World*. From the perspective of sacramental and sophianic eschatology, the whole created world becomes the Body of Christ in the process of sacramental transmutation as suggested by Sergei Bulgakov: "This transfiguration of creation, corresponding to the Savior's second coming, is accomplished in the Divine Eucharist *mysteriously* or *sacramentally*, that is visibly only for the eyes of faith, upon the eucharistic matter. That which is accomplished in the sacrament will be accomplished, at the end of time, in the whole world, which is the body of humankind. And the latter is the Body of Christ," *The Holy Grail and Eucharist*, 137–38. Italics in original.

us that Christian theology "needs to supplement its classic sacramentalism with an anticipatory vision of the universe."[28] Instead of static sacramentalism and the cult of the eternal now, Haught argues in favor of retrieving the eschatological hope that is found in the scriptures:

> Our sacramental spirituality, I suggest, must now meet up again with the spirit of the Bible. Every sacrament needs to be seen as a promise, an opening not so much to what once was, or to what is vertically above, or even to what is deep within, as to what is coming from up ahead. [. . .]Understood in a fully biblical context, a sacrament is not just an epiphany of the eternal now, but also an anticipation of the not-yet. The *parousia* for which we long is not so much a perfect presence as a transforming *adventus*.[29]

It matters, then, what kind of power dynamic and eschatological trajectory the eucharistic mystery reveals and models because like all other theological concepts, the Eucharist "functions"—as liturgy, as theological imaginary, and as ritual performance. And this is where transubstantiation—not just one way of insisting on a "really" real presence of Christ in the Eucharist, but also an insistence that a certain change is necessarily a part of sacramental transformation—should be explored as a really stimulating idea for postcolonial sacramental reflection.

Of course, a lot depends on what we mean by "transubstantiation!" Again, it is neither feasible nor necessary to rehearse here the long and even tortuous genealogy of this Western notion of sacramental presence and sacramental change, including all the variables of interpretation that have emerged from the twelfth century onwards. However, one thing seems to be clear. As Gary Macy observes from a historical perspective, the prominence of the doctrine of transubstantiation grew exponentially alongside the centralization of clerical power in Western Christianity (among other philosophical and cultural factors) "to make Christ present in the Eucharist."[30] As with the sacramental "numbers game," transubstantiation, too, is a concept that emerged only in the second millennium. It belongs to a distinctly Western theological mentality which, from the Middle Ages onward, produced eucharistic theologies deeply enamored with, and embedded in, soteriologies privileging sacrificial atonement—a development that the Jesuit theologian Robert Daly has recently—and rightly—described as a "theological tragedy."[31]

28. Haught, *Resting on the Future*, 14.
29. Ibid. Italics in the original.
30. Macy, "The Medieval Inheritance," 18, 22.
31. Daly, "The Council of Trent," 179.

The lack of explicit scriptural origin and a very close—yet dispensable—entanglement with images of sacrificial propitiation were the reasons why Protestant reformers ditched transubstantiation as their favored way of talking about the real presence of Christ in the Eucharist. Instead, the preferred imaginaries of Christ's sacramental presence and agency were modeled upon certain versions of the hypostatic union in terms of Chalcedonian Christology (Martin Luther), or re-envisioned in various pneumatological settings (Huldrych Zwingli, Jean Calvin)—or sidelined altogether (some Radical Reformation movements). Considering the customary rejection of transubstantiation even among the most sacramental of Protestants, despite recent ecumenical conversations on this complicated topic,[32] it might appear strange for someone like me (i.e., a Lutheran) to highlight it. After all, the scriptural institution narratives of the Last Supper accommodate an exceptionally wide and polyphonic hermeneutical horizon. Why, then, talk about transubstantiation at all?

It all boils down to the role of—and even the very desire for—change in a theological imaginary. For postcolonial theologies, the notion of change—transformation, transition, transmutation, transsignification, transelementation, and other such images—is of paramount significance. Change is an empancipatory matter in postcolonial perspectives. In sacramental context, Eucharist represents the most intense and the most intimate revelation of what salvific change, salvific *metanoia*, is all about on this side of the beatific vision. Hence it is the most paradigmatic revelation, too, of what is possible, desirable, virtuous, and healing for human life and all the deepest tissues of created material reality as a whole within the panentheistic economy of "deep incarnation" and, equally, "deep resurrection."

In this sense, the question about eucharistic change is a question about how a truly emancipatory transformation can happen and ought to happen across the relational interface among the Uncreated and the created. Emancipatory change is a real, substantial, actual, embodied, and experientially accountable change. It is not merely a change of rhetoric or ritual. It is a question about the nature of power relationships on a planetary scale that sacramental transformation simultaneously signifies and has the potential to effect. For the Eucharist, like all theological images and concepts, also "functions." It "functions" as the template, the *Leitmotif*, the summary, indeed a gateway or sign *par excellence*, for the whole planetary interface

32. The documents of the Lutheran-Roman Catholic ecumenical dialogue indicate areas of divergent contrasts in eucharistic matters, for example, see "Declaration on the Way: Church, Ministry, and the Eucharist," (2015). See also George Hunsinger's recent initiative to resurrect ecumenical conversations on possible convergences regarding the presence of Christ in the Eucharist, *The Eucharist and Ecumenism*.

that some of us call sacramentality, and which is patterned in tune with the Third Space of hypostatic union. In short: in whatever way qualitative change happens in the eucharistic mystery—as far as we can even begin to articulate it—then that is the way a genuinely transformative, ethically sound, and truly liberating change should happen, because that is how the divine agency works.

The marginalization of sacramental change in the Lutheran (and in other versions of Protestantism, even more so) tradition is very unfortunate. As noted before, *unio sacramentalis* is not a triumphant or aggressive imaginary. It revels in opacity, or what Chauvet describes as the "consent to mediation," and renounces the idolatrous and necrotic temptations to crave for a full, unmediated, and thus manageable presence of God.[33] It does not capitalize on the disordered human fixation with competitive hierarchies of being and acting, and on controlling the being and acting of others. It does not obsess about who among us can produce what kind of divine presence, or who can exclusively act *in persona Christi* to "make" him present *ex opere operato*—and then usually through the toxic imaginary of sacrifice. *Unio sacramentalis* is not an either/or imaginary—otherwise so typical in the Lutheran valorization of dialectical, and thus often lamentably dualistic, extremes and their conflictual grind. All that being said, the peaceful and mutually fecund conviviality of bread and body, the human and the Divine, the material and the spiritual, the one and the many, all within the redemptive opacity of sacramental union, is simply not quite enough.

It is fortunate that Martin Luther's approach (and that of other Protestant Reformers) does not mandate anything material and created to be annihilated (as if by a colonial conquest), or sacrificed, or destroyed, or replaced, or substituted. But in a world that is unrelentingly structured in dominance, hegemony, abuse, ruthless competition, and victimization, only an idea of a profound change can signify a counter-hegemonic alternative for life, and cause a healing transformation of all the seemingly intransigent ills that are of human making- not to mention those that are simply part and parcel of the messy evolutionary process ever on the edge of unpredictable and creative chaos and failed trial runs.

The question of sacramental change should no longer be ignored in postcolonial theology, especially in its Protestant expressions, as a topic of importance only for "high church" traditionalists and snobbish liturgical

33. Chauvet, *Symbol and Sacrament*, 173–77. Chauvet remarks that "the liturgy is the powerful pedagogy where we learn to consent to the presence of the absence of God, who obliges us to give him a body in the world, thereby giving the sacraments their plenitude in the 'liturgy of the neighbor' and giving the ritual memory of Jesus Christ its plenitude in our existential memory," 265.

purists. Realizing that his statements go against the habitual grain of most Protestant theology, Theodore Runyon has pointed out the worth of not ditching the notion of transubstantiation too soon, provided it is carefully nuanced: "Although it may be surprising for a Protestant to make this point, there is one element within the doctrine of transubstantiation that is well worth retaining, the emphasis upon transformation and change. Traditionally Protestants have not looked kindly upon this aspect of the doctrine."[34] That being said, the interesting aspect of transubstantiation is precisely that the change here is "an intrinsic rather than an extrinsic or forensic change of the type familiar to Calvinists and Lutherans from the doctrines of election and justification" since the change involved in consecration is "a sanctifying, not just declaratory, action."[35] If Eucharist is, as Theodore Runyon argued, a real communion with Christ, then "where the kingdom breaks through, even provisionally, it brings change in this world. Thus a sacrament that mediates the power of the new age in Christ must be affected at its very core by the kingdom-reality of which it is a part."[36]

Runyon's interpretation highlights the necessary caution to carefully guard against the fetishizing of the Eucharist. He suggests a model of transubstantiation that might be described as a variation of transvaluation or transelementation. Christ's intentionality and agency "raises" the material realities of the Eucharist "to a new power, he transforms them into their original and eschatological destiny."[37] Most importantly, "the focus is not upon change for its own sake but for the kingdom's sake. This change is at one and the same time the transformation of the world and the empowering of the sanctified world to be the bearer of Christ to as many as will receive him. . ."[38] The change that must characterize a postcolonially colored transubstantiation is a genuinely transformative change that empowers rather than displaces, detaches, or annihilates created material reality.

TRANSUBSTANTIATION . . . WITH A POSTCOLONIAL TWIST

From a postcolonial perspective, the idea of transubstantiation is as theological as it is political—and cosmic. There is no such thing as a theology

34. Runyon, "The World as the Original Sacrament," 505.
35. Ibid.
36. Ibid., 506.
37. Ibid.
38. Ibid.

that is not always already a theopolitics, as Catherine Keller reminds us.[39] Transubstantiation witnesses to the deep, mystical audacity to hope against hope that an alternative to the world's ills is possible. It affirms that such an alternative is possible at least in a proleptic manner, even here and now, if only sporadically and if only through experientially opaque glimmers of healing, renewal, peace, justice, and fulfillment.

Above all, the idea of transubstantiation gestures toward an alternative which is not just the mightiest image of uncontrolled omnipotence that our imagination can conjure up and then project onto divinity, but one that works within an ethical ontology of relation and that is expressed through a liberating and whole-making, not subjugating or conquering, agency. In this world, such an idea alone might suggest something miraculous without in any way invoking Aristotelian or apologetic pyrotechnics. But the point here really is that something in this reality, as we know it, has to genuinely, though not necessarily violently or by violation, change—whatever that change might mean and entail—in order for that alternative world to emerge from the long shadow of the Cross. After all, transubstantiation is not just about any change. It is about revolutionary change in the blunt words of Herbert McCabe: "The doctrine of transubstantiation, as I see it, is that the bread and wine suffer a revolutionary change, not that they change into something else, they become more radically food and drink. . ."[40]

So far, so good. The big issue, though, is what type of power dynamic might this sort of change require in order not to replicate, even if unconsciously and unintentionally, the type of imperialistic "change" that has shattered so many lives? What type of relational conviviality among the Uncreated and the created ought to be envisioned to facilitate a change that is non-hegemonic, perhaps indeed counter-hegemonic and decolonial?

Postcolonial imaginaries of power express particular concern about dualistic and antagonistic patterns of power. Power dynamics play out in the world of starkly uneven differences, be they human, non-human, or divine. Divine transcendence is encountered and interacted with throughout this very complex terrain of a world structured in dominance. In R. Radhakrishnan's words, it is a "world that occludes the big O[ther] and seeks to possess the Real in the name of dominance."[41] Our functional concepts of divine transcendence are never exempt from this entanglement. As Mayra Rivera points out, there can be no compartmentalizing of various realms of exis-

39. Keller, *God and Power*, 135.

40. McCabe, *God Matters*, 126.

41. Radhakrishnan, *Theory in an Uneven World*, 120. In addition: "The political is too much with us, but unfortunately any gesturing towards the Real that bypasses the political can only be a pseudo-gesture," ibid.

tence; the sociopolitical is inextricable from the theological and vice versa.[42] Of course, there is always a temptation to ignore or disguise the "close connection between interhuman values and metaphysical structures."[43]

The postcolonial perspective underscores that o/Otherness and difference do not need to imply antagonism, exclusion, and a habitual oppositionality that inscribes its divisive "either/or" understanding of power in human and trans-human relations. As Wonhee Anne Joh puts it, postcolonial approaches call for dismantling "our impulse to kill or erase the other in order to feel we exist. . ."[44] Be it intersubjective, intercultural, or trans-ontological, postcolonial imaginaries of power endorse reciprocal transcendence. This perspective arises out of subaltern imaginary of power that holds its own symbolic authority that challenges the symbolic authority of dominant discourse. Radhakrishnan observes:

> there are good and bad instances of transcendence. Lusty or greedy transcendence would be one in which one point of view preying on another establishes a binding and normative relationship with the Real on behalf of all perspectives. It is a logic whereby I say that I don't have the responsibility of proving the benevolence and the legitimacy of my God so long as I have the ability and the power to desecrate or destabilize the authority of your God. What makes my perspective axiomatic and universally binding is not the justice or fairness of its vision but its power to destroy or depoliticize other perspectives. The lust of the dominant desire is posited on the objectification of the other and the nihilation of the right to pleasure of the other. It is through this process of nihilation that the dominant participants name their desire as the Real of the encounter, and their lack as the semantic body of the Real. The other in this experiential nexus ceases to have the right to name the experience and interpret it. The ultimate trope of such an encounter is of course rape, where the other is both implicated and silenced in the dominant self's expression.[45]

To summarize the spectrum of postcolonial concerns, Radhakrishnan describes a postcolonial transcendence and its template of power as follows:

> Transcendence is intended as a qualitative movement that acknowledges the specificity of the location that inaugurates

42. Rivera, "God and Difference," 35.

43. Ibid. 33.

44. Joh, "Violence and Asian American Experience: From Abjection to *Jeong*," 152.

45. Radhakrishnan, *Theory in an Uneven World*, 103–4.

> the transcendence, while at the same time marking that very location or state of being as one to be left behind. At the other end of the arc of transcendence is the other as activated and eroticized by the desire of the self. Is the other as self violated by the desire of the self undertaking the transcendence? Why should the "other self" be available for transcendence at all unless the transcendence is mutually effected? I do not mind being the object and terminus of your transcendence so long as you consent to being the object and terminus of my transcendence. It is only within such a context of reciprocal transcendence and the ethical obligation that it entails that the question of freedom can even begin to be posed contrapuntally against the reality of objectification.[46]

What questions might these postcolonial visions of non-hegemonic encounter between divine transcendence and our created world bring to the discussion about transubstantiation? It probably goes without saying that a postcolonial imaginary of transubstantiation would distance itself as far as possible from any intimations that the bread and wine, the material elements of the Eucharist—liturgically and cosmically—are annihilated or destroyed[47] as they "suffer the revolutionary change" in the process of eucharistic conversion. A postcolonial transubstantiation cannot be a violent, imperialistic, and competitive change where the divine colonizes material creation by devastating force. As such it would certainly find a friendly conversation partner in the Aquinas of the *Prima Pars* of *Summa Theologiae*: grace does not destroy but rather perfects—and not just simply builds upon—nature.

Postcolonial visions of transubstantiation ought to resist with all their might the toxic sacrificial imagery of propitiatory atonement and all the theological and ethical metastases that this ruinous teaching has unleashed in mainstream Western Christianity over almost a millennium. From the post-totalitarian context of Central and Eastern Europe, the Czech theologian Ivana Noble has called for extreme vigilance regarding sacrificial imagery in theological constructs of power and agency. Proceeding from a Girardian perspective of post-communist theological inquiry, Noble argues that "we have to avoid any form of positive divine assent Christ's sacrificial killing, and reject any, even if passive, participation in the destruction of the

46. Ibid., 104.

47. Daly in his "The Council of Trent" offers a very poignant critique of the sacrificial annihilation and destruction models of transubstantiation as laid out, for example, by Robert Bellarmine.

other or the self. . ."[48] Hence, "a celebration of life does not happen when victims are produced, when injustice is done or even overlooked, when people are deprived of hope. This applies not only to the less traditional ways of celebration of life, but also to liturgy."[49] Noble exhorts cultural critiques of sacrificial belonging and communion that only succeed in producing victims. Instead, she advances an imaginary of "non-sacrificial love—and that includes not sacrificing oneself at the deepest level of being. Only then is communion possible."[50]

Furthermore, if salvation is liberation from the self-perpetuating mechanism of violence and victimization then, Noble argues, as such it must entail "a ban on sacrificial relationships."[51] Postcolonial visions of eucharistic change and conviviality resonate very deeply with the dynamic of non-sacrificial love. A genuinely eschatological and genuinely eucharistic idea of sacramental conviviality and sacramental change, while always hypersensitively remembering the "wretched of the earth," could be accountably rooted in what Noble articulates as the eucharistic vision wherein no one is required to give up anything or anyone sacrificially, not even oneself, but rather where abundance has the last and fulfilling word. Noble finds such a vision expressed in the eucharistic eschatology of the Brazilian theologian Luiz Carlos Susin who argues that,

> love will be the sole translation of the eternal eucharist: abundance of life is abundance of human and creaturely relations, in heartfelt communion with God. Pure abundance, with nothing lacking and no deformations, is expressed—is glorified—as a perfect act of thanksgiving, the praise of the universe. All sacrifice will be abolished, for sacrifice is not the religious act *par excellence*. It is not the sacrifice of human victims, or of substituting victims, or even the sacrifice of oneself in historical and crucified love, but only a gift, without victims, that constitutes the eschatological eucharist.[52]

48. Noble, *Theological Interpretation of Culture in Post-Communist Context*, 124.

49. Ibid., 133.

50. Ibid., 191.

51. Ibid., 192.

52. Susin, *Assim na terra como no céu*, 192. Quoted in Noble, *Theological Interpretation of Culture in Post-Communist Context*, 165.

IN LIEU OF CONCLUSION

To conclude my reflections, there are a few pointers that can be useful in elucidating the models of sacramental change that postcolonial theology could entertain as it starts finding its sacramental voice in years to come.

First, if we are talking about a mysterious, radical, and even revolutionary change then this sort of sacramental change, or "transubstantiation," must be articulated within an intrinsically interrelational, dynamic, planetary, and ethical cosmology of power. As Mayra Rivera points out, we should start with the (panentheistic) presupposition that always and already "all creation is grounded in and linked to God, who is its source . . .relation is not something external or superadded to reality, but something inherent to reality."[53] If so, then a postcolonially colored transubstantiation would need to take place under the auspices of a transcendence which,

> pushes forward and retains—the future emerges from within the matrices of relations that characterize created life, which include sociopolitical relations as well as the organic energies that sustain life and evolution in the cosmos. . . the old does not predetermine the new, but supports it. The future emerges not simply by unfolding spontaneously from culturally or genetically inherited potentiality, but it is never independent from, or external to, the organic processes. Transcendence in history implies that new things emerge that are not predetermined by biological legacies, but they come in and through the physical, vital reality that we call nature: a reality that is grounded in the divine.[54]

Second, a postcolonial worldview is not allergic to crossing and transgressing borders. Sterile transitions are not the postcolonial cup of tea. Here the notion of hybridity can help sketch the contours of how change materializes. In many postcolonial perspectives, hybridity emerges as a "catholic" preference for the both/and rather than either/or imaginary. To reiterate once more, in Robert Young's words:

> Hybridity . . . makes difference into sameness, and sameness into difference, but in a way that makes the same no longer the same, the different no longer simply different. In that sense, it . . . [is] a breaking and joining at the same time, in the same place: difference and sameness in an apparently impossible simultaneity.[55]

53. Rivera, "God and Difference," 40.

54. Ibid., 39.

55. Young, *Colonial Desire*, 26–27.

It is hard to imagine a postcolonial imaginary of eucharistic change or "transubstantiation" that would endorse not just annihilation or destruction of created materiality through a miraculous colonization, but also a permanent and finalized displacement or dislocation of the integral structure of creation, perhaps we could call it "substance," as somehow irrelevant and redundant in the process of salvific transformation. Regardless of how the concept of substance or essence might be interpreted,[56] postcolonialism does not need to have Monophysite, or Nestorian leanings. Asymmetrical as it may be, the integrity of created reality is irreducible even in the process of its own salvation. A model of transubstantiation that in any way replaces or substitutes one identity/substance for another with a unilateral and unidirectional finality is a problematic concept in the worldview where conviviality and reciprocity are recognized as life-giving values. And this is where a postcolonial approach to transubstantiation must look beyond sacramentality and liturgyalone.

Third, transubstantiation, postcolonially speaking, is an eschatological matter. It already unfolds in the sacramental mysteries, but is not yet fulfilled. It dwells in, with, and under sacramental opacity where the bread, wine, water, oil, touch, taste, smell, sound, and the whole of material creation communes with the Divine, using the famous words of Alexander Schmemann, as "the material of one all-embracing eucharist."[57] It coexists and co-creates together with Christ, asymmetrically but nevertheless reciprocally. As such it is a revelatory glimmer of the "new heaven and a new earth" (Rev 21:1).

Here I must again return to Runyon's analysis. The change, which the idea of transubstantiation gestures toward, is really about "the proleptic renewal of the order of creation and the reconciliation of humankind through [Christ's] body."[58] In this sense, transubstantiation cannot be said to be complete or finalized in a ritual sense alone because the mystery of Eucharist, and whatever type of sacramental change it may entail, is not exclusively or

56. The vociferous debates about the definition of "substance" and what it might refer to in a non-Aristotelian philosophical and cosmological framework have not ceased in the early twenty-first century theology. Even though the Aristotelian "substance metaphysics" has come under a heavy critique in the Western postmodern milieu, the question about the nature and, as it were, the ecology of sacramental change remains relevant. Even if the "substance" or "essence" of any given created reality is ultimately an immensely complex network of relations as the Buddhist ontological perspectives suggest, the issue of how change happens, what it involves, and how it impacts the integrity of that reality remains as significant as when the conventional concepts of substance are used.

57. Schmemann, *For the Life of the World*, 15.

58. Runyon, "The World as the Original Sacrament," 506.

even primarily about what happens to a piece of bread and a mouthful of wine on a certain altar. Yes, it is about the bread and wine. But it is equally about a qualitative transformation within and throughout the convocation of Jesus' disciples. In other words, it is about what happens to those followers of Jesus Christ who are gathered and convoked by the Holy Spirit into the movement of *metanoia* to become Christ's true Body in the world.

Fourth, and furthermore, the Eucharist is about the salvific transformation of all life precisely as created, as unfinished, as evolving and emerging. This emergence is accompanied by the profound and often debilitating biological, historical, cultural, and psychospiritual "groaning" (Rom 8:20–22). Thus, "if the Supper is to be a true eschatological sign, it must signify the restoration of the created world as well as the reconciliation of the human world."[59] Such a restoration and reconciliation, obviously, is far from anything even remotely resembling a *fait accompli* in the world as we know it now.

It is in this context—and against the powerful inertia to prematurely emphasize semiotic transparency—that the opacity of all sacramental signification and agency must be upheld. It is not just a matter of deep postcolonial sensitivity to and resistance against the cultural and psychospiritual homogenization that Glissant has unmasked and defied so masterfully. It is, once again, a matter of eschatological vigilance to remember that, as Haught aptly cautions, an immoderate, i.e., gleeful, sacramentalism is irresponsible since it mistakes eschatological promise for historical actuality. Thus, blanking over the eschatological dimension in sacramental thought "cannot easily accommodate the shadow side of nature" and therefore (mis)takes every present state of affairs as an already realized epiphany of God.[60] Sacramental revelations and relations, real and meaningful as they can be, are and will be opaque in the evolutionary world even as it "nurture[s] a promise of future perfection."[61] For now, Haught argues, we live with eschatological ambiguity "as a partner to promise."[62] Both accountable ecotheology and sacramental theology would fall prey to the gullibility of romanticism were they to try to escape the need to recognize the intense eschatological striving toward the promise of new heaven and new earth. For, as Haught admonishes, "the world, including that of nonhuman nature, has not yet arrived at the final peace of God's kingdom, and so it does not merit our worship. It does deserve our valuation, but not our prostration."[63]

59. Ibid.

60. Haught, *The Promise of Nature,* 111.

61. Ibid., 110.

62. Ibid., 111.

63. Ibid.

The matter of eucharistic change is of supreme planetary and cosmic—and not only liturgical and devotional—importance. When it is conceived according to the root note and tonic key of Christ, the crescendo of sacramental pluriverse and the incarnate Third Space of hypostatic union, and the contrapuntal hybridity of *unio sacramentalis*, then it can indeed manifest as "a proleptic participation in the eschaton" which "preserves the integrity of the creature while exhibiting the power of the kingdom."[64] Consequently, with Runyon, it can only be underscored once more:

> No more fundamental change is imaginable. Nor could the presence of Christ be more faithfully portrayed than as his presence in the power of the in-breaking kingdom which restores the world to its creaturely integrity. Thus the Eucharist enables us to participate in the very recreation of the cosmos that in being effected in Christ Jesus.[65]

Fifth, transubstantiation tries to articulate, imperfectly as all our concepts, images, and semiotic events always do, the interactive, of the Eucharist. Eucharist as a semiotic event is a hybrid sacramental mystery of non-hegemonic convergence and synergy of divine, human, and nonhuman agencies in order to signify and effect a meaningful, if ever mysterious, transformation. It is a semiotic and synergistic mystery ever in progress. Within the fold of this mystery, it not just about God and humanity. Rather, a planetary postcolonial theology will want to steer clear of what Haught calls the "anthropocentric exaggeration of our own importance" in sacramental discourses.[66] As such, it cannot—it may not—leave anything that is not radically evil or functionally destructive "behind" as redundant or irrelevant. It may not, for obvious biblical reasons, leave behind the *Ursakrament* of creation since God "saw everything that [God] has made and indeed, it was very good" (Gen 1:31).

Obviously, bread and wine, the hybrid gifts of biological creativity as well as human intelligence and agency, are not radically evil or functionally destructive—nor is the material creation from which they come and to which they return. To extend the semiotic trajectory of the Eucharist as a redemptively opaque foretaste of cosmic transformation, it can be said that the whole creation participates in this eucharistic mystery precisely as "good"—not perfect or fully realized, but nevertheless "good" enough for such a transformation. Of course, the Christian tradition has always,

64. Runyon, "The World as the Original Sacrament," 508.

65. Ibid., 508–9.

66. Haught, *The Promise of Nature*, 41.

however clumsily most of the time, insisted that the creation is "good" even in its incompleteness, wastefulness, unpredictability, and rich opacity.

Rather than skidding down the route of Manichean dualisms or Docetic reductionism, postcolonial perspectives envision the Eucharist as an interactive semiotic event—a cosmic, planetary, synergistic, and contrapuntal hybridity. Within such a hybridity, a truly transformative change happens only when no one's integrity and agency is violated, or sacrificed, or colonized, or undercut—even for an ostensibly beneficial cause and allegedly "for their own good." In this context, postcolonial sacramental imagination can enthusiastically join hands with the feminist discourses which lift up the vision of divine power, presence, and action as the presence which "would not be one of a domineering, potentially threatening God which could be used diabolically to justify the domination of a few human persons over other humans, nor the exploitation of the common environment."[67]

Last but not least: as Emmanuel Levinas sighs, "of peace there can only be eschatology."[68] Likewise, of transubstantiation there also can properly—indeed, only—be an eschatology. The vector of *epektasis* toward salvation is long and slow. Liturgical bells should be ringing only to remind us that such a longing and straining is far from accomplished. Transformative sacramental change—some might want to call it transubstantiation—in this world is a decidedly unfinished symphony. Any triumphalist theological claims or liturgical postures that mystify us into thinking that transubstantiation is a transparent *fait accompli* which we can manage, comprehend, enshrine, and control—on altars, in tabernacles, in dogma, in ritual, in institutions, in relationships, in mindscapes, and powerscapes—are premature, presumptuous, and dangerous.

67. Roll, "Baptism," 255.

68. Levinas, *Totality and Infinity*, 24.

CODA

Postcolonial Ressourcement and Diasporic Method

Reimagining the Sacramental Signature of All Things

The signature of all things: method.[1]

Giorgio Agamben

. . .the magisterial texts can now be our servants, as the new magisterium constructs itself in the name of the Other.[2]

Gayatri Chakravorty Spivak

Finally, and once more with feeling—postcolonial sacramental *ressourcement* is a relevant, vigilant, and timely endeavor. In this brief Coda, I will summarize the challenges and promises of postcolonial retrievals of Christian sacramental discourse. To underscore the particular leads and liabilities of my constructive trajectory, I will briefly point out, this time explicitly, the contours of a diasporic postcolonial method—indeed, the

1. Agamben, *The Signature of All Things*.

2. Spivak, *A Critique of Postcolonial Reason*, 7.

"signature" of the diasporic and postcolonial imaginary in theological reflection. I will wrap up these concluding remarks with an epigrammatic plea for a methodological *ressourcement* of sacramentality—and not just particular sacramental doctrines or rituals—to reinvigorate theological imagination precisely as an endeavor of postcolonial planetarity.

SACRAMENTALITY: IS IT WORTHY OF POSTCOLONIAL RESSOURCEMENT?

Despite the awareness that the contemporary veracity and salvific vocation of Christian sacramental theology is overshadowed and increasingly questioned by the painful gravity of postcolonial histories and memories, sacramental sensibilities have endured throughout the global postcolony, both in locations "from above" as well as "from below." They continue to glimmer in the metropolises and margins alike. Sacramental sensibilities have been modulated—and mutilated—throughout the lifeworlds of Western colonial modernity and postmodernity. Sacraments and sacramental imagination have been betrayed by violence, arrogance, racism, and patriarchy woven into many an imperialistic and abusive theological and ecclesiastical formation that are far from extinction today. Sometimes sacramental teachings and practices have even enabled and legitimized injustice, violence, and abuse. These unholy histories point to the reason why postcolonial studies and postcolonial theologians have been reclusive to engage sacramental theology.

That being said, postcolonial theology can no longer afford to make a wide berth around the sacramental tradition in Christianity. If for no other reason, realizing that sacramental imaginaries can be fruitful conversation partners amid the unfolding planetary ecological crisis should generate interest. As I argued throughout this study, the constructive resonances between postcolonialism and sacramental theology are not limited to environmental issues. Particularly, through the notion of hybridity, Saidian contrapuntality, and diaspora discourses, sacramental modes of reasoning and imagination harbor a significant potential for mutually enriching constructive conversations not only regarding ecological justice but also social, economic, and gender justice.

Recognizing the historical and cultural ambiguities of longstanding (and longsuffering!) Christian enmeshment with colonial and imperial escapades, I persevere in the belief that postcolonial *ressourcement* of the Christian sacramental imaginary *can* vigilantly and creatively retrieve the life-giving impulses of vital and profoundly convivial, reciprocal, non-dualistic, and non-coercive relationality that the notion sacramentality is really all about. The impulses of such reality and relationality may well be opaque to many contemporary eyes in the post-ecclesial era and much more fragmentary than our liking. But they do speak *sotto voce* through nuances, through the fragments and glimmers percolating deep in the crevices and on the outer margins of conventional Occidental theologies. Sometimes they hide in plain sight within well-known theological canons waiting to be retrieved and appreciated. Occasionally they are strategically camouflaged in the very midst of so-called "popular" religious practices and even in spiritual practices that have been untethered from conventional religious settings.

At the same time, no postcolonially accountable constructive retrievals of sacramentality can be done without guarding against the perils of theological and ecclesiastical nativism, be it geopolitically or liturgically inspired. Postcolonial sacramental imagination insists that the divine power, precisely as sacramental power, does not operate within the limits of our ecclesiastical-ritual sacraments alone—however we count, number, or demarcate them. As I have argued, sacramentality is not an imaginary of colonizing and hegemonizing power unless it gets seduced by the idolatrous mimicry of imperialism. And seduced it indeed has been: the sinister entanglement of Christian sacramental liturgies with colonial and imperial histories in various cultures and continents demonstrates that these liturgies are often incapable of performing a critical self-analysis, as my explorations of Latvian history—among a multitude of other postcolonial locations—show.

Steffen Lösel highlights the issue of fundamental importance for postcolonial sacramental and liturgical studies. Lösel does not represent an explicitly postcolonial perspective. However, his questions—"can ritual truly incorporate its prophetic critique" and "can critique and reform of ritual . . . ever be part of a ritual itself. . . or must they not rather come from outside the world of ritual?"[3]—are particularly relevant to the decolonial thrust of postcolonial sacramental theology. Lösel concludes that, in light of Christian history, the liturgical *ordo* itself "cannot provide the necessary incentive for inner reform" out of its own resources and therefore "require[s] the second critical principle."[4]

Such "second critical principle" must embody some form of resistance to the necrotic temptations of (self) idolatry in worship and religious practice in general. It requires what Emmanuel Levinas would call exteriority.[5]

3. Lösel, "What Sacred Symbols Say about Strangers and Strawberries," 646.

4. Ibid., 647.

5. Levinas, *Totality and Infinity*.

From a postcolonial point of view, that exteriority in general is the ethics of theology (David Ngong) and the hypersensitivity to the marginalized, colonized, imprisoned, and the poor (Namsoon Kang). Specifically, it is the ethics of decolonization or, as Nelson Maldonado-Torres articulated it, "de-colonial justice."[6] Postcolonial imaginary prioritizes ethics, hence ethics can provide such indwelling exteriority, a planetary exteriority, an exteriority which always asks, how, historically and at the present time, do theological images and concepts actually "function?" Who do they empower and lift up and who do they disempower and disinherit? Who do they heal and who do they sin against? What do they change—or not—and to what end? How do they effect change?

Among the constructive priorities of postcolonial sacramental theology is the recuperation of the sacramental *as* the ethical. In light of postcolonial *anamnesis,* the vital entanglement of the sacramental with the ethical has been molested in Christian history with lamentable regularity. Past and present molestations notwithstanding, a fruitful recuperation of this fragile yet pivotal counterpoint of sacramentality and ethics can nevertheless be re-orchestrated again through creative crosspollinations between sacramental and postcolonial modes of reflection.

By affirming the hybrid and liberative dynamics of sacramental mysteries not as ancillary but as constitutionally indispensable across the God-world relational interface, postcolonial sacramental imagination by the same token affirms that sacramentality, as the relational interface mediating the encounter between the Uncreated and the created, must itself be, in a certain sense, ethics. In other words, sacramentality does not simply equal certain historical and institutionally demarcated rituals of the past or present forms of Christianity. Nor is it circumscribed, exhausted, or fully realized in such rituals. Sacramentality can be conceptualized as ethics in the sense of being the theological articulation of relationality that is asymmetrical yet reciprocal; powerful yet not hegemonic; effective yet not coercive and conquering; whole-making yet not patronizing; unifying yet not totalizing; differentiating yet not discriminating; inviting yet not imposing; persuading

6. As Maldonado-Torres explains decolonial justice, it is "a justice oriented by the trans-ontological dimension of the human. Decolonial justice opposes the preferential option for imperial Man by the preferential option for the *damnés* or condemned of the earth," "On the Coloniality of Being," 260. According to Maldonado-Torres, "the de-colonial turn involves interventions at the level of power, knowledge, and being through varied actions of decolonization and 'des-gener-accion'. It opposes the paradigm of war which has driven modernity for more than five hundred years, with a radical shift in the social and political agent, the attitude of the knower, and the position in regards to whatever threatens the preservation of being, particularly the actions of the *damnés*," 262.

yet not converting; robust yet not rude; challenging yet not idolatrously competitive; paradoxical yet not decadently dialectical.[7]

Can postcolonialism afford to steer clear of such an imaginative partnership as a new planetary "magisterium constructs itself in the name of the Other?"[8] And can Christian sacramental theology afford to ignore postcolonialism as an unrelenting global *anamnesis* of the "wretched of the earth" and the ethical claim their victimization lays upon theology? For, in the world as postcolonial experience knows it,

> God's light is. . . obscured in a twofold way: through the desperation of wandering have-nots, and the excess of possibilities of free-wheeling tourists. As long as this split remains there as an open wound, the presence of God—and of life as a gift, for that matter—shows only its disfigured appearance. I can scarcely imagine an abundance of sacramental presence in a world at large, in which on the one hand excessive glamour neutralises God's light, and dire misery, on the other hand, cries out for mercy. Those who have not experienced gratuity in real life can hardly be expected to understand the meaning of divine gratuity expounded in learned discourses.[9]

ON THE METHODOLOGICAL SIGNATURE OF POACHING, FRAGMENTS, AND DIMINUTIVE POLES

Everything that I have argued for so far has been instinctually and organically ("always already") but also, at a reflective level, intentionally "polluted" and "braided" by the hybridities of my diasporic and postcolonial lifeworlds. As I argued in Part I, these existential actualities are not shunned in the methodological galaxies of postcolonialism and diaspora. Rather, postcolonial diasporic imaginary is a relatively homeless and multipolar mindscape, soulscape, and spiritscape which emerges and becomes aware of its own deepest predilections and homing desires precisely through a deliberate transposition of lived experience into a matrix of theoretical sensuality. And the lived experience in question is precisely this: hybrid, braided, polyphonous, multipolar, and contrapuntal, even though not necessarily harmonious like the Third Space of the hypostatic hybridity of peace—Christ. Small

7. On the difference between paradox and dialectic, see Žižek and Milbank, *The Monstrosity of Christ*, 160–216.

8. Spivak, *A Critique of Postcolonial Reason*, 7.

9. De Schrijver, "Postmodernity and the Withdrawal of the Divine," 62, 64.

wonder, then, that the methodological inclination is to poach boldly (Part I), like a theological magpie, from multiple streams of sacramental traditions and from intellectual disciplines as seemingly incompatible as possible, and to dive for the pearls of great value in multiple sources of wisdom wherever they might come from—and, ultimately, metabolize it all, through the "diminutive poles" and the "cardinal fragments" of one's own existential engagement with places, people, identities, pain, hope, desire, and all the irreconcilabilities of one's own inimitable history.

Theologizing through these diminutive poles of diasporic life is a stealthy and nimble undertaking. At times, it may look almost the same as the dominant narratives and imaginaries—but not quite. What distinguishes it from the dominant narratives is the diminutive yet cardinal shifts in scale, intensity, and repetition with a difference which is not mindless replication. The aspiration of diasporic theologizing in diminutive poles and through cardinal fragments is rather, to invoke Wilson Harris again, "to unravel a thread that may sustain us to cope with an abysmal otherness whom and which we dread but which may also bring resources to alter and change the fabric of the imagination in the direction of a therapeutic, ceaselessly unfinished genesis."[10]

In this study, I have migrated in and out, across and beyond multiple theological, liturgical, sacramental, and historical traditions. I am a sojourner in several of them while the desire for "a better homeland" (Heb 11:16, New Jerusalem Bible) runs even deeper than them all for "here we have no lasting city, but we are looking for the city that is to come" (Heb 13:14). "Western" and "Eastern," Protestant and Catholic, Eastern European and North American, postsoviet and postcolonial, metropolitan and "oriental," native and immigrant—all of these locations, influences, allegiances, and identities braid together and play off one another in the native borderlands of diasporic imaginary. Diasporic method emerges from a mindscape and bodyscape whose roots, to borrow Gloria Anzaldúa's image, are "portable and potable as the diasporic roots clinging to immigrants' feet and carried from one community, culture, or country to another."[11]

But how did that exactly play out in this study? When writing about the Eucharist, for instance, for me it is always and inescapably a hybrid Eucharist of the inherited historical palimpsest in an ongoing dialogue with new layers of migration, displacement, and emplacement. This Eucharist may not be sufficiently pure according to certain canons of confessional and liturgical authenticity, be they "Western" or "Eastern," Lutheran, Anglican

10. Harris, "The Fabric of Imagination," 182.

11. Anzaldúa, *Light in the Dark*, 67.

or Catholic, academic or devotional, mainstream or marginal. If this Eucharist—and all my theological musings so far—is in any sense properly localized and rooted, then its place is one of relentless polyphony within a creolized *ordo*. And it is a hyphenated and heterolocal *ordo*!

It seems rather unworkable for a diasporic theologian to chase after tight confessional univocity, or an exclusionary belonging, or an absolutized "authenticity" that some Christian liturgical and sacramental traditions deem desirable and even normative. As Anzaldúa notes, for those who live in the *nepantla*, the borderlands in between cultures and languages, "the process of making yourself whole requires all your parts—you can't define yourself by any single genetic or cultural slice"[12]—or, theologically speaking, by any single liturgical or confessional slice.

Ironically for a diasporic sensibility, there comes a point when it feels inauthentic to try to artificially force oneself, as if through self-effacing mimicry, into the dominant narratives of authenticity. Not only does it feel like being squeezed into an alien(ating) procrustean bed, but in the long run, it only results in promoting what Arjun Appadurai in another context described as the imagination and "language of incarceration."[13] Uncontaminated localities—including doctrinal and ritual localities—are hegemonic and often violent locations on this side of the beatific vision, even if such spaces and communities actually exist only as an imaginative outlet of anxious desire and for the convenience of institutional inertia.

Diasporic "authenticity" and its theological method resides precisely in the discerning embrace of, sometimes unwillingly and often by necessity more than by choice, the polyphonic hybridity of life as a *locus theologicus*. After all, as Chauvet reminds us, in the incarnational vision of Christianity, materiality and corporeality of "the anthropological is the place of every possible theological. And the sacramental—can it be anything else but the arch-symbolic space for this economy?"[14] The diasporic anthropological—and here I must insist on keeping Chauvet's anthropocentrism and hypertextuality in check by emphasizing that diasporic hybridity, in all its intricacy and idiosyncrasy, is embedded, embodied, and enabled by the planetary horizon of an unfinished cosmo-evolutionary genesis and not just language —is the theological precisely according to a sacramental vision of reality. The theological—the revelatory, the salvific, and the transformative—is mediated through and woven within the ever changing web of planetary materiality. It cannot be sacramentalized into our reality otherwise

12. Ibid., 89.

13. Appadurai, "Putting Hierarchy in Its Place," 37.

14. Chauvet, *Symbol and Sacrament*, 152.

than through the ambivalence, the materiality, and the opacity ("through a glass, darkly") of history and culture. And what is matter anyway in an incarnational imaginary if not "a mystery of ever-increasing connections?"[15] The sacramental pluriverse, apart from which anything theological is only a disembodied abstraction, is not a mere playground of rationality. It is, equally, a dense semiotic of flesh—a galaxy of materiality and sensuality through which grace is continually mediated.

For diasporic theology, its integrity is interstitial and its method is pollution, code-switching, and poaching—a hybridity indeed of cultural and experiential crescendos as well as the hardly categorizable, stealthy small voices whose imaginary homelands are signified and elicited by diminutive poles like wild carrots and cardinal fragments of blue cornflowers from the borderlands between the "East" and "West." Such diasporic hybridity does feel quite at home in the opaque sacramental planetarity of the Eucharist—the hybrid sign of the salvific Third Space of Christ, Word and Wisdom incarnate, crucified, and resurrected, and the instrument of the Spirit, ever moving, ever renewing, and ever unoverloardable like the wind.

Ultimately, diasporic method in sacramental theology becomes genuinely postcolonial when it abides in "these three: Word, Sacrament, and suffering human beings."[16] The ethical integrity of postcolonial theology abides in sounding these three theological constants always and everywhere *together*: simultaneously, contrapuntally, tenaciously, and vicariously with, among, and for the "wretched of the earth."

TOWARD A CHAMBER METAPHYSICS OF SACRAMENTALITY: A FINAL SUPPLICATION

The dominant inclination in postmodern Western sacramental theology has been to keep as great a distance as possible from anything smelling like ontology (i.e., "ontotheology" or foundationalism) and to focus instead on particular sacraments as rituals, texts, communicative spaces, and language events. Such an approach, innovative as it might have been, is a theologically shortsighted option. The intense focus on the particularity and communal performance of sacramental liturgies rode the wave of postmodern sensibilities cherishing unfettered semiotic diversity, the disruption of totalizing metanarratives and truth claims, a fascination with aesthetics and the ludic hermeneutics of liturgy as well as an almost messianic enchantment with the polar opposites of logocentrism and the "metaphysics of presence."

15. Chryssavgis, *Light Through Darkness*, 112.

16. Saliers, *Worship as Theology*, 230.

Consequently, the notions of absence, deferral of meaning and efficacy, emptiness, and even trauma took central stage in the most creative sacramental reflections.

Without doubt, these contributions offered valuable philosophical, ethnographic, and pastoral dimensions to liturgical and sacramental studies across the ecumenical arena and an inspiration for the renewal of worship in many local communities of faith, at least in the so-called liturgical traditions. Yet, the absolute majority of the most prominent Western postmodern re-envisagements of particular sacraments, precisely as rituals and dynamic relational/sign/language events, never really went beyond the confines of the respective confessional "numbers game" even though critical rumblings about the limitations of such restricted systems sometimes bubbled up alongside the realization that the disjunction between sacramental liturgies and the praxis of justice is a problem of profound and mounting proportions. At least in passing, lamentations do surface about how constricted, juridical, static, and culturally and philosophically dated certain institutionally operative definitions and practices of sacraments appear to be today. While the technicalities of institution, validity, duration, and other such intricacies continue to claim the attention of professional liturgists, widening disenchantment with and unease around the institutionalized forms of Occidental Christian sacramentality is becoming more pronounced outside the shrinking inner circles of piety.

Yet this, (peculiarly Occidental) crisis of reified sacramental traditions does not necessarily spell unmitigated disaster. Rather, it presents an opportunity for Christians to self-critically reassess and reimagine not just the ritual, cultural, and linguistic expressions of sacramental rites, but to take a more thorough look at what is in need of renewal and constructive retrieval at a new, considerably more complex, inclusive, and indeed planetary level of sacramentality.

What is in such a need of existentially momentous renewal is a whole new theological *compositio loci*—the sacramental imaginary as a whole, as a methodological comportment and as a worldview that Christians, particularly those in the Occidental theological orbit, could develop to engage with other religious and cultural traditions of wisdom in the context of ecological degradation. To propose such a methodological shift is not to take the typical—and far from the trendiest—path in contemporary Western sacramental theology. It is also to challenge the reigning primacy of rituality, (hyper) textuality, and the valorization of fragmentation in Occidental sacramental discourses. And yes, it gets even more quirky: it is to propose bringing ontological reflection back to the forefront of sacramental theories and practices.

It is not feasible to present here a full-blown argument as to why sacramentality ought to be considered as the preferential methodological option for Christian theologies committed to the incarnational vision of God and world. What is, I believe, sufficiently persuasive to consider here at face value is a possibility of a chamber metaphysics (in Mikhail Epstein's sense, as presented in the Introduction) of sacramentality as a contender for the role of a shared and planetary imaginative grammar of interrelatedness, interdependence, and wholesome transformation. It is the ethical exigency of environmental degradation and its nascent entanglement with the already preexisting global octopus of injustice, violence, inequality, and systemic disempowerment which calls for a robustly theo-ethical response. Intentional and vigilant re-envisioning of the sacramental imaginary is, I submit, the most promising and potentially most fruitful response that Christian theology can offer today.

In that sense, I wholeheartedly lift up David Brown's ostensibly eccentric plea for a more rigorous return to the sacramental understanding of reality that was characteristic of the first Christian millennium. Critiques notwithstanding, this is what has actually started to happen, albeit obliquely, when some twentieth century theologians ventured forth with ideas like Christ being the *Ursakrament* or primordial sacrament and the Church as the *Grundsakrament* or basic, foundational, sacrament. Brown argues that rather than the "sacramental being seen as essentially ecclesiastical or narrowly Christian, it should instead be viewed as a major, and perhaps even the primary, way of exploring God's relationship to our world."[17] My study is a postcolonial and diasporic attempt to make a case for the sacramental signature of all things as an incarnationally consistent and ethically consequential methodological comportment for Christian theology in this time of planetary crisis.

The crux of the matter is this: sacramental imaginary matters. It matters precisely because it is a worldview, a consciousness, and a chamber metaphysics which articulates a wholistic yet non-totalitarian vision of the dynamic and open-ended interrelatedness and inter-accountability of all planetary lifeforms in relation to God and among themselves. From the Eastern Orthodox perspective, John Chryssavgis has aptly pointed out that the sacramental principle—a more conventional (inconspicuous?) way of expressing what I have termed the chamber metaphysics of sacramentality—in connection with the idea of the world as sacrament can engender a worldview that resonates very strongly with postcolonial planetarity. Chryssavgis argues that "indeed, if there exists today a vision able to transcend

17. Brown, *God and Enchantment of Place*, 6.

and transform all national and denominational tensions, it may well be that of *our world understood as sacrament.*"[18] Somewhat uncannily resembling Gayatri Spivak's approach, Chryssavgis calls attention to the perhaps startling truth that, instead of sacramental discourse being the most churchy or inward-looking slice of traditional(ist) Christianity, the world should be seen as a sacrament of planetary solidarity. The world as sacrament is "the common ground that we all tread as the source of our solidarity and as the ultimate sign of communion that we share."[19]

What is at stake in choosing to reclaim and retrieve sacramentality as the primary way of exploring the ultimate meaning of creation and its relation to the Uncreated Wellspring of its very existence is the possibility of a radically consequential affirmation of life, liberation, and wholeness by Christians for the life of the whole creation. It is all unfolding precisely when our human community is becoming agonizingly aware of our planetary fragility and the possibility of wholesale self-destruction through nuclear annihilation or environmental degradation.

In this context and with appreciation, I lift up the undeservedly overlooked call by Kevin Irwin to restore—but I am more inclined to say, inaugurate and consistently prioritize—"sacramentality as the basic principle" and as the "foundational and reflective" new paradigm in theology.[20] Irwin has argued for the restoration of "the overarching notion of the sacramental economy."[21] Such a sacramental economy—yet another postmodernly understated metaphysical vision—"would make creation the ground of theology, both natural and revealed, and would order a study of sacraments as based on how the God of creation and redemption is incarnated in the world and therefore discovered in the world and in all of human life."[22] Although Irwin's proposal is more narrowly focused on Roman Catholic sacramental theology, the scope of his plea goes well beyond Western Catholicism and the subdiscipline of sacramental-liturgical theology. For, what is at stake here is precisely the retrieval of "the credibility of our sacramental structure so that what is celebrated in liturgy is based on how we always experience God—in nature, creation and human life and love."[23]

18. Chryssavgis, "The World as Sacrament," 1. Italics in original.

19. Ibid., 2.

20. Irvin, "Sacramentality and the Theology of Creation," 164–65. See also his "Liturgical Actio: Sacramentality, Eschatology and Ecology," 114–17.

21. Ibid., 169.

22. Ibid., 173.

23. Ibid.

Sacramentality is most emphatically not about churchiness or nostalgic piety. Sacramentality today is about the audacity to seek, sense, taste, and find the Holy Mystery that underlies all that exists in all that exists, from intergalactic vastness to the least of *les damnés de la terre*. But until and unless there occurs a "signature" methodological shift in theological inquiry and, indeed even more vitally, in a groundswell of lived spirituality to foreground the sacramental principle (i.e., the ontological and epistemological priority of sacramentality which precedes, grounds, and exceeds any socio-culturally or religiously articulated sacramental rites), mere adjustments of ritual and religious language alone will not effectively address the planetary crisis of ecology and justice. Nor will it reorient the growing disenchantment with conventional sacramental expressions in Western Christian communities which, like it or lump it, will play a significant even if no longer presumptuously unipolar and self-aggrandizing, role in the very viability and sustainability of life for the whole planetary community.

When all is said and done, what is worth seeking is an integral vision of God and all things—native, diasporic, hybrid, metropolitan, exilic, subaltern, thriving or wretched—in relation to God and in God, that ultimate triune and perichoretic hybridity of which the Word and Wisdom incarnate is the sacramental and contrapuntal crescendo, and the eschatological Third Space of *shalom* who dwelled among us so that we all "may have life and have it abundantly" (John 10:10).

Bibliography

Abraham, Susan. "The Pterodactyl in the Margins: Detranscendentalizing Postcolonial Theology." In *Planetary Loves: Spivak, Postcoloniality, and Theology*, edited by Stephen D. Moore and Mayra Rivera, 79–101. New York: Fordham University Press, 2011.

———. "Queering the Pitch: Sacramental Challenges to Catholic Feminist Theology." *CTSA Proceedings* 67 (2012) 42–45.

Acheraiou, Amar. *Questioning Hybridity, Postcolonialism and Globalization*. New York: Palgrave, 2011.

Ackerman, Denise M. *After the Locusts: Letters from a Landscape of Faith*. Grand Rapids, MI: Eerdmans, 2003.

Agamben, Giorgio. *The Signature of All Things: On Method*. New York: Zone, 2009.

Allmen, Jean-Jacques, von. *Prophétisme sacramentel*. Neuchatel: Delachaux et Niestle, 1964.

Ang, Ien. "Can One Say No to Chineseness? Pushing the Limits of the Diasporic Paradigm." *Boundary 2* 25:3 (1998) 223–42.

———. "Together-In-Difference: Beyond Diaspora, Into Hybridity." *Asian Studies Review* 27:2 (2003) 141–54.

Ansell-Pearson, Keith, et al. "Introduction." In *Cultural Readings of Imperialism: Edward Said and the Gravity of History*, edited by Keith Ansell-Pearson et al., 8–27. New York: St. Martin's Press/Lawrence and Wishart, 1997.

Anzaldúa, Gloria E. *Light in the Dark/Luz En Lo Oscuro: Rewriting Identity, Spirituality, Reality*. Edited by Analouise Keating. Durham and London: Duke University Press, 2015.

Appadurai, Arjun. "Putting Hierarchy in Its Place." *Cultural Anthropology*, 3:1 (1988) 36–49.

Appiah, Anthony Kwame. "Is the Post- in Postmodernism the Post- in Postcolonial?" *Critical Inquiry* 17: 2 (1991) 336–57.

Arac, Jonathan. "Criticism between Opposition and Counterpoint." *Boundary 2*. Special Issue on Edward W. Said. 25:2 (1998) 55–69.

Ashcroft, Bill. "Introduction: Spaces of Utopia." *Spaces of Utopia: An Electronic Journal* 2:1 (2012) 1–17.

———. "Threshold Theology." In *Colonial Contexts and Postcolonial Theologies: Storyweaving in the Asia-Pacific*, edited by Mark G. Brett and Jione Havea, 1–20. New York: Palgrave Macmillan, 2014.

Bahri, Deepika. "Raising the Profile of Southeastern Studies." *Khabar* (July 2008) 14–20.

Бахтин М. М. Вопросы литературы и эстетики. Москва: Худож. лит.,1975.

Bakhtin, Mikhail. *The Dialogic Imagination: Four* Essays. Edited and translated by Michael Holquist and Caryl Emerson. Austin: University of Texas Press, 1981.

Bal, Mieke. *The Practice of Cultural Analysis: Exposing Interdisciplinary Interpretation.* Stanford: Stanford University Press, 1999.

Balasuriya, Tissa, O.M.I., *The Eucharist and Human Liberation.* Maryknoll, NY: Orbis, 1979.

Banerjee, Mita. "Postethnicity and Postcommunism in Hanif Kureishi's *Gabriel's Gift* and Salman Rushdie's *Fury*." In *Reconstructing Hybridity: Post-Colonial Studies in Transition*, edited by Joel Juortti and Jopi Nyman, 307–24. Amsterdam and New York: Rodopi, 2007.

Barenboim, Daniel. "Foreword." In Edward W. Said, *Music at the Limits*, vii–x. New York: Columbia University Press, 2007.

Bauman, Whitney, A. "Opening the Language of Religion and Ecology: Viable Spaces for Transformative Politics." In *Inherited Land: The Changing Grounds of Religion and Ecology*, edited by Whitney A. Bauman, et al., 80–101. Eugene, OR: Wipf and Stock, 2011.

Bauman, Zygmunt. *44 Letters from the Liquid Modern World.* London: Polity, 2010.

Beattie, Tina. *New Catholic Feminism: Theology and Theory.* New York: Routledge, 2006.

Benavides, Gustavo. "Modernity." In *Critical Terms for Religious Studies*, edited by Mark C. Taylor, 186–204. Chicago and London: The University of Chicago Press, 1998.

Benjamin, Walter. "Theses on the Philosophy of History." In *Illuminations: Essays and Reflections.* Edited by Hannah Arendt, 253–264. New York: Schocken Books, 1985.

Berger, Teresa. "Spying in the Promised Land: Sacramental Signs Through Women's Eyes." *CTSA Proceedings* 67 (2012) 28–41.

Bernasconi, Robert. "African philosophy's Challenge to Continental Philosophy." In *Postcolonial African Philosophy: A Critical Reader*, edited by Emmanuel Chukwudi Eze, 183–96. Oxford: Wiley-Blackwell, 1997.

Bhabha, Homi K. *The Location of Culture.* Reprint edition. London and New York: Routledge, 2006.

———. "Preface: In the Cave of Making: Thoughts on Third Space." In *Communicating in the Third Space*, edited by Karin Ikas and Gerhard Wagner, ix-xiv. New York and London: Routledge, 2008.

———. "The Third Space. Interview with Homi Bhabha." In *Identity: Community, Culture, Difference*, edited by Jonathan Rutherford, 207–21. London: Lawrence and Wishart, 1990.

Bisong, Kekong. "A Postmodern Response to Sacramental Presence." In *Celebrating the Sacramental World: Essays in Honour of Emeritus Professor Lambert J. Leijssen*, edited by Kekong Bisong and Mathai Kadavil, 40–64. Leuven: Peeters: 2010.

———, and Mathai Kadavil, "Introduction." In *Celebrating the Sacramental World: Essays in Honour of Emeritus Professor Lambert J. Leijssen*, edited by Kekong Bisong and Mathai Kadavil, 7–10. Leuven: Peeters: 2010.

Blomkvist, Nils. *The Discovery of the Baltic: The Reception of a Catholic World-System in the European North (AD 1075–1225).* Leiden and Boston: Brill, 2005.

Boersma, Hans. *Heavenly Participation: The Weaving of a Sacramental Tapestry.* Grand Rapids: Eerdmans, 2011.

———. *Nouvelle Théologie and Sacramental Ontology: A Return to Mystery.* Oxford: Oxford University Press, 2009.

Boff, Leonardo. *Christianity in a Nutshell*. Translated by Phillip Berryman. Maryknoll, NY: Orbis, 2013.

———. *Cry of the Earth, Cry of the Poor*. Translated by Phillip Berryman. Maryknoll, NY: Orbis, 1997.

———. *Die Kirche als Sakrament im Horizont der Welterfahrung*. Paderborn: Bonifacius Verlag, 1972.

———. *Sacraments of Life, Life of the Sacraments*. Translated by John Drury. Beltsville, MD: Pastoral, 1987.

Bong, Sharon A. "Theologies of, for, and by Asians: Reformulating Dialogue." In *Decolonizing the Body of Christ: Theology and Theory After Empire*, edited by David Joy and Joseph F. Duggan, 79–106. New York: Palgrave Macmillan, 2012.

Bonhoeffer, Dietrich. *Ethics*. Dietrich Bonhoeffer Works, Vol. 6. Edited by Wayne Whitson Floyd, et al. Minneapolis: Fortress, 2005.

Brah, Avtar. *Cartographies of Diaspora: Contesting Identities*. London and New York: Routledge, 1996.

Brah, Avtar, and Annie E. Coombes, editors. *Hybridity and Its Discontents: Politics, Science,* Culture. London and New York: Routledge, 2000.

Brilioth, Yngve. *Eucharistic Faith and Practice: Evangelical and Catholic*. Translated by A.G. Herbert. London: SPCK, 1965.

Brock, Rita Nakashima. "Cooking Without Recipes: Interstitial Integrity." In *Off the Menu: Asian and Asian North American Women's Religion and Theology*, edited by Rita Nakashima Brock et al., 125–43. Louisville and London: Westminster John Knox, 2007.

———. "Interstitial Integrity: Reflections Toward an Asian American Woman's Theology." In *Introduction to Christian Theology: Contemporary North American Perspectives*, edited by Roger A. Bradham, 183–96. Louisville: Westminster John Knox, 1997.

Broeck, Sabine. "White Fatigue, or, Supplementary Notes on Hybridity." In *Reconstructing Hybridity: Post-Colonial Studies in Transition*, edited by Joel Kuortti and Jopi Nyman, 43–57. Amsterdam and New York: Rodopi, 2007.

Brown, David. *God and Enchantment of Place: Reclaiming Human* Experience. Oxford: Oxford University Press, 2004.

Bulgakov, Sergei. *The Holy Grail and Eucharist*. Translated by Boris Jakim. Hudson, NY: Lindisfarne, 1997.

Burghardt, Walter J., S.J. *Justice: A Global Adventure*. Maryknoll, NY: Orbis, 2004.

Burns, Stephen, and Clive Pearson, eds. *Home and Away: Contextual Theology and Local Practice*. Eugene, OR: Pickwick, 2013.

Butulis, Ilgvars, and Antonijs Zunda. *Latvijas Vēsture*. Rīga: Jumava, 2010.

Cattoi, Thomas. "What Has Chalcedon to Do with Lhasa?" *Buddhist-Christian Studies* 28 (2008) 13–25.

Cavanaugh, William T. *Migrations of the Holy: God, State, and the Political Meaning of the Church*. Grand Rapids, MI: Eerdmans, 2011.

Certeau, Michel, de. *Practice of Everyday Life*. Berkeley: University of California Press: 1984.

Chauvet, Louis-Marie. *The Sacraments: The Word of God at the Mercy of the Body*. Translated by Madeleine Beaumont. Collegeville, MN: Liturgical, 2001.

———. *Symbol and Sacrament: A Sacramental Interpretation of Christian Existence.* Translated by Patrick Madigan and Madeleine Beaumont. Collegeville, MN: Liturgical, 1995.

Cho, Lily. "The Turn to Diaspora." *Topia* 17 (2007) 11–30.

Chow, Rey. *Ethics After Idealism: Theory-Culture-Ethnicity-Reading.* Bloomington and Indianapolis: Indiana University Press, 1998.

Christiansen, Eric. *The Northern Crusades.* New Edition. New York: Penguin, 1997.

Chryssavgis, John. *Light Through Darkness: The Orthodox* Tradition. Maryknoll, NY: Orbis, 2004.

———. "A New Heaven and a New Earth: Orthodox Christian Insights from Theology, Spirituality, and the Sacraments." In *Toward and Ecology of Transfiguration: Orthodox Christian Perspectives on Environment, Nature, and Creation*, edited by John Chryssavgis and Bruce V. Foltz, 152–62. New York: Fordham University Press, 2013.

———. "The World as Sacrament." *Pacifica* 10:2 (1997) 1–24.

Clifford, James. "Diasporas." In *The Postcolonial Studies Reader*, edited by Bill Aschcroft et al., 451–54. Second edition. New York: Routledge, 2006.

Coakley, Sarah. "What Does Chalcedon Solve and What Does it Not? Some Reflections on the Status and Meaning of the Chalcedonian 'Definition.'" In *The Incarnation: An Interdisciplinary Symposium on the Incarnation of the Son of God*, edited by Stephen T. Davis, et al., 143–63. Oxford: Oxford University Press, 2002.

Condee, Nancy. "The Anti-imperialist Empire and After: In Dialogue with Gayatri Spivak's 'Are You Postcolonial?'" *PMLA*, 121:3 (2006) 829–31.

Congar, Yves. *The Mystery of the Temple, or, The Manner of God's Presence to His Creation from Genesis to the Apocalypse.* Translated by Reginald F. Trevett. London: Burns & Oates, 1962.

Cooper-White, Pamela. *Braided Selves: Collected Essays on Multiplicity, God, and Persons.* Eugene, OR: Cascade, 2011.

Daly, Robert J., S.J. "The Council of Trent." In *A Companion to the Eucharist in the Reformation*, edited by Lee Palmer Wandel, 159–82. Leiden and Boston: Brill, 2014.

Danneels, Godfried Cardinal. "Liturgy 40 Years After the Council." *America* (August 27-September 3, 2007) 11–14.

———. "Liturgy Forty Years After the Second Vatican Council: High Point of Recession?" In *Liturgy in a Postmodern World*, edited by Keith F. Pecklers, S.J., 7–26. London and New York: Continuum, 2003.

Davies, Oliver, et al. *Transformation Theology: Church in the* World. Bloomsbury T&T Clark: 2008.

Deleuze, Gilles, and Félix Guattari. "What is a Minor Literature?" *Mississippi Review* 11:3 (1983) 13–33.

DeLisio, Therese B. "Considering the Cosmos as Primary Sacrament: A Viable Basis for an Ecological Sacramental Theology, Liturgy, and Ethics?" *NAAL Proceedings* (2006) 160–84.

DeLoughrey, Elizabeth, et al. "Introduction." In *Global Ecologies and the Environmental Humanities: Postcolonial Approaches*, edited by Elizabeth DeLoughrey, et al., 1–32. New York: Routledge, 2015.

Dirlik, Arif. "Bringing History Back In: Of Diasporas, Hybridities, Places, and Histories." *The Review of Education, Pedagogy, Cultural Studies* 21:2 (1999) 95–131.

D'Sa, Francis X., S.J., "Sacramentum Mundi: Preface to a Cross-Cultural Re-Vision of Sacraments." In *The World as Sacrament: Interdisciplinary Bridge-Building of the Sacred and the Secular. Essays in Honour of Joself Neuner on the Occasion of his 90th Birthday,* edited by Francis X. D'Sa, SJ, et al., 239–93. Pune: Jnana-Deepa Vidyapeeth Theology Series, 1998.

———. "The World as Sacrament." In *Celebrating the Sacramental World: Essays in Honour of Emeritus Professor Lambert J. Leijssen,* edited by Kekong Bisong and Mathai Kadavil, 24–39. Leuven: Peeters, 2010.

Dube, Musa W. "Postcolonial Feminist Perspectives on African Religions." In *The Blackwell Companion to African Religions,* edited by Elias Kifon Bongmba, 127–39. Oxford: Wiley-Blackwell, 2012.

Dziesmusvētki. "Dziesmusvētki." http://www.dziesmusvetki.tv/lv/par/vesture/.

Eggemeier, Matthew T. *A Sacramental-Prophetic Vision: Christian Spirituality in a Suffering World.* Collegeville, MN: Liturgical, 2014.

Eihmane, Eva. "The Baltic Crusades: A Clash of Two Identities." In *The Clash of Cultures on the Medieval Baltic Frontier,* edited by Alan V. Murray, 37–51. Farnham and Burlington: Ashgate, 2009.

———. "Christianisation of the Local Peoples of Livonia: Cultivation of God's Vineyard or Brutal Subjugation under the Cover of Religion?" *Latvijas Universitātes Raksti.* 725 (2009) 9–28.

El-Tayeb, Fatima. "The Forces of Creolization: Colorblindness and Visible Minorities in the New Europe." In *The Creolization of Theory,* edited by Françoise Lionnet and Shu-mei Shih, 226–253. Durham and London: Duke University Press, 2011.

Epstein, Mikhail. Философия возможного. Санкт-Петербург: Алетейя, 2001.

———. "Minimal Religion." http://www.emory.edu/INTELNET/e.pm.minim.religion.html.

———, et al. *Russian Postmodernism: New Perspectives on Post-Soviet Culture.* Translated and edited by Slobodanka Vladiv-Glover. New York and Oxford: Berghahn Books, 1999.

Etherington, Ben. "Said, Grainger and the ethics of polyphony." In *Edward Said: The Legacy of a Public Intellectual,* edited by Ned Curthoys and Debjani Ganguly, 221–38. Carlton: Melbourne University Press, 2007.

Ezigbo, Victor Ifeanyi, and Reggie L. Williams. "Converting a Colonialist Christ: Toward an African Postcolonial Christology." In *Evangelical Postcolonial Conversations: Global Awakenings in Theology and Praxis,* edited by Kay Higuera Smith, et al., 88–101. Downers Grove, IL: IVP Academic, 2014.

Fanon, Frantz. *The Wretched of the Earth.* Translated by Richard Philcox. New York: Grove, 2004.

Farley, Wendy. *Gathering Those Driven Away: A Theology of Incarnation.* Louisville: John Knox, 2011.

Feldmanis, Roberts. *Latvijas baznīcas vēsture.* Rīga: Luterisma Mantojuma Fonds, 2011.

Felski, Rita. "The Doxa of Difference." *Signs* 23:1 (1997) 1–21.

Fonnesberg-Schmidt, Iben. *The Popes and the Baltic Crusades 1147–1254.* Leiden and Boston: Brill, 2007.

Forsdick, Charles. "Edward Said After Theory: The Limits of Counterpoint." In *Post-Theory: New Directions in Criticism,* edited by Martin McQuillan, et al., 188–99. Edinburgh: Edinburgh University Press, 1999.

Gandhi, Leela. *Postcolonial Theory: A Critical Introduction*. New York: Columbia University Press, 1998.

Garrigan, Siobhán. *Beyond Ritual: Sacramental Theology After Habermas*. New York and London: Routledge, 2004.

Gilroy, Paul. *Against Race: Imagining Political Culture Beyond the Color Line*. Cambridge, MA: Bellknap, 2002.

———. *The Black Atlantic: Modernity and Double Consciousness*. Cambridge: Harvard University Press, 1993.

———. *Postcolonial Melancholia*. New York: Columbia University Press, 2006.

Glissant, Édouard. *Caribbean Discourse: Selected* Essays. Translated and edited by J. Michael Dash. Charlottesville, VA: University Press of Virginia, 1999.

———. *Le Discours antillais*. Paris: Gallimard, 1997.

———. *Poetics of Relation*. Translated by Betsy Wing. Ann Arbor: University of Michigan Press, 1997.

———. *Tout-monde*. Paris: Gallimard, 1993.

Godzieba, Anthony J., et al. "Resurrection-Interruption-Transformation: Incarnation as Hermeneutical Strategy. A Symposium." *Theological Studies* 67:4 (2006) 777–815.

———. "'Stay with us. . .' (Lk 24:29)—'Come, Lord Jesus' (Rev 22:20): Incarnation, Eschatology, and Theology's Sweet Predicament." *Theological Studies* 67:4 (2006) 783–95.

Goldberg, David Theo, and Ato Quayson. "Introduction: Scale and Sensibility." In *Relocating Postcolonialism*, edited by David Theo Goldberg and Ato Quayson, xi-xxii. Oxford: Wiley-Blackwell, 2002.

Gregersen, Niels Henrik. "Deep Incarnation and *Kenosis*: In, With, Under, and As: A Response to Ted Peters." *Dialogue: A Journal of Theology* 52:3 (2013) 251–62.

———. "Deep Incarnation: Why Evolutionary Continuity Matters in Christology." *Toronto Journal of Theology* 26:2 (2010) 173–87.

———. "The Extended Body of Christ: Three Dimensions of Deep Incarnation." In *Incarnation: On the Scope and Depth of Christology*, edited by Niels Henrik Gregersen, 225–51. Minneapolis: Fortress Press, 2015.

Grīnfelde, Māra. "Definitions of Religion: Annotation." In *Reliģiski filozofiskas idejas Latvijā 20.gs., 1. Puse. Pirmā grāmata. Reliģijas skaidrojumi*, edited by Māra Grīnfelde, 180–87. Rīga: Latvijas Universitātes Filozofijas un socioloģijas institūts, 2013.

———. "Ievads. Reliģijas skaidrojumi." In *Reliģiski filozofiskas idejas Latvijā 20.gs., 1. Puse. Pirmā grāmata. Reliģijas skaidrojumi*, edited by Māra Grīnfelde, 18–46. Rīga: Latvijas Universitātes Filozofijas un socioloģijas institūts, 2013.

Groot, Rokus, de. "Edward Said and Polyphony." In *Edward Said: A Legacy of Emancipation and Representation*, edited by Adel Iskandar and Hakem Rustom, 204–26. Berkeley, Los Angeles, London: University of California Press, 2010.

Guha, Ranajit. "The Small Voice of History." In *Subaltern Studies IX: Writings on South Asian History and Society*, edited by Shahid Amin and Dipesh Chakrabarty, 1–12. Delhi: Oxford University Press, 1996.

Gustafson, Hans. *Finding All Things in God: Pansacramentalism and Doing Theology Interreligiously*. Eugene, OR: Pickwick, 2016.

Hall, Stuart. "Minimal Selves." In *Identity: The Real Me: Postmodernism and the Question of Identity,* edited by L. Appignanesi, 44–46. London: Institute of Contemporary Arts Documents 6, 1987.

———. "When Was 'The Post-Colonial'? Thinking at the Limit." In *The Post-Colonial Question: Common Skies, Divided Horizons,* edited by Iain Chambers and Lidia Curti, 242–60. London and New York: Routledge, 1996.

Hancock, Brannon. *The Scandal of Sacramentality: The Eucharist in Literary and Theological Perspectives.* Eugene, OR: Pickwick, 2014.

Handley, George B. *Postcolonial Ecologies: Literatures of the Environment.* Edited by Elizabeth de Loughrey and George B. Handley. New York: Oxford University Press, 2011.

Harris, Wilson. "The Fabric of the Imagination." *Third World Quarterly* 12:1 (1990) 69–79.

———. *The Radical Imagination: Lectures and Talks by Wilson* Harris. Edited by Alan Riach and Mark Williams. Liege: L3—Liege Language and Literature: 1992.

Hart, David Bentley. "The Gnostic Turn." *First Things.* July 27, 2009. http://www.firstthings.com/web-exclusives/2009/07/the-gnostic-turn.

Hart, John. *Sacramental Commons: Christian Ecological Ethics.* Lanham: Rowman and Littlefield, 2006.

Haught, John F. *The Promise of Nature: Ecology and Cosmic Purpose.* New York and Mahwah, NJ: Paulist, 1993.

Heschel, Abraham. *God in Search of Man: A Philosophy of Judaism.* New York: Doubleday, 2007.

Higgins, Kathleen Marie. *The Music of Our Lives.* Philadelphia: Temple University Press, 1991.

Higton, M. A. "'A Carefully Circumscribed Progressive Politics': Hans Frei's Political Theology." *Modern Theology* 15:1 (1999) 55–83.

Himes, Michael. "'Finding God in All Things': A Sacramental Worldview and its Effects." In *As Leaven in the World: Catholic Perspectives on Faith, Vocation, and the Intellectual Life,* edited by Thomas Landy, 91–104. Franklin, WI: Sheed and Ward, 2001.

Honold, Alexander. "The Art of Counterpoint." In *Edward Said's Translocations: Essays in Secular Criticism,* edited by Tobias Doering and Mark Stein, 187–204. New York: Routledge, 2012.

Huggan, Graham, and Helen Tiffin. *Postcolonial Ecocriticism: Literature, Animals, Environment.* New York: Routledge, 2015.

Hunsinger, George. *The Eucharist and Ecumenism: Let Us Keep the Feast.* Cambridge: Cambridge University Press, 2008.

Ignatius of Loyola. *Spiritual Exercises and Selected Works.* The Classics of Western Spirituality. Edited by George E. Ganss. New York, Mahwah, NJ: Paulist, 1991.

Irenaeus of Lyons. *Against Heresies.* Book IV, 18:5. http://www.newadvent.org/fathers/0103418.htm.

Irving, D. R. M. *Colonial Counterpoint: Music in Early Modern Manila.* Oxford: Oxford University Press, 2010.

Irwin, Kevin W. "Liturgical Actio: Sacramentality, Eschatology and Ecology." In *Contemporary Sacramental Contours of a God Incarnated,* edited by Lieven Boeve and Lambert Leijssen, 111–23, Leuven: Peeters, 2001.

———. "A Sacramental World: Sacramentality as the Primary Language for Sacraments." *Worship* 76:3 (202) 197–211.

———. "Sacramentality and the Theology of Creation: A Recovered Paradigm for Sacramental Theology." *Louvain Studies* 23 (1998) 159–179.

———. *The Sacraments: Historical Foundations and Liturgical Theology*. New York, Mahwah, NJ: Paulist Press, 2016.

Jacoby, Russell. *Picture Imperfect: Utopian Thought for an Anti-Utopian Age*. New York: Columbia University Press, 2005.

Jagessar, Michael N. and Stephen Burns. *Christian Worship: Postcolonial Perspectives*. Sheffield and Oakville: Equinox, 2011.

Jankélévitch, Vladimir. *Music and the Ineffable*. Translated by Carolyn Abbate. Princeton and Oxford: Princeton University Press, 2003.

Jenson, Robert, W. *Systematic Theology. Vol. 1 The Triune God*. New York and Oxford: Oxford University Press, 1997.

Joh, Wonhee A. *Heart of the Cross: A Postcolonial Christology*. Louisville and London: Westminster John Knox, 2006.

———. "Violence and Asian American Experience: From Abjection to *Jeong*." In *Off the Menu: Asian and Asian North American Women's Religion and Theology*, edited by Rita Nakashima Brock et al., 145–162. Louisville and London: Westminster John Knox Press, 2007.

Johnson, Elizabeth A. *Abounding in Kindness: Writings for the People of God*. Maryknoll, NY: Orbis, 2015.

———. "Community on Earth as in Heaven: A Holy People and a Sacred Earth Together." *Santa Clara Lectures* 5:1, 1–15. Santa Clara, CA: Santa Clara University, 1998.

———. *Friends of God and Prophets*. New York: Continuum, 1998.

———. "Presidential Address: Turn to the Heavens and the Earth: Retrieval of the Cosmos Theology." *Catholic Theological Society of America Proceedings 1996 Vision and Values: Ethical Viewpoints in the Catholic Tradition*. Edited by Judith A. Dwyer, 53–69. Washington DC: Georgetown University Press, 1999.

———. *She Who Is: The Mystery of God in Feminist Theological Discourse*. New York: Crossroad Herder, 2000.

———. *Women, Earth, and Creator Spirit*. New York: Paulist Press, 1993.

Jong-Kumru, Wietske, de. *Postcolonial Feminist Theology: Enacting Cultural, Religious, Gender and Sexual Differences in Theological Reflection*. LIT Verlag, 2013.

Julian of Norwich. *Showing of Love*. Translated by Julia Bolton Holloway. Collegeville, MN: Liturgical Press, 2003.

Kadavil, Mathai. *The World as Sacrament: Sacramentality of Creation from the Perspective of Leonardo Boff, Alexander Schmemann and Saint Ephrem*. Leuven: Peeters, 2005.

Kala, Tiina. "Rural Society and Religious Innovation: Acceptance and Rejection of Catholicism among the Native Inhabitants of Medieval Livonia." In *The Clash of Cultures on the Medieval Baltic Frontier*, edited by Alan V. Murray, 169–190. Farnham and Burlington: Ashgate, 2009.

Kalme, Guntis. "Izdziedāt, svinēt un apliecināt." *Delfi.lv*. July 6, 2013. No pages. Online: http://www.delfi.lv/news/comment/comment/guntis-kalme-izdziedat-svinet-un-apliecinat.d?id=43461693

Kalniņš, Jānis. *Latvju Krusta Ceļš*. Rīga: San Estera, 2012.

Kalra, Virinder S. et al. *Diaspora and Hybridity.* London, Thousand Oaks, New Delhi: Sage, 2005.

Kang, Namsoon. *Diasporic Feminist Theology: Asia and Theopolitical Imagination.* Minneapolis: Fortress Press, 2014.

Karavanta, Mina, and Nina Morgan, editors. *Edward Said and Jacques Derrida: Reconstellating Humanism and the Global Hybrid.* Cambridge: Cambridge Scholars Publishing, 2008.

Kavanagh, O.S.B., Aidan. *On Liturgical Theology.* New York: Pueblo, 1984.

Keller, Catherine. *Face of the Deep: A Theology of Becoming.* London and New York: Routledge, 2003.

———. *God and Power: Counter-Apocalyptic Journeys.* Minneapolis: Fortress Press, 2005.

———. *On the Mystery.* Minneapolis: Fortress Press, 2008.

———, and Laurel C. Schneider, editors. *Polydoxy: Theology of Multiplicity and* Relation. London and New York: Routledge, 2011.

Keller, Catherine, et al, editors. *Postcolonial Theologies: Divinity and Empire.* Saint Louis: Chalice Press, 2004.

Kelertas, Violeta, editor. *Baltic Postcolonialism.* Amsterdam and New York: Rodopi, 2006.

Kennedy, Valerie. *Edward Said: A Critical Introduction.* Malden, MA: Blackwell, 2000.

Kilmartin, Edward, S.J. *The Eucharist in the West: History and Theology.* Collegeville, MN: Liturgical Press, 1998.

Kolb, Robert and Timothy J. Wengert, editors. *The Book of Concord: The Confessions of the Evangelical Lutheran Church.* Minneapolis: Fortress Press, 2000.

Kraidy, Marwan. M. *Hybridity, or the Cultural Logic of Globalization.* Philadelphia: Temple University Press, 2005.

Krishna, Sankaran. *Globalization and Postcolonialism: Hegemony and Resistance in the Twenty-first Century.* Lanham: Rowman and Littlefield, 2009.

Krūmiņa-Koņkova, Solveiga. "Priekšvārds /Foreword." In *Reliģiski filozofiskas idejas Latvijā 20.gs. 1. Puse. Pirmā grāmata. Reliģijas skaidrojumi,* edited by Māra Grīnfelde, 5–17. Rīga: Latvijas Universitātes Filozofijas un socioloģijas institūts, 2013.

Kuortti, Joel, and Jopi Nyman. "Introduction: Hybridity Today." In *Reconstructing Hybridity: Post-Colonial Studies in Transition,* edited by Joel Kuortti and Jopi Nyman, 1–18. Amsterdam and New York: Rodopi, 2007.

Kwok, Pui-lan. "Ecology and Christology." *Feminist Theology* 15 (1997) 113–25.

———. *Introducing Asian Feminist Theology.* Sheffield: Sheffield Academic Press, 2000.

———. *Postcolonial Imagination and Feminist* Theology. Louisville, KY: Westminster John Knox, 2005.

———. "A Theology of Border Passage." In *Border Crossings: Cross-Cultural Hermeneutics,* edited by D.N. Premnath, 103–117. Maryknoll, NY: Orbis, 2007.

Lachman, Kathryn. "The Allure of Counterpoint: History and Reconciliation in the Writing of Edward Said and Assia Djebar." *Research in African Literatures* 41:4 (2010)162–186.

Lai, Pan-chiu. "A Mahāyāna Reading of Chalcedon Christology: A Chinese Response to John Keenan." *Buddhist-Christian Studies* 24 (2004) 209–228.

Lartey, Emmanuel Y. *Postcolonizing God.* London: SCM, 2013.

Lathrop, Gordon W. *Holy People: A Liturgical Ecclesiology.* Minneapolis: Fortress, 1999.

Leo the Great. Sermon 74:2 "On the Lord's Ascension." Christian Classics Ethereal Library. http://www.ccel.org/ccel/schaff/npnf212.ii.v.xxxviii.html.

LETA. "Latvijā reliģiskā dažādība visaugstākā starp postpadomju valstīm." *Delfi.lv*. April 18, 2016. http://www.delfi.lv/news/national/politics/latvija-religiska-dazadiba-visaugstaka-starp-postpadomju-valstim.d?id=47331847.

Levinas, Emmanuel. *Difficult Freedom: Essays on Judaism*. Translated by Sean Hand. Baltimore: Johns Hopkins University Press, 1997.

———. *Totality and Infinity: An Essay on Exteriority*. Translated by Alphonso Lingis. Pittsburgh, PA: Duquesne University Press, 2002.

Levy, Daniel, et al., editors. *Old Europe, New Europe, Core Europe: Transatlantic Relations After the Iraq War*. London and New York: Verso, 2005.

Lionnet, Françoise. *Postcolonial Representations: Women, Literature, Identity*. Ithaca and London: Cornell University Press, 1995.

———, and Shu-Mei Shih. "Introduction: Thinking through the Minor, Transnationally." In *Minor Transnationalism*, edited by Françoise Lionnet and Shu-Mei Shih, 1–23. Durham and London: Duke University Press, 2005.

Lieberman, Benjamin. *Remaking Identities: God, Nation, and Race in World History*. Lanham and Plymouth: Rowman and Littlefield, 2013.

Lindbeck, George. *The Church in a Postliberal Age*. Edited by James Buckley. Grand Rapids, MI: Eerdmans, 2003.

Livonijas Indriķis. *Indriķa Livonijas hronika/ Heinrici Cronicon Lyvoniae 1180–1227*. Translated by Ābrams Feldhūns. Edited by Ēvalds Mugurēvičs. Rīga: Zinātne, 1993.

Lösel, Steffen. "What Sacred Symbols Say about Strangers and Strawberries: Gordon W. Lathrop's Liturgical Theology in Review." *Journal of Religion* 85 (2005) 634–48.

Lott, Bret. *Jewel*. New York: Washington Square, 1999.

Louw, Daniel J. "Sacramental Presence within and African Context: Toward a *Theologia Africana* in Pastoral Theology." In *The Presence of Transcendence: Thinking 'Sacrament' in a Postmodern Age*, edited by Lieven Boeve and John C. Ries, 199–211. Leuven: Peeters, 2001.

Lubac, Henri, de, S.J. *Corpus Mysticum: The Eucharist and the Church in the Middle Ages*. Translated by Gemma Simmonds C.J., et al. Edited by Laurence Paul Hemming and Susan Frank Parsons. Notre Dame, IN: University of Notre Dame Press, 2006.

Luther, Martin. "The Babylonian Captivity of the Church." In *The Annotated Luther. Church and Sacraments*, Vol. 3, edited by Paul W. Robinson, 13–129. Minneapolis: Fortress Press, 2016.

———. "Table Talks," Nr. 46. In *Luther's Works*, Vol. 54, edited by Theodore G. Tappert, 7. Philadelphia: Fortress, 1967.

———. "A Treatise On the New Testament, That Is, the Holy Mass." In *Luther's Works*, Vol. 35, edited by E. Theodore Bachmann, 75–111. Philadelphia: Fortress, 1960.

MacCulloch, Diarmaid. *Silence: A Christian History*. New York: Penguin, 2013.

Macy, Gary. "The Medieval Inheritance." In *A Companion to the Eucharist in the Reformation*, edited by Lee Palmer Wandel, 15–37. Leiden and Boston: Brill, 2014.

———. "Theology of the Eucharist in the High Middle Ages." In *A Companion to the Eucharist in the Middle Ages*, edited by Ian Christopher Levy, et al., 365–98. Leiden: Brill, 2011.

Maldonado-Torres, Nelson. *Against War: Views from the Underside of* Modernity. Durham and London: Duke University Press, 2008.

———_. "On the Coloniality of Being: Contributions to the development of a concept." *Cultural Studies*, 21:2–3 (2007) 240–70.

Marcus, Gary. *Kluge: The Haphazard Construction of the Human* Mind. Boston and New York: Houghton Mifflin, 2008.

Marion, Jean-Luc. *God Without Being*. Translated by Thomas A. Carlson. Chicago: University of Chicago Press, 1995.

Martin, Ralph. "Post-Christendom Sacramental Crisis: The Wisdom of Thomas Aquinas." *Nova et Vetera* 11:1 (2013) 57–75.

Martos, Joseph. *Doors to the Sacred: A Historical Introduction to Sacraments in the Catholic Church*. Revised and updated edition. Ligouri, MI: Ligouri, 2001.

———. *The Sacraments: An Interdisciplinary and Interactive Study*. Collegeville, MN: Liturgical Press, 2009.

Matthews, David. "The Art of the Fugue. Expended Version of a review of 'The Art of Fugue' by Joseph Kerman." http://david-matthews.co.uk/writings/article.asp?articleid=42

Mbmebe, Achille. *On the Postcolony*. Berkeley, Los Angeles, London: University of California Press, 2001.

———. "On the Postcolony: A Brief Response to Critics." *African Identities*, 4:2 (2006)143–78.

———. "Provincializing France?" *Public Culture* 23:1 (2015) 85–119.

McBrien, Richard P. *Catholicism*. New Edition, Completely Revised and Updated. San Francisco: Harper, 1994.

McCabe, Herbert, O.P. *God Matters*. Revised edition. Mowbray, 2000.

———. *New Creation*. New York and London: Continuum, 2010.

McDougall, Dorothy C. "The Cosmos as Primary Sacrament: An Ecological Perspective for Sacramental Theology." In *Contemporary Sacramental Contours of a God Incarnate*, edited by Lieven Boeve and Lambert Leijssen, 233–41. Leuven: Peeters, 2001.

———. *The Cosmos as the Primary Sacrament: The Horizon for an Ecological Sacramental Theology*. New York: Peter Lang, 2003.

McGuckin, John Anthony. "Gregory Palamas (1296–1359): Triads in Defense of the Holy Hesychasts." In *Christian Spirituality: The Classics*, edited by Arthur Holder, 136–47. London and New York: Routledge, 2010.

———. *The Orthodox Church: An Introduction to its History, Doctrine, and Spiritual Culture*. Oxford: Wiley-Blackwell, 2011.

Metz, Johannes Baptist. "The Future in the Memory of Suffering." In *New Questions on God*, edited by Johannes B. Metz, 9–25. New York: Herder and Herder, 1972.

Mignolo, Walter D. *The Darker Side of Western Modernity: Global Futures, Decolonial Options*. Durham and London: Duke University Press, 2011.

———. "Delinking: TheRhetoric of Modernity, The Logic of Coloniality and the Grammar of De-coloniality." *Cultural Studies* 21:2–3 (2007) 449–514.

———. "Introduction: Immigrant Consciousness." In Rodolfo Kusch, *Indigenous and Popular Thinking in America*, translated by Maria Lugones and Joshua M. Price, xiii-liv. Durham and London: Duke University Press, 2010. S

———. *Local Histories/Global Designs: Coloniality, Subaltern Knowledges, and Border Thinking*. Princeton, NJ: Princeton University Press, 2000.

———. "On Pluriversality." http://waltermignolo.com/on-pluriversality/

———, and Arturo Escobar, editors. *Globalization and the Decolonial Option*. London: Routledge, 2013.

———, and Madina V. Tlostanova, "The Logic of Coloniality and the Limits of Postcoloniality." In *The Postcolonial and the Global*, edited by Revathi Krishnaswamy and John C. Hawley, 109–23. Minneapolis: University of Minnesota Press, 2008.

Miles, Margaret R. "Foreword: The Eye of the Beholder." *The Subjective Eye: Essays in Culture, Religion, and Gender in Honor of Margaret R. Miles*, edited by Richard Valantasis, xix-xxix. Eugene, OR: Pickwick, 2006.

———. "The Resurrection of the Body: Re-imagining Human Personhood in Christian Tradition." In *Theology, Aesthetics, and Culture: Responses to the Work of David Brown*, edited by Robert MacSwain and Taylor Worley, 42–52. Oxford: Oxford University Press, 2012.

Min, Anselm, K. "The Church as the Flesh of Christ Crucified: Toward an Incarnational Theology of the Church in the Age of Globalization." In *Religion, Economics, and Culture in Conflict and Conversation*, edited by Laurie Cassidy and Maureen H. O'Connell, 91–107. Maryknoll, NY: Orbis, 2010.

———. *Paths to the Triune God: An Encounter Between Aquinas and Recent Theologies*. Notre Dame, IN: University of Notre Dame Press, 2005.

———. *The Solidarity of Others in a Divided World: A Postmodern Theology after Postmodernism*. New York and London: T&T Clark International, 2004.

Misāne, Agita. "Latvijas kristianizācija." *Latvijas Luterānis*. May 31, 2013. http://www.latvijasluteranis.lv/2013/05/31/latvijas-kristianizacija-ko-tas-isti-nozime/.

Mitchell, Nathan D. *Meeting Mystery: Liturgy, Worship,* Sacraments. Maryknoll, NY: Orbis, 2006.

Moslund, Sten Pultz. *Migration Literature and Hybridity: The Different Speeds of Transnational Change*. New York: Palgrave, 2010.

Mutambara, Maaraidzo. "African Women Theologies Critique Inculturation." In *Inculturation and Postcolonial Discourse in African Theology*, edited by Edward P. Antonio, 173–91. New York: Peter Lang, 2006.

Nandy, Ashis. *The Intimate Enemy: Loss and Recovery of Self Under Colonialism*. Oxford and Delhi: Oxford University Press, 1983.

Nesaule, Agate. *A Woman in Amber: Healing the Trauma of War and* Exile. New York: Penguin, 1995.

Ngong, David T. "Christianity in Africa." In *The Wiley-Blackwell Companion to African Religions*, edited by Elias Kifon Bongmba, 208–19. Chichester: Wiley-Blackwell, 2012.

———. *Theology as Construction of Piety: An African Perspective*. Eugene, OR: Resource, 2013.

Noble, Ivana. *Theological Interpretation of Culture in Post-Communist Context: Central and East European Search for* Roots. Farnham and Burlington: Ashgate, 2009.

Oh, Jea Sophia. *A Postcolonial Theology of Life: Planetarity East and* West. Upland, CA: Sopher, 2011.

Orobator, Agbonkhianmeghe., S.J. "A Global Sign of Outward Grace: The Sacramentality of the World Church in the Era of Globalization." *CTSA Proceedings* 67 (2012) 14–22.

———. *Theology Brewed in an African* Pot. Maryknoll, NY: Orbis, 2009.

Osborne, Kenan B., OFM. *Christian Sacraments in a Postmodern World: A Theology for the Third Millennium*. New York and Mahwah, NJ: Paulist, 1999.

———. "Euro-American Sacramental Theology—It's Need for Asian Help." Paper presented at the Asian Theology Consultation, Catholic Theological Society in America. 2012 Annual Convention in St. Louis, Missouri, June 9, 2012.

Padinjarekuttu, Isaac. "Sacrament in Catholic History." In *The World as Sacrament: Interdisciplinary Bridge-Building of the Sacred and the Secular*, edited by Francis X. D'Sa, S.J., et al., 17–37. Pune: Jnana-Deepa Vidyapeeth Theology Series, 1998.

Painter, Karen. "Contested Counterpoint: 'Jewish' Appropriation and Polyphonic Liberation." *Archiv für Musikwissenschaft*, 58. Jahrgang; H.3 (2001) 201–30.

Pandey, Gyanendra. *Routine Violence: Nations, Fragments,* Histories. Stanford, CA: Stanford University Press, 2006.

Papanikolaou, Aristotle. *The Mystical as Political: Democracy and Non-Radical Orthodoxy*. Notre Dame, IN: University of Notre Dame Press, 2012.

Parappally, Jacob, M.S.F.S. "The World, God's Primary Sacrament." In *Celebrating the Sacramental World: Essays in Honour of Emeritus Professor Lambert J. Leijssen*, edited by Kekong Bisong and Mathai Kadavil, 77–87. Leuven: Peeters 2010.

Park, Andrew Sung. "The Bible and Han." In *The Other Side of Sin: Woundedness from the Perspective of the Sinned-Against*, edited by Andrew Sung Park and Susan L. Nelson, 45–60. Albany: State University of New York Press, 2001.

Parker, David. "Diaspora, Dissidence and the Dangers of Cosmopolitanism." *Asian Studies Review* 27:2 (2003) 155–79.

Parry, Benita. "Countercurrents and Tensions in Said's Critical Practice." In *Edward Said: A Legacy of Emancipation and Representation*, edited by Adel Iskander and Hakem Rustom, 499–512. Berkeley, Los Angeles, and London: University of California Press, 2010.

———. *Postcolonial Studies: A Materialist Critique*. London and New York: Routledge, 2004.

Phan, Peter C. "Embracing, Protecting, and Loving the Stranger: A Roman Catholic Theology of Migration." In *Theology of Migration in the Abrahamic Traditions*, edited by Elaine Padilla and Peter C. Phan, 77–110. Palgrave, 2014.

———. *In Our Own Tongues: Perspectives from Asia on Mission and Inculturation*. Maryknoll, NY: Orbis, 2003.

Pieterse, Jan Nederveen, and Bhikhu Parekh, "Shifting Imaginaries: Decolonization, Internal Decolonization, Postcoloniality." In *The Decolonization of Imagination: Culture, Knowledge and Power*, edited by Jan Nedervesen Pieterse and Bhikhu Parekh, 1–19. London and New Jersey: Zed, 1995.

Pieris, Aloysius, S.J. *An Asian Theology of Liberation*. Maryknoll, NY: Orbis, 1988.

———. "A Liturgical Anticipation of a Domination-free Church: The Story of an Asian Eucharist." *East Asian Pastoral Review* (*EAPR*) 43:3 (2006). http://eapi.admu.edu.ph/content/east-asian-pastoral-review.

Plakans, Andrejs. *A Concise History of the Baltic States*. Cambridge: Cambridge University Press, 2011.

Pordzik, Ralph. *The Quest for Postcolonial Utopia*. New York: Peter Lang, 2001.

Pound, Marcus. "Eucharist and Trauma." *New Blackfriars* 88 (2007) 187–94.

Prabhu, Anjali. *Hybridity: Limits, Transformations, Prospects*. Albany: State University of New York Press, 2007.

Prakash, Gyan. "Science between the Lines." In *Subaltern Studies IX*, edited by Shahid Amin and Dipesh Chakrabarty, 59–82. Delhi: Oxford University Press, 1996.

Pramuk, Christopher. *At Play in Creation: Merton's Awakening to the Feminine Divine.* Collegeville, MN: Liturgical, 2015.

Probyn, Elspeth. *Outside Belongings*. New York: Routledge, 1996.

Purs, Aldis. *Baltic Facades: Estonia, Latvia, and Lithuania since 1945*. London: Reaktion, 2012.

Radhakrishnan, R. *A Said Dictionary*. Malden and Oxford: Wiley-Blackwell, 2012.

———. "Derivative Discourses and the Problem of Signification." *The European Legacy*, 7:6 (2002) 783–95.

———. "Globalization, Desire, and the Politics of Representation." *Comparative Literature*, 53:4 (2001) 315–32.

———. "Postcoloniality and the Boundaries of Identity." *Callaloo* 16:4 (1993) 750–71.

———. "Postmodernism and the Rest of the World." In *The Pre-Occupation of Postcolonial Studies*, edited by Fawzia Afzal-Khan and Kalpana Seshadri-Crooks, 37–70. Durham and London: Duke University Press, 2000.

———. "Race and Double-Consciousness." *Works and Days* 45/23:24 (2006) 45–67.

———. *Theory in an Uneven World*. Malden and Oxford: Blackwell Publishing, 2003.

Rahner, Karl, S.J. *Theological Investigations*. Vol.1. Translated by C. Ernst. New York: Crossroad, 1982.

Ramazani, Jahan. "Modernist Bricolage, Postcolonial Hybridity." *Modernism/Modernity*, 13:3 (2006) 445–63.

Rivera, Mayra. "Elemental Bonds: Scene for an Earthy Postcolonial Theology." In *Postcolonial Interventions: Essays in Honor of R.S. Sugirtharajah*, edited by Tat-siong Benny Liew, 347–60. Sheffield: Sheffield Phoenix Press, 2009.

———. "Flesh of the World." *Concilium: International Journal of Theology*. Special Issue: Postcolonial Theology, edited by Hille Haker et al., (2013:2) 51–60.

———. "Ghostly Encounters: Spirits, Memory, and the Holy Ghost." In *Planetary Loves: Spivak, Postcoloniality, and* Theology, edited by Stephen D. Moore and Mayra Rivera, 118–35. New York: Fordham University Press, 2011.

———. "God and Difference." In *Building Bridges, Doing Justice: Constructing a Latino/a Ecumenical Theology*, edited by Orlando O. Espin, 29–44. Maryknoll, NY: Orbis, 2009.

———. *The Touch of Transcendence: A Postcolonial Theology of* God. Louisville and London: Westminster John Knox, 2007.

Roll, Susan K. "Baptism: New Thinking from Women-identified Perspectives." In *Contemporary Sacramental Contours of a God Incarnate*, edited by Lieven Boeve and Lambert Leijssen, 242–55. Leuven: Peeters, 2001.

———. "Sacraments as Energy: A Search for a New Paradigm." *Feminist Theology* 21:3 (2013) 259–68.

Ross, Melanie C. *Evangelical Versus Liturgical? Defying a Dichotomy*. Grand Rapids, MI: Eerdmans, 2014.

Ross, Susan A. *Extravagant Affections: A Feminist Sacramental Theology*. New York: Continuum, 1998.

Runyon, Theodore. "The Sacraments." In *Keeping the Faith*, edited by Geoffrey Wainwright, 209–23. Minneapolis: Fortress, 1994.

———. "The World as the Original Sacrament." *Worship* 54:6 (1980) 495–511.

Rushdie, Salman. *Imaginary Homelands: Essays and Criticism 1981–1991*. London: Granta, 1991.

Quayson, Ato. "Introduction: Area Studies, Diaspora Studies, and Critical Pedagogies." *Comparative Studies of South Asia, Africa and the Middle East,* 27:3 (2007) 580–90.

Said, Edward, W. "Criticism, Culture and Performance: An Interview with Edward Said." *Performing Arts Journal* 37 (1991) 21–42.

———. *Culture and Imperialism.* New York: Vintage, 1994.

———. *The Edward Said Reader.* Edited by Moustafa Bayoumi and Andrew Rubin. New York: Vintage, 2000.

———. *Freud and the Non-European.* London and New York: Verso, 2003.

———. "Invention, Memory, and Place." In *Landscape and Power,* Second Edition, edited by W.J.T. Mitchell, 241–60. Chicago: The University of Chicago Press, 2002.

———. *Music at the Limits.* New York: Columbia University Press, 2007.

———. *Musical Elaborations.* New York: Columbia University Press, 1991.

———. *Out of Place: A Memoir.* New York: Knopf, 1999.

———. *Power, Politics, and Culture: Interviews with Edward W. Said.* Edited by Gauri Viswanathan. New York: Pantheon, 2002.

———. *Reflections on Exile and Other* Essays. Cambridge, MA: Harvard University Press, 2002.

———. *Representations of the Intellectual.* New York: Random, Vintage: 1996.

Saliers, Don. E. *Worship as Theology: Foretaste of Glory Divine.* Nashville: Abingdon, 1994.

Schneider, Laurel C. *Beyond Monotheism: A Theology of Multiplicity.* Abingdon and New York: Routledge, 2007.

———. "Promiscuous Incarnation." In *The Embrace of Eros: Bodies, Desires, and Sexuality in Christianity,* edited by Margaret D. Kamitsuka, 231–45. Minneapolis: Fortress, 2010.

Schneiders, Sandra, I.H.M. *Written that You May Believe: Encountering Jesus in the Fourth Gospel.* Revised and Expanded Edition. New York: Crossroad, 2003.

Schmemann, Alexander. *Church, World,* Mission. Edited by Alexander Schmemann. Crestwood, NY: St. Vladimir's Seminary Press, 1979.

———. *For the Life of the World: Sacraments and Orthodoxy.* Crestwood, NY: St. Vladimir's Seminary Press, 2002.

Schrijver, Georges, de, S.J. "Experiencing the Sacramental Character of Existence." Translated by Susan Roll. *Questions Liturgiques* 75 (1994) 12–27.

———. "Postmodernity and the Withdrawal of the Divine: A Challenge for Theology." In *Sacramental Presence in a Postmodern Context,* edited by Boeve and Lambert Leijssen, 39–64. Leuven, Paris, Sterling: Leuven University Press, 2001.

Schwartz, Regina Mara. *The Curse of Cain: The Violent Legacy of Monotheism.* Chicago: University of Chicago Press, 1997.

———. *Sacramental Poetics At the Dawn of Secularism: When God Left the World.* Stanford: Stanford University Press, 2008.

Scott, Derek B. "Edward Said and the Interplay of Music, History and Ideology." In *Edward Said and the Literary, Social and Political World,* edited by Ranjan Gosh, 104–23. New York: Routledge, 2009.

Skultans, Vieda. "Theorizing Latvian Lives: The Quest for Identity." *The Journal of the Royal Anthropological Institute* 3:4 (1997) 1–20.

Šnē, Andris. "The Emergence of Livonia: The Transformations of Social and Political Structures in the Territory of Latvia during the Twelfth and Thirteenth Centuries."

In *The Clash of Cultures on the Medieval Baltic Frontier*, edited by Alan V. Murray, 53–72. Farnham and Burlington: Ashgate, 2009.

Snyder, Timothy. *Bloodlands: Europe Between Hitler and Stalin*. New York: Basic, 2010.

Soja, Edward W. "Thirdspace: Toward a New Consciousness of Space and Spatiality." In *Communicating in the Third Space, Communicating in the Third Space*, edited by Karin Ikas and Gerhard Wagner, 49–61. New York and London: Routledge, 2009.

Spekke, Arnolds. *Latvijas vēsture*. Rīga: Jumava, 2003.

Spivak, Gayatri Chakravorty. *An Aesthetic Education in the Era of Globalization*. Cambridge, MA: Harvard University Press, 2013.

———. *A Critique of Postcolonial Reason: Toward A History of the Vanishing Present*. Cambridge and London: Harvard University Press, 1999.

———. *Death of a Discipline*. New York: Columbia University Press, 2003.

———. "In Memoriam: Edward W. Said." *Comparative Studies of South Asia, Africa and the Middle East* 23:1&2 (2003) 6–7.

———. *Outside in the Teaching* Machine. New York and London: Routledge, 2009.

———. "Reply." *PMLA* 123:1 (2008) 247–49.

Šterns, Indriķis. *Latvijas Vēsture 1180–1290: Krustakari*. Rīga: Latvijas Vēstures institūta apgāds, 2002.

Streufert, Mary J., editor. *Transformative Lutheran Theologies: Feminist, Womanist, and Mujerista* Perspectives. Minneapolis: Fortress Press, 2010.

Strods, Heinrihs. *Latvijas katoļu baznīcas vēsture 1070.-1995*. Rīga: 1996.

Stuart, Elizabeth. "Exploding Mystery: Feminist Theology and the Sacramental." *Feminist Theology* 12:2 (2004) 228–36.

Sugirtharajah, R. S. *Exploring Postcolonial Biblical Criticism: History, Method, Practice*. Oxford: Wiley-Blackwell, 2012.

———. *Postcolonial Configurations: An Alternative Way of Reading the Bible and Doing Theology*. London: SCM, 2003.

Suna-Koro, Kristine. "Once More on (the Lightness of) Postcolonial Naming: Which Europe and Whose Eurocentrism?" *Journal of Postcolonial Theory and Theology* 1:4 (2010) 1–58.

———. "Not With One Voice: The Counterpoint of Life, Diaspora, Women, Theology, and Writing." In *Women, Writing, Theology: Transforming a Tradition of Exclusion*, edited by Emily A. Holmes and Wendy Farley, 207–32. Baylor University Press, 2011.

———. "Postcolonially Bittersweet in America: Ecojustice and Sacramental Agency." *Journal of Postcolonial Theory and Theology*, 4:2 (2013) 1–47.

Susin, Luiz Carlos. *Assim na terra como no céu: brevilóquio sobre Escatologia e Criação*. Petropolis: Vozes 1995.

Tanner, Kathryn. *Christ the Key*. Cambridge: Cambridge University Press, 2010.

Thatamanil, John J. "Front endorsement." In John Philip Newell, *A New Harmony: The Spirit, the Earth, and the Human Soul*. San Francisco: Jossey-Bass, 2011.

———. "How Not to Be a Religion: Genealogy, Identity, Wonder." In *Common Goods: Economy, Ecology, and Political Theology*, edited by Melanie Johnson-de Baufre et al., 54–72. New York: Fordham University Press, 2015.

Theokritoff, Elizabeth. *Living in God's Creation: Orthodox Perspectives on Ecology*. Crestwood, NY: St. Vladimir's Seminary Press, 2009.

Thieme, John. *Post-Colonial Studies: The Essential Glossary*. London: Arnold, 2003.

Tillich, Paul. "The Nature of Religious Language." In *The Essential Tillich: An Anthology of Writings of Paul Tillich*, edited by F. Forrester Church, 44–55. New York: Collier and Macmilan, 1987.

Tlostanova, Madina. Деколониальные гендерные эпистемологии. Москва: Маска, 2009.

———. "The Imperial-Colonial Chronotope: Istanbul-Baku-Khurramabad." *Cultural Studies* 21:2–3 (2007) 406–27.

———, and Walter D. Mignolo. *Learning to Unlearn: Decolonial Reflections from Eurasia and the Americas.* Columbus, OH: The Ohio State University Press, 2012.

Toolan, David, S.J. "The Voice of the Hurricane: Cosmology and a Catholic Theology of Nature." In *'And God Saw That It Was Good': Catholic Theology and the Environment*, edited by Drew Christiansen, S.J. and Walter Grazer, 65–103. Washington DC: United States Catholic Conference, 1996.

Torres-Saillant, Silvio. *An Intellectual History of the Caribbean.* New York: Palgrave Macmillan, 2006.

Travis, Sarah. *Decolonizing Preaching: The Pulpit as Postcolonial Space.* Eugene, OR: Cascade, 2014.

Trinh, T. Minh-ha. *When the Moon Waxes Red: Representation, Gender and Cultural Politics.* New York: Routledge, 1991.

———. *Woman, Native, Other: Writing Postcoloniality and* Feminism. Bloomington and Indianapolis: Indiana University Press, 1989.

Vīķe-Freiberga, Vaira. *Kultūra un latvietība.* Rīga: Karogs, 2010.

———. *Pret Straumi: Runas un Raksti par Latvietības Tēmām* 1968–1993/*Against the Current: Essays on Latvian Identity.* Montreal: Helios, 1993.

Vena, Osvaldo D. "My Hermeneutical Journey and Daily Journey into Hermeneutics: Meaning-Making and Biblical Interpretation in the North American Diaspora." In *Interpreting Beyond Borders.* The Bible and Postcolonialism 3, edited by Fernando Segovia, 84–106. Sheffield: Sheffield Academic, 2000.

Viswahathan, Gauri, editor. *Power, Politics, and Culture: Interviews with Edward W. Said.* New York: Pantheon, 2001.

Walcott, Derek. "The Caribbean: Culture or Mimicry?" In *Postcolonialisms: An Anthology of Cultural Theory and Criticism*, edited by Gaurav Desai and Supriya Nair, 257–64. New Brunswick, NJ: Rutgers University Press, 2005.

Ware, Kallistos. "Through Creation to the Creator." In *Toward an Ecology of Transfiguration*, edited by John Chryssavgis and Bruce V. Foltz, 86–105. New York: Fordham University Press, 2013.

Westhelle, Vítor. *After Heresy: Colonial Practices and Post-Colonial* Theologies. Eugene, OR: Cascade, 2010.

White, James F. *Sacraments as God's Self Giving.* Nashville: Abingdon, 2001.

Williams, Raymond. *Marxism and* Literature. Oxford: Oxford University Press, 1977.

Wing, Betsy. "Translator's Introduction." In Édouard Glissant, *Poetics of Relation.* Translated by Betsy Wing, xi–xxiii. Ann Arbor: University of Michigan Press, 1997.

Yang, Lingyan. "Theorizing Asian America: On Asian American and Postcolonial Asian Diasporic Women Intellectuals." *Journal of Asian American Studies*, 5:2 (2003) 139–78.

Yap, Fu Lan, "Living the Eucharist in Asia: A New Habitus: Reflection on the Final Statement of the 9th Plenary Assembly of the FABC in the Indonesian Pastoral

Context." *East Asian Pastoral Review* 47:4 (2010). http://eapi.admu.edu.ph/content/living-eucharist-asia-new-habitus.

Yarnold, Edward, S.J. "Transubstantiation." In *The Eucharist in Theology and Philosophy: Issues in Doctrinal History in East and West from the Patristic Age to Reformation*, edited by Istvan Perczel et al., 381–94. Leuven: Leuven University Press, 2005.

Yearsley, David. "Alchemy and Counterpoint in an Age of Reason." *Journal of the American Musicological Society* 51:2 (1998) 201–43.

Yeo, K. K. "Biblical Christologies of the Global Church: Beyond Chalcedon? Toward a Fully Christian and Fully Cultural Theology." In *Jesus Without Borders: Christology in the Majority World*, edited by Genre L. Greene et al., 162–79. Grand Rapids, MI: Eerdmans, 2014.

Young, Robert J. C. *Colonial Desire: Hybridity in Theory, Culture and Race*. London and New York: Routledge, 1995.

———. "Edward Said: Opponent of Postcolonial Theory." In *Edward Said's Translocations: Essays in Secular Criticism*, edited by Tobias Döring and Mark Stein, 23–43. New York and London: Routledge, 2012.

———. "Postcolonial Remains." *New Literary History* 43 (2012) 19–42.

———. *Postcolonialism: A Historical Introduction*. Oxford: Blackwell, 2001.

———. *Postcolonialism: A Very Short Introduction*. Oxford and New York: Oxford University Press, 2003.

———. "The Void of Misgiving." In *Communicating in the Third Space*, edited by Karin Ikas and Gerhard Wagner, 81–95. New York and London: Routledge, 2009.

Zemītis, Guntis. "Kultūru saskarsme un komunikācija Latvijas teritorijā 12./13. gadsimtā pēc Indriķa Livonijas hronikas ziņām." In *Latvijas vēsture: Krustcelēs un jaunu pieeju meklējumos*. Latvijas vēsturnieku I kongresa materiāli, 172–94. Rīga: LU Akadēmiskais apgāds, 2014.

Žižek, Slavoj, and John Milbank. *The Monstrosity of Christ: Paradox or Dialectic?* Edited by Creston Davis. London and Cambridge, MA: MIT Press, 2009.

Made in the USA
Middletown, DE
22 July 2017